THE ILLUSTRATED HISTORY OF
SCIENCE FICTION

UNGAR WRITERS' RECOGNITIONS SERIES

Science Fiction / Fantasy

Selected list of titles in this series:

Complete list of titles in the series
available from the publisher on request.

THE ILLUSTRATED HISTORY OF
SCIENCE FICTION

DIETER WUCKEL
AND BRUCE CASSIDAY

UNGAR · NEW YORK

1989
The Ungar Publishing Company
370 Lexington Avenue, New York, N.Y. 10017

Originally published as *Science Fiction:*
Eine Illustrierte Literaturgeschichte
Copyright © 1986 by Edition Leipzig

English translation by Jenny Vowles.
Additional material and American adaptation
Copyright © 1989 Bruce Cassiday

Printed in the German Democratic Republic

Library of Congress Cataloging-in Publication Data

Wuckel, Dieter.
     The illustrated history of science fiction.

     (Ungar writers' recognitions series)
     Translation of: Science fiction, eine illustrierte
Literaturgeschichte.
     Bibliography: p.
     1. Science fiction—History and criticism.
I. Cassiday, Bruce. II. Title. III. Series.
PN 3433.8.W 8313   1989   809.3'876   87-19113
ISBN 0-8044-2984-7

CONTENTS

Science Fiction in the Second Half of the Twentieth Century 153

Themes, Subjects, and Motifs in Modern Science Fiction 217

Conclusion 241

Appendix 243

PREFACE

It has been said that books need no special introduction, for, as Aleksandr Herzen optimistically remarked, they find their ground themselves. I am nevertheless writing a few introductory sentences, mainly because when I used to tell friends I was writing about a work of Thomas Mann or Christa Wolf, or problems of space and time in the epic, this was accepted without surprise even by those who never look into such literature. But ever since I have admitted I am working on a history of science fiction, the response has been one of astonishment. Such a study, some friends comment, is surely unworthy of a serious scholar! After all, isn't this type of fiction just adventure stories for adolescents? On the other hand, some people—mainly the young—are terrifically enthusiastic and are of the unhesitating opinion that such a project is of historic importance. Even these fans are in the main possessed of only the vaguest idea of the wide spectrum that science fiction literature encompasses.

I have likewise become wary of the cries of joy expressed by fanatical fans of science fiction, for whom no other genre exists.

Then there are the many who have but little notion of what science fiction is, and therefore are reticent about giving any opinion at all. It was, nevertheless, members of this last group who often posed the most interesting queries; it was they whom I imagined my research would be most able to help.

The result of many years of occupation with science fiction lies in this volume. It is meant not only as a history of the genre, but also as a guide to the reader in choosing his or her reading and to encourage further delving into the science fiction genre. I have also attempted to clarify certain aspects of the literature and set them in their proper context.

Of course, there is much that remains outside the scope of this book. For example, it is impossible to give the names of all relevant authors and books; a selection must be made. This selection must on the one hand be as representative as possible so that major trends can be convincingly presented; but on the other hand its subjectivity must be apparent enough for my own personal opinions and evaluations to shine through and encourage readers to compare my preferences with their own. It is equally unlikely that one single author could pay adequate tribute to all the many national varieties and trends: one could only successfully undertake such an exercise after many years of international research. There is also the problem of the major gaps in all collections and libraries, particularly related to "trivial" literature.

To get the most out of this book it is important to be aware of the omission of authors whose area is that of more "normal" fantasy and horror literature—for example, H. P. Lovecraft or J. R. R. Tolkien—although they are often mentioned in the literature secondary to science fiction.

This work will use the original titles with the English translations given in brackets when it is mentioned for the first time. The transliteration of Russian language titles follows common practice. The year of publication given (except where the text specifies otherwise) is the first edition in the world, regardless of the language.

In order to make for easier reading, I have avoided footnotes. The superscript numbers after quotations and references refer to the notes at the end of the book.

To avoid inconsistencies, transliterations of Russian names essentially follow the so-called popular system.

At this point I would like to thank all those persons and institutions who lent items that have been used in the illustrations for the book. My special thanks must also go to my children Uta and Uwe for their help.

—Dieter Wuckel

BEGINNINGS

SCIENCE FICTION OR SCIENTIFIC FANTASY: WHAT IS IT?

When a commentator undertakes to write about science fiction, it is necessary to explain clearly what exactly is meant by the term. It signifies different things to different people, so much so that some definitions are in total contradiction with one another, while many more seem to rephrase the question rather than offer a direct answer.

Eike Barmeyer takes a narrow view and defines science fiction simply as "an example of highly marketable literature for mass consumption, a part of the entertainment industry even when it reaches beyond the realms of mere entertainment."[1]

Kingsley Amis understands the short science fiction story to be a "class of prose narrative treating of a situation that could not arise in the world we know, but which is hypothesized on the basis of some innovation in science or technology, or pseudo-science, or pseudo-technology, whether human or extra-terrestrial in origin."[2]

The Reader's Encyclopedia of American Literature stresses the fact that science fiction is primarily a short-story medium "in which the seemingly impossible is made to appear possible by the introduction of alleged scientific hypotheses and discoveries and of still uninvented mechanical contrivances. It is characteristically a dream of the future; sometimes the dreams come true."[3]

Against this one must compare Dieter Hasselblatt's statement: "Science fiction sketches not the future, but an alternative, it leaps into another reality, it refers not to the future but to the present. Science fiction should not be viewed as referring to the future so much as to all possibilities."[4]

According to the Yugoslavian critic Darko Suvin, science fiction is a literary genre "whose one necessary condition is the availability and the complex interaction of alienation and familiarity, and whose main formal trick is its use of an imaginative framework which functions as an alternative to the empirical environment of the author."[5]

Hans-Jürgen Krysmanski, on the other hand, believes that the phenomenon of science fiction is approachable from the perspective of the twentieth-century utopia, and introduces the term "utopian method" into the discussion.[6]

Bernd Ulbrich, an author of the German Democratic Republic (East Germany), places his cards on the table with aplomb: "What is SF? Above all it is literature. . . . Fiction, to which some fool or perhaps a crafty businessman has appended the word science, but which would do better without its appendage—yes, I think this does the genre a disservice and restricts its scope."[7]

According to this view, the dilemma is to be solved by reference to "the estrangement that transcends reality."[8]

Peter Wilfert, editor at the renowned Goldmann publishers in the Federal Republic of Germany (West

1

Germany), suggests: "The differentiation of the three kinds of literary fantasy, namely, horror, science fiction, and fantasy, has hitherto been best delineated by the Russian Yuri Lotmann in a short essay. In a concise and schematic description, he says the key is the depiction of one element (nature, place, knowledge) in the real everyday world of the reader relative to one element of the fictive system in the world of the book. Horror literature begins by describing the real world and then the way in which it is broken up by some hidden supernatural cosmos with ghosts and demons whose existence is negated by the real world. Science fiction sketches a nonreal world in which however elements of the life experience of the reader—albeit expanded and set in the future—do have a role. Fantasy, at least in its pure form, describes a world that has no correspondence with our cosmos. The setting, times, and figures of these novels have no reflection in the lives of the reader. The author makes a personal system of truths that no longer bears upon any empirical basis."[9]

In the novel *His Master's Voice*, Stanislaw Lem has his scientist Dr. Rappaport read American books in "that popular genre . . . called, by a persistent misconception, 'Science Fiction.'"[10] Peter Hogarth explains somewhat cryptically in the book his disappointment over the monotonousness of science fiction: "The authors of pseudo-scientific stories offer the public what it wants."[11]

From here it is but a small step to the polemical statements of Michael Pehlke and Norbert Lingfeld: "With science fiction it is necessary to take into account what the publishers feed to the market under this label."[12]

There have been attempts to retrieve the situation and renew the genre under the name "science creation,"[13] and also the heavily sarcastic "science triction."[14]

These uncertainties and differences of definition are the result of the fact that science fiction is a historical phenomenon. Its roots reach far back into literary history. It originated under distinct cultural and historical conditions and was built upon live tradition.

Spaceships in docking maneuver. Painting by Andrei Sokolov.

In the course of its maturation, certain characteristics faded from importance, and others burgeoned to take their place. Science fiction has had distinct peaks; one can trace marked upswings alternating with phases of stagnation and decline. In this historical process, the genre may be compared with a stream whose waters gather from several sources. It winds along and, swelled by tributaries, becomes a river that then loses a portion of its volume in side streams, some of which later rejoin the main flow. Every so often a rivulet peters out and becomes extinct. In some, the water stands as cloudy, evil-smelling pools. But the main flow grows nonetheless, so that in the course of the centuries it broadens as a river so wide it is hardly visible in its entirety from any one vantage point. Such is the state and history of science fiction as it is known today.

What position can I myself adopt in my attempt to write the history of science fiction? To gather so many

Venusian city. Painting by Andrei Sokolov.

3

works under a general definition is surely impossible. Such a history must in my opinion demonstrate the wealth of science fiction by reference to the essential books and authors of the past, and also recapitulate the current situation. In that area, there is an almost incomprehensible mass of science fiction literature, isolating certain key themes, topoi, and motifs, that must be highlighted to outline the most important developments.

A further premise: the chosen works must without question be classifiable under the title "fantasy." This is already clear from the term "scientific fantasy," so often used as an alternative to "science fiction." The difficulty lies only in the fact that the nether regions of the area defined as fantasy (which term indeed almost defies definition) are extremely vague.

Close to the Moon. Painting by cosmonaut Aleksei Leonov.

Stanislaw Lem offers the following thoughts on fantasy: "Thus for example a dwarf, a native of Jupiter, or a flying snail, are unreal, fantastical things. African deities, two-headed dogs or computers that hypnotize humans are, on the other hand, realistic things (i.e., things that could exist), which are still nevertheless considered fantastic by many."[15]

Nonexisting objects can thus be fantastic, as can objects to which one is not yet accustomed, or those that belong to a foreign culture, or things only potentially possible.

Recently two authors representing different areas of literary study, from each of the two great social systems of today, have given their opinion on fantasy. The Kirgiz author Chingis Aitmatov says, in connection with his novel *I dol'she veka dlitsja den' (The Day Outlasts the Century)*, "When it comes to the meaning of fantastical fiction, Dostoyevski says that the fantastic in art has limits and rules: the fantastic must come close enough to the real so as to become almost believable. Dostoyevski here has exactly formulated the law of the fantastic. In fact, whether it is mythology from olden times or the realistic fantasy of Gogol, Bulgakov, Garcia Marquez, or even scientific fantasy, all these in their different ways convince through the exactness with which fantasy and reality intersect. The fantasy extrapolates excessively certain aspects of reality and demonstrates it with the aid of its "rules of play," philosophically generalized, thereby exposing its developmental processes to the full."[16]

These deliberations lead him on to the following: "The fantastic is a metaphor of life, which presents itself with the help of the fantastic in a new and unexpected guise. The metaphors of our own century are especially revealing, and not only because the scientific and technical achievements in the fantasy of yesteryear are now upon us in real life, but now particularly because the world in which we live is like a fantasy—torn as it is by economic, political, ideological, and race-based contradictions."[17]

The famous American science fiction writer Ursula K. Le Guin takes the opposite point of view. At about the same time the above was written, she wrote a comment on her novel *The Left Hand of Darkness*, in which she defines science fiction as "extrapolative

4

A science fiction film now produced as a comic.

as "scientific." The metaphors of life in science fiction are dressed up in pseudoscience. Whereas in the fairy tale the witch can simply ride away on a broomstick, or rub a magic ring to fulfil a wish, in science fiction the author must attempt to provide adequate cause for such effects and give for them a solid and rational explanation even when this may at times involve "inventing" technological, scientific, or social developments to suit. Particularly in the twentieth century, with the ever-finer differentiation in our mental and spiritual life, more new scientific disciplines are entering the field to make the metaphors of fantasy more believable—for example, cybernetics, electronics, and psychoanalysis.

Today, three different historic eras are postulated among students of science fiction for the emergence of the form as a new and distinct genre. The first identifies science fiction with the fantasy literature of all peoples and therefore sees it as beginning with myths, fairy tales, and the earliest records of human history. At the other end of the spectrum is the school of thought that sees science fiction as being born only in the year 1929 or thereabouts, when Hugo Gernsback coined the term. This latter position leads to indescribable difficulties with authors such as Jules Verne and H. G. Wells (and indeed Gernsback himself whose novel *Ralph 124 C 41 Plus* was written before World War I). Since to exclude such as these is clearly undesirable, one would be forced to view them as precursors and trailblazers. The third view places the evolution of science fiction as contemporaneous with the Industrial Revolution in the nineteenth century. Few who subscribe to this view would be as inconsistent as Brian Aldiss, author of *The Billion Year Spree*, who, despite his suggestion of a very long history in his title, goes on to state that science fiction was born in 1818, the year that Mary Shelley produced *Frankenstein*.

My own opinion is that science fiction was first born in that epoch when the problems, achievements, and discoveries concerning the potential of the natural sciences—and, above all, the social sciences—were beginning to force their way into the traditional fantasy story. That trend developed during the Renaissance, and this study of the genre will therefore begin with this fruitful period in history when self-

literature." She characterizes her own work as an experiment in thought, whose purpose it is to describe the reality of the present-day world. She says that science fiction does not preempt, but describes.[18] She then expands on this point and comes to the conclusion that all literature is metaphor as it embodies an alternative form of society, just as the future does. In literature, she goes on to say, the future is itself a metaphor.

Between the metaphors of other fantastic genres and those of science fiction there are a mass of borrowings and mixings; even in the works of one author the two branches may mingle, so that an exact dividing line is not always able to be drawn.

As a rule of thumb however, one may say that science fiction stands apart from other fantasy genres by virtue of the singular way in which it is designated knowledge and self-confidence blossomed, when man set sail for the unknown, and when nature was so successfully harnessed for human purposes. The sources of fantasy and those authors who paved the way and handed down traditions will not be dealt with explicitly here, but will be touched upon where necessary to demonstrate how science fiction even in its use of familiar motifs and themes differentiates itself both from the fantasy of prescientific ages, and from newer types of fiction.

Science fiction enters history as a prose form, but in the course of the years the dividing lines between it and other literary forms have been overstepped, as is the case with any art form. Thus one must look at novels, tales, novellas, short stories, sketches, and fairy tales, as well as poems, radio plays, drama, television productions, and film scenarios. Some paintings, music, films, and sculpture will also earn a mention. The range is from humanist works of world literature down to banal, shallow—indeed inhumane—products of the lowest trivial reaches.

This multiplicity baffles a strict historically ordered presentation as surely as it exercises an unfailing attraction for the reader.

CLASSIC SOCIAL UTOPIAS
AND FANTASIES

Science fiction's roots lie deep in the Renaissance, an epoch characterized above all by violent changes in the forces of production.

These changes touched every facet of social life. On the one hand there were the discoveries, the inventions, the artistic activity, and the wonderful achievements of the humanists; on the other hand there was the wrenching transition to capitalism. The working population became employees; the means of production were concentrated in the hands of the few and *became* capital. These preconditions for capitalist production were not achieved without violence.

The explosive technological development seen during the Renaissance was intricately bound up with the progress of science in opening up the world. The new methods of research that were thereby perfected were founded upon experiment, observation, and experience. The most important fact established at this time was Copernicus's scientific proof of a heliocentric cosmos. Gutenberg's invention of the printing press with movable type enabled new knowledge and new ideas to spread widely and rapidly through the printing of many copies.

The overland route to the land of spice and all wonders—"India" (by which was meant really the whole of Asia)—was rendered extremely perilous by the Islamic world that lay in its way. The search for alternative routes was fueled by the need for the craved-for commodities to be obtained more easily, safely, and cheaply. This search was the decisive motivating factor in the period's discoveries and ventures. In the early Renaissance, the Italians, who at that time had the most experience in seafaring, were welcomed in Spain and Portugal, and later in England too, as masters who could pass on their expertise in the art of maritime navigation.

Some of the most important voyages were the discovery of America (Christopher Columbus, traveling between 1492 and 1504), the discovery of a sea route to India around the Cape of Good Hope (Vasco da Gama 1497–99), and the first circumnavigation of the world by Ferdinand Magellan and de Elcano, who assumed Magellan's mantle after the latter's death (circa 1522). This last finally proved that the Earth *was* a sphere, and gave practical proof or rebuttal to many a hypothesis.

Each was an immense achievement in its own right; together they were the basis for a flowering of the sciences, arts, and literature on an unprecedented scale.

The alterations in the means of production led to a transition from a theocentric to an anthropocentric world view. The emphasis was now on people and the power of the personality, the might of the individual. The revolutions of the epoch became the objective sources for the later humanist movement and for the

6

Man breaks free from the confines of the ancient world. German woodcut, circa 1530.

development of a deeply humanist view of the world and mankind. "People began to rely upon their own will and their own ability in the world, which was now viewed as the sphere of human activity and the field for human energy. It thus became necessary for mankind to comprehend the world in its reality."[1]

Philosophy strove for the liberation of humanity from the fetters of theological dogma. The temporal character of state and society shone clearly through; Renaissance art did away with medieval conventions and turned towards the realities of life, to the activities of humans in their changing world.

From these contradictory processes new forms and genres of literature peculiar to the new age sprang up. The modern novel began to crystallize; the epic was already losing its importance. The Renaissance gave rise to the gradual merging of traditional imaginative fantasy with scientific ideas, or pseudoscientific ideas. Thus the Renaissance saw the birth of scientific fantasy, or, what is now called science fiction.

At first scientific fantasy showed itself as a mingling of literature, science, and social theory. As with many Renaissance novelties, science fiction can be

7

traced back to examples in classical literature. In some authors, particularly some of the Greeks, ideas related to social utopias had already made their appearance. Hesiod (fl. circa 800 B.C.) in his *Dreams of the Golden Age* and Aeschylus (circa 525–456 B.C.) give hints of a new morality. Aristophanes (circa 450–circa 388 B.C.) also investigated fundamental problems by distancing them through fantasy, as in *The Birds, The Frogs*, and the *Ecclesiazusae (Parliament of Women)*.

Social utopias rose to special importance in the prehellenist period. In the fifth century B.C. up to the beginning of the fourth century B.C. Hippodamos of Miletus and Phaleas of Chalcedon sketched hierarchical social models, which anticipated some of the thoughts of Plato. These early utopias were born without exception under a conservative star.

Nicholas Copernicus.

More revealing is the utopian sketch *Hiera Anagraphe* by Euhemerus who lived circa 340–260 B.C. In this work one still finds the hierarchical stratification of society, but now the problem of private wealth is addressed for the first time.

Sharply contrasted with Euhemerus's elitist society, Jambulos's (circa 200 B.C.) fairy-tale utopia, disguised as a story of travel, describes a radical enforcement of the equality principle. The work is not extant but an outline of its contents survives in the writings of the historian Diodorus Siculus (circa 80–30 B.C.). Equality informs Jambulos's ideas not only in social standing within the community, the sharing of produce, and the organization of production, but also in the realms of culture and intellectual work, and even to the extent that neither marriage nor familial structures were allowed. Collective child care and collective living dominate. This society was set in seven islands dedicated to the Sun God, to the south of Arabia Felix (Yemen), somewhere in the Indian Ocean, a place at the time quite unexplored—an example of another fundamental trait of so many later utopian fictions, set, as they were, outside the known world.

Jambulos was one major source for social utopia in the Renaissance; the philosopher Plato (427–347 B.C.) was the other, with *The Republic*, especially in its formal device of epic dialogue, which Plato perfected. In his social utopia, the idea of the equality of mankind was completely dismissed and replaced by a supposedly "natural" ordering in three social tiers. Only the two superior tiers, according to Plato, were to be advanced through the abolition of private wealth and the introduction of a kind of consumer communism.

Thoughts of social utopia by authors closely associated with Christian belief are of lesser significance in the history of literature. Saint Augustine the church father took up ideas like those of the Thousand-Year Reich no more than sporadically.

These social conditions were simply described and gave rise to a reaction in the form of utopian teachings, often under the mantle of Christianity that strove to establish the kingdom of God here on Earth. The poor and dispossessed became ardent followers of preachers with this message. The Reformation,

8

as it spread through Europe along with uprisings, struggles, and rebellions, fell on fertile ground. In England there was John Wycliffe (1324–84); in Bohemia Jan Hus (1369–1415); in Zurich Huldreich Zwingli (1484–1531); in Geneva John Calvin (1509–64); in Germany Martin Luther (1483–1546) and Thomas Müntzer (1490–1525). The attempt to translate ideas of utopia into the workaday world was, however, doomed to failure even though the dream of a world of justice and equality persisted. Literature has indeed preserved finely rounded sketches of believable humanist societies.

The first and most important utopia of the Renaissance was written by the English humanist Thomas More (1478–1535). In 1519, Erasmus of Rotterdam wrote a letter to Ulrich von Hutten containing a detailed description of More's character.[2]

Thomas More was born into a well-to-do family. At the finish of his studies he was a highly respected lawyer. In 1504, he entered Parliament; in 1509 he became under-sheriff and a judge with many responsibilities. In the years 1515–16, he traveled on missions abroad for Henry VIII, one with a legation to Bruges in the Netherlands to discuss trade and commerce with the representatives of the later Charles V. His duties also took More to Antwerp where he was able to visit his friend Peter Giles (Petrus Ägidius), the town clerk of Antwerp.

After his return home Thomas More began work on his book *Utopia*, consisting of two parts and including descriptions of his travels in the Netherlands presented as a letter to Giles—a favorite literary ploy of the humanist writers.

Two years later, when More settled a dispute concerning papal ships' freight to the approval of all parties, Henry VIII summoned him to state duty. From treasurer of the exchequer, More rapidly rose to become chancellor of the Duchy of Lancaster, and in 1529, on the fall of Wolsey, he was appointed lord chancellor. He thus gained a political influence in the realm second only to that of the king himself.

More accepted the post of lord chancellor against his own strong reservations, for he knew he was being brought face to face with a situation he had discussed in his *Utopia*. And his doubts were to be proved well-founded only a few years after his promotion.

Thomas More. Portrait from 1689 edition of *Utopia*.

Henry VIII severed the English church from Rome's influence for a combination of personal and political reasons. He was supported by the Archbishop of Canterbury and by the Chancellor of the Exchequer Thomas Cromwell. The clergy lost all its powers. Henry was divorced and remarried; the king was made head of the Anglican church (Act of Supremacy 1534) and the succession to the throne rearranged.

Thomas More was opposed to these measures, and in May 1532 he resigned on health grounds from his position as lord chancellor. Though he was thrown

Io. Clemens. Hythlodæus. Tho. Morus. Pet. Aegid.

The main characters in *Utopia* in conversation, from Basel edition of 1518.

into jail, he remained true to his convictions and resisted compromise. He was accused of high treason and executed on July 6, 1535, in London—sent to his death for his religious convictions, which were inseparable from his humanist concept of life. One observing this history from some distance can identify More's outlook as a conservative one, for, despite all his arbitrary use of power, Henry VIII and the English bourgeoisie (considerably strengthened under his care) embodied the spirit of social progress.

The writings of Thomas More, published in Latin in Antwerp, are important for several reasons. His *Utopia* is consciously related to the classical utopian tradition; Plato in particular is mentioned several times. As in Plato, More sets his ideal society on an island at the very edge of the known world.

Another noteworthy point is that More overreaches the boundaries of classical utopia in that he clothes his fiction in authenticity to make it believable. He introduces the work with the above-mentioned letter to Peter Giles in which he asserts that both he and Giles learned the facts of the book through a certain "Raphael"—a fictional character. Part 1 of the book takes the form of a Plato-like dialogue between More, Giles, and Raphael Hythloday (Greek: *hythlos* = farce; *daios* = tub-thumper, zealot, or gasbag). Raphael was, according to the book, the constant companion of Amerigo Vespucci "in the iii last voyages of those iv that be nowe in printe and abrode in every mannes handes."[3] On the final journey, twenty-four of the sailors are left behind on the eastern coast of Brazil to form a permanent trading post. Raphael explains that he was one of those twenty-four. By traveling "through and aboute many

Map of the island of Utopia, Basel edition of 1518.

10

Amauroti vrbs.

Fons Anydri.

Ostium anydri.

Hythlodaeus.

Countreyes,"[4] he and five companions chance upon Utopia, later on upon Taprobane (Sri Lanka), from whence he goes to Caliquit (Calicut, or Kozhikode), where he boards a Portuguese ship bound for Europe. These geographical details reflect the then current belief that the land Columbus had discovered and the magical land of India were one and the same.

Finally, the "authenticity" of More's book is further enhanced by his detailing and condemnation, in part 1, of aspects of contemporary England—for instance, the laws by means of which the rural population was forced to work as serfs for wages, thus laying the foundations for the expropriation of the peasantry.

While More thus lards part 1 of *Utopia* with a close criticism of the deplorable state of affairs at home, he builds up in part 2 a picture of an alternative state that is portrayed as ideal. The very word *Utopia* is supposed to derive from the name of the first conqueror of the island, one King Utopus. The island was originally a peninsula in America; Utopus directed that a stretch of ground fifteen miles wide be "cut and dugged up,"[5] thus creating an island, Utopia (Greek: U = nowhere; *topos* = land; thus *Utopia* literally means nowhereland), two hundred miles wide and five hundred miles in circumference, with fifty-four "large and faire cities."[6]

Employing many details, More mirrors his ideal—read, utopian—order. The most far-reaching difference is that the basis for all concerns is the dismantling of private ownership—that is, of the means of production. For this reason, Utopia "alone of good right maye claime and take upon it the name of a commen wealth. But every man procureth his owne private gaine. Here where nothinge is private, the commen affaires bee earnestly loked upon."[7]

From these premises—that is, economic and social equality—it is possible to establish all political and educational institutions, all laws, and so on, according to the principles of true justice. More describes the organization of labor, the life in town and country, marriage, care of the ill and infirm, the upbringing and training of children and young people, the structure of the society, the practice of crafts, travel, the low emphasis placed on money, the treatment of crime and criminals, and the role of each Utopian in the defense of the island. He finishes with a de-

scription of the fictional religion, the chief aim of which is to develop a sense of moral virtue. At the center of the book is the problem closest to More's heart: justice, warfare, and religious tolerance.

Utopia is a clear-sighted optimistic profession of faith in humanity, the fortune of mankind. This is shown in a hexastich, a six-line verse, supposedly written by the Utopian poet laureate Anemoleus, nephew of Hythloday by his sister, which says that this land should be called "not Utopie, but rather rightly / My name is Eutopie."[8]

Thomas More's social utopia is thus, as he himself indicates, a "eutopia"—that is, a beautiful, desirable land—and is the first of a whole row of portrayals of happy, humane works in the literature of the ensuing centuries.

The second important early utopia is *Civitas Solis (The Sun State)* by Tommaso Campanella, which was the product of a quite different society.

Campanella was born Giovanni Domenico in 1568 in a poor family in Calabria. At fifteen he entered the Dominican order, adopting the cloister name Tommaso. More than once he had to defend himself against charges of heresy. In 1599, he was among the leaders of a revolt against Spanish domination, for which he was cruelly tortured and condemned to lifelong incarceration in jail. Most of his philosophical writings stem from his years of confinement; he was not released from prison until the winter of 1628–29, but even then was allowed no peace. A threat of further imprisonment forced him to flee to France under a false name. He lived in a Dominican monastery in Paris from 1634 until his death in 1639, greatly admired by the king for his anti-Spanish sentiments, and equally lauded by intellectual circles for his philosophical publications.

Civitas Solis was written during Campanella's darkest hours, the period between his arrest and his trial when he was ceaselessly interrogated and tortured. There are basic similarities between this book and More's *Utopia*, particularly in their respective conceptions of a true communal humanist society. For Campanella, as for More, a just social order is founded on the idea of no private ownership; such conditions are the basis of the common good and productive work and as such are the goal of each citizen.

12

Children are brought up with this aim in mind, and they are trained not so much in the disciplines popular at the time but rather, to use a twentieth-century term, are given a polytechnic education. During their early years children are introduced to all the various crafts, in situ, so that the particular interests and talents of each child can be more easily recognized.

Campanella's system is aimed at the all-round development of the personality. In *Civitas Solis*, the emphasis on physical training is even more marked than in More's *Utopia*, and every individual is expected to contribute meaningfully to the defense of the community in times of conflict or war.

The spirit of communalism informs not only working patterns and mealtimes in Campanella's world, but all aspects of life are communally based. As in Plato, marriage itself has quite a new character. The women have their own separate organization.[9] Two people are given in marriage by the leader of the

Tommaso Campanella.

state; they are chosen according to astrological charts. Eugenics is also taken into account.

Unlike More, Campanella does not base his book on a recital of the concrete social wrongs of his own time, though of course his utopia contains an inherent criticism. His chief concern is to weave his social ideas into his philosophical vision. He emphasizes the unity of all existence; central is "the thought that the rank, the degree of perfection of the individual, is based on how near he or she is to the perfection of the holy spirit."[10] Thus the highest position in the country is always given to the citizen who has come closest to perfection.

Campanella writes in the form of a dialogue between the administrator of a monastic hospice and his guest. The guest, true to tradition, is a well-traveled sailor who relates his tale of the ideal community on an island at the furthermost reaches of the known world. Its center is the *Civitas Solis*, the sun country, which is formed in seven concentric circles of beautiful palaces on a mountain, at the peak of which is a temple illuminating the whole. Jambulos's seven islands probably influenced the seven circles of Campanella, and the latter's choice of title may also be traceable to the former's portrayal of sun worship.

More and Campanella set an example that was to be studied for centuries—above all in England and France, but also in other countries. Many utopian works in their mold followed, though it was not until the nineteenth century that the name of More's book became a generic title for the form. The *Staatsroman* of German literature and the *voyages imaginaires* of French literature are often works of social utopia, or at the very least contain related ideas. In France, the number of such books grew so rapidly that, on average, in the eighteenth century, "ten to twenty new such books every year, or even thirty in some years, flooded onto the market."[11] The vast majority of these are forgotten, or at most are of academic interest to specialists. Because it is so difficult to draw a clear dividing line between the escapist and the philosophical (which by rights belongs in a history of science fiction literature), this volume will avoid a mere listing of titles bearing upon the theme, and offer instead commentary on a few examples to illustrate the range of this literature.

NOVA
ATLANTIS
PER
FRANCISCUM BACONUM,
Baronem de Verulamio,
Vice-Comitem S. Albani.

ET FLORE — ET FRUCTU

VLTRAIECTI

Apud Ioannem à VVaesberge,
Anno cIɔ Iɔ c XLIII.

Title page of an old edition of Francis Bacon's *New Atlantis*.

The search for happiness was in these years inextricably linked with utopian aspirations. It is therefore not to be wondered at that even the great Renaissance novels like Rabelais's *Gargantua and Pantagruel* contain utopian elements (for instance, the Abbey Theleme) or Cervantes's *Don Quixote*, and even more so, *Persiles and Sigismunda*.

A work of great influence in its day was *Christianopolis*, written by Johann Valentin Andreae in 1619, with its Christian social outlook. In the first real French utopian novel, the 1678 *History of Sevaram-ben*, by Denis Vairasse d'Alais, a group of shipwreck survivors find an apparently uninhabited island. After a while it becomes evident that there are people living there, and in an ideal community. Some extra piquancy is lent to a few episodes in the book by the fact that only one in five of the survivors are women.

There are some works that tend to be linked to More's *Utopia* or Campanella's *Civitas Solis*: for example, the philosopher Francis Bacon's *New Atlantis*, an incompleted fragment, written in 1623 and published posthumously in 1627. Bacon founded his philosophy on empiricism. Thus, despite all religious scruples, he became, according to Engels, the true father of English materialism and all modern experimental sciences.[12] The one extant utopian fragment in the work centers on Plato's Atlantis, an "island" under the sea enjoying a high cultural life.

The polishing up of the fable delivers few original elements. A boat encounters a storm as it sails from South America towards Japan and is beached on the shores of an island called Bensalem by its inhabitants. Only when the newcomers profess to being Christians are they allowed to land and stay for six weeks. Some two thousand years before a sage by the name of Salomon has given to the island its laws and founded the "Order of the Wise," a kind of academy of arts. It is a rescued sailor who describes life on the island, thus conforming to the established literary pattern.

But Bacon's book is arguably not a utopian work. He does not challenge the existing class hierarchy. At the time of the writing the bourgeois structure of English society was already established. There are those with property and those without, the ruled and the rulers, the lower orders and the upper echelons. It is not until the last few pages of the fragment that the author's philosophy becomes clear. Bensalem is a massive laboratory where all nature is being investigated. In the "House of Solomon" the origins and developments, as well as the harnessed powers of nature, are traced to their source to extend the limits of human knowledge as far as possible. Much energy is spent on the invention of important machines and devices—for example, stronger telescopes and other optical aids, machines and instruments for all kinds of transport, even including air travel. In addition, much attention is paid to the development of new and better

14

animal stocks. Also undertaken are experiments with light and sound and anatomical investigations.

Bacon's scientific utopia is indirectly a social utopia even though it lacks a spontaneous socialist insight. In *New Atlantis* it is emphasized that for the new bourgeoisie and the new nobility of England scientific knowledge is the route to political power.

In 1688, England's "glorious revolution" occurred under the banner of puritanism and the ideology of the bourgeois, but in the end it proved to be little more than a coup d'état in which the masses of the people exchanged one ruler for another. England then witnessed a historical compromise between the nobility and the bourgeoisie. A parliamentarian constitution became the basis for the development of bourgeois politics. "It was a time of radical changes in which the rules of the market place began to inform every area of the economy, state, administration, culture, and social intercourse. . . . Puritans provided a commercial populace, learning to venerate its sense of

Francis Bacon.

Robinson Crusoe. Woodcut after Grandville, 1850.

method and strong discipline, with a fitting list of virtues including a sense of duty, energy and enthusiasm, a sense of measure and economy, all of which served its own ends admirably." [13]

A child during this time of social turbulence, Daniel Defoe (1660–1731) later created a particular type of literary utopia that found devotees and imitators throughout the eighteenth and nineteenth centuries—one especially developed in outer space by Jules Verne in the twentieth century. In 1719, after economic and social ups and downs and tireless work in a multitude of fields, Defoe at fifty-nine published his book, *The Life and Strange and Surprizing Adventures of Robinson Crusoe of York*. This book owes its origins to the Renaissance sailor-discoverers and the picaresque fictions of many literary predecessors, and to various portrayals of island life. Actual examples of marooned sailors such as the story of Alexander Selkirk were widely known; Defoe drew freely on these and other elements in his story of the shipwreck of his hero and of his twenty-eight years of solitary life on the island.

Unlike the established mode of sailors' tales, this new book was more than a tale of action and adventure with glimpses of a multitude of exotic settings. At the opening of the book the reader is confronted by the shipwreck and the dilemma of the hero as its sole survivor. The adventure of this lonely individual then takes center stage as he triumphs over his unique situation. Defoe avoids unadulterated fantasy. The hours, days, weeks, and years pass and are documented in plain fashion, filling out a history of nearly thirty years. It follows the philosophy of John Locke, that nature and common sense are the motivating forces at the source of all individual and social evolution. But

Title page for *Robinson Crusoe*, Daniel Defoe's enduring classic of travel and survival.

ROBINSON CRUSOE

HIS LIFE AND
STRANGE, SURPRISING ADVENTURES

BY
DANIEL DEFOE

———

WITH SEVENTY ILLUSTRATIONS

———

NEWARK, N. J.
CHARLES E. GRAHAM & CO.
NEW YORK

Illustration for early edition of *Robinson Crusoe*.

nature and common sense are also seen to be in conflict in Defoe's book. Common sense is shown as the ability to gather, to compare, and to assess, and then make good productive use of experience. This is the kernel of the story. Robinson Crusoe gathers experience in his world, assessing the plants and animals, food, clothing and shelter, space and time, tools, instruments, wild animals, and becomes active through contact with that world. The right to own land and to own objects is thereby won, but also, as is shown in the example of his man Friday, the right to own people. Knowledge won from experience triumphs, and achieves success for the individual. The form in which Defoe relates the story—that is, by letting the fictional hero tell his experiences in the first person by presenting extracts from a supposed diary—is a major element of the book's success. Accuracy and exactness of style was particularly congenial to the English reading public at the beginning of the eighteenth century.

Despite this apparently total commitment to realism, Defoe's novel belongs to the annals of science fiction. He had only to turn to the unreal, the utopian, and his story would have been one in which the good of the individual and that of the community coincides completely and harmoniously. A fantasy element is present in the figure of the hero. Contemporary experience and reports indicated that lonely and lost survivors of shipwrecks very soon adapted an animal-like life-style, as was the case with Alexander Selkirk, and almost all forget the lessons of civilization. Crusoe, the first-person narrator of the book, is an example of the opposite—a towering individual who tames first external nature and then human nature itself, in the person of Friday. By choosing a lone individual on which to concentrate his story, Defoe avoided the questions of private ownership, class divisions, and differences of interest that are usually at the core of full-fledged utopian works. But at the same time the precondition for Crusoe's survival is that the distant bourgeois society of the time informs his life through its ideology. At the very moment Crusoe leaves his isolation and reenters "normal" life, he sheds anything he has of the unusual about him. It is not surprising that a second volume of the book, *Farther Adventures*, published in the same year (1719), contains nothing akin to the adventure and travel exploits of the first. A third volume, *Serious Reflections*, published in 1720, contains some verbose moralizing on Defoe's part, and falls far short of the literary level of volume 1.

The story of Crusoe's shipwreck and island existence opened the floodgates to untold numbers of "island utopias." Most of them were insignificant as literature and fell far below Defoe's imaginative work. Books such as *Die Insel Felsenburg (Felsenburg Island)*, by Johann Gottfried Schnabel (originally titled *Wunderliche Fata einiger Seefahrer, absonderlich Alberti Julii, eines geborenen Sachsens . . . [The Wonderful Tales of Sailors, in Particular Albertus Julius of Saxony]*, the shorter title first becoming current in the following century when a new edition was published by Ludwig Tieck), a four-part work first published in 1731–42, tended not to be as artistic as the English model, but their social criticism was in general sharper. Schnabel's novel concerns a group utopia, as opposed to Defoe's individual utopia. His heroes are stranded in a world of pure nature, and there they regain their lost common sense. Schnabel develops an island community with distinct threads of primitive communism and protestantism. The community is based on active religion, such as that practiced by the pietists.

Seven years after Daniel Defoe's *Robinson Crusoe*, there appeared the second famous book of English enlightenment literature, Jonathan Swift's *Travels into Several Remote Nations of the World*, by Lemuel Gulliver, "first a surgeon and then a captain of several ships," published in 1726. In this work, Swift subjected to rational analysis the English system of government, the economic and social aspects of the postrevolutionary age in England. He also wanted to expose the oppression practiced by England on Ireland.

Like Defoe, Swift had recourse to traditional travelogue literature; but while the former wrote in praise of the virtues of the English puritans who managed to found a British colony in the face of nature's resistance, the latter wrote not simply a grim satire on receding feudalism, but what could be called the first literary study of capitalism.

Swift develops both the biting critique of existing conditions and the picture of a humane way of life that emerges through encounters with "aliens." At first Gulliver's adventures led him into lands where the "otherness" of the inhabitants is evident in their altered sizes. The Lilliputians' are one-twelfth Gulliver's. The tables are turned however in the kingdom of Brobdingnag, a land of giants. The author thus develops a geometric utopia, based on the philosophical teachings of René Descartes. Swift shared his contemporaries' conviction that human properties would remain unchanged if dimensions were altered in equal proportion. This geometric utopia was the means by which Swift dissected the afflictions by his time. "In Gulliver's journey to Lilliput, Swift describes the misery of human size. In Gulliver's journey to the land of giants, he describes the size of human misery," Jan Kott wrote in the 1954 German edition of the book.

17

with "horse" sense—Swift takes a new look at the idea that mankind in the so-called civilized world is nothing more than a more cultivated, even more dangerous, version of the Yahoos. In the development of science fiction, however, Swift's satire and utopianism are of less importance than his portrayal of the individual and society as it is reflected by alien beings and customs.

Gulliver sights the flying island of Laputa, from London edition of 1815.

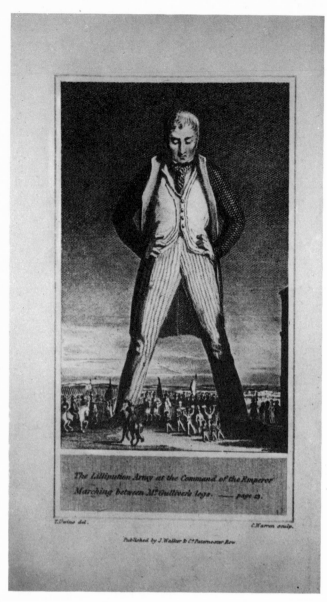

The Lilliputians march through Gulliver's legs, from London edition of 1815.

Gulliver's other travels take him to the flying island of Laputa, and to the land of talking animals. The motif of setting animals above humans is a staple of classical literature. But it is precisely in this humane land of aliens that Swift places the Yahoos—his distorted representation of humans that stands the well-known concept of the "noble savage" on its head. In confrontation with the Houyhnhnms—humans

Around the middle of the eighteenth century, extensive tracts of the world were opened up and charted, many countries were colonized by the emerging colonial powers, and thus naïve fictions of "true" utopias became less and less convincing. Writers were forced to invent new scenarios to create their social utopias.

These years witnessed the establishment of pietism in Denmark, which stressed Bible study and personal religious experience. Community life was devoid of gaiety; comedies were banned from the theaters. In these very years Denmark's most important theatrical writer and creator of the Danish theater, Ludvig Holberg, produced some twelve comedies in three years. In 1738, however, a royal decree brought his work to a halt, and Holberg had to earn his living for the next twenty years through academic writing. During this period he wrote a novel *Nicolai Klimii iter subterraneum (Niels Klim's Subterranean Journey)*, drawing on the work of his literary heroes, the Greek writer Lucian (circa A.D. 125–circa 190) and Jonathan Swift (1667–1745). The book, in Latin, was published in 1741 in Leipzig, but was quickly

The Yahoos, a caricature of humanity, by Josef Hegenbarth, 1954.

Gulliver and a Houyhnhnm, by Josef Hegenbarth, 1954.

translated into many other languages. The hero, Niels Klim, wishes to investigate a cave near his Norwegian hometown of Bergen. The rope breaks and a rush of air blows him down into the Earth, where he finds a new planet called Nazar. The inhabitants of Nazar are plants, intelligent trees. Thus Holberg develops two new elements of scientific fantasy: first, a new environment that is not on the surface of Earth, and second, "aliens" not of human or animal form. The pal-

ace of this well-organized and peaceful planet bears the significant name of "Potu"—that is, "Utopia" spelled backwards. Two aspects of Holberg's detailed description of life in Nazar stand out. In Denmark a farmer had the status of a serf with no rights at all; in Holberg's underground world the farmer was the first citizen of the state both in terms of contribution and respect accorded. The other noteworthy reordering in the book is that man and woman is given exactly the same status: women are numbered even among the judges.

The picture of Nazar is enriched by several technical details not necessarily essential to the plot. For instance, Holberg's boat travels the seas in this under-

ad Cap. 4.

Abbildung eines Bürgers
in Rotu.

Early varieties of aliens in science fiction—tree people, minstrels, and ape men, from a Copenhagen and Leipzig edition of 1753.

ground world with the aid of hidden machinery, without sail or rudder, though the fictional narrator Klim is unable to explain how.

As a contrasting scenario, Holberg introduces other underground states to caricature our world. In one, Klim establishes a tyranny, with the help of a powder-powered lethal weapon. When the people rise against him, he tries to bury himself in a cave—and suddenly he is back where he first entered this strange world ten years previously. This book today still holds valuable lessons, even though the political and philosophical nudges appear quite harmless in comparison to Swift's stinging satire.

Less philosophical, political, and sociological—but more purely fantastical—was *The Life and Adventures of Peter Wilkins, a Cornishman* (1751), an adventure novel along the lines of *Robinson Crusoe*, written by Robert Paltock (1697–1776), a London attorney. In the Antarctic regions, the hero's ship becomes trapped in a tidal current that sucks it down into an underwater cavern, where it drifts through stygian darkness to emerge in a huge vaulted world peopled by winged humanlike beings. This "world" is not set up as a utopian environment. Wilkins falls in love with Youwarkee, who, injured, falls from the sky in front of his tent; he heals her, marries her, and

21

has seven children by her. Not as wide-ranging as Klim's adventures, but good fantasy fare nonetheless.

An obscure French work, *Malle Bossé* (loosely, *Express Mail*), unsigned but probably written by Alexis Piron, had appeared in 1747, offering a parallel between the eighteenth and twenty-fourth centuries. This novel was the forerunner of Louis Sébastien Mercier's vision of a perfect society in the guise of a dream, *L'an deux mille quatre cent quarante (The Year 2440)*, published in 1770. The hero, an Englishman grown weary of Parisian city life, sinks into a deep sleep to awake like Rip Van Winkle to see an obelisk with the year 2440 carved into it. All of 670 years have passed him by! Reforms that were to Mercier most desirable were included in his vision of the future. This work is interesting in the history of science fiction for its inclusion for the first time of changes effected during a long sleep or trance. Hitherto, descriptions of a social utopia were displaced geographically rather than temporally, set at the edges of or beyond the known world, or underground, as in Holberg; but now a social utopia appeared displaced in the time stream.

More writers followed Mercier's lead. In 1781 Legopanov and Aletovitz, two members of the Russian Imperial Academy, wrote a discussion of current literature. Dated 2001, these pamphlets supposedly originated in Constantinople, which, as explained in the text of the pamphlet, had in the meantime come into Russian hands. Rétif de la Bretonne used the same idea of a utopia set in the future in his comedy *The Year 2000*, first performed in 1790—in the midst of the French Revolution—outlining a people's monarchy based on bourgeois principles. In the nineteenth and twentieth centuries, utopias displaced in time and in space through time warps came to be an independent branch of science fiction.

Relative to this mixture of reality and fantasy, the introduction of technical wonders at the beginnings of science fiction is of small significance. As already indicated, many books contain sections where the bounds of contemporary knowledge or experience are overreached; but on the whole, science fiction up to the end of the eighteenth century follows the established mode. The idea of physically leaving the Earth's surface appeared of course in antiquity, though always in

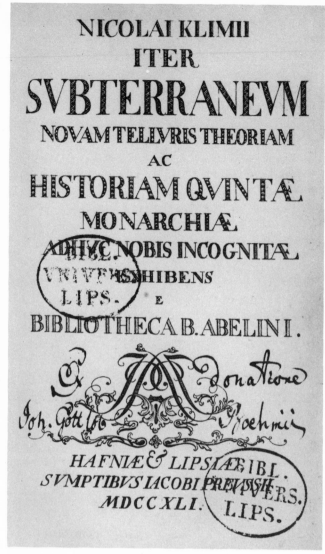

Title page of the Latin edition of Ludvig Holberg's *Niels Klim*, 1741.

a way linked to the flight of birds. Thus the swan maidens or the magic ravens in fairy tales can fly only when endowed with their feathers. Daedalus created for himself and his son Icarus a set of wings made from birds' feathers, flax thread, and wax, in order to escape from Crete. In the Germanic saga of Thidreks, the crippled smith Wieland manages to flee with the aid of a suit of artificial feathers. Lucian's Mennipos, in his "Icaromennipos," a story of the storming of heaven, takes one wing each from the vulture and the eagle, in an attempt to fly. He breaks his journey by

22

landing on the Moon, where he meets Empedocles. This meeting is used as a background for a critical examination of the various schools of philosophy and sociological conditions on Earth. Lucian here set an example eagerly followed in the eighteenth century during spiritual and intellectual struggles of the enlightenment. Mennipos then continues his journey, passing by the Sun and the stars, at last reaching the portals of heaven. There ensues a satirical exchange both with heaven and again with contemporary and older philosophies. Zeus eventually orders to take away Mennipos's wings and then to have him taken back to Earth by Hermes, the messenger of the gods (who wears winged shoes). In Lucian's "True Stories" (of course, a collection of lies) a ship is tossed into the sky by a storm, and many adventures in strange lands follow, in particular on the Moon with its emperor, Endymion. Lucian here strangely foreshadows a "war of the worlds"; he has the Moon and the Sun waging battle over the question of the colonization of Venus. Strange people ("alien" life forms) confront the reader, who must be swallowed by a whale to see a whole new world there.

To these and other works of literature the authors of fantasy fiction could and did turn for ideas between the fourteenth and the eighteenth centuries. Often, as in Lucian, a technological utopia was used as a vehicle to criticize philosophical leanings—especially the gradual spread and finally the acceptance of the Copernican system of the universe.

In 1638 John Wilkins published his argument for a heliocentric system, *Discovery of a New World: or a Discourse That It's Probable There May Be Another Habitable World in the Moon*. In the same year came the posthumous publication, *The Man in the Moone: or a Discourse of a Voyage thither by Domingo Gonsales*, by Bishop Francis Godwin (1562–1633) (originally titled *A View of St. Helena, an Island in the Ethiopian Ocean in America with an Account of the Admirable Voyage of Domingo Gonsales, the Little Spaniard, to the World of the Moone, by the Help of Several Gansas or large Geese. An Ingenious Fancy, Written by a Late Learned Bishop*). In this "ingenious fancy" by the "late learned Bishop," Gonsales successfully completes his flight with the help of large, specially trained geese, which pull his wagon through the air. But Gonsales has made a mistake, and instead of landing as planned in a faraway country, he travels up into the sky to land on the Moon.

Godwin's work was quickly translated into various languages; the book received much attention in France. From the French it was translated into the German by Hans Jacob Christoffel von Grimmelshausen.

This line of development opened up by Godwin was carried on by Savinien Cyrano de Bergerac (1619–55) in his *L'autre monde ou les états et empires de la lune (The Other World, or the States and Empires of the Moon)* (1656) and *L'histoire comique des états de la lune et du soleil (The Comic History of the States of the Moon and of the Sun)* (1662), known collectively in English as *Other Worlds*. *Moon* appeared before *Sun*—both being published posthumously. *Moon* may have been written in 1642, but *Sun* could not have been written before 1650, the year of Descartes's death, since Descartes appears among the philosophers gathered on "the other side" as the most recently deceased. The philosophy of Pierre Gassendi (1592–1655) is unmistakably the foundation upon which Cyrano built; Cyrano de Bergerac was, along with Molière, a pupil of Gassendi. The influence of Descartes himself is also well marked, and in parts Cyrano appears to be attempting to combine the two systems. The book, written in a gloriously satirical style, shows the author sketching out a materialist theory of the creation of the world and expressing deep thoughts on politics, religion, and nature.

While interesting, the speculations on space travel are rather comic to a modern reader. In *Moon*, the narrator's flying machine has bottles filled with dew attached to it, which is sucked up by the Sun, thereby lifting him above the Earth. Because his destination is the Moon, and not the Sun, he breaks the bottles one by one, thereby descending to Earth again. But the Earth has meanwhile spun silently on, owing to its spherical shape, and the narrator lands in Canada (at the time a land the French earnestly sought to be explored). The hapless narrator crashes into a second construction; he must salve his wounds with ox marrow. But his vehicle turns up again in the market place of Quebec, surrounded by rockets, destined to be part of the midsummer celebrations. In order to

Daedalus and Icarus. Fresco from Pompeii, before 79 A.D.

The flight of Francis Godwin's Domingo Gonsales.

rescue his machine, he jumps into it at the exact moment the rockets fire; thus he initiates the first motorized lift-off into space. The rockets burn out very soon. Gravity brings the craft back to Earth once more. But Cyrano has not finished yet: the ox marrow turns out to be attracted to the Moon! Once on the Moon, Cyrano finds not only paradise, with the tree of life, but also other living forms. The indigenous centaurlike creatures mistake the narrator for a female ape, and shut him up in a cage with a male to breed. The male turns out to be none other than Godwin's Spaniard! Among the many philosophical paragraphs in the book, there is a great deal of technological fantasizing: The idea of moving cities whose

houses and town walls are on wheels to be blown forward by sails and bellows; and the idea of glowworm lamps—glass balls that provide sunlight without warmth. When at last the devil comes to claim a soul on the Moon, Cyrano hangs on to the soul, trying to save him. By this means he is transported back to Earth, in Italy, where the entrance to hell is situated in a volcano.

At the opening of *Sun*, Cyrano is imprisoned in a tower. Trying to escape, he takes less than eight days to design and build a complicated flying machine. "It was a large very light box that shut very exactly. It was about six feet high and about three wide in each direction. This box had a hole in the bottom. Over the

24

roof, which was also pierced, I placed a crystal vessel with a similar hole made globe shape but very large, whose neck terminated exactly at and fitted in the opening I had made at the top. The vessel was expressly made with several angles, in the shape of an icosahedron. As each facet was convex and concave, my globe produced the effect of a burning mirror."[14] In the morning this machine is exposed by Cyrano at the top of his tower, and, settling onto a lightweight board, he waits until "the Sun emerged from the clouds and began to shine on my machine [and] the transparent icosahedron received the treasure of the

Encounter with a "Moon man." From the 1913 German edition.

Flying with Cyrano de Bergerac. Rolf Winkler's illustration for the 1913 German edition (Munich and Leipzig) of Cyrano de Bergerac's utopian novel.

Sun through its facets and transmitted the light through the globe into my cell. . . . Then suddenly I felt my entrails stirred in the same way a man feels them stir when he is lifted up by a pulley. I was about to open the door to find out the cause of this sensation, but, as I was stretching out my hand, I looked through the hole in the floor of my box and saw my tower already far below me; and my little castle in the air thrusting upwards against my feet showed me in a twinkling Toulouse disappearing into the earth."[15]

Of course, the flight does not go absolutely according to plan; Cyrano climbs up into the realm of the Sun. During the flight it is possible to observe and describe the rotary movement of the Earth, as well as

25

to muse "on the causes of the construction of this great Universe."[16] On the Sun, the philosophical debates and propositions are once again presented through contact with bizarre animals—for instance, birds (a notion derived from Aristophanes); salamanders (appropriately enough they are supposed to be borne of heat itself); and the "remora," or ice-animal. There was also the idea of a new, full-size youth created out of many little people; this was then quite new, and an idea that was to be used often later in science fiction. The extent to which Cyrano de Bergerac was known and loved in his own time and even later is suggested by the fact that the French dramatist Edmond Rostand wrote a highly successful play with him as hero (1897).

One hundred years later, in 1752, Voltaire's philosophical tale *Micromegas* appeared, in which a native of Sirius eight miles tall is seeking Saturn. He uses his size and the laws of gravity to launch himself into space, and then with a fellow Sirian of equal size, travels through our solar system. They land on Earth among what they view as tiny humans. Voltaire (1694–1778) is satirizing Thomas Aquinas's (1225 to 74) *Summa Theologica*, with its picture of a man-centered universe. Likewise in *Candide* (chapter 18), Voltaire introduces a bit of scientific fantasy: a kind of flying machine (there are few details of its supposed construction) is the means by which the travelers return from the legendary South American land of El Dorado.

The middle of the eighteenth century saw the end of the Renaissance phase of social utopia and early technological fantasy; it was then that science fiction slowly began to emerge as a branch of literature in its own right.

The Industrial Revolution brought about not only an increase in productivity to hitherto unprecedented levels, but also a far-reaching effect on the social structure, and indeed all areas of social, intellectual, and spiritual life. Science fiction was therefore not alone in entering a new phase of development at this time.

26

THE INDUSTRIAL
REVOLUTION AND ITS REFLECTION
IN FANTASY

ANIMAL MAGNETISM,
MONSTERS,
AND AUTOMATONS

The second great epoch of development for science fiction literature is closely related to the scientific and technical, political and social, military and intellectual developments witnessed by civilization during the nineteenth century. These were based on the breakthroughs achieved in science and society in the eighteenth century—for instance, the first industrial machinery that revolutionized techniques, especially in the textile industry (improved looms, Cartwright's mechanical loom, Hargreaves's "Spinning Jenny"). Wind and water were no longer adequate as prime sources of energy to keep such machines working at full capacity. The search was on for a new power source that could be stationed anywhere and that would be able to run a large number of machines equally and effectively.

This problem was finally solved by a university engineer from Glasgow named James Watt, who was able to bring together the work of previous pioneers to bear new fruit. In 1776, the first machine to use his system of steam power was installed and put into service. In England alone, the number of such machines operating by the end of the century was 1,500, with improvements being developed and incorporated into the design every day. The influence of these machines was profound—not simply on engineering and the economy, but on the very structure of society. In fact, the steam engine introduced onto the stage of history the modern Industrial Revolution.

Against this backdrop of the flowering of a technical civilization in the most important industrial countries of Europe and America, one can trace the second state of development of scientific fantasy that was to end only with World War I. Literature shows something of the other side of the Industrial Revolution, the extent of the mass misery and poverty, though of course by its very nature it tends to concentrate on scientific and technical developments. Most authors were deeply impressed by the fact that the new machines were able to multiply a hundredfold the muscle power of the worker, that new secrets were being wrung from nature every day, that products were being moved to and fro on the world market quicker than ever before, and that radio created the means of immediate communication worldwide. The belief soon surfaced that science alone would be able to bring into being a superior mode of life. Thus this second phase of science fiction is characterized primarily by its sense of euphoria. The main trust of most science fiction written at this time is its optimism in regard to technological progress.

As a result of the economic, political, and social changes since the eighteenth century, the literary utopia fell into a distant second place in science fiction, along with many of the dominant social criticisms raised by the enlightenment. With the independence of the United States and the proclamation of the great humanist aims of the French Revolution

27

("liberty, equality, and fraternity," and the 1793 declaration of civil and human rights), the belief in the progress and ability of mankind seemed to be substantiated so that the desire to escape into a wonderful utopia was no longer very strongly felt.

There were still some works that devolved upon the wished-for utopia of a former age: the fragment *The Year 4338*, written in 1838 (though not published until 1926!) by the Russian Count Vladimir Fedorovich Odoyevski. At the outset of the new epoch, new elements were seen to be characteristic of scientific fantasy. The works of the authors of the Romantic era were so fond of mixing pure fantasy with scientific fantasy that it is difficult to draw a line between the two. Ernst Theodor Amadeus Hoffmann (1776 to 1822), for instance, wove into most of his novels and stories allusions to scientists, and discoveries and developments that had been of considerable import to his own age and the recent past. Indeed, in some of his books the "scientific" thread of fantasy is so strong that it would be fair to include them as works of true science fiction.

Hoffmann was intensely preoccupied with the problem of animal magnetism. This question had first been tackled by the theologist and doctor Franz Mesmer in the 1770s; later it was explored further in France. Animal magnetism was supposedly related to metallic magnetism; the theory was that a fluid found in the human organism could exercise a comparable influence on other living organisms. Widely accepted in Europe in the latter years of the eighteenth century, animal magnetism was attributed with wonderful powers of relieving certain diseases. Such a theory proved very attractive to bourgeois intellectuals, especially to those with Romantic poetical natures who already retained an open mind on the supernatural and the inexplicable.

Also this era witnessed the strange doings of the alchemist and necromancer Count Alessandro di Cagliostro (real name Giuseppe Balsamo) who in 1785 played a part in the notorious affair of the diamond necklace of Marie Antoinette.

In 1813 E. T. A. Hoffmann wrote his story "Der Magnetiseur" ("The Magnetist") to develop some of the elements of animal magnetism in a fantasy vein; his purpose was to warn against some of the dangers of the technique as a healing method, and to publicize some of its inhuman elements and disastrous consequences. The connection between this and the questions of the time regarding the natural sciences and technology is distinct and unmistakable. Hoffmann also raised the issue of Mesmer's "science" in other works, for instance in "Das öde Haus" ("The Deserted House") (written 1816/1817) and "Der unheimliche Gast" ("The Sinister Guest") (1818). Obviously, it was a matter of grave concern to Hoffmann. "The Sinister Guest" offers not only a similar scenario and identical cast of characters as in "The Magnetist," but also the same central theme: the ghostly element in animal magnetism as a psychic principle dealing in the unknown. The latter book rings the changes on the earlier only in its close, "The Sinister Guest" ends happily, but "The Magnetist" ends tragically. In these stories, Hoffmann tapped a rich seam nowhere nearly exhausted to this day, involving telepathic children, clairvoyant aliens, or mutants with supernatural powers—all now well-established in the world of science fiction literature.

Hoffmann was also very interested in the building of machines, especially in the field of music, his first love. In 1769, in Pressburg (Bratislava), one Wolfgang von Kempelen built a machine, the famous chess-playing Turk, which caused a great sensation—that is, until the secret was discovered, and the midget who had been hidden in the casing was let out. This is a motif that crops up again and again in Hoffmann. In his fantasy novel *Lebensansichten des Katers Murr* (*Standpoints of the He-cat Murr*) there are references to such occurrences—for instance, a blind girl who reads fortunes in a crystal ball turns out to be the victim of torture in a complex business swindle.

In the story "Die Automate" ("The Automaton") (written in January 1814), Hoffmann describes, quite factually, von Kempelen's mechanism, though this time as the "fortune-telling automaton." He also goes on to write about other "intelligent machines," for example "Ensler's horse-rider," and figures from the collection of the Danzig Arsenal; even the fictive musical automaton developed by the demoniac "Professor X" is later explained. For this part of the story Hoffmann

E. T. A. Hoffmann.

28

E.T.A.
HOFFMANN

had inspected to great effect the famous Kaufmann musical automaton in Dresden in 1813, describing how in the middle of an elevation there stood, next to a large grand pianoforte, a life-size male figure with a flute in its hand, on whose left there sat a female figure before a clavierlike instrument. Behind the latter are two youths, one with a large drum and the other with a triangle. In the background the heroes of the story espy the orchestrion, with which they are already familiar, along with various musical clocks. The professor seats himself at the grand piano and begins to play, very softly, a slow andante march, at the reprise of which the flutist raises his flute to his mouth and takes over the melody, the drummer begins to

The automaton on stage: Olympia from *The Tales of Hoffmann*, by Jacques Offenbach, in a production at the Leipzig Municipal Theater.

30

mark the beat with gentle taps on the drum, and the triangle player begins to strike his instrument to make a barely perceptible tone. Suddenly the woman begins to join in with full-blooded chords, bringing forth a harmonicalike sound by depressing the keys! And now the whole room becomes more excited and lively; the musical clocks begin to chime in concert with the drummer and the note of the triangle rings through the room—the orchestrion blazes into a grand fortissimo that makes everything shudder and shake; until the professor, with his machine, ends the whole with a massive unison on the final chord.[1]

If one examines these and other scenes in greater detail, Hoffmann's mechanical figures are nothing more nor less than the early prototypes of the humanoid robots of twentieth-century science fiction, but designed along the lines of an earlier technology. Here, however, Hoffmann is not alone. In John Paul's writings similar figures appear in the "Court of the Machine King."

Such tales bear witness, on the one hand, to interest in mechanical works of art, and on the other, to a repugnance for distorted images of the human spirit and human creativity.

In a passage following the one referred to above, Hoffmann's hero describes how he has long been impressed, mystified, and even horrified by the connection of humans with dead figures that ape people in their appearance and movement. He sees the striving of inventors to imitate human organs in bringing forth musical sounds, or to replace them with mechanical means, as a declaration of war against the intellect and spirit.

An extreme example of this attitude can be found in Hoffmann's story "Der Sandmann" ("The Sandman") (original version 1815; revised version 1816). This is a story that closes with the hero's going mad—made so by a "living doll." The doll, "Olympia," was later immortalized in Offenbach's opera *The Tales of Hoffmann*.

Other fantasy tales by Hoffmann contain ideas both peripheral and central that play important roles throughout science fiction: vampirism; strange beings in animal form able to speak or write; second sight; dead bodies found after years never to have decayed; and much more.

Wolfgang von Kempelen's chess-playing Turk of 1769.

While Hoffmann was writing in Germany, the nineteen-year-old Mary Wollstonecraft Shelley was writing a book not entirely unlike Hoffmann's insofar as it developed the centuries-old dream of creating a living being by giving it a pseudoscientific foundation; this was of course her book *Frankenstein; or the Modern Prometheus* (1818).

Mary Godwin was born in London in 1797, and grew up in an atmosphere of intense intellectual energy, where the ideas of the Enlightenment and those of the Romantic age mingled. When she was seventeen, she ran away with Percy Bysshe Shelley, already a major poet who was to leave an indelible mark on English Romantic ideas and poetry.

During a second stay on the Continent, between May and August 1816 at Lord Byron's Villa Diodati on Lake Geneva, a series of conversations took place from which came the central theme of *Frankenstein*, and the first version of the tale. Mary Shelley finished the book in May 1817, and it was published in March 1818. This book laid the foundation for the literary fame of this very unusual woman. Distortions of her ideas and work were produced immediately by her

31

Mary Wollstonecraft Shelley.

Percy Bysshe Shelley.

contemporaries, and the flow has never since ceased. The many theatrical productions of the nineteenth century and the thirty or so films made between 1910 and 1982 have only added to the distortion, so that nowadays the word "Frankenstein" is used simply as a byword for a monster or horror story.

But Mary Shelley's first object in her work was by no means to inspire horror and fear. From the beginning, her monster is not malicious, as he was to be portrayed in the 1931 film, given the brain of a criminal by accident. Mary Shelley's monster is a later variant of the type already familiar from such books as *Robinson Crusoe*—the "noble savage." For two years the monster lives with the De Lacey family, and he is well-behaved, warm-hearted, always willing to help. He becomes malicious only gradually because his rights as a human being are not recognized by society, because he is rejected and therefore condemned to

unmitigated loneliness. The depth of this rejection by society, and more so, the rejection by Frankenstein the experimenter himself, is equalled only by the depth of the monster's hatred and resentment. He destroys all whom he finds guilty of causing his plight, including Frankenstein, the "modern Prometheus."

Mary Shelley developed three central ingredients of science fiction. First, she created in *Frankenstein* an important archetype of science fiction literature—namely, the restless scientist not to be deflected from his own research and experimentation. In this field Mary Shelley's creation is one of a long line of literary figures, including even that most convincing and inspiring example of a single-minded questor, Christopher Marlowe's *Faust*. Like his famous predecessor, Frankenstein is concerned only with his scientific ambition, ready to sacrifice anything and everything to break down the boundaries of knowledge, giving not a

THE INDUSTRIAL REVOLUTION AND FANTASY

moment's thought to consideration of the rightness or morality of his activities. Not satisfied with half solutions or compromise, he must aim directly at the summit, become a godlike figure, a second creator of human life. This over-reaching, of course, means his eventual fall is so much the greater.

This theme of creating life reaches far back into the early traditions of mankind. In practically all myth systems and religions, there are stories of how the first

Title page of an English edition of *Frankenstein* of 1831, showing Frankenstein's farewell.

Frankenstein flees from his creation. Illustration from the 1831 edition.

humans were formed, in accordance with contemporary technical knowledge, usually from some workable material—clay for instance—and given life by the secret craft of the creator. Figures that are assembled from discrete parts and then spring to life abound in fairy tales.

Following these primitive versions, new variations on the theme appeared, but no longer of human beings so much as beings acknowledged as copies of humans. Such ideas were already to be found in myth—for example, Pandora—but they gained in importance through the centuries to displace the less ambiguous form. Thus came the Jewish legend of the being created from loam dating from the Talmud period (between the third and fifth centuries A.D.). The name of "golem" for such a creation is found first in the Middle Ages. Such legends were in fact plentiful, one of the best known being that of the creation of the

33

The "monster" and the child. *Frankenstein*, 1931 film version.

inexperience of anatomy, and thus he studies and traces the processes of decomposition of the various bodily sections of corpses. At last he discovers the key: "I could bestow animation upon lifeless matter."[5] This stage occupies him for many long months, until at last the hour comes in which the monster is born, a monster some eight feet tall and with a girth to match. The horror of his own creation causes Frankenstein immediately to sink to the floor.

The second important contribution Mary Shelley made to the development of science fiction, was the

Boris Karloff as Frankenstein's monster in the 1931 American film version.

Polish Rabbi Elijah of Chelm (sixteenth century). This story is the first such tale to include the "schem," written on a strip of paper and wrapped around the brow of the being's head. The golem is by this means brought to life and given supernatural powers, and in the few final seconds the rabbi must tame the creature. Probably, the most popular legend is that of the Prague Rabbi Low and his golem.[2]

The alchemists' search for the source of life was second only to their search for the philosophers' stone that could transform all base metals into gold. Dreams of the homunculus recur time and again in their writings. These were later to be turned on their heads by Marlowe and Goethe in *Faust*.[3]

While Hoffmann had introduced into literature artificial human creatures, Mary Shelley was the first to portray in science fiction the process of making a human being from organic substances. Her hero, Frankenstein, narrates the tale in the first person, a procedure presumably suggested by the alchemist authors in the heretical works. The book cites Cornelius Agrippa, Paracelsus, and Albertus Magnus.[4] It was through these authors that Frankenstein's attention was drawn, he says, to the possibilities of creating life. He has studied mathematics and physics, and then, to complete his knowledge, he has turned to what was then still a relatively new discipline—chemistry. The only thing now keeping him from his ambition is his

34

West German film version of *Frankenstein* with Omar Sharif.

blending of a story concerning the scientific creation of life with the new contemporary genre of the Gothic novel. Horace Walpole (1717–97), in *The Castle of Otranto* (1764) had started the craze. Hot on his heels followed Clara Reave with *The Old English Baron*, Mrs. Radcliffe's (1764–1823) *The Mysteries of Udolpho* and, shortly afterwards, *The Italian*, and Matthew Gregory Lewis's (1775–1818) famous book, *The Monk*. After Mary Shelley's *Frankenstein*, this line was continued by Charles Robert Maturin's *Melmoth*. Later exponents of the genre include Gaston Leroux (1868–1927), with *Le Fantôme de l'Opéra (The Phantom of the Opera)*, of course Bram Stoker, the author of *Dracula*, and other writers.

Mary Shelley, in introducing the hideous, the heinous, the cryptic, and the criminal into literature, and combining them with "scientific" elements, gave science fiction a flavor that became part of its very fiber, ever present in succeeding works. Very often, particularly amongst the trivial works of science fiction, the portrayal of horrific effects becomes more drastic with each succeeding work. In film adaptations there is no longer any clear line to be drawn between science fiction pictures and horror pictures—thanks in no small way to the genius of Mary Shelley.

The third important achievement of Mary Shelley relevant to the story of science fiction is her use of the ancient motif of the sorcerer's apprentice, such as Lu-

35

cian had introduced in his satirical *True Stories*, and which was brought to full maturity in Goethe's ballad *Der Zauberlehrling (The Sorcerer's Apprentice).*[6]

Here the sorcerer bewitches the spirits conjured up by the apprentice. In the many science fiction variants that followed Mary Shelley's book, the point is made that sin rebounds upon its originator. Here a parallel may be drawn with E. T. A. Hoffmann. The homunculus is no less horrifying or threatening than the automaton. The creation will always in the end turn against the creator, and kill him, though the cre-

Mary Shelley's novel remains popular in print today.

Modern horror-film adaptation of *Frankenstein.*

ation dies with him. This is a fundamental thread running through science fiction literature.

Soon the territory mapped out by E. T. A. Hoffmann and Mary Shelley was opened up and exploited by other writers. It is remarkable how often it has been authors concentrating their efforts in other fields of literature—pure fantasy, adventure, crime, or Gothic horror—who have made the most significant contributions to the field of science fiction, almost, as it were, in passing.

Among these was Edgar Allan Poe, born in Boston in 1809. After the publication of his early volumes of poems went unnoticed, he turned in 1832 to publishing prose. He became famous for his theories on the "short story," but he really made his mark in his tales of horror and fantasy, and for his creation of the eccentric detective Dupin, who solved the mystery of "The Murders in the Rue Morgue" by exercising his talent for observation and power of logic, and recovered "The Purloined Letter," and thus became the literary ancestor of many fictional detectives. In Poe's rich œuvre are also to be found tales with pseudo-

THE INDUSTRIAL REVOLUTION AND FANTASY

scientific elements that may be called science fiction—for instance, "The Unparalleled Adventures of One Hans Pfaall" (1835), "A Descent into the Maelström" (1841), "Some Words with a Mummy" (1845), as well as the single full-length novel, albeit left uncompleted, *The Narrative of Arthur Gordon Pym of Nantucket* (1838).

In the story of Hans Pfaall's journey to the Moon, Poe mixes elements of fantasy with satire, as for instance in the introductory sequence, describing a "little gentleman" seen flying over Rotterdam in a balloon, who throws down a letter from Hans Pfaall and then disappears into the clouds. This balloon is made out of dirty pieces of newsprint, reminiscent in shape of a gigantic upturned fool's cap—it is through such scenes that Poe's satirical intention is made clear. In the letter itself, Hans Pfaall relates in the minutest detail the balloon journey he has undertaken three years previously, and it is not by chance that Poe has the whole escapade begin just April 1! The flight ends on the Moon. What is interesting and new here is that the journey, modeled on a bird's flight, is described as a trip through the air in which the pilot is aided, at the point where the air becomes too thin, by a "very strong, perfectly airtight, but flexible gum-elastic bag"[7] into which air is pumped by means of a "condensator." This idea of Poe's appears to be the first of innumerable descriptions of space suits in literature. The story ends fairly abruptly, for Pfaall's messenger, the little moon manikin, is swept away again by his fear of the people of Rotterdam, without waiting to collect their reply.

In "Some Words with a Mummy," a well-preserved but five-thousand-year-old Egyptian mummy is brought to life by means of an electric current. It later becomes clear that it was not dead but had fallen into a deathlike trance (a motif familiar since Mercier), and survived through the long interval owing to the Egyptian prowess of preserving bodies. Here Poe fashions a variation on the theme of time travel, with a person from the past witness to the modern age, rather than one from today traveling forward in time to glimpse the future. Thus he sidesteps any descriptions of utopian communities. For him, social commentary is a peripheral consideration; what he prefers to focus on is the combining of freedom of time constraints and the reburgeoning of life. These ideas are both carried a stage further in Edward Bellamy's *Looking Backward: 2000–1887* (1888). Eventually space travelers would be more usually settled into an artificially induced sleep under low-temperature conditions with a computer programmed to reanimate them just before arrival at their destination—usually a strange galaxy.

"A Descent into the Maelström" is the story of a ship wrecked in a furious whirlpool that was, in the world of the story, known to recur at intervals. The narrator, who by dint of precise scientific observations during the horrendous moments in the center of the maelström, draws the correct conclusions that enable him to save himself.

Poe was drawn to the theme of his unfinished *The Narrative of Arthur Gordon Pym of Nantucket* by the many difficulties and mysteries associated in his time with the area around the polar regions. After Captain

Edgar Allan Poe.

James Cook's voyages of 1773 and 1774, exploration in the outer Antarctic was an established practice—seal-hunting, for instance, became quite an industry. In 1819–21, a scientific expedition led by Bellinghausen and Lazarev sailed all the way around Antarctica; but in Poe's lifetime the interior of the continent still held many secrets, not to say puzzles, about its nature. In the preamble to his book, the narrator Arthur Gordon Pym explains how he met the publisher of the *Southern Literary Messenger*, one E. A. Poe, to whom he gave permission to print the first section of the story of his adventure in that journal. The opening pages of the book abound in the standard elements of sea stories—stowaways, escape from severest danger,

Robert Louis Stevenson.

mutiny, storm and shipwreck, shark-infested waters, rescue by a passing ship, and much more. These set pieces from the annals of tales of adventure and travel are then increasingly combined with elements of scientific fantasy. The ship sets forth into a hitherto undiscovered sea, with black natives and black animals. At this point, most of Pym's companions are killed in a landslide, which turns out not to have been natural in origin. Next comes the story of Pym's flight in a small boat, and his encounter with a gigantic snow-white creature. At this point the novel breaks off, with a note from the supposed publisher to the effect that the succeeding chapters will be published when they are forthcoming.

Poe's contribution to science fiction travel literature is largely confined to this volume. It was not by chance that Jules Verne, considering that the latter was indebted above all to Edgar Allan Poe, wrote his own conclusion to the fragment in 1897, extending the Antarctic journey and giving his own version of Pym's ending in his novel *Le Sphinx des Glaces (The Ice Sphinx)* but translated also as *The Sphinx of the Ice Fields* or *An Antarctic Mystery*.

In 1886, thirty-seven years after Poe's death, *Doctor Jekyll and Mr. Hide*, by the Scottish poet Robert Louis Stevenson (1850–94), was published. Following Mary Shelley to some extent, Stevenson places at the center of the action Dr. Jekyll, a scientist obsessed with his pursuit of knowledge and enlightenment. Unlike Frankenstein, however, Jekyll does not manufacture a monster, but under the influence of certain potions of his own invention, he himself is temporarily changed into a monstrous alter ego. Such a theme is not new, but Stevenson's introduction of it through pseudoscientific means lays the foundation for an investigation into the duality of human nature by splitting it clearly into good and bad. The potion more than gives free rein to the "bad" side of the hero's character: it also alters his external appearance. As Dr. Henry Jekyll, he is a kindly man; but when transformed into his repulsive and horrifying criminal alter ego, he appears as the vicious, snarling Edward Hyde. His undoing is inevitable as the period of time in the person of Dr. Jekyll becomes shorter, and the potion is drained more and more often. As the potion is used up, no more transformation is possible—Mr. Hyde

THE INDUSTRIAL REVOLUTION AND FANTASY

Strange sacrificial rites in the "lost" country ruled by She are watched by Ayesha (She) from her crystal throne.

perishes, totally disoriented. He takes with him his "creator," Dr. Jekyll: yet another variant on the sorcerer's apprentice motif.

Other writers were following the lead of Poe and Stevenson in blending adventure with science for stunning effect. The literature of travel had never really faltered in its popularity, and many kinds of writers continued to take advantage of the adventure format, not only to exploit the ideas of social "utopias," but to implant their own scientific ideas in the public mind.

One firm believer in the evolutionary theories of Charles Robert Darwin as put forward in his *Origin of Species* (1859) and *The Descent of Man* (1871) was

H. Rider Haggard, born in 1856 in Norfolk, England. As secretary to a titled aristocrat, Haggard traveled in his early years in South Africa, where he became acquainted with the Dark Continent first-hand. As a writer of fiction, Haggard was nowhere nearly as influential or critically acclaimed as Poe or Stevenson, yet he wrote thirty-four novels of history and adventure, usually set in foreign locales and in remote times. His concept of "utopia" took on a slightly different tone from earlier tracts, concentrating as it did on the discovery of "lost races." *She* (1887) tells the story of a tribe of people in Africa cut off from the civilized world. One familiar utopian element in *She* is Ayesha's immortality, fueled by a "life-giving" flame that

39

Shangri-La, probably the most popular conception of utopia known in the twentieth century, as it appears in movie *Lost Horizon.*

capitulates phylogeny"—from a smashingly beautiful woman to a two-thousand-year-old ugly, hump-backed ape. Thus Haggard's bow to Darwin. In the literature of a later date, Ayesha's memorable transformation in death recurs in the mainstream utopian novel *Lost Horizon* (1933), by James Hilton—called by some a potboiler—when a beautiful "immortal" woman living well beyond her years in the salubrious atmosphere of Shangri-La (somewhere in Tibet) leaves her home with her new English lover only to turn wrenchingly into an ugly, aged crone during her passage out. Made into a classic motion picture by Frank Capra, the utopia of Shangri-La prompted President Franklin D. Roosevelt to name his Presidential hideaway near Washington D.C. "Shangri-La." It is now, of course, called "Camp David." The utopianism of Shangri-La was its ingenious combination of the careless rapture of an unpolluted "magic" atmosphere and the practice of passive Eastern mysticism. But that was all to come much later. To return to Haggard, he played with the time-tested science fiction theme of doomsday when "the world will end in ice" in *Allan and the Ice-Age,* published posthumously in 1927. He also explored the science fiction motif of Lost Atlantis in *When the World Shook* (1919).

When the author of *She* and *King Solomon's Mines* was only six years of age—long before James Hilton was born—the first classic writer of science fiction literature, Jules Verne, had already risen to maturity and published his first book, *Cinq semaines en ballon (Five Weeks in a Balloon)*. Verne's literary debut was a clear indication of the direction that science fiction would be taking in the succeeding decades of the nineteenth century.

seems strangely prophetic of nuclear power. The memorable fantasy element in the book is her surprising death as she bathes herself in the flame and slowly reverts—in a reverse of Darwinian "ontogeny re-

JULES VERNE AND HIS "VOYAGES EXTRAORDINAIRES"

The first classical writer of science fiction literature, as has been said, was the Frenchman, Jules Verne. He was born on February 8, 1828, into an age when the most developed countries of the world, at whose head were England and France, were introducing factory production redesigned on mechanized lines after the

experimentation and discoveries made in the eighteenth century. The new means of production was provided by the Industrial Revolution of the preceding years, and itself became the basis of the explosive development of production and of the further technical and technological research of succeeding years.

40

Jules Verne died in Amiens on March 24, 1905, and thus in his lifetime saw major breakthroughs achieved in science, the greater part of which found at least a mention in his books.

The last century saw little if anything of the possible negative side effects of these developments, and so it is that the era in which Verne was writing was an era of unbounded belief in science—even, it may be said, of euphoria. Mankind ruled the natural world and the limitless power of technology was the tool through which he ruled. This was the credo of the nineteenth-century bourgeoisie, and was the formula according to which Jules Verne created the characters in his fictions.

The changes in production not only had a disturbing effect on the social structure of the population, but

Jules Verne.

also caused a major redefinition of literature's attitude to itself and to its audience. In the eighteenth century the free-lance writer had been the exception, such a life being somewhat risky; after the Industrial Revolution in the nineteenth century, however, freelancing in literature became the rule and most authors held a high status. New laws covering the production of goods and the ever-increasing division of labor were not without effect even in the marketing of books. The breakdown of the link between a publishing house and its own retail outlet was a fait accompli early on; the close relation that was until that time paramount had suddenly become unnecessary. The speedily expanding bookshops chose their stock with far more of an eye to its commercial value than to its origin. Under these conditions, the novel, always till then overshadowed by other genres of literature, was able to begin its victorious rise—which led, incidentally, to the foundation of popular light fiction as a major genre at the beginning of the century.

Enlightenment had paved the way for compulsory education which—according to the demands of the new forms of production—was accomplished in more and more countries and led to the growth of the reading public. The need for information in all classes of society, but especially the new middle classes, continued to increase with the growth of international trade—and as traveling became easier. Apart from books, there were newspapers and magazines of all kinds, and in particular, family journals, which bridged the gap between knowledge and entertainment, all of which performed an essential function. This was the reason why so many authors financed their "independent" existence—some occasionally, others constantly—by working as journalists.

The now very high turnover in books helped finance research in paper production and in printing itself—for example, new English paper-making machinery, a new steam press patented by Friedrich König in 1810/11, and machine-aided bookbinding methods. Through such developments, book production was simplified and the product made cheaper to buy. Print runs multiplied. The structure of the literary genres was irrevocably changed with more and more authors working for the press. New forms of publicity, pamphlets and early eye-witness reports had

41

an effect on the purer forms of storytelling: the serialization of novels, stories, and travel books in magazines was tried, first of all in France, and found to be highly popular. Writers adapted their techniques to these new conditions by developing literary methods of creating and maintaining suspense.

When Jules Verne first stepped onto the literary stage, publishing houses had already set about specializing, and the first of the large-scale commercial publishing houses were already in existence. Nevertheless, the sale of belletristic literature in book form was still relatively low, so around the middle of the century the story serializations and magazines were of special importance. Other fundamental aspects for sale were the increasing members of new lending libraries spreading like wildfire; their needs and requirements caused a thorough overhaul of thought in the publishing industry.

Only when set against this background can the far-reaching effectiveness of Jules Verne's work be fully appreciated. He refashioned the old traditions of centuries-old travel fantasy (*"voyages imaginaires"*) to suit the modern temperament, and, above all, the tastes of the newly developed reading public. "In the early eighteen sixties, France witnessed the drawing to a close of the anti-liberal liaison between Napoleon III and Pope Pius IX; the French education system was progressively secularized and the press censorship considerably relieved; the novels of Jules Verne, in their idealized way, were eagerly appreciated during this period characterized by a hitherto suppressed hunger for a new scientifically based yet entertaining literary mode."[1]

Verne superimposed the very real problems of contemporary technological development and scientific exploration on the well-loved fable structures and motifs of adventure and travel fantasy. According to the practice of the time his works were published in fortnightly episodes in the *Magazin d'éducation et de récréation*. Only later were the early novels made available in book form, published by Hetzel in the *Bibliothèque d'éducation et de récréation*, as part of a library called *"voyages extraordinaires."*

The greatest influence on Verne was Edgar Allan Poe. This is evident not only in Verne's sequel to Gordon Pym's story *(The Ice Sphinx)*, or in the introduc-

tion of the point from *Trois dimanches dans la semaine (Three Sundays in the Week)* into the story *Le tour du monde en quatre-vingts jours (Around the World in Eighty Days)*, but also in the preference Verne showed for cryptograms and their unraveling. Verne himself was the creator of some four thousand crosswords and alphabetical puzzles of profound difficulty. Jules Verne was preoccupied with the conflict of good and evil so familiar from and fundamental to the fairy tale, and nearly all his characters can be readily identified as being on one side or the other of the moral divide. The social consequences of contemporary technological and scientific advances are presented in Verne's novels as relatively uncomplicated and hardly ever negative. The villains in his books as well as his heroes are for the most part ordinary citizens with great scientific gifts. They embody the ethical and moral ideals of the eighteenth century. Jules Verne very rarely acknowledged that the new developments of the nineteenth century were in contradiction to humanist ideals such as "liberty, equality, and fraternity." Society other than the bourgeoisie was

Jules Hetzel, Jules Verne's publisher.

JULES VERNE

CINQ SEMAINES

EN BALLON

VOYAGE DE DÉCOUVERTES EN AFRIQUE

Par trois Anglais

Rédigé d'après les notes du docteur Fergusson

TRENTIÈME ÉDITION

Ouvrage couronné par l'Académie française

BIBLIOTHEQUE

D'ÉDUCATION ET DE RÉCRÉATION

J. HETZEL ET CIE, 18, RUE JACOB

PARIS

—

Tous droits de traduction et de reproduction réservés

Five Weeks in a Balloon. Title page of the volume in Hetzel's *Bibliothèque d'éducation et de récréation.*

made up of largely irrelevant bystanders: loyal servants, honest sailors, humble underlings, the almost anonymous comrade at arms—for example, of Captain Nemo and his like, who willingly perform duties set by their mentors or some incredibly gifted engineer.

Verne's attitude to the nationalist movements of the age was contradictory. His sympathy lay with the northern states in the American Civil War, as an opponent of slavery. On the other hand, he wrote books (for example, *The Steel Elephant*) in which he thoroughly endorsed colonialism. Nonwhites, in the world of Verne's writings, occupy a lowly position, with the exception of Prince Dakkar, who has become immortal as the secretive Captain Nemo. In many books Verne's views are shown to be open and unprejudiced on other peoples, and in others a nationalistic, even chauvinistic, tone is unmistakable. This latter element strengthened after the War of 1870–71. In the positive as in the less savory sides to his character, in his achievements as in his mistakes, Jules Verne was very much a child of his time.

The son of a well-respected lawyer, Verne was born and spent his childhood and youth in Nantes.

Felix Tournachon, photographer and caricaturist known as Nadar.

43

JULES VERNE

DE LA TERRE À LA LUNE

AUTOUR
DE LA LUNE

VOYAGES
EXTRAORDINAIRES

COLLECTION HETZEL

After attending school, he stayed there to continue his education, only moving to Paris after attaining a doctorate in law. The secure life of a civil servant appeared to be his. But, as he himself put it: "Because of my natural leanings towards literature, I left the path that had been prepared by my father. When I was just twenty-one, I was fortunate enough to see my first theater piece *Les pailles rompues (The Broken Straws)* staged in the Theater Vaudeville in 1850. Then several other pieces followed."[2] These comedies are now forgotten.

Verne's interest in balloon flight was soon awakened. Aeronautics was still considered a great risk, although the successful first flight of the brothers Montgolfier was already eighty years in the past (1783). The writer, photographer, and caricaturist Nadar (real name, Felix Tournachon) was a friend of Verne's and had a desire to make an ascent in a balloon. Verne worked at this project with immense enthusiasm, involving himself with all stages of construction. But the project never got off the ground as Nadar's balloon crashed. Around the time of Verne's growing enthusiasm for scientific experimentation, the newspapers were publishing numerous reports on David Livingstone's explorations in Africa—in particular his successful crossing of South Africa from west to east in 1856. Jules Verne combined the two themes and in 1863 he wrote a book about a balloon journey across the African continent and related the "experiences" of the airborne explorers. This book, *Five Weeks in a Balloon* was the first example of a new literary genre named by Verne (in 1902) the "scientific-didactic novel."[3] This was the first of Verne's *"voyages imaginaires"* or *"voyages extraordinaires,"* to be followed by some hundred more novels and tales that all followed the basic structure of his first and almost all of which concentrated on such imaginary journeyings.

The Parisian publisher Hetzel, who had sown the seeds of the first book and financed it, immediately placed Jules Verne under contract for further productions. With his iron discipline and boundless energy, the author trod further along his newly chosen path.

Underwater action in 1971 film version of Jules Verne's *20,000 Leagues under the Sea.*

His plan was to bring out a new book every six months. He had a gift for exploiting and incorporating new scientific trends in each story. He noted on innumerable slips of paper anything of interest in the fields of engineering, industry, physics, biology, and other subjects. With his admirable imagination he managed to isolate and weave into his adventures the newest ideas in science, pulling his heroes through the most unusual and challenging experiences. The technical revolution had left a gap in the book market that Jules Verne found himself able to occupy with his novels of technological wizardry. Scientific novelties were primarily responsible for the immediate and worldwide success that his books enjoyed.

From approximately the end of the 1860s onwards, doubts were growing as to the absolute validity of the premise that progress in scientific knowledge was in itself sufficient to ensure the general progress of humankind. Verne did not omit to deal with such problems; in more than one work he contemplated the dangers inherent in the uncontrolled development of science, and the risk that knowledge might fall into the wrong hands. To his dying day, Verne remained on the side of the bourgeois humanists, those champions of the old progressive ideas. In his later works there are even antiutopian elements: in *L'éternel Adam (The Eternal Adam)* published posthumously, Verne reworks the main theme of newer science fic-

Cover of a Hetzel edition of the two Moon books of Jules Verne.

45

20,000 Leagues under the Sea. Contemporary illustration by A. de Neuville in a Hetzel edition.

tle (usually hard to decipher, or damaged and incomplete, so that the hero must first make many mistakes before his goal is within sight). In the message in a bottle in *Les enfants du capitaine Grand (The Children of Captain Grant)* the longitude is illegible; there is a similar loss of information as regards longitude and latitude in *Les mirifiques aventures de maître Antifer (The Magnificent Adventures of Master Antifer)*; in *Voyage au centre de la terre (Journey to the Center of the Earth)* there is a message in an unknown runic script; and in *La Jangada* there is a confession written in code. In characterizations, Verne makes free use of contemporary cliché. Again and again, one meets the silent, totally unflappable English gentleman, from Samuel Fergusson in his first novel to Phileas Fogg in *Around the World in Eighty Days* and the chess-playing British officer in *Hector Servadac* (sometimes called *Off on a Comet*); or the agile North American in his shirtsleeves; the patriotic,

Cover of an 1874 luxury edition of *Around the World in Eighty Days*.

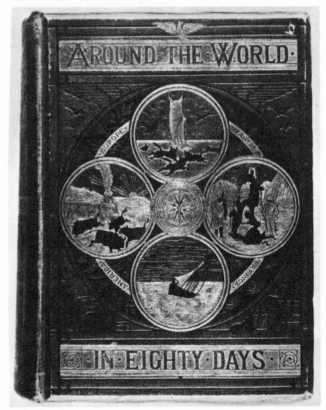

tion, namely the doomsday plight of the last humans on Earth after some great catastrophe.

Most of Verne's books are based on the model that gave him his first success. In the first phase of the plot, the journey that forms the main story line is initiated through some special occurrence, thus setting a train of events in motion. Often an idea that meets with ridicule or opposition—a wager can dramatize almost anything!—sets the story going. The preparation for the journey, long or short, forms the opening section of the typical Verne adventure, and leads into the journey itself.

Another opening gambit is the discovery of a secret manuscript, or the contents of a message in a bot-

46

The ocean landing after the Moon journey. Illustrated Hetzel edition.

Quixote with the hero's appendage Sancho Panza. Verne's Samuel Fergusson has a follower, Joe, in *Five Weeks in a Balloon*; Professor Lidenbrook has as a guide the good Hans Bjelke from Iceland in *Journey to the Center of the Earth*; on his journey around the world, Phileas Fogg is accompanied by Jean Passepartout; Nab the Negro looks after his master Cyrus Smith in *L'île mystérieuse (The Mysterious Island)*, and so on.

In order to provide excitement and tension in the story, the competitor or opponent of the main figure sometimes takes part in thwarting the hero or even in celebrating the hero's failure as his own triumph, for example, in *De la terre à la lune (From the Earth to the Moon)*, and in *Au tour de la lune (Back from the Moon)*. In other cases, crimes are committed and over-eager police detectives jump to the erroneous conclusion that the hero is the perpetrator of the evil, and so the chase is on; thus the chief of police suspects Karl Dragoch in *Le pilote du Danube (The Danube Pilot)* of being the leader of a band of river thieves; Fix, the detective in *Around the World in Eighty Days* likewise suspects the hero. Because the authorities are thus anxious to halt the journey, Verne is able to give much added tension to that inherent in his story's time, place, and circumstance.

It is notable that Verne's basic plan for his novels includes precise data as to the dates of events in the story, serving the readers as guides for their own benefit. Mostly Verne gives dates that fall immediately before the date of the first edition. A few examples demonstrate this.

Date of 1st Edition	Title	Date given for events in book
1863	Five Weeks in a Balloon	Action begins on January 14, 1862
1864	Journey to the Center of the Earth	Journey leaves base on May 22, 1864
1865	From the Earth to the Moon	After end of American Civil War (1865)
1867–68	The Children of Captain Grant	Search in 1854–55

ultracultivated Frenchman; or many variations on the comic yet rather dangerous "ugly German" (for instance, the Bavarian baron Weissschnitzerdörfer who wears his shaving brush in his hat in *Claudius Bombernac* or Professor Schultze of Jena in *Les cinq cents millions de la Begum,* [usually *The Begum's Fortune*] who of course, as a typical German, eats sausage and sauerkraut, drinks beer, and, through his founding of the Steel City, even endangers the peace of the world).

Jules Verne carried on traditions inherited from world literature that affected his handling of themes and characterization. He had a propensity for giving each hero a loyal factotum as is so often seen in picaresque novels—above all in the incomparable *Don*

1869	Twenty Thousand Leagues under the Sea	1866–67
1870	The Mysterious Island	Hurricane early March 1865, then several years living on island
1873	Around the World in Eighty Days	Journey begins October 2, 1872, and ends December 21, 1872
1879	The Begum's Fortune	Sarrasin hears of inheritance on October 28, 1871; action of story continues until Autumn 1878

The Czech film director Karel Zeman combined live film and animation in a movie after Jules Verne's *Face to the Flag*.

THE INDUSTRIAL REVOLUTION AND FANTASY

By this device, the reader is led to believe that the events described are almost part of the news of the day. Verne draws on new discoveries, experiments in physics and chemistry, and technological discoveries of the immediate present, and, with the help of fantasy, weaves them together into an exciting plot involving the hero, the villain, and all the details of the journey. The newest technological facts that Verne collected out of the newspapers month by month were incorporated into the stories as accepted practice; thus the reader's appreciation of the "scientific" nature of the fiction was strengthened.

Verne led his characters to parts of the world that at the time were largely unknown and unexplored. Precisely *because* of their novelty, these backgrounds enhanced the exotic nature of the adventures described. For instance, Verne describes Africa *(Five Weeks in a Balloon)*; the Amazon region *(La Jangada)*; the delta swamps of Florida *(Nord contra Sud [North against South])*; Siberia and China *(Claudius Bombernac; The Courier of the Tsar, Michel Strogoff)*; the Balkan countries *(The Danube Pilot; Mathias Sandorf)*; the Arctic and the North Pole *(Aventures du capitaine Hatteras [The Adventures of Captain Hatteras])*; India *(Around the World in Eighty Days)*; the Baltic *(Un drame en Livonie [A Drama in Livland])*; the lands bordering the Black Sea *(Keraban le têtu [Keraban the Obstinate])*. Verne divulges full details of the lands and their peoples in the course of his narratives, and readers feel that they are roaming the whole globe with the author as their guide. Then the author penetrates even further. The depths of the ocean are plunged *(Twenty Thousand Leagues under the Sea)*, and the center of

49

Jules Verne continues popular with the motion picture public as this advertisement attests.

the Earth itself explored, access being gained by means of a volcanic crater. Hector Servadac and his comrades go on a journey through space on the back of a comet, and with four hundred thousand pounds of gun cotton, Barbicane's manned rocket is blasted to the Moon. And with his own flash of genius, Verne anticipated the effects of weightlessness that would be experienced later on such real flights.

Verne made use of favorite themes of adventure literature from down the centuries, giving them a new dimension. Shipwrecks were an especial love of his, with various Crusoe-like results. There is for instance the tale of Ayrton, put off his vessel for villainy, who becomes while fending for himself quite wild, and, through the same process, purified. There is also the tale of the group shipwreck on *The Mysterious Island*, where—as opposed to Crusoe's experience—all new inventions and experiments are understood

and practiced, and, in short, nothing is impossible. Even the unrecognized and self-depreciating helper turns out to be the one-time Captain Nemo!

Motion and transport are important themes in Verne's books. He uses all kinds of agencies: animals, carts, railways, row boats, big ships, carriers, even tightrope walkers—and, of course, balloons. But he also made many forecasts in this field: the most famous after the launch of the rocket must be the secret submarine *Nautilus* by Captain Nemo. And in *Robur le conquérant (Robur the Conqueror)* he introduces a primitive kind of helicopter.

Verne can describe the battle between the ichthyosaur and the plesiosaur *(Journey to the Center of the Earth)* with as much excitement and imagination as he can the quasi-military attack of the icebears *(Hatteras)*.

Rogues figure often in Verne's dramatis personae, as do pirates, kidnapers, and gangs of thieves. These all contribute to the danger through which the hero moves, appearing to put the outcome in doubt, and delaying the successful return home as well as constituting a threat to life itself. The most abominable of these villains are those who exploit their private inventions or discoveries or sudden acquisition of wealth for their own ends or who attempt to conquer the world *(Face au drapeau [Face to the Flag]; The Begum's Fortune)*. But the good and fair in Verne will always triumph—though usually only in the nick of time! The villain is routed—balance is restored.

The novels of Jules Verne's last ten years testify to their author's increasing sense of sympathy with oppressed peoples *(Mathias Sandorf, A Drama in Livland, The Danube Pilot)*, which he manages to incorporate in his tried and tested formula.

All his novels have neat endings: the main plot is resolved, what is sought is found, the outcast is rescued, suspicion is lifted from the innocent, humanity rescued from terror and—most of all—the race is won, the journey is brought to a successful conclusion. In these closing sections of his books, Verne often uses an effect made popular in the theater, when the tension is wound so tight the whole structure seems in danger of snapping.

The story reaches a climax where failure is imminent and appears inevitable, the destination of the trav-

50

elers is lost from sight, the villains are poised on the very point of total triumph. But then at the very last moment the tables are turned and the moral world is once more established.

Since Jules Verne was so extraordinarily successful with this basic structure, it is really not to be wondered at that many writers sought to borrow his formula, and that they were promoted by various publishers as "the German Verne," "the Hungarian Verne," and so on. But none of these achieved the high quality of the original. Elements of Verne's concepts were common in adventure fiction up through the middle years of our own century, especially in the realms of popular literature.

Jules Verne did not confine his writings to fiction. Between 1870 and 1878 he and Théodore Lavallée produced a six-volume work, *Histoire des grands voy-ages et des grands voyageurs (History of Great Voyages and Great Voyagers)*.

Verne's best works still rank at the forefront of science fiction. Every year, his books are reprinted (albeit in shortened, reworked, or modernized forms) and they remain popular among young audiences as well as elders. Versions are produced on stage, on film, or on television, famous actors do not turn down the chance to play the parts of Verne's immortal creations. The roots of this success may be traced to Verne's skill in combining strenuous and exciting action with accurate observation of human capacity and value under the most difficult circumstances. The immense optimism conveyed in his books (and in those of his immediate successors) was to be found again only in the books of socialist science fantasy and in western science fiction during the John Campbell era.

THE GIANT OF SCIENCE FICTION:
H. G. WELLS

Some three years after Verne's first major success with *Five Weeks in a Balloon*, on September 21, 1866, Herbert George Wells, one of the most important pioneers of modern science fiction, was born in Bromley, then a small town in Kent though nowadays a suburb of London.

When H. G. Wells was twelve, his mother became the main breadwinner of the family when his father, a professional cricketer, broke his leg. She worked as housekeeper for one Miss Bullock of Up Park, and it was there that Herbert George Wells spent his early teens. The library of the house had an irresistible attraction for the boy, and even when he visited it in later years, he turned to the library again for the works of Voltaire, Thomas Paine, Swift, and Plato. He first met the social criticism of Dickens through an uncle who kept a hostelry by the Thames, who also introduced his nephew to the plethora of trivial literature of the day. In particular, Wells at this time seriously considered Eugène Sue's *The Secrets of Paris* one of the most important books ever written.

After a basic education, Wells tried to find his feet in trade for a living—joining in turn a draper, a chemist, and also trying his hand as an assistant teacher.

The most significant post he held during this period was at Midhurst, where he worked as a teacher and continued his own education. He passed all his examinations and thereby earned himself a free place at the Normal School of Science (later the Imperial College of Science) in South Kensington. It was there that Wells's ideas began to form under the influence and tuition of one particular professor. As a student teacher, he studied biology for one year with Thomas Henry Huxley, the grandfather of Aldous and Julian Huxley. The profound respect Wells had for Huxley is clear from a passage in his book *Mr. Blettsworthy on Rampole Island* where, borrowing the voice of the hero's uncle, Wells gives a thumbnail sketch of Huxley, describing how the bishops in the House of Lords have lost much of their influence at the hands of this mental athlete, this through-and-through right-thinking man.

Professor Huxley was an energetic opponent of religious orthodoxy, and a passionate advocate of the ideas of Darwin. Wells, whose religious doubts had been evident even in his childhood, became, under the influence of Huxley, a convinced atheist.

After the retirement of Huxley, Wells continued his studies in physics and biology with considerably less enthusiasm. His interest turned to history. Meanwhile, old habits dying hard, he continued to read any and every book that fell into his hands. At this time he attended and spoke at debating society meetings. With all these extracurricular interests, he failed his college examinations. This forced him to switch from science to the arts.

During his student days and afterwards, Wells came into intimate contact with all the social movements of the day. At the beginning of the 1880s, the working class in England was experiencing a new upswing. The Fabian Society, formed in 1883–84, supported the theory of the gradual development of

Caricature of H. G. Wells by Max Beerbohm.

Herbert George Wells.

socialism. The Fabians were identified with some of England's leading intellectuals: Beatrice and Sidney Webb for instance, and George Bernard Shaw, who despite their differences, were all agreed in putting Marxism to one side. Wells however became an influential person with his developing theory of ethical socialism. Only with the split in the Fabians in the first decade of the twentieth century did Wells leave the society, and subsequently began to attack its ideas in his writings. (The Fabian Society was, with the trade unions and other parties, one of the groups that founded the British Labour Party. Immediately, the Fabians became the focus of the right-wing party and the union leaders.)

Wells's attitude, as evidenced in his early work, developed around his atheism, his belief in Darwin's evolutionary theory, and in the ethical socialism of the Fabian Society. In the ten short years between 1895 and 1905 most of Wells's science fantasy was published, and his fame was assured. Some of these works first appeared in the *Strand Magazine* (published by George Newness from 1891), and in them Wells

52

of a machine that can move freely through space and time. The theory is substantiated by experiment with a working model of the machine, but this does not wholly convince. One week later, the main protagonists gather together again—the Time Traveler puts in a somewhat tardy appearance, "in an amazing plight." [1] And the others foregather to hear the story of the journey through time.

The time machine has taken the first time traveler in literature forward to the year 800 000 or so. Wells's picture of the future of mankind is gloomy in the extreme. The social structure of England at the end of the nineteenth century is extrapolated to grotesque proportions. There are now just two "classes": the Eloi, who live in the upper world; childlike, playful, not to be persuaded to engage in purposeful employment; and the Morlocks, who live alongside

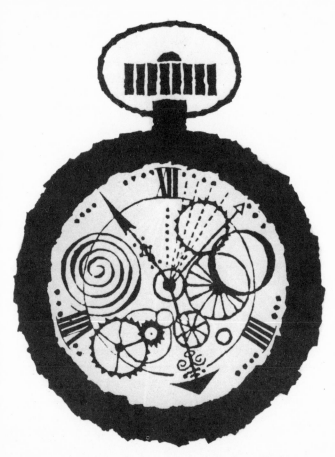

A modern German-language version of *The Time Machine*.

Thomas Huxley, an early adherent of Darwinism in Great Britain.

made significant strides forward from the Vernian model of science fiction. He did not confine himself to the fictional conquest of geographical areas of the natural world known to exist though as yet still not fully explored. Wells toyed with ideas wholly new—time travel, man-eating plants, contact with other beings, aliens, wars between worlds, and so on. He thus first introduced into literature those ideas and themes that for nearly a century have formed the basis of science fiction throughout the world and that still inspire authors now to try new variations.

Even his first "Scientific Romance," as he termed it, was a literary achievement. *The Time Machine* (1895) includes references to contemporary scientific speculation on time as a fourth dimension. Wells opens the book with his "Time Traveler" involved in a general discussion that lays down the theories on which a great experiment is founded: the construction

53

heavy machinery, confined to an enormous underground network of dark wells and tunnels. The Time Traveler supposes that the Morlocks have to work as slaves to the privileged of the upper world. But the inexorable degeneration under the oppressors' rule has ensured that the Morlocks, protected by the night, are always usurping the power of the Eloi. Eventually, it becomes clear to the Time Traveler that the Eloi are only suffered to exist at all as "mere fatted cattle, which the antlike Morlocks preserved and preyed upon."[2]

The story is lightened by the inclusion of a love interest, a chase, a visit to a museum, and numerous other episodes that climax in a battle with the Morlocks—followed by escape at the last moment.

By mishandling the machine, the Time Traveler journeys even further forward in time to find only some monstrous crablike life forms, and again further forward to an era when no life remains save for lichens, and finally to a time when there is nothing at all. The Earth is then a freezing, dead planet, shortly to dissolve entirely. This is Wells's gloomy projection.

At the end of the book, the Time Traveler starts out anew: "The Time Traveller vanished three years ago. And, as everybody knows now, he has never returned."[3]

Wells was by no means the first writer to confront the present with either the past or the future. Mark Twain's humorous novel, *A Connecticut Yankee in King Arthur's Court*, was published not long before *The Time Machine* in 1889, and tells the tale of an American from the age of hectic industrialization who is propelled by a blow on the head into the wonderful Celtic world of King Arthur and his Round Table, and who eagerly introduces to that world many of the "achievements" of the nineteenth century. This technical trick enables Mark Twain, and the reader, to stand back and examine the outrages of his own age. Edward Bellamy's *Looking Backward* (1888) sketches a utopian world of a society that has achieved socialism, not through revolution but by means of general education and reform. In this book, the protagonist is transported to the future through an unnaturally long sleep (an idea used by Wells himself later in his novel *The Sleeper Awakes*, a revision of an earlier version, *When the Sleeper Wakes*). *The Time Machine*, however, is the first such work wherein a machine is envisaged that enables travel through time at will, and it is this aspect that it can legitimately claim to be the first example of a new branch of science fiction. Since this book was first produced, the number of time travelers has been legion, and their conveyances have been of infinite variety—but they can all be traced back in their origins to their Wellsian prototype. In fact some authors emphasize their

An earlier version of Wells's 1895 time machine: Mark Twain's 1889 time-warp fantasy of Camelot.

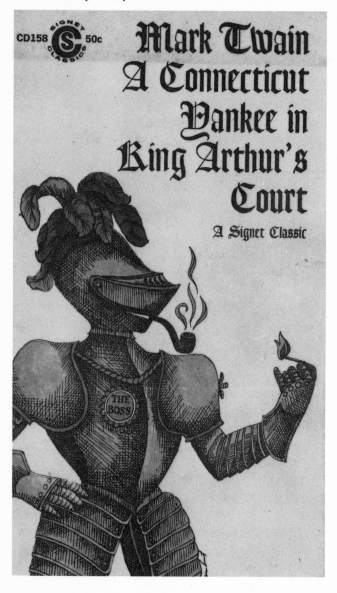

CD158 50c SIGNET CLASSICS

Mark Twain
A Connecticut Yankee in King Arthur's Court

A Signet Classic

THE BOSS

54

his island he creates men out of animals. He overturns evolution at a stroke. The changed animals living on the island must without fail obey Dr. Moreau in everything. They have to recite, prayer-fashion, the island's laws, which are all precepts on behavior towards "Him" (Dr. Moreau)[4] who is a godlike figure. Wells, like all authors of such tales, is here working out a variant of the sorcerer's apprentice theme. Dr. Moreau, by the end, can no longer control his creations—some are even turned into vampires—and Moreau himself is eventually savaged to death by a puma on which he is experimenting. The return to the jungle proceeds apace. The terrified witness to the saga, a shipwreck victim, flees to a boat that drifts

The recovered "time machine" of Wells in Bastiné's novel.

The time machine in Carl Grunert's novel. Illustration by Stein, 1908.

debt by having their heroes find the lost time machine of Wells and travel in it anew—for example, Carl Grunert's *Pierre Maurignac's Abenteuer (Pierre Maurignac's Adventure)* (1908); Wilhelm Bastiné's *Die wiedergefundene Zeitmaschine (The Recovered Time Machine)* (1914); and Egon Friedell's posthumous novel, *Die Rückkehr der Zeitmaschine (The Return of the Time Machine)* (1946).

The second novella of H. G. Wells, *The Island of Doctor Moreau*, kindled a wave of indignation soon after its publication in 1896, and soon became a bestseller. The book is as relevant to us today as it was when written for its pertinent view of such problems as genetic engineering and its consequences.

Dr. Moreau is a vivisector, like Frankenstein before him, who wants to be a creator of new life. On

Bundled up to appear visible, the invisible man, Claude Rains, causes consternation in an English pub.

ashore and is eventually rescued. His nephew frames the story, releasing it to the public only after the "death" of his uncle, Charles Edward Prendick.

This book threads together the mythology of creation, elements of horror literature and the Gothic novel, and aspects of current scientific disputes raging around the issue of vivisection. All are melded together with motifs of the adventure story (the cruel ship's captain, his mutinous crew, and the shipwreck itself) into a coherent and successful whole.

Wells's third book, *The Invisible Man* (published in 1897 and referred to by Wells as a grotesque romance) is of lesser significance in the growth of

science fiction as a genre and likewise of lesser significance in demonstrating either Wells's effectiveness as a writer or his social/scientific concerns. In this book Wells taps the rich resources of the sorcerer's apprentice theme once again. An expert in optics, the hero, Griffin, conducts research to isolate a substance that will make him invisible. His chemical process has changed "only the living tissue," he explains, "and only for as long as [he is] alive."[5] The work centers on the situations that arise as a result of the invisibility of the hero (only his clothing and as yet undigested food remain visible): a burglary at the vicarage, a case of arson, stealing clothes in a shopping emporium, a

THE INDUSTRIAL REVOLUTION AND FANTASY

huge brawl, and at the end the general pursuit of the "invisible man." He is wounded and wants revenge; he lays deep plans for murder to heighten general fear. Thus Griffin instigates his fight against the world at large, and lays the seeds of his own downfall. His corpse slowly makes "that strange change to visible fleshliness."[6]

Of much more importance is *The War of the Worlds*, published in 1898. This novel was the basis of the famous American radio play with Orson Welles (script by Howard Koch), whose first broadcast on October 30, 1938 led to a general panic when many listeners took the report of the attack from Mars as a genuine news flash.

Wells starts from the premise that the Martians are creatures quite different from ourselves, who have as a result of the very harsh natural conditions on their native planet developed an outstanding degree of intelligence. They are now trying to colonize a new home: on Earth. This means war. Thus begins the Martian attack with their spacecrafts, against the weaponry of which humanity has no defense, and the attackers make steady inroads. Then there comes a turning point in the fighting: the enemy is not resilient against bacteria found on Earth, and they succumb in great numbers to dreadful illnesses. Wells's pacifism shines through in his descriptions of the atrocities of war: thousands of humans flee before the battle; bombs, flying machines, and artillery blacken the skies; poisonous gases are released. In the epilogue[7] the narrator explains that mankind has learned a thing or two from the Martians—for example, that it is possible to build airplanes and that mankind's vision of the future will never be the same again.

Wells's *Invisible Man* has spawned many film versions—for instance, Harry Piel's *The Invisible Man Comes to Town.*

The radio script that made Orson Welles a household name in America—courtesy the imagination of another Wells.

With this book a procession of innumerable novels telling the tale of war in the universe was set in motion. In the more trivial science fiction works this basic story line is made to carry the wildest fantasy and often quasi-fascist ideology. Wells's conception of his novel was a kind of warning to humanity to identify certain nonpacific tendencies and particularize their consequences.

The serious tone of this book is unmistakable, and in Wells's subsequent works it becomes even more pronounced. The general political situation at the turn of the century, the rattling of sabres, the (as yet localized) wars, the economic and social pressures on the poor in society—Wells's appreciation of all these factors led him in 1899 or thereabouts to turn his pen more to serious speculation on the future of mankind. He did not entirely forsake science fiction, but he fixed his attention more on works of a sociocritical content. He also published an increasing number of theoretical works.

This change was already noticeable in the novel *When the Sleeper Wakes* (1899)—later revised as *The Sleeper Awakes*. The hero, Graham, falls into a kind of hypnotic trance. In the 203 years of this

Illustration of a Martian in Wells's *The War of the Worlds* in *Pearson's Magazine*, illustrated by Goble.

THE INDUSTRIAL REVOLUTION AND FANTASY

trance, his small property so grows that when he wakes he owns practically the Earth, for his private estate encompasses half the world. The sleeper's property is being administered by a high official. Owing to the fact that increase in money means increase in power, arguments between various factions have developed. The novel propounds late nineteenth-century ideas on utopia; it differs from most such books (for example, Bellamy's) in projecting no changes in social structure. The traditional inequalities still obtain, only they are now even starker. An oppressed rebellion, led by Ostrog, moves against high officialdom. It is during this period of turmoil that the sleeper awakes—ostensibly disturbed by Ostrog so that he may authorize the distribution of goods.

However, Ostrog has orchestrated the whole episode in order to inherit power. He has used a massive airplane to gather together the "Blacks." (Here one finds racist elements; the Blacks are portrayed as ignorant and brutal.) Graham, who has learned how to pilot an airplane in a matter of days, enters the fight against Ostrog's massive flying transport in his own small "aeropil." He is able to destroy several of Ostrog's huge machines, including even the aeropil in which Ostrog has been planning to make his escape. The betrayal is avenged, and the people victorious. At the end of the book, Graham falls into a kind of abyss—a floating between dream and reality.

The descriptions of the battles are built up by details of the technical achievements of a distant future: heavy machinery for all uses, moving pavements, cylindrical "books," television, cafeterias, fluorescent advertisements, a machine approximating modern radio, a specially designed day home for young children, and as a final comfort to the old, euthanasia for a fee. All industrial plants are underground. The workers have hollow cheeks, weak muscles, tired eyes, and terrible skin diseases (because of strong chemicals and the like).

What is so special about *The Sleeper Awakes* is the manner in which Wells adopts aspects of ancient folk tales of prolonged sleep—for example, the German myth of Kaiser Barbarossa—and mingles this with the "world redeemer" motif as in the English tale of King Arthur who will appear just at the right moment to put the world to rights. Wells takes up this

motif and demonstrates in Graham, the sleeper, the tragedy of the idealist who must be defeated by the realities of power. The presentation of a "Golden Age" heralded by the world redeemer when "the sleeper awakes" is shown in all its hollowness. With this novel, Wells issued a new warning to the world.

In the book *The First Men in the Moon* (1901), Wells derives from Verne's *From the Earth to the Moon* the necessity for an airtight chamber to a moon rocket. Wells's two astronauts, Cavor and Bedford, are not shot into space, but launched by means of Cavorite, an antigravity substance. The body of the craft is made of two spheres: the inner one houses the two

Illustration for H. G. Wells's *The War of the Worlds.* An armory is destroyed (chapter 9).

59

astronauts, and the outer one is made of movable segments through which the vehicle can be steered. The book contains a description of the journey and of the fantastical life on the Moon, including enormous Moon calves, in comparison with which the Selenites, or Moon people, seem antlike, and an extraordinary flora consisting of quick-growing thorns and the like, with a variety of fungus definitely hallucinatory in effect. There is the further description of underground worker stations, and of the journey to Earth. For Wells another aspect is rather more important: Cavor stays behind on the Moon (he feels at home there), and reports by radio signals on the natural history of the Moon, the rise of the Selenites, their language and art, their social structure, and finally, of his contact with the Grand Lunar, the master of the Moon community. In his discussion with the Grand Lunar, Cavor describes the ability of mankind and the "orders and ceremonies of war,"[8] and shortly thereafter the radio messages cease. This peaceful world has its own way of protecting itself from the aggression and disruptiveness of the Earth's inhabitants.

Just one year after *The First Men in the Moon* was published, the new universal art form of film availed itself of this material, combined with motifs from Verne. Georges Melies, a Frenchman, made a fifteen-minute film *The Journey to the Moon*—the first science fiction movie.

Alongside the novels of Wells's early period are several short stories that are also worthy of enumeration among the classics of science fiction. Most of them date between 1895 and 1904. "Ugh-Lomi—a Story of the Stone Age" is an illustration of a cultural history that offers the reader an insight into the world of our ancestors as Wells's study and imagination saw it. Another such story is "Through a Window" (recalling E. T. A. Hoffmann's "The Cousin's Window"), in which the observer's passivity is broken as the story relates many typically nineteenth-century adventures with Asiatics running amok—and with rescue only at the very last moment.

Stories such as "The Country of the Blind," "The Magic Shop," "The Truth about Pyecraft," and "The Wonderful Suit" are not science fiction in the narrower sense. They are rather examples of contemporary tales of fantasy. Among these can also be counted "The Man Who Could Work Miracles," although here a science fiction motif plays a large role (Mr. Fotheringay wishes that the Earth would stop turning, "but made no stipulation concerning the trifling moveables upon its surface,"[9] and everything is "jerked and smashed and utterly destroyed"[10]).

In the best of his stories, Wells draws motifs, ideas, and themes into the general fund of science fiction material so that later science fiction authors may till a richer ground. "The New Accelerator" introduced the idea of absolute acceleration of life, with the natural pace being stepped up many thousandfold. This is an open-ended situation where many ideas may be explored—noise is no longer audible; window curtains appear stationary despite the blowing wind; with such abnormally fast movement possible there may be a danger of clothes spontaneously catching fire. At the close of the story, the inventor Gibberne is working on a brake, or retarder, which should counter the effects of the accelerator. This story is the first science fiction short story to throw off the chains of mankind's biological system. Something similar is achieved in "The Plattner Story," in which the hero can be proven by reference to photographs to have been perfectly normal until the age of twenty-one. But then, because of the explosion of a certain powder, he is lost for fourteen days. After his "return" it is found that his anatomical structure is reversed—certain symmetrical parts of his body have been swapped to the opposite side. During his fortnight's absence, Plattner was in another strange and dreamlike world where curious life forms observed mankind incessantly.

"The Remarkable Case of Davidson's Eyes" documents an instance of telesight. For some weeks, whenever Sidney Davidson opens his eyes, he sees before him scenes occurring on the other side of the world. "The Strange Orchids" is a story concerning plants that suck blood and murder people.

"The Sea Raiders" tells the tale of struggles between humans and colonies of the mighty kraken—sea monsters that rise out of the deep. After killing eleven people, the monsters vanish back into the ocean leaving no trace. A different kind of contact with fantastic creatures is experienced by Butcher, the hero of the story "Aepyornis Island." He not only dis-

60

Scene from the first science fiction film, *The Journey to the Moon*, 1902.

covers bones, but also three eggs preserved in a bog. In spite of all kinds of dangers, one egg manages to survive and eventually hatches the aepyornis, a long-extinct species. For two years the animal is good company for the shipwrecked Butcher, but later it grows quarrelsome and dangerous and Butcher is obliged to protect himself by trapping it and killing it.

"The Crystal Egg" concerns a method of making contact with life on Mars, the crystal egg of the title being something like a television. In "In the Abyss," an engineer named Elstead descends in a kind of bathysphere to find a parallel world, to which he falls victim on a second descent.

"A Dream of Armageddon" describes, in the form of a dream, a horrific vision of a war that rages over the entire world and from which there is no refuge. Wells recalls an apocalyptic terror, in particular the passage in the New Testament at Revelation 16:16 where Armageddon, a mountain by Megiddo, is named, and where three unclean spirits, spirits of devils, challenge the kings of the Earth at the Last Judgment. In later years Armageddon became a well-worn symbol of total destruction in science fiction writing. The book *Armageddon—2419 A. D.* by Philip Francis Nowlan is notable for containing the first story of the cosmic hero Buck Rogers. In cosmic painting too the same theme is present in many impressive paintings of galactic slaughter and battle (for instance in the work of Michael Whelan).

Wells follows an old tradition in his story "Mr. Elvesham." In this tale a person attains immortality by slipping into the body of a much younger man, who must meanwhile inhabit his more grizzled form. As a result, the young man commits suicide. The irony of the tale is that the newly youthful Elvesham had been run over by a hansom cab twenty-four hours before. The exchange of bodies can protect him from much, but not this.

In 1897 Wells wrote his story "The Star," which relates events occurring when a strange planet enters our universe. The end of the world appears nigh, but then the new body miraculously changes course for the Sun. Wells goes deep into the circumstances of the scare and its effects: earthquakes and other natural disasters abound, causing mass evacuations and—happily—a new sense of fraternity.

In "The Lord of the Dynamos," Wells deals with events when the Asian Azuma-zi, because of his mythical background, sees the dynamo machine he works at as a god, and brings it human sacrifices. Soon, however, he traps himself by touching certain parts of the machinery, causing his own death. This motif of the collision of mythical ideas with highly developed technological apparatus was to bear much fruit in later science fiction. In "The Wonderful Visit," an angel is sent out of heaven, and must learn to adapt to earthly life. Wells, like Verne before him, kept a watchful eye on new scientific discoveries and theories, and used them in his writing whenever he could, as is shown in his story "The Stolen Bacillus." This story was published in 1895, only eleven years after Robert Koch in Germany had isolated the cholera bacillus. The story tells of an anarchist who steals a bacterical culture, aiming to set the world in fear and terror by the threat of cholera. The comedy of the story lies in the fact that the thief has made a mistake, and instead of the cholera has taken bacteria that color blue anything with which it comes into contact. Through the discoveries of the latter half of the nineteenth century, the study of bacteriology attracted much interest, as is demonstrated by Wells's incorporation of such themes into many of his plots.

61

The novels Wells produced after 1904–05, which have to do with scientific fantasy, have less liveliness and originality than his earlier work. In his later years he concentrated more and more on probing ethical and moral problems.

In *The Food of the Gods* (1904), a substance is discovered that leads to enormous growth. This "heracleophorbia" produces giant wasps, earwigs, creepers, and vines, and, above all, giant children. Wells describes how the normal people, now by comparison small, attempt to oust the giants and how the giants rise and rebel. Although some giants are killed by cannon fire, they are victorious and spread the heracleophorbia around London so that everyone becomes their size. Wells believed that the two "races" must live with one another in peace—generations later the giants and the normal-size people will still exist alongside one another. "The little will hamper the great and the great will press upon the little. So it must needs be."[11] "We fight not for ourselves, but for growth, growth, that goes on for ever."[12]

The tendencies evident in these later works became ever more fixed, as for instance in *A Modern Utopia* (1905), and *In the Days of the Comet* (1906). In this latter novel, the green gas emanating from a comet passing very close to the Earth makes humanity at last peaceable. This wisdom is enough to transform society to socialism without turmoil or violence.

The sense of impending unrest already evident by 1908 influenced Wells to write *The War in the Air*, in which a world war between Germany and the United States is anticipated; there are airplanes in the battle, with whole cities (New York for example) being bombarded.

Wells was forced to be even clearer in his descriptions by 1914. In *The World Set Free*, he incorporates the research of Rutherford and others and describes in the first chapter of that book a new energy source, which is actually what is now termed nuclear energy. Wells immediately recognized how this research could be put to use in the weapons industry, and his novel describes a war in the middle decades of the twentieth century that causes untold human destruction. It was a warning to the world, delivered immediately before the outbreak of World War 1.

In World War I, Wells's anticipations of evil were more than fulfilled in the craze for murder and mayhem, and although he was in succeeding years an unflagging propagandist for peace, international relations, and utopian world government, his works in the science fiction genre bear unmistakably pessimistic threads. In 1923, in his *Men Like Gods*, he attempted a satire on imperialism, but here the utopian idea can no longer be taken seriously. This novel is chiefly interesting for its use of an idea that Wells was to employ with increasing frequency—a small group of people finding themselves in another world some three thousand years further advanced. It is noteworthy that this more advanced society has achieved a kind of communism through gradual social evolution. There has been an ongoing development of greater and greater economic organizations that have eventually led to this utopian society in which huge groupings of people are no longer considered, but only individuals. "It is a life of a demi-God."[13]

The hero of *Men Like Gods*, Barnstaple, and several others, are then returned to our world. Barnstaple is fundamentally altered by the experience of that other world and immeasurably removed from the friction and bustling of everyday life on Earth. For he knows that in three thousand years our own planet *could* be like that other, if . . . .

This book reveals that Wells, despite his passionate commitment, was no longer fully in touch with the conditions that would underlie twentieth-century developments. Another testament to this loss of touch was Wells's wrong assessment, during his fortnight's sojourn in Petrograd and Moscow in the autumn of 1920, of the new opportunities opened up by the Soviet experiment. In his early works Wells had sketched the future with great imagination, but he was unable to grasp the essence of the social changes under the surface in the Soviet Union and behind the postwar suffering. The prejudice of the ethical socialist against Marxism is evident in his *Russia in the Shadows*. But even so, Wells makes characteristic observations on the newly begun revolution in culture and the changes in educational policy that give hints as to the possible wider opportunities for the future. In Wells's report on his meeting with Lenin he refers to him as "the dreamer in the Kremlin." Wondering

62

H. G. Wells visits V. I. Lenin in the Kremlin, 1920.

whether he had made himself fully aware of all that had already been achieved in Russia, for instance in the electrification program, Wells muses that Lenin, like the good orthodox Marxist he is, has while throwing out all that is "utopian," fallen victim to the utopian—namely the utopia of electrification. Wells complains that Lenin has put his whole influence behind the realization of a plan to create gigantic power stations throughout Russia in order to provide complete provinces with light, means of transport, and electricity for industrial purposes. Lenin explains that two wide areas were already fully electrified as a pilot scheme. Wells wonders what project could be more extreme than one to provide electricity to such an im-

measurably enormous country with so many forests inhabited by illiterate peasants, with no water power, with no technological base, and whose trade and industry is thoroughly underdeveloped. Wells scorns the idea of envisaging such a process for Russia, claiming that it is too much for the imagination to encompass. He says that he finds it impossible to foresee the completion of such a project in the dark crystal of Russia. Lenin's power of imagination was such, Wells says, that he was almost enticed into believing it himself.

The early fantasies of Wells have already been overtaken by the reality of today. Few of his later works are of significance in the history of science fic-

Raymond Massey, a visitor from outer space, in the 1936 film of H. G. Wells's prophecy of the future—*Things to Come.*

tion. For instance, the novel *The Dream* (1924), set some two thousand years in the future, tells the story of a man who, after seeing the ruins and the mummified corpses (through gas) of the last war of a previous age, dreams of life in this (our own) cruel era of the twentieth century. Another book with some limited relevance is *Mr. Blettsworthy on Rampole Island* (1928), dedicated to the "immortal ideas of Candide." Wells opens this book by addressing the reader with his ideas on its theme: it is meant to be the story of an educated and refined man who suffers shipwreck and is totally isolated from human company for many years except cruel and raw cannibals. The story is meant to show how he observes other animals' behavior; how he goes mad; how he eventually by strange means escapes the terror and barbarism of Rampole Island, arriving back in the civilized world just in time to fight in World War I; and how he later comes to the point of wanting to return to his island forever. The story is also meant to illustrate, according to this introductory section, much that may amuse or edify concerning morals, habits, convictions, warmongering, crime, and a storm at sea. The reader is then forewarned that the book closes with ethical observations on life in general and contemporary life in particular.

At the outset this novel, after a longish peroration on the hero's upbringing, appears to be in the same vein as *The Island of Doctor Moreau.* Here also the hero is shipwrecked on an island. But, unlike in the earlier story, Rampole Island turns out to be a dream, a delusion. It is nothing less than the real world, rising behind the mist of the hero's illusions. The power structure of the island—namely cannibalism, the death of enemies, the narrow-mindedness of the warriors (whose motto is that "all warriors are equal")—all these constitute a model for the world situation as Wells perceived it. This warning is made the more concrete by Wells's idea of drawing a parallel between cannibalism and the worldwide reaction to the judicial murder of Sacco and Vanzetti in the United States.

In this book Wells takes the idea of development into the realms of the absurd. The balance of his thinking is that evolution allows to survive the species that is least suited for continuing progress. This is demonstrated by the natural history of the giant sloth, which seems to show that the survival of juveniles is far less evident than the slow pace of adaptation.

There are still elements of scientific fantasy in the later books of H. G. Wells, as in *The Happy Turning* (1945), where, in the hereafter, imaginary conversations take place with Jesus, as a revolutionary generally shunned by mankind. These traces of science fiction are small indeed. The development of the genre of science fiction literature had meanwhile taken other paths leading away from Wells.

64

THE INDUSTRIAL REVOLUTION AND FANTASY

Some countries witnessed a revival in novels and short stories featuring social utopian themes during the years when Verne and Wells were writing. In basic structure and general range, they followed the paths trodden by the classic writers of the genre in the sixteenth to eighteenth centuries. If, however, Thomas More and Campanella, each from his own point of view, wrote works that genuinely offered an alternative to the "unsocial" order they found around them, this is the case only to a limited extent with the later utopian writers.

Socialist utopians like Saint-Simon, Fourier, and Robert Owen, had attempted to describe the changes that had come about with the Industrial Revolution, and to find ways of assimilating or overcoming them. Karl Marx and Friedrich Engels refined socialism to a science relating social development to the laws of nature, thereby producing what seemed to be a rational prognosis for the future of mankind. This eventually pulled the rug out from under the feet of the real utopian writers.

For the new experimenters in the genre, there now existed only limited possibilities if they chose to stay within the old established structure. One alternative was to describe a social structure that expressly conformed with the ideas of Marxism. Then it was only necessary to fill in the details of social organization and technological progress within the order, so that it could seem worth striving for when compared with contemporary life. Another alternative was for authors to try, from an antisocialist standpoint, to portray current societies, Candide-like, as the best of all possible worlds in which there are just a few aspects that need change. Increasingly such an outlook tended to take a more pronounced antisocialist stance. A third alternative was to avoid and ignore any reference to social science and present an individual message of salvation.

The basic structure of such stories remained true to its roots. This is the more to be wondered at when one considers that in the meantime most of the globe had been cartographed, with now only a few blank spaces left. Despite this, the new utopians found odd areas where they could situate their Earthly paradise. The hero—scarcely a believable individual anymore—now had the dual function of narrator and source of the story; he comes by some unusual way into the new utopia (for example, in unexplored Africa, he will cross mountains wreathed in taboos,

Edward George Earle Lytton, first Baron Lytton of Knebworth.

or channel through a system of caves). He wanders through a wondrous landscape, learns about the customs and mores of the people and their social structure and then returns, usually after negotiating a number of additional obstacles. These works have in common with the old utopias the motif of a central conflict between the world of the book and the world of the real. It is thus understandable that the hero of such a work tends to be "colorless," and fails to come to life, for the author will tend to place little value in him as a character, preferring simply to use him to express the detailed descriptions of the ideal society in the author's mind. In order better to convince the reader, the hero is usually given an unbelieving, skeptical outlook at the onset, and is made to doubt the opportunities afforded by such an ideal society, only to become gradually a convinced adherent of the ideas underlying the utopian state. He retains only the fondest memories of the place after his return, mourning his loss.

In 1871 appeared *The Coming Race*, by Lord Edward Bulwer-Lytton (Edward George Earle Lytton, first Baron Lytton of Knebworth, 1803–75). This novel is a textbook example of the attempt to imagine a world truly divorced from the conflicts that beset the author's age. An engineer and his friend, mountain climbing, enter a strange new world remote from civilization. The friend dies; the engineer finds retreat impossible. Bulwer-Lytton proceeds to describe the world inside the Earth, including its people, its animals, and even some machines that look and act something like humans (in fact, a type of robot). The head of state of this new world explains that war has long been eradicated—all through the secret power of "Vril." Thanks to Vril, people are even able to fly, and with Vril they can counter any attack (they have a spearlike weapon powered by Vril that in some respects anticipates a laser-beam gun). Vril, in this fiction, is a secret natural power that supports everything and also affords everything unlimited power. Bulwer-Lytton adds to the interest of the story by including a love plot: the beautiful and clever Zee falls in love with the narrator. When, however, the daughter of the head of state *also* falls prey to his charms, the hero's life is threatened. Then Zee forces an opening through a rock to the ordinary world and carries

him through. After his return to his own world, the engineer learns from a doctor that he has very little time to live. He decides to write down his experience as a warning to the world against the danger that this underground race might one day emerge into the light of day, and, with the help of Vril, destroy mankind. It is easy to recognize among the technological ideas ascribed to the future in this work certain motifs and ideas that later were to become favorites among lesser science fiction writers.

One year later, in 1872, Samuel Butler (1835 to 1902) published his novel *Erewhon, or Over the Range*, followed in 1901 by a sequel called *Erewhon Revisited* (later published together under the general title of *Erewhon*). This book is often considered in

Title page of Samuel Butler's utopian classic.

 EREWHON

AND

EREWHON REVISITED

BY
SAMUEL BUTLER

INTRODUCTION BY
LEWIS MUMFORD

THE
MODERN LIBRARY
NEW YORK

66

Title page of Edward Bellamy's utopian classic.

relation to *The Coming Race*, but this might be adjudged inappropriate, for Butler's manuscript was ready before Bulwer-Lytton's novel was available or even advertised. Less problematical is the deciphering of the title *Erewhon* as a backwards rendition (almost) of the word "nowhere," carrying on the tradition established by More's use of the word "utopia."

The similarities between Butler and Bulwer-Lytton lie in the fact that both envisage a future in which the social structure they know stays largely unchanged and both have little belief in the possibility of a social flowering of mankind. They unite against the loss of individual identity, and place their hope for change principally in the use of technological and scientific discoveries.

Samuel Butler subjects the morals and everyday attitudes of Victorian England one by one to a thorough investigation and exposes their obsolescence. He does not introduce any miracle substance like Vril, but prefers to criticize direct normal human common sense. His hero, George Higgs (who, strangely enough, remains unnamed and hardly even defined throughout the first volume) arrives in Erewhon over the mountains and experiences this unknown society as a stark contrast to contemporary European society, especially in its English form. That Butler's new society is developed not from the scientific penetration of political and social problems but rather from the individual extrapolation of Darwinian ideas and laws is made clear by chapters 23 to 25, concerning machines. It is a variant of the old theme of Ludditism.

In the preface to his new edition of August 1901, the author wrote: "There is no central idea underlying *Erewhon.* . . . In *Erewhon* there was hardly any story, and little attempt to give life and individuality to the characters."[1]

Hence the essaylike flavor of the book. Butler himself had certainly realized the inconsistency inherent in his method, and presumably this is why he allowed thirty years to elapse before writing the sequel. In *Erewhon Revisited,* Higgs's son, meanwhile grown up and educated in England, is the narrator and commentator. This time however, *Erewhon* is no longer an unknown country, taking away much of the tension of the earlier book. Butler's Erewhon inhabitants are found to have succumbed to the same weakness of character as Europeans; this is seen as a general failing of humanity at a particular stage of development. In an afterword to the 1981 Berlin edition of the book in translation, Joachim Krehayn wrote, "Thus Butler takes back some part of his original criticism. At the end of the whole work there remains the hope that future generations will learn from the mistakes of their parents. People will be reconciled and together build a better world."

In 1888, Benjamin Tickner published a book in Boston, the success of which has completely overshadowed all other modern utopias—*Looking Backward* by Edward Bellamy (1850–98). In the US alone, more than 400,000 copies were sold immediately, and the book's fame spread throughout the world by

67

means of translations within only a very few years. In Germany, for instance, Clara Zetkin was instrumental in making the book available by not only writing a deeply appreciative notice on it, but also authoring the translation that is still authoritative.

Edward Bellamy was born in Chicopee Falls, Massachusetts, a small industrial town in the northeast of the country, the son of a liberal Baptist minister. Although he was a sickly child, his mother's discipline and the high school he attended in a neighboring town gave him a good education at an early age. Added to this was his own observation of the crass social contradictions in his hometown, which permeated American society throughout the second half of the nineteenth century following the Civil War (1861–65). On the one hand there was a massive surge of belief in America as the land of unlimited opportunity, while on the other hand the misery of the lower classes was intensified. Workers' organizations formed, pursuing indefinite, often quasi-religious socialist ideas.

Hartmut Lück says that in this situation of unrelenting class antagonism the people wondered what the future held—a question answered here in the form of a socialist utopia.

In 1868, Edward Bellamy accompanied a rich cousin on a trip to Europe. It was during this journey, while staying in Dresden, that Bellamy first came into contact with socialist ideas. Returning to America, he worked for some years as a journalist, but had to give this up as tuberculosis began to take its toll. From 1880 he and his brother Charles produced a paper whose aim it was to tell the truth about economic and political events, avoiding the sensationalism of much of the current literature.

Throughout the 1880s, Bellamy was forced to see that his homeland was drifting ever farther from his ideal of a humane democracy. Already in the 1870s, according to his own diaries, he was playing with the idea of writing a novel depicting a radically different future for America. He then turned to the idea of a "prose poem," a project that he soon relinquished, choosing finally the novel form, which he eventually considered best suited for his aims.

Inspired by the thoughts expressed in the American sociologist Laurence Gronlund's *The Co-opera-*

William Morris.

tive Commonwealth in Its Outline, An Exposition of Modern Socialism (1884), Bellamy realized his project in 1886–87. His first object was to educate rather than entertain his public; the didactic elements in the book are heavily emphasized, and they are the driving force behind the success of the book. As in other utopian novels, the characters are not given much individuality; in fact their only raison d'être is to facilitate Bellamy's didactic aims.

Just as H. G. Wells was to do over a decade later, in *The Sleeper Awakes*, Bellamy projects his hero into the future by means of a prolonged cataleptic sleep. Julian West, a young entrepreneur from Boston in the year 1887, has himself put into a deep trance by a "Professor of Animal Magnetism,"[2] or mesmerist, to cure a bout of insomnia. In order to remain undisturbed, his sleeping quarters are hidden away under the foundations of his house. One morning he fails to wake up, and the next thing he knows, it is 113 years

68

later. He is then wakened by the owner of a new house built over the ruins of his own, and emerges to find a wholly new state run along socialist lines. Julian West learns about his new surroundings first through his own observation and second through his companions' explanations, which are presented for the most part in dialogue. He goes to the roof garden, for instance, where he is shown a transformed Boston landscape (lacking the chimneys and their smoke!); he visits shops, a major hotel, and so on. This enables Bellamy to draw comparisons between the harmony attributed to the year 2000 and the problems of 1887. The author's main thrust however is in his detailed analysis of the future way of life—including technological predictions—through which he tries to emphasize to the reader the necessity for changing contemporary society. Much of Bellamy's criticism is still pertinent today: for example, his description of the arrangement of residential areas in cities (far more widely dispersed); his ideas on the upbringing of children and their multifaceted education; the role of women in the family and in society; physical training and sport; justice and punishment; and trade and international exchange of goods.

In all, Bellamy sketches a picture of a society that he envisaged as the product of a socialist system. He was no Marxist: he believed in the peaceful growth of socialism under the leadership of an organization of a "national party." Bellamy writes, as if in fairy-tale style: "In the time of one generation men laid aside the social conditions and practices of barbarians, and assumed a social order worthy of rational and human beings. Ceasing to be predatory in their habits, they became co-workers, and found in fraternity, at once, the science of wealth and happiness."[3]

Bellamy produces an especially fine effect in the last chapter of the novel, where the hero dreams that he has been returned to his own inequitable society of the nineteenth century, and finds it excruciating after his experience in the future. But this return is just a bad dream, and Julian wakes up restored to the twentieth century, where he will live out the rest of his life in that harmonious world.

The fourth major utopian novel written just before the turn of the century was *News from Nowhere, or: An Epoch of Rest* (1891) by William Morris (1834–96), once referred to by Engels (in a letter to Friedrich Adolph Sorge) as a socialist through his feelings. Unlike Bellamy, Morris was part of the social struggle of his age. He studied painting at Oxford, and took up and extended the thoughts of John Ruskin in the field of social reform and the arts. In the 1880s he was an active participant in the political force of the English working classes. He was for a while a member of the Social Democratic Federation, and in 1884 he became leader of the Socialist League. He made a study of economics at the time of political activity.

In many literary works in a wide variety of genres Morris gave expression to his deep belief in a better, socialistic future for mankind; Morris brought together some of the Marxist theory and the coopera-

The first page of Morris's *News from Nowhere*.

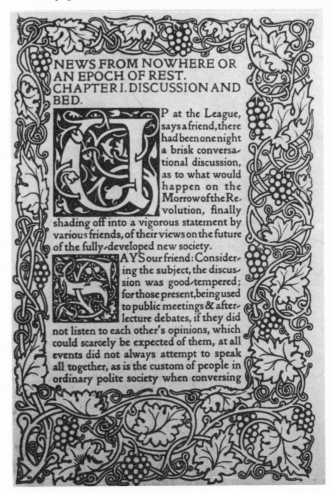

tive utopian visions of Fourier. To this eclectic mixture of ideas, Morris remained true to the end of his life.

The most important of his writings is his novel *News from Nowhere*. Morris differs from Bellamy in that he sets his novel in his own age, and in a London socialist club. A friend tells him a tale he has heard from another source, and for the sake of simplicity in narration, this tale is given in the first person. Only at the end is it made clear that it is all a dream.

In the tale, the reader is taken to the England of 2100 or thereabouts—that is, a century after Bellamy's fictional Boston. For Morris, the socialistic future is a kind of rural idyll. The major cities are gone, the people live in country communities or in parklike areas. The overcoming of capitalism leads immediately to the wide-scale suppression of industry and machinery. The people work with their hands in small cooperatives, which is felt to be almost a kind of bliss.

A comparison between the futures envisaged for mankind by Morris and by Bellamy reveals clearly that it is the American author who was gifted with more insight into the necessity of industrial development and had a deeper understanding of property relations and technology. Morris's Arcadia evidences a fundamental misunderstanding of the economic conditions of human development.

In contrast, however, Morris is far more precise than Bellamy on the question of how a socialist society may be established: there is no peaceful transition for him, but a full revolution led by a form of workers' party, the "Committee of Public Safety." The bourgeois state and its institutions are revealed as the rulers' instruments of power. Morris describes this process as "war from beginning to end,"[4] until at last the might of capital was crushed: the first prerogative in forming a socialist society.

Besides these four important utopian novels, the closing years of the nineteenth century saw the production of many other attempts at such hypothesizing, but they are mostly weak rehearsals of the same old ideas.

TECHNOLOGICAL FANTASY AND PLANET STORIES

The Franco-Prussian War of 1870–71 and its immediate repercussions (the struggles of the Paris Commune, the founding of the German Reich) mark an important turning point in history. One era came to an end, the era when bourgeois society established and secured its political supremacy. Now the first signs of a new era were becoming visible, during which the bourgeoisie gradually lost its position as the decisive leading power.

Industrial and scientific advances created an explosive rise in productivity. An ever closer linkage between factory production, transport, education, and science is the key to this new stage of development. The process of capital concentration in the banks and in production accelerated in giant steps. In the industrially developed countries the changes were obvious: huge manufacturing centers and the terrible slum ghettos of the multiplying army of workers with their inevitable consequences in society and the nations'

health became the new face of the cities. Smoke and a smoggy haze, visible from afar, showed the locations of the industrial centers.

Railways, bridges, stations, telegraph poles and wires, and paved roads—the landscape even outside the towns was permanently changed. Industrial landscapes were created showing only the work of the human hand obeying the laws of profit and utility. Questions of beauty, harmony, happiness, and wholesomeness stood for little.

Despite these developments, or perhaps because of the perceptible changes all around, the age was characterized by optimism and hope of further technological advance, and belief in a better future that would be achieved with the help of new knowledge to make all things possible and solve all problems.

Thus it is not to be wondered at that science fiction now produced a new variant specializing in stories based on newly opened vistas. One can even

70

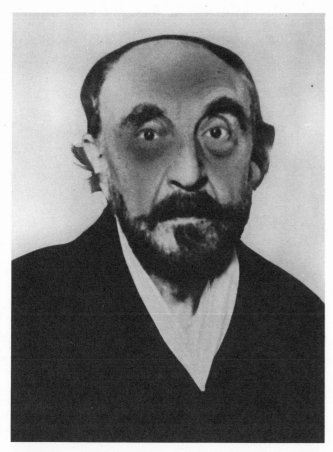

Joseph-Henry Rosny the Elder.

claim, and with justice, that the "novel of the technological future" dominated science fiction at this time.

It was to the tried and tested model of Jules Verne that authors turned for inspiration, sometimes adapted, or even stole. The social background was projected in many cases in the image of the ideals prevalent at the time of writing and based on the author's own surroundings, sometimes even revealing nationalist tendencies. Many authors however took great pains to avoid social questions altogether and set their books in a future based on existing social structures and political institutions.

Sometimes the writer's utopian dream was set on the Moon, or one of the planets such as Mars. This latter was the object of wide public interest at this period owing to the discovery of the "Martian canals" by the astronomer Giovanni Schiaparelli. There were enough novels of a type to be identified as another

sub-genre of science fiction—the "planet novel." Between 1889 and 1915 more than fifty-five such books were published in English, and no less than forty-eight in German.[1] Similar figures could be quoted for French and other languages.

This development of science fiction into a genre dealing with the technology of the future was not confined to the writers in Great Britain and America. Parallel tendencies are to be found to a greater or lesser extent in authors from many different nations. France was naturally at the forefront in developing the traditions of Jules Verne. Even during Verne's lifetime, it is possible to identify authors who were influenced by his ideas and technique. One such is Albert Robida (1848–1926), and another is Joseph-Henry Rosny the Elder (or, J.-H. Boex, 1856–1940). Rosny found great favor in France just before the turn of the century with his books *La guerre du feu (Fire War)* and *La mort de la terre (Death of the Earth)*. Even more widely read was the work of Maurice Renard (1875–1939), the writer most often nominated to second place after Verne. He deviated more than his contemporaries from the shining example of Verne by avoiding "extraordinary journeys," instead trying to represent in his novels, under cover of fantasy, the effect of scientific discoveries on people. His novels *Le docteur Lerne, sous-dieu (Doctor Lerne, God Figure)* (1908), and *Le péril bleu (The Blue Peril)* (1910), as well as his later books such as, *Les mains d'Orlac (The Hands of Orlac)* (1920) and *Un homme chez les microbes (Man of the Microbes)* (1928) are of importance in science fiction because they anticipate the problems of transplantation and explore the ethical questions raised by such activity. Renard's Dr. Lerne is an expanded version of Wells's Dr. Moreau. Renard is first in the ranks of many science fiction writers to have scientists perform transplants of human brains. Orlac, on the other hand, is a pianist, who after an accident receives the hands of a murderer transplanted. The hands are not under the control of their new owner, and force him to acts totally foreign to his personality. *The Blue Peril* explores a new and important theme in science fiction—the concept that mankind is not the result of natural evolution, but is being carefully bred and monitored by an extremely advanced civilization elsewhere in the cosmos.

71

In Russia, science fiction as a genre was born in the first half of the nineteenth century, as in other European countries. Here as elsewhere, straight fantasy and scientific fantasy are so closely related that it is hardly possible to draw the line between them. Wilhelm Küchelbecker, one of the Decembrists, published a story set on the Moon ("The Land of the Headless") as early as 1824, and the succeeding decades saw many new editions of *The Fantastical Travels of Baron von Brambäus* by Senkovski, which tells of travels to the core of the Earth and to an island near the North Pole.

Alexander Weltmann's novel *Aleksandr Philipovich Matsedonski* (1836) takes us, albeit without the aid of a time machine, into the past. In the work of many authors of the nineteenth century, themes and motifs common to science fiction are to be found in abundance, for instance: Nikolai Chernyshevski ("The Fourth Dream of Vera Pavlova," in the novel *Chto delat'? [What to Do?]*, 1863); Nikolai Gogol, Ivan Turgenev, Mikhail Saltykov-Shchedrin, and Fedor Dostoyevski.

In the last decade before the turn of the century, Russian scientific romance gradually switched in emphasis to science and technology for the basis of its plotting and setting. Some of the most important works dating from this time are: "In the World of the Future" (1892) by Shelonski, Chikolev's "No True Story, but Equally no Fairy Tale: An Electrical Story" (1895), and Rodnykh's *Samokatnaya podzemnaya zheleznaya doroga mezhdu Sankt-Peterburgom i Moskvoyu (The Automatic Underground Train from St. Petersburg to Moscow)* (1902). In the three chapters of this "novel," a quite straight tunnel between

Conrad Veidt in the film *The Hands of Orlac*, 1924, adapted from the novel by Maurice Renard.

THE INDUSTRIAL REVOLUTION AND FANTASY

two cities—one that ignores the curvature of the Earth—is postulated. On releasing the brakes, the train passes through the first half of the tunnel going faster and faster, gathering sufficient momentum to travel the second half of the distance towards its destination. This energy-saving plan is meant to be taken not too seriously, and the author invites readers who are curious to know more, to apply to him direct.

Planet stories and tales were also produced, for example by the Father of Space Travel, Konstantin Tsiolkovski, in his "On the Moon" (1893), and "Dreams of the Earth and the Heavens" (1895). There are many others worth a mention: "The Worlds' Fight" (1900) by Kholodny, "The Journey to Mars" (1901) by Afanasev, "On Another Planet; a Story from the Life of Martians" (1901) by Infantev. Semenov's "astronomical" novels *The Empress of the World* and *The Rulers of the Air* were published in 1908 and 1909 respectively, followed by Krasnogorski's *On the Air Waves* in 1913.

In his smaller works even the major Russian author Aleksandr Ivanovich Kuprin (1870–1938) made use of science fiction motifs, for instance in his story "The Star of Solomon" (first published in 1920) and in his novella *Liquid Sun* (1912). Of most importance to him were the consequences for the fate of mankind of scientific research, contrasting with the more action-packed novels of Renard in France that share the same concern. In this connection, Kuprin investigates the question of the responsibility for the discovery born by the inventor. His short story, "The Toast" (written in 1906 but not published until 1917), is set in New Year 2906—that is, about a thousand years into the future. Kuprin makes this the year 200 of a new time scheme, which reckons dates from the month when "the last country organized as an independent state, the most stubborn, conservative and musty of all countries, namely Germany, at last decided to give up its outdated and pathetic notion of national independence, and joyfully took membership of the anarchical World Band of Free People, to the jubilation of the whole world."[2] Kuprin envisages the world as having, after thirty years of immense labor, been turned into an electromagnetic coil. The central stations are at the North and South Poles, and "the incredible power of the Earth's magnetism produces

Kurd Lasswitz.

enough power for all factories, workshops, agricultural machines, railways and ships."[3] At the New Year, the connection is demonstrated on screens from the North to the South Pole. While giving his speech, the chairman tells of what he has read in a book about the twentieth century and the monstrous and haphazard life of his forefathers. Pictures are shown on the screens demonstrating this, along with scenes of how such a situation gave rise to outcry and revolution. A toast is duly drunk to the "Martyrs of the Past."[4] But the author makes his point by having a beautiful woman weeping and whispering how she "would have liked to live at that time, together with those people, with them."[5]

This humanist strain, showing affection for the world and its people in his own time, is not unique to Kuprin, but informs nearly all the works of Russian science fiction before World War I, and the tradition was continued in the 1920s by Soviet writers.

Lasswitz's tales in a new edition in the series "SF-Utopia," Berlin, 1982.

Contemporary with the above and of equal importance are two novels by Aleksandr Bogdanov, *Krasnaya Zvezda (The Red Star)* (1908) and *Manny the Engineer* (1913). In the latter many technological discoveries are adumbrated, for example the conquest of gravity, rockets driven by atomic power, and so on. But it was *The Red Star* that had the greatest influence on succeeding generations of science fiction writers, for it was in this novel that for the first time in Russian literature the excitement of science and discovery were linked with the utopian picture of a communist society achieved through revolution. This novel also contains details of blood transfusions undertaken by Martian doctors.

Writers from other parts of Europe who contributed to the growth of science fiction at this period include the Czech writer Jakub Arbes ("Saint Xaverus" [1873]; "Newton's Brain" [1877]; "The Last Days of Mankind" [1895]), the Pole Sygurd Wisniowski—whose tale "The Invisible Man" ("Niewidzalny") was published in 1881, that is, a full sixteen years before Wells's novel on the same subject!—and his compatriots Antoni Lange, Wladyslaw Uminski ("the Polish Jules Verne"!), and Jerzy Zulawski, who was the author of a trilogy set on the Moon; the Hungarian Mor Jokai ("Oceania: The Story of a Sunken Continent," "The Book of Future Centuries," "Twenty Thousand Years under the Ice"), the Belgian Henri Proument, and others.

Especially effective in their flights of technological fancy are the works of some German writers, for instance the short stories of Carl Grunert, including "Feinde im Weltall" ("Enemies in Space") and "Im irdischen Jenseits" ("The Earthly Hereafter") (1905), "Menschen von morgen" ("Tomorrow's People") (1905), and "Der Marsspion" ("The Martian Spy") (1908). Also in this collection is "The Adventure of Pierre Maurignac," which describes a young man who finds Wells's time machine and uses it to travel to the distant past and tells of his meeting with primitive man and cave bears. Other popular stories and novels dealing with the technological world were written by Max Eyth: "Der Schneider von Ulm" ("The Tailor of Ulm"), the story of an attempt to fly, two hundred years too soon (1906), "Der Kampf um die Cheopspyramide" ("The Battle for the Pyramid of Cheops") (1902), and so on. Most popular of all though are the stories of Kurd Lasswitz, and Bernhard Kellermann's *Der Tunnel (The Tunnel)*.

Kurd Lasswitz (1848–1910) is today fully acknowledged to be one of the major figures in science fiction writing before World War I. His books include: *Bilder der Zukunft—Zwei Erzählungen aus dem 24. und 39. Jahrhundert (Pictures of the Fu-*

Lasswitz's most important novel, *On Two Planets*, in an edition of 1913.

THE INDUSTRIAL REVOLUTION AND FANTASY

Kurd Lasswitz

Auf zwei Planeten

ture—*Two Tales of the Twenty-Fourth and Thirty-Ninth Centuries*), published in 1878, which included the stories "Bis zum Nullpunkt des Seins" ("To the Rockbottom of Being"), and "Gegen das Weltgesetz" ("Against the World's Laws") (1877); his "modern fairy tale" "Seifenblasen" ("Soap Bubbles") (1890), the novel *Auf zwei Planeten (On Two Planets)* (1897), "Nie und immer: neue Märchen" ("Never and Forever—New Fairy Stories") (1902), a collection of short pieces "Aspira—Roman einer Wolke" ("Aspira—the Story of a Cloud") (1905), and "Sternentau—Die Pflanze vom Neptunmond" ("Star Dew—The Plant from the Neptune Moon") (1909). His output also includes many other stories published individually in various magazines and journals.

Lasswitz was a teacher in Gotha from 1876 to 1907, and thus the first in the long line of science fiction authors whose primary occupation was something other than writing, the favored areas being mathematics, physics, or philosophy. Lasswitz's fictional fantasies were a kind of by-product, by means of which he wished to convey his ideas on philosophy, science, and nature. This aim indeed was included as the fourth conclusion of his research thesis—"The Natural Sciences Can and Must Be Popularized."[6]

Much of the effect of Lasswitz's stories is lost on the modern reader, for whom they tend to appear rather old hat, or just eccentric, particularly where he personifies occurrences and laws of nature. But one must not overlook his consistent linking of scientific and technological speculation with the basic question of morality and humanity. He never abandons his stance with regard to the social consequences of the continual broadening of technological boundaries. He is capable of humor too, as in his first story written while still a student, "To the Rockbottom of Being," published in two parts in a local newspaper in Silesia, and his imagination is fertile enough for him to write of some fine anticipatory scientific inventions including flying machines whose vanes could be positioned horizontally, enabling them to stay still in the air helicopterlike (this was a very short time after Verne's story of Robur the conqueror); tall buildings on solid pillars whose lower stories house workshops and factories, above which are the living quarters, while roof gardens afford a place to relax; he puts the whole Earth to agriculture both arable and stock-raising; artificial weather manipulation; day trips from Europe to see the Niagara Falls are a matter of course; telegrams and the like are common, as are the first attempts to intercept and nullify the effects of gravity; air sprays are a new kind of artillery effective at two hundred or more kilometers; he speaks in detail of aerodynamic wing design, and also of a new dance craze, the "Hullu-Kullu," "the point of which was to crash everybody's heads together."[7]

The enduring contribution of Lasswitz for the history of science fiction is his novel *On Two Planets*, which predates Wells's *War of the Worlds* by one year, having first been published in 1897 in an edition of two thousand. New editions followed immediately, and have in fact not ceased yet. By 1918 some 25,000 copies in the original German had been sold, and between 1898 and 1914 it was translated into Danish, Swedish, Dutch, Hungarian, and Czech. It is a large two-volume novel with a good number of didactic asides, in which a band of hapless Arctic explorers in a balloon discover at the North Pole a station that turns out to be an observation point set up by visitors from Mars. The explorers are given the opportunity to visit Mars and find it to be a highly civilized and cultivated society. The Martians live in an ideal state and are unacquainted with the notion of enmity. If an individual does not like where he or she is living, it is always possible to move belongings and even abode (movable houses figure even in Cyrano de Bergerac) somewhere else. Thus in order to retain its population, any particular area must strive for the best social organization possible. However, despite this insight into the demands of good sense, the Martians succumb to the allurements of power and plan to conquer Earth in order to establish a neighboring planet with their high culture and civilization. The visitors are impressed by their example, and proceed to build a similar state and society, in which "order reigns not through the egotistical violence of individual classes, but through the living social sense of all communally."[8] People must then, however, throw off the yoke of foreign rulers.

Lasswitz does not introduce Wellsian bacteria against the Martians, but they are corrupted by the

76

relative mildness of the climate and through the exercise of power itself. The Earthlings secretly build a fleet of airships in America, making use of the technology rejected by the Martians—for instance, "nullity spheres" and "repulsing artillery." The outcome however is not total war between the worlds; good neighborliness and peaceful relations between the two civilizations triumph, especially since one of the "Numen"—airships—sacrifices itself in order to avert the danger to mankind threatened by the gravitational instability of the polar station.

The novel is broadened in scope by utopian ideas, which have the outlook of a bourgeois-liberal German teacher of the time of Kaiser Wilhelm but on a bigger scale. Nationalist tendencies are clear. It is Germans who are invited to visit Mars; the then "enemy," England, is shelled by the Martians and obliterated as a world power. Lasswitz borrows ideas from the natural philosophers, especially Gustav Theodor Fechner's teachings concerning the soul in nature, and Darwin's teachings on human evolution.

Many other authors followed in Kurd Lasswitz's footsteps, even during his lifetime. One of his most important successors was an electrical engineer, Hans Dominik, who had been a pupil of Lasswitz at Gotha and who shows his master's influence, especially in his early work "Technische Märchen" ("Technological Fairy Tales") (1901). Lasswitz had set himself the task of introducing elements of the natural sciences into his tales, thereby helping children's understanding. Dominik carries this one step further. He personalizes objects, instruments, blood cells, and so on, and thus simplifies physical, chemical, and biological ideas so that the tales read like those of fussy old nanny in the style of "What the little snowflake saw and did on its way down to Earth." His method changed however, and the tales published from 1907 onwards in children's annuals (for example, "Neues Universum" ["New Universe"]) are different. Technical details are offered in a clearly didactic way, but things are no longer personified and given childlike attributes. Dominik now explores themes and subjects that will figure in his postwar novels with increased conviction.

In publishing these technical short stories Hans Dominik found himself part of a group of authors preferring to project their scenarios of the future against the background of a massive technological experiment. Structurally, many of these books are quite similar, often opening with the attempt to find backers for the experiment or project—fellow researchers, financial backers, state support. Opposition to the plan is often on a huge scale, leading to the core of the work, the fight to realize the plan. Natural and technical difficulties must be overcome. Many such novels also include other problems—for example, sabotage and other organized opposition, or strikes—often as a kind of tension at the last moment, a hitch when all

The Tunnel was the most important technical science fiction novel before World War I.

77

Bernhard Kellermann.

seems to be going well, just before the final break-through. The finales, or closing sections, appear in a wider variety of shapes and forms. Much favored is the triumphant close, in which the project is completed for the benefit of mankind at large, or at least for the particular country concerned. Sometimes however the story ends in failure, resistance to the project being too great. The hero may attempt to subvert the

threatened disaster, often paying with his life. This usually gives a wider perspective to the tale: his sacrifice is not in vain, for his work is then carried on by others.

This basic structure common to so many novels exploring technology and its future is the skeleton onto which many different kinds of literary flesh is attached. Sometimes elements from detective and ad-

78

venture stories are brought in, or even the clichés of romantic fiction. In this last case the ending often involves overcoming additional obstacles so that the lovers may live happily ever after. An example of such plotting may be seen in Hugo Gernsback's novel *Ralph 124 C 41 Plus*, serialized in 1911–12, in which an American scientist named Ralph falls in love with Alice, a beautiful girl from Switzerland.

But by far the most important such novel is *The Tunnel* by Bernhard Kellermann (1879–1951). This book, first published in 1913, has since been translated into more than twenty-five languages. Kellermann's fantasy tells of a tunnel dug out under the Atlantic Ocean connecting Europe and America. That the book was an immediate and sensational success worldwide is mainly due to its superior literary merit, far in advance of most other novels of the type written at the time. On top of that, it followed the spectacular sinking of the *Titanic* in the Atlantic by only two years. The impression of this catastrophe was still vivid in the minds of readers, rendering them particularly receptive to the notions of the author with his suboceanic burrowings.

This novel celebrates the creative individual, the inventor-engineer enamored of his gigantic idea. But Mac Allan is no inventor of the Verne-travelogue school. He is at one and the same time manager, organizer, and publicizer of his plans. He is a "self-made" man whose origins lie amongst the lowest of the low, socially speaking—he is a stableboy in the style of Uncle Tom—and this enables him to inspire the workmen to supreme efforts.

The then dominant picture of America as the land of unlimited opportunity is the background for Kellermann's "epochs of iron and electricity, the major human deeds of all time"[9] as the book says. At the same time, Kellermann convincingly argues his case that, without the power of money, an engineer is nothing. Thus at every step the close bond between capital and labor is stressed, and the achievement of the engineer

The first film version of *The Tunnel* followed hot on the heels of the book's publication.

Film-Kurier

DER TUNNEL

Paul Hartmann as Mac Allan in the 1933 German film.

of the work that is perhaps the novel's greatest narrative achievement.

In the seventh year of work, an explosion occurs that destroys three miles of the tunnel, claiming the lives of nearly three thousand workers. A raging mob, demanding vengeance, stones Allan's wife and small daughter.

The construction work resumes, but now at a sluggish pace. The treasurer of the syndicate has speculated privately: suicide is his last attempt to escape responsibility. Thousands of small investors are ruined as the project collapses and the syndicate goes bankrupt. At the end, Mac Allan marries Ethel Lloyd although he recognizes that by doing so he is selling himself out. Now Lloyd alone finances the construction. Twenty-four years after the work had begun, the first train runs through the tunnel, the completion of which in the end has claimed the lives of some nine thousand workers. Mac Allan, whose triumph it is, is grown old before his time—paying heavily for his success.

Apart from the concessions to the age in which he lived (for example, antisemitic elements, which are incidentally also to be found in the work of Jules Verne), this novel is a model of the science fiction novel exploiting futuristic technology. Kellermann presents on the one hand the possibilities inherent in modern industrial society, and on the other explores the dangers that threaten humanity through its existing contradictions. His proffered suggestion for a solution is for the individual, through sheer activity and through proving himself or herself in the struggle for technological progress, to overcome and neutralize such contradictions. Kellermann fêtes the unceasing technological and scientific evolution in the work of Mac Allan as the touchstone and criterion for human achievement. The workers appear to the author at this time still as "ant-like masses led by the nose by advertisements, in the thrall of spontaneity and a fantastical yen for revenge."[10]

A special kind of technological vision is to be found in the stories and novels that appeared on the market in industrialized countries in the final two decades preceding World War I—especially those in which authors portray future war. On three important points most of these books agree.

is set against the closely observed background of procurement of capital, the fever of speculation, and the ruination of countless small fry. The true social nature of the time was not within Kellermann's ability to elucidate clearly. In this aspect, his work remains rather less impressive than the major works of H. G. Wells.

The plot follows the general outline of the genre as described above. The engineer Mac Allan persuades Charles H. Lloyd, the most powerful man in America, to back his project of building a tunnel between New York and France, via Bermuda, the Azores, and northern Spain. Lloyd's daughter, Ethel, falls in love with Mac Allan and helps to make a convert of her father. Thus the Atlantic Tunnel Syndicate is founded.

Work on the project, which Allan has been planning for fifteen years, starts simultaneously at the five sites. The hazardous work is described in exciting and vivid detail, as is every aspect of the construction. It is this intriguing depiction of the hectic pace and rhythm

80

Social origins are largely excluded from these works. Shown instead is the introduction through the media of a particular country of manipulatory clichés identifying friends and enemies in grossly simplified terms—for example, there are "terrible Germans," "perfidious Albion," or the "French Arch-Fiend."

This preoccupation with war is concentrated on technical developments and "novelties" (Zeppelin attacks, airplanes, heavy gunnery, gas, and so on), but acts of cruelty are also featured. However, none of these fantasies, based as they were on past war experience, ever approached the actual atrocities that were to be unleashed on the countries involved in World War I. In general these literary visions of "future warfare" ensured that the enemy would be routed. Victory was assured for the home country of the author. Such presentations of technological fancy helped psychologically to prepare the ground for war. Warnings, such as those produced by H. G. Wells, were the exception to this general rule.

In the main, these fantastic wars are fought out in works of literature in the more popular vein.

THE DESCENT
INTO THE TRIVIAL

The gradual implementation of popular education is one of the most significant achievements of the bourgeois liberation movement. Relevant laws had been passed at least in part already during the eighteenth century (for example, in most of the German lands, or states, the rules for general education had been laid down by 1800), but many decades were to pass before regular attendance at school by all children was to become a reality in Europe. In poorer families, the earning power of children often meant the difference between survival and destitution—especially in agriculture, in cottage industries, and in the textile business—which meant in turn that during the last century not even half of those children by law entitled and obliged to be educated in school were able to attend regularly. Some help was offered in the form of factory schools, in which children were to be taught late in the evening after what might be a twelve-hour working day. Sunday schools were another alternative form of schooling. Pressure to overcome these educational difficulties was exerted by workers' groups and the newly organized social democratic parties.

Progressive developments were creating a huge new readership for the book market—millions of extra people were now registering a need for educational material. Against this background some features need special elucidation in order to explain fully the explosive increase in the readership of books and journals.

Important discoveries, laws, and new kinds of organizations offered answers to the continuously expanding needs of this huge new readership, and at the same time exerted continuous fresh stimulation—for example, rotary presses, new typesetting machinery, large factories producing cheap paper, and relaxation of trade restrictions. The introduction of industrial methods enabled the price of newspapers, magazines, and books to remain so low that most of the population was able to buy them.

In the second half of the nineteenth century literature thus became a mass product for mass consumption. In Germany, the number of new titles published per year exceeded 10,000 for the first time in 1870.[1] ("Book production climbed from 4,000 titles in the year 1800 to more than 10,000 [1840] and then to 30,000 [1908].")[2]

Progressive publishers performed a great service at this time by producing the great works of world literature in cheap editions, thus bringing valuable material to the masses. In Germany for instance, Reclam publishers had a "Universalbibliothek" ("Universal Library") and the publishers Bibliographisches Institut edited many classic works. But since the field of literature was now in effect a business, it became an area where competition was at work. Gaps were searched out and filled with the searcher's product. All countries had a wealth of local, regional, and national newspapers that acted as channels for mass

81

communication. In closely fought battles for subscriptions and readers, editors and publishers successfully utilized light, popular, belletristic literature. Short stories, travel books, novellas, tales, and full-length novels were—mostly in serialized form—published in a bid to answer the demand for entertainment and to stimulate a particular newspaper's circulation. In Germany alone newspapers published during the last decade of the nineteenth century some twenty thousand serials annually.[3] The situation was comparable in other major industrialized countries.

This state of affairs led to a dilution of aesthetic standards, to a shift of artistic taste in many groups of readers, and to a general loss of quality in some fields of literature. Of course, there was already a variety of material of lower quality available: romances of chivalry, novels of "good" robbers in the Robin Hood tradition, pirate stories, Gothic novels, and other such thrillers structured primarily for plot tension. These new publishing conditions caused a division of literature into "true," or "mainstream," literature as recognized and studied by professors, and escapist literature for entertainment purposes, as read by millions but sometimes low in artistic quality and "commercialized."

In these new market conditions, a mass literature of the moment developed. The overwhelming mass of science fiction fell into this "of the moment" category; because of this, one assumes, science fiction as a whole was from then on generally dismissed as being of little or no value.

In addition to the serialization of fiction in so many newspapers and magazines—primarily in the many "family journals"—there was a trend in all parts of Europe for cheap sensationalism in novels. Such "sensational" fiction was mainly produced in book form rather than in serials, and became a new genre of popular literature. These productions were written for amusement only, and, for the most part, were of no literary value whatsoever, aiming as they did at tension, shock, and sensation. "Serious" bookshops did not handle them. They were peddled door-to-door by salespeople. The audience for such literature was composed of serving maids, young people, women in the working-class districts, and so on—people of limited financial resources; they seldom crossed the

Title page of an American (half-) dime novel.

threshold of a bookshop. Such books became known as "backstairs books" in Germany. In France they were called *littérature bleue*. Just as there were many groups at which such literature was aimed, there were also many varieties in the product. One type concentrated on an illusory, dreamy, and sentimental view of "life", showing true love and peace found at last by the hero who has managed to climb from humble origins to the heights of society. The real life of the reader, almost unendurable in its poverty, is "escaped" for a pseudoworld of harmony, justice, good, and fulfilled love. Later on Hollywood exploited such material for its products.

The other main variant of this sensational literature concentrated on "escape" from the misery and sorrow of life in the industrialized world. Taking into

82

account such factors as inadequate education and the narrowness that constricted so many people—particularly the "proletariat" (laborers) and the "petit bourgeoisie" (white-collar clerks)—during the upheavals of the nineteenth century, it becomes understandable why so many young people wanted nothing more than to escape their misery and make a name for themselves. Pandering to this dream, publishers produced romantic adventure stories that dealt mainly with literary heroes who would break out, establish their individual worth, and become "names" in society. Their "adventures" involve the exploration of exotic and little-known areas, peopled by wild tribes and frequented by villains of all kinds. The open sea, or later, extraterrestrial travels in the air, or on other planets and stars—places where the everyday social afflictions of the reader, such as compulsory class distinctions, were blurred or nonexistent—became favorite sites for adventure tales. In these fictions the law of the jungle obtains; strength is the sole arbiter. In many cases, this is combined simultaneously with a residual and general moral outlook on good and evil, so that the hero becomes a fearless and unblemished knight whose aim it is to work on the side of justice, ridding society of criminals and punishing malefactors. According to the particular backdrop against which such a tale is set, and the time from which it dates (both of which naturally affect the particular form of tension-tightening technique employed), one can differentiate the seeds that were to flower as several distinct genres: the American Western, the English detective novel, the adventure novel, the pirate story, and the latest such genre to develop—the science fiction tale.

There is a problem in that the aesthetic value of any piece of writing is not immediately obvious from the generic name given to that particular type of work. In literature as a whole there are among Westerns, detective stories, and romances, including of course science fiction, works with radically varying quality, ranging from the "mainstream," through harmless novels for the young, "kitsch" literature devoid of artistic value (but not necessarily morally undermining to the reader) right down to trash that has lost any grip on morality and appeals to the lowest instincts and antihumanist tendencies of the reader.

In the United States, European novels had at first no chance of success. Even a great science fiction writer like Jules Verne was at first published in single isolated volumes, achieving a full collection only in 1911.

At the same time the sensational novel was reaching a zenith in Europe just before the turn of the century, in America another form of mass literature was developing—the serial published in pamphlet form. The price of a single pamphlet was low; they became known as "dime novels." Later parallel developments in other countries were to appear. Germans became readers of "Groschen novels" (1 Groschen = 10 Pfennigs). The main difference between the American dime novel and its European counterpart lay in the fact that the American model allowed a single hero to

Robert Kraft.

stamp his personality on a whole series of independent adventures published one at a time. This occasioned certain differences in the treatment and structure. In the "sensational" novel (as in newspaper serializations) each part had to end with some kind of cliff-hanger, to create a tension and curiosity as to the outcome of the adventure, satisfied only by the purchase of the next number. In a series of separate adventures, this device becomes pointless; the structure as a whole must engender a wish in the reader to follow the hero's adventures further, chiefly by encouraging the reader to identify with the hero and his escapades. Thus every number had to satisfy certain expectations, leading to widespread use of clichés and stereotypes that came to be associated with particular pamphlet productions.

Dime novels were available for purchase in the US as long ago as the middle of the nineteenth century. At first they were mostly adventure subgenres like pirate stories and shipboard tales, detective novels, travel stories, and, increasingly as time went on, tales of the "frontier,"—pioneering romances of the opening of the west. Only in the latter years of the nineteenth century did science fiction adventure stories join the ranks of these serial pamphlets.

Sam Moskowitz points out how more than three-quarters of all the hundreds of "prophetic dime novels"[4] to be published in the last thirty years or so of the nineteenth century in the US were written by one single author—Luis Philip Benares. He is thought to have written 1,500 serial stories under some twenty-seven pseudonyms. In many of his works, the young hero undertakes an adventure "with all manner of vehicles, all constructed by himself, from mechanical horses to helicopters, using any kind of apparatus. . . . Some of the best of these series are 'Frank Reade,' 'Frank Reade, junior,' 'Tom Edison, junior,' 'Bulger Boom the Inventor,' 'Electric Bob,' 'Jack Wright,' and, just after the turn of the century, 'Tom Swift.'"[5]

While the sensationalist writings of Europe made little impact in America, the American dime novels gave an important new lease on life to mass literature. Pamphlet serializations on the US model soon sprouted in profusion. In 1901, for instance, a new series was started, called "From the Wealth of Fantasy." The author was Robert Kraft, already well known for his sensational literature. "Under titles such as *Der letzte Höhlenmensch (The Last Cave Man), Die Totenstadt (The City of the Dead), Der Weltallschiffer (The Space Ships), Das Stahlross (The Steed of Steel), Die Ansiedlung auf dem Meeresgrunde (The Civilization of the Sea Bed),* Kraft systematically borrowed and reworked all the clichés prevalent in the science fiction of the time."[6]

Individual tales were held together, as was generally the case with serial stories, by maintaining one main figure. This is one of the few areas where Kraft was atypical, in that his hero was a lame schoolboy, who *dreamed* fantastic adventures (always the right length to fill just one pamphlet). In his stories Kraft portrays very few original ideas. In this he was quite characteristic of the mass of popular science fiction writers. In general he seizes the well-worn motifs of fairy tale and adventure story and then updates and enriches them through technological additions and reworkings. Manfred Nagl's opinion, that in these trivial works second-hand mythologies are present not only in the ideological sense but also in the technique of the writing and story structure, is fully justified. He says that "a parasitical method of storytelling [dominates, in which] the old 'written out' genres of popular literature . . . are utilized once more with changes of scenery, renewed by complication, and by alienation."[7] This was the case to the extent that successful authors of science fiction of the calibre of Verne, Wells, and Lasswitz, were themselves plagiarized time and again.

Besides Robert Kraft's pamphlets and books, for example, *Der Herr der Lüfte (The Master of Air), Im Aeroplan um die Erde (Around the World in an Aeroplane), Im Panzerautomobil um die Erde (Around the World in a Tank), Im Zeppelin um die Welt (Around the World in a Zeppelin), Die Nihilit-Expedition (The Nihilit Expedition),* and, above all, *Loke Klingsor. Der Mann mit den Teufelsaugen (Loke Klingsor: The Man with the Devil's Eyes),* Germany especially took to the series "Wunder der Zukunft. Romane aus dem dritten Jahrtausend" ("Wonders of the Future—Novels of the Third Millennium"). This series was started in 1909 and each book contained more than the smaller pamphlets that cost literally one Groschen.

84

Dust jacket for A. Conan Doyle's fantasy classic.

Single copies cost 1 Mark, but they accordingly offered better contents. The first number offered a "sequel" to H. G. Wells's *Invisible Man (Der unsichtbare Mensch aus dem Jahr 2111 [The Invisible Man from the Year 2111])*, and *Die über und unter der Erde (Above and Below the Earth)*; the second number offered the story of *Der rote Komet (The Red Comet)* and its terrifying consequences. This story was not based on the red glow of the planet Mars, but rather on the symbolic import of the color red for the socialist movement. At the same time the title unmistakably defers to H. G. Wells, of whose work this is a copy. The influence of the red comet, according to Robert Heymann, the author of this elaborate invention, is the opposite of Wells's described in *In the Days of the Comet*, published three years earlier. A war is fought between Germany on one side, and France and England on the other. Of course, Germany wins, and she can dictate the terms of peace. But at the same time the red comet is the cause underlying certain tumult and revolt in Germany. The mob takes to the streets. Heymann paints a terrifying picture of events that he delineates under the term "revolution." But the victorious armies return from the war and—God be praised!—restore order as before. Because the red comet is now drawing away from the Earth once more, the action taken to defray tension succeeds totally. At the beginning of the novel the comet had been discovered by Romulus Futurus, who by the end of the story has lost his senses. Encapsuled in this warning picture of what revolution can do to a state is also the terrible story of Futurus's development of a wonderful photographic plate that is able to picture people's secret wishes.

There were innumerable such series in the years before World War I in the industrialized countries. Since they were not available through the normal book-buying channels, and were also not the kind of product collected by libraries, it is no longer possible to give an accurate rundown of all their forms and variations. Even accurate estimates of their circulation figures are impossible, for the extant figures calculated by the publishers themselves may have been secretly lowered for the sake of the tax collector, or the figures given by competitors might have been overestimated. Because of this uncertainty over the figures, the estimates for the number of such dime novels before World War I vary from 40,000 to 100,000 per week.

But there have always been movements aimed at checking the ever-increasing flood of popular literature at this low level. Usually it is the progressive teaching groups, organizations of "serious" bookshops, workers' groups, and women's groups who spearhead this opposition. In the United States in the 1900s a boycott of most dime novel publishers forced them to retract their operations. Popular literature found a new home however in the following decades in another publishing format: the "pulp magazine" (so called because they were printed on cheap paper made of pulp). Such magazines were the direct descendants of the French publisher Hetzel's *Magazin d'éducation et de récréation* and similar publications. The pulps largely avoided articles dealing with popular science, as Hetzel's did. They were in fact modern short-story magazines, and in terms of genre stood halfway between the magazine and the serial pamphlet.

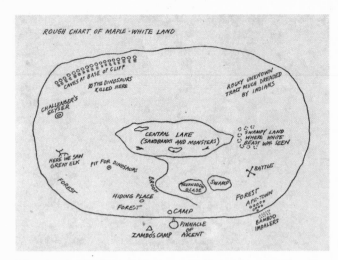

Map showing findings of Professor Challenger's group. Drawing by Gil Walker.

A typical copy of a pulp magazine would contain a number of stories of various popular genres. These might include love stories, detective stories, westerns, and, last but not least, science fiction stories.

Pulp magazines, published periodically, also contained larger works of fiction in serial form, rather in the way newspapers and magazines had done for years. Most American science fiction novels at the time achieved their first editions in serial form. The majority of these magazines, such as *All-Story, Argosy, Blue Book, Cavalier,* and *Scrap Book* were in the hands of the uncrowned king of the New York pulp scene, Frank A. Munsey.

In Europe, there were parallel developments. Antiobscenity laws closed many of the serial producers prior to World War I, helped by raids in schools, and by concerted efforts at exchanging them. One attempt at weighting the scales in favor of more serious literature—above all where young readers were concerned—was the introduction of tension and adventure at a higher aesthetic literary level. Thus were born the yearbooks *New Universe,* or *Library of Amusement and Knowledge,* and many others, all built on the model developed by Hetzel. They were published monthly or annually and contained educational papers, hints for leisure-time activities, and entertainment—all in a balanced mix. The literary contributions to such products were mainly sentimental love stories, adventure stories, or detective tales. But

there were, as in the American pulp magazines, also science fiction short stories. These were for the most part stories set in the future and oriented towards technical sensationalism or the portrayal of imminent war techniques in worldwide confrontations.

Despite all the differences found in publication form as to style and content of such products, there is one constant factor in all the popular literature of the years leading up to World War I. Because of the laws of production, there are on the one hand authors who become salaried writers (with the publisher's freedom to apportion work among writers and assign more than one writer to any series where only the general type of story is fixed), and on the other hand readers considered conformist and sheeplike, on no account to be disturbed from this passive state. The link that holds the two together is the item of "trivial" litera-

Arthur Conan Doyle.

THE INDUSTRIAL REVOLUTION AND FANTASY

ture, produced and sold at a fixed price and in fixed format with contents varying only minimally with the stereotype hero fighting through one clichéd situation after another.

Understandably, the success of the serials and the pulp magazines helped increase the publication of science fiction literature in book form. Some authors now transferred certain successful principles from other genres into science fiction writing. The books and short stories of the English author Sir Arthur Conan Doyle about the superlatively gifted Sherlock Holmes and his loyal assistant Dr. Watson had been a great success in the second half of the 1880s; Conan Doyle also tried his hand at a science fiction series based on the figure of Professor Challenger. One of these novels is *The Lost World* (1912), his most important contribution to the literature of science fiction. In this book, Professor Challenger ventures into a South American jungle, into a secret and "lost" world locked in a prehistoric state of development. Challenger is again the hero of *The Poison Belt,* and of a number of stories grouped together after the death of the author under the general title of "The Professor Challenger Stories." Some of Conan Doyle's science fiction works date from after World War I, and these too have been included in various collections.

THE GROWTH OF SCIENCE FICTION
AFTER WORLD WAR I

DREAMS OF WORLD REVOLUTION
AND THE
"FANTASY OF THE NEAR FUTURE":
SOVIET SCIENCE FICTION BETWEEN 1917 AND 1956

Immediately after World War I, science fiction in the Soviet Union underwent far-reaching changes. With the revolution in October 1917, a great experiment was begun to establish a social system in reality, about which earlier generations had only dreamed. The entire country was engaged in the new order, the masses filled with enthusiasm and inspiration. Of course there were also doubters and those made timid by the sheer size of the task, and those so reactionary that they turned away from anything new. Each individual was now forced to make his or her own decisions every day, indeed every hour. At the same time as the social, political, and economic changes were confronting the people, there were also new challenges to be mastered, which in other industrialized countries already in the progressive phase of bourgeois development had been successfully met. These included the combating of illiteracy. To this aim, national and international traditions were able to assist, along with new educational and pedagogic methods set in practice to rid the country of the hitherto rampant educational privilege of only the well-to-do. New strata in society now had access to higher education; to further the establishment of a new intelligentsia academic teaching was open to all. And all this in a land in a state of unimaginable backwardness by the tsarist regime! Most urgently of all, it was necessary for scientific and technological knowledge to be spread so that efficient and widespread training of engineers, technicians, and factory workers could take place; in this manner the basis of the country could be renewed in the shortest possible time.

All artists, including of course authors, were drawn into the newly effervescent life of the state. In their works they declared their new allegiance. New classes of readership were hungry for books that could offer answers to their many questions. New literary genres were developed to speak to and for the people, old forms were resurrected with new content and new forms experimented with all the time.

Subjects and motifs based on scientific fantasy found a wide public. Against this background came the first great flowering of science fiction literature in the Soviet Union. The main threads of Soviet science fiction (retaining some connections with the old Russian social utopian story) was used to suggest and anticipate changes and features of the communist future. This involved writers in critical assessments of the philistinism of the old-fashioned bourgeoisie, of their constrictive behavior, and of their patterns of living. Fantasy became the literary form most capable of expressing divergence from the developments of the bourgeois order of western countries; and science fiction became not only a means of popular education and enlightenment but also a means of spreading technological propaganda and information. And lastly, very early on in the new system, a new kind of poetic fantasy became established, classed today as pure fantasy. An example of this last would be the work of Aleksandr Stepanovich Grin (or Grinevski).

These main threads of science fiction are to be found in so many forms in individual works that a pure example of each can hardly be selected. The following descriptions of authors and their works are organized according to the dominating characteristics of each.

Yevgeni Brandis, one of the leading theorists of science fiction in the USSR, points out in an article published in 1969 that the critic Jakov P. Perelman even as early as the beginning of the 1920s used the generic title *nauchnaya fantastika* (science fantasy) in the magazine *Masterskaya Prirody* (Nature's workshop), using it primarily for technological fantasy. But it was not until later on that the term came into general usage, probably under the pressure and influence of international science fiction, and became a recognized literary term. Thus, the words of another theorist, Yuli Kagarlitski, are also correct: "The modern term 'science fantasy' . . . is the inexact, but apt, meaning of the English term 'science fiction,' rather than 'scientific literature.'"[1]

Naturally, there are to be found in the literature of the new Soviet state some works that express disappointment with early developments, because these diverged from the dreams of the ideal communist society. Some of these feelings found their way into science fiction literature as authors looked back to the forms of social criticism in earlier Russian literature and expressed their anxieties about the concept of "the masses" and the loss of individualism in society. Such is the gist of Yevgeni Ivanovich Zamyatin's dystopic (i.e. anti-utopian) novel *My (We)*. But such novels stayed at the periphery of Soviet science fiction and were sometimes published abroad by emigrant printers only, and had therefore no impact inside the Soviet Union.

The majority of Soviet authors were filled with the optimistic feeling that a new world was in the making. In these early years it was felt that nothing was impossible. Advances were being made at a tremendous pace. Everyone knew that in reality many years must pass before their new world would be complete, but equally everyone felt that this achievement was very near. Thus it was natural to seek a glimpse of that new world, for which the foundations had already been laid. This turbulent impatience was equally characteristic of readers and writers, and was indeed one of the main impulses behind the boom in literature.

Public institutions of the new Soviet state also put their weight behind such developments. One of the new young writers of the time, Valentin Petrovich Katayev, recalled some forty years later, in 1962, that "in the Press Department we had to remember that in the provinces hardly any newspapers were read. We came to a decision to print exciting serialized novels. Authors were sought."[2]

The appeal for writers to create Soviet adventure stories found a large response. It is also the reason why early science fiction literature in the USSR is intimately connected with crime stories and adventure tales. Forms and genres were borrowed, including the clichés of such popular literature, to convey the main thematic ideas: the literary exposition of the embittered battle against the old order in every area of life, and the description of the new world to be born in the struggle.

This movement brought forth some really strange works. A weekly magazine of the time, *Ogonek*, edited by Mikhail Yefimovich Koltsov, published in the first half of 1927 a collectively written detective novel called *The Great Conflagrations*, in a total of twenty-five parts, each part being the work of a different writer. The whole amounts to a detective novel very critical of those slow to accept the Soviet's "New Economic Policy." At the same time, however, the predominant naïve simplifications of the world situation were taken to heart and the already recognizable style of Soviet literature parodied. Understandably, reference was also made to writers of science fantasy, such as the first volume of Marietta Shaginyan's trilogy *Mess Mend* and Tolstoi's *Aëlita*. This last author was a member of the authorship collective along with such well-known authors as Aleksandr Grin, Isaac Babel, Konstantin Fedin, Mikhail Soshchenko, Vera Inber, and Venyamin Kaverin.

One of the earliest Soviet science fiction stories is *Otkrytiye Rielja (Riel's Discovery)* by Vivian Asarievich Itin (1894–1945). This work was first planned in 1917, and published in 1922 under the title *Strana*

89

Gonguri (Gonguri's Land). Two prisoners condemned to death—the aged Doctor Mitchell and the young, imaginative Helios, a gifted poet—are locked in a cell by members of the White Guard. The doctor lays siege to the time and the place, though without resorting to the "Wellsian vehicle of the fourth dimension,"[3] but by putting Helios in a deep hypnotic trance. When he wakes up, Helios narrates his imagined adventures on distant stars as the personage "Riel." He tells of the beauty of the stars and contrasts them with the cruelty still widespread on Earth. This glimpse of a better future and the knowledge that life throughout the universe will develop to ever new heights helps Helios on his last journey to be executed by Czech legionnaires of the White Guard.

Although for Itin the society of the future can only be depicted through displacement in time and setting, for his fellow author Jakov Markovich Okunev (1882–1932) a gas is "discovered" in his book *The World of the Future* (1923) that can suspend life in humans for years. The first part of the novel offers an action-packed introduction to the story. Professor Moran puts his terminally ill daughter, and a young man, into a deep sleep. As his secret gradually leaks out, others become interested, including wealthy members of the old order. Professor Moran attempts to flee to Canada with his sleepers packed securely in coffins. The ship breaks up on an iceberg (this surely owes something to the still fresh memory of the disaster of the *Titanic*) and sinks.

In the second part of the novel, which has the function of a bridge, Okunev shows in simplified form, the symbolic struggles of the proletariat and the property owners, ending with a successful world revolution. The final section of the book, set in 2123, describes the awakening of the hypnotized pair into a world of fully effective communism. The action of the book retreats into the background, and descriptive passages now dominate, to a certain extent a development of the ideas in Bellamy's *Looking Backward*.

A very different kind of novel is Sergei Budantsev's *Squadron of the World Commune*, published in 1925, though it shares the fact of being set in the future. This time the date of the action is 1944. Almost the whole world is by now communist and under the leadership of a central government stationed in London. The last reactionaries have gathered together, including such notorious people as Rockefeller, Mussolini, and so on, on the island of Madagascar. The story takes the form of a war fantasy, in which both sides have access to "new" technology. After the main representatives of the old order are exterminated, the last bastion of opposition is converted to communism.

Marietta Sergeevna Shaginyan (1888–1982) wrote the book *Mess Mend* as her contribution to Soviet adventure literature, and it has enjoyed considerable success abroad as well as at home. It is a trilogy: part 1 is called *Mess Mend: or a Yankee in Petrograd* (1923; a film version was also produced that year); part 2 is *Lois Len, the Metal Worker* (1924); and part 3 is *The International Wagon, or the Way to Baghdad* (1925). In all three parts, the author makes unselfconscious use of clichés and situations fre-

Mikhail Bulgakov.

quently met with in "trivial" literature. Mixed in with these are motifs from science fiction; for example, there is a strange dark ball that induces sleep, and a very secret metal, "Lenium" by name. In fact, the whole work is such a melting pot of influences that it can only be called a science-adventure-detective fantasy. It is of particular interest in that it contains the first gleanings of antifascism to be found in science fiction. The direction of its message is also made clear by the author's choice of name for her central persona—Jim Dollar.

Other authors began at this time to forge their own paths with science fiction material, which they mainly used for satirical purposes. Examples are Andrei Platonovich Platonov's *The City of Cities* (1927) and other volumes; Vsevolod Vyacheslavovich Ivanov's *The Secret of Secrets* (1927), in which the author attempts to make the thread of the story mankind's subconscious; Viktor Borisovich Shklovsky's *Yprit* (1925), written in collaboration with Ivanov after returning home from exile; Yefim Sosulya's *The Gramophone of the Centuries*, in which a machine is able to reproduce long forgotten sounds; and Mikhail Afanasevich Bulgakov's work (1891–1940).

Bulgakov's short stories from this period were collected into one volume in 1925, and published under the general title of *Diaboliade*. Included is "Rokovye yaitsa" ("The Fateful Eggs") written in 1924, one of the acknowledged classics of Soviet satire. After a concise description of the development of Professor Persikov, positively dripping with irony, the author describes his discovery: a ray under the influence of which amoebas become superactive and breed at a fantastic rate. The effect of the ray is comparable to the consequences of H. G. Wells's heracleophorbia in *The Food of the Gods*. At any rate, Wells's food is directly mentioned in the third chapter of Bulgakov's book. Persikov wishes to undertake further investigations and manages to order reptile eggs from abroad in the west. At the very same moment, fowl-initiated pestilence spreads among the whole stock of poultry throughout the republic. With the agreement of the ruler of the land, Alexander Scare (as his name might be translated) fetches three ray guns from a research laboratory. He has conceived a plan of using the rays to boost hen stocks into unprecedented heights of

Ilya Ehrenburg.

production. For this purpose, hen's eggs have been ordered from abroad. Of course the packages are mistaken for each other. Thus, after a short while at the sovkhoz (state farm) "Red Beam," enormous snakes, crocodiles, lizards, and other reptiles slither out, multiply, grow larger and larger, and cause something of an invasion of the republic. Only the advent of freezing weather halts the grotesque charade and averts the danger to land and people.

Unfortunately, in the fracas, the only existing ray guns are destroyed, and Persikov is murdered by the furious crowd. Bulgakov's satire is directed against bureaucracy and self-seeking ambition, and the misuse of scientific knowledge. (Notice the use too, of the sorcerer's apprentice theme once again.)

Later on in his life, Bulgakov again used motifs from science fiction—for example, in the stories "Rapture" and "Ivan Vasilevich." Filmed under the ti-

Valentin Katayev.

tle of *Ivan Vasilevich Swaps Careers*, the story concerns an exchange made by a time machine. The Moscow concierge Ivan Vasilevich is returned in time and substituted for Ivan the Terrible, who is brought forward to the present day as Vasilevich. Since the two men are almost identical in appearance, the confrontation of the characters with the new social structure gives rise to many a comic situation, all fully exploited by the author. Bulgakov's masterpiece, *Master i Margarita (The Master and Margarita)*, published posthumously in 1969, also draws on topoi from fantasy and science fiction.

Ilya Grigorevich Ehrenburg (1891–1967) wrote his book *Trust D. E.; or the History of the Decline of Europe* (1923) as a support to his novel of 1921, *The Amazing Adventures of Julius Jurenito and His Boys*. The 1923 book is a fantasy tale about American financiers who manage to destruct the whole of Europe. Using satirical hyperbole, Ehrenburg defines the danger inherent for mankind in the old social order, making it believable by a wealth of description and detail. In 1961, the author said he could just as well have written his satire at that time, changing the subtitle to *Episodes from the Third World War*.[4]

When Valentin Petrovich Katayev (1897–1986) took up his pen in response to the call for indigenous Soviet adventure stories, he used Ehrenburg's novel as a target for his own satire in *Ehrendorf Island*. This novella was first published in serial form in July and August 1924 in an Omsk daily paper. The no-

vella describes how Professor Grant has come to the conclusion that the whole world, but for one tiny island, is going to be ruined in the near future. Matapal, who is very rich, wants to found on this island the future ideal capitalist society and turns away all those who seek refuge there. Then comes catastrophe: the island is lost while the rest of the world remains safe. The blame for the false prophecy is found to lie with a particular adding machine that had got its pluses and minuses mixed. Katayev introduces into his tale elements drawn from science fiction—for example, safety zones, machines that produce force fields, and other accessories common to the genre, besides other borrowings from adventure stories and sentimental love stories. In another novel, *The Commander of Steel* (1924), Katayev once again combines ideas from adventure stories with caricatures of muddles and naively simplified ideas of the progress of social development and world revolution.

Even the great Russo-Soviet poet, Vladimir Vladimirovich Mayakovski (1893–1930) worked more

Vladimir Mayakovski (third from left) with Meyerhold, working on the production of *The Bathhouse*.

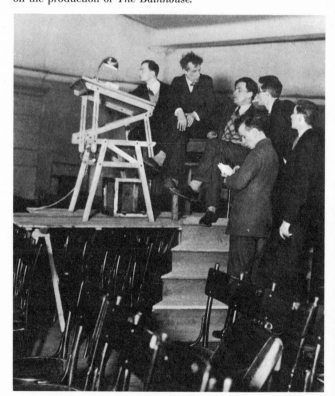

than once with the ideas and materials of science fiction. As early as 1918, he wrote into his *Mystery Bouffe* (second edition 1921) an allegorical parable based on bible stories, depicting his ideas on workers' power and revolution. The later comedies *Klop (The Bedbug)* (1928) and *Banya (The Bathhouse)* (1929), which were given their premieres in the world-famous Meyerhold Theater, are masterpieces of science fantasy and satire against bourgeois values and bureaucracy. Both plays derive from satirical poems. In *The Bedbug*, the action centers on "a former Party member, former worker and now [a] fiancé"[5]—that is, the kind of person particularly caught by the New Economic Policy.

During a turbulent bourgeois wedding, the bride's clothing is set afire, and it immediately flares up and it takes two hours for fire engines to arrive on the scene. However, the water jets, when applied, freeze the groom to a block of ice. Thus encased, the hero survives to witness a classless society of the year 1979. He is resuscitated and subjected to intense study for his strange habits that excite astonishment and aversion. Eventually he is caged in a zoo as a relict of backward notions, labeled *bourgeoisius vulgaris*. A similar relict is Comrade Pobedonosikov in *The Bathhouse,* a bureaucrat liable to confuse sense with nonsense and thus hinder progress. A phosphorescent woman appears from the future and examines people unerringly according to their actions. All willing and active people are sent on into the world of the future, while bureaucrats are shown to be mere ballast. The unresolved question on which the play ends is also the key to the author's intention: "How did you get here? Why am I suffering?"[6] He and his sort are perhaps unfitted to communism.

Science fiction motifs and codes were borrowed too during the 1920s by a group of lyrical poets who called themselves "Cosmics." Their aim was to introduce an abstract cosmic romanticism into Earthly life. One member of the group was the important Russian poet Boris Leonidovich Pasternak.

For all the authors mentioned so far in this chapter, science fiction works form only small periodic deviations from their main oeuvre. The really typical pieces of early Soviet literature in the science fiction genre were written by Alexei Nikolayevich Tolstoi, Vladimir Afanasevich Obruchev, and Aleksandr Romanovich Belyayev.

Alexei Tolstoi (1883–1945) was not involved in the October 1917 Revolution and was estranged from the new aims and struggles. He left his home and emigrated to France, staying in western Europe for some years. Those years abroad were for him the most difficult of his life. He was disappointed by the social decay he found, and was alienated by the anti-Soviet sentiments of fellow exiles who rejected all that their homeland now stood for. He was racked by yearning for Russia. Gradually he came to a decision to return to the Soviet Union. The first step was to move to Berlin in 1921, where he was offered asylum in the Soviet embassy until all the formalities were completed. There he wrote his Martian novel *Aëlita*.

Work on this project was for Tolstoi the turning point on his way back home. In it he wove his newly won knowledge as to the need for and the meaning of revolution in the historical process. This realization Tolstoi poured into his portrayal of the figure of Gusev, a member of the Red Army, who accompanies Los, an engineer, on a rocket launch to a neighboring planet. The ruler of Mars, Tuskub by name, whose outlook on life is characterized by feelings of doom, wants to sacrifice the lives of millions of Martians so that he may rule unhindered over the few remaining inhabitants of the planet who accept and follow his ideas. By creating such a figure, Tolstoi registers his opposition to philosophers like Oswald Spengler, who argued in his morbidly prophetic book *Untergang des Abendlandes (The Decline of the West)* (1921–22) that mankind was on the path to certain destruction as the result of advancing civilization. (Here there are also hints of Ilya Ehrenburg's satire on the decline of Europe.) The Red Army soldier Gusev becomes the opponent of this apostle of doom. He spurs the Martians to thrust off their fear and lethargy; revolution follows. At the point when Tuskub and his followers appear to have the upper hand, Gusev becomes even more convinced that his optimistic belief in a better world is justified. Los, the inventor of the rocket, carries weight in the book owing to his love for Aëlita, the young and beautiful daughter of the Martian ruler, who is caught by terrible spiderlike beasts in the labyrinth of the fearful Magr, and is lost.

93

Mayakovski's *The Bedbug* in the Meyerhold production of 1929.

The fairy-tale stories of Aëlita, which are incorporated into the novel, deal with the origins of the Martians and their early development. According to these legends, the Martians date back to the loss of Atlantis on Earth and the recovery of some few of its inhabitants who are then flown by spaceship to Mars. In these passages, Tolstoi is referring to a current pseudotheory concerning Atlantis, which also inspired some other writers (for instance, the German O. W. Gail, author of *Der Stein vom Mond [The Stone from the Moon]*). The film of Tolstoi's novel, made by Protasanov in 1924, is one of the very first Soviet science fiction films.

After his return to his homeland, Alexei Tolstoi published more novels, among them *The Band of Five* (1924) and *Giperboloid inzhenera Garina (The Hyperboloid of Garin the Engineer)* (1925), which has become better known under its German title,

which translates as *Secret Rays*. This novel deals with a "wonder weapon" developed by the power-hungry engineer Garin, who, along with his American financier friend named Rolling, hankers for world power. In the character of Garin early intimations of the fascist dictator figure emerge. His plans are only obstructed through the might of the Soviet Union and international workers' solidarity. This novel has particular impact when seen as a warning to humanity about the increasing dangers of the growing cult of fascism.

In all three books Tolstoi testifies to his belief in science fiction as an artistic means of investigating philosophical problems and his own attitudes to the questions of the time and developments currently in progress.

The aims of Obruchev and Belyayev differ from those of Tolstoi. They tend to use science fiction

94

mainly to propagate by means of belletristic literature large scientific questions, identifying the possibilities inherent in them and in the boundaries of current research and knowledge. They develop the prewar genre of the technological novel of the future, and take the older traditions, especially those laid down by Verne and to a lesser extent by Wells, a stage or two further.

Vladimir Afanasevich Obruchev (1863–1956) belongs to the large group of science fiction authors also practicing as professional scientists. He graduated from the St. Petersburg Mining Institute in 1886 and took part in numerous expeditions destined to study and chart the geological structure of Siberia and northern China. His most important contributions to science fiction literature are his novels *Plutoniya* (*Plutonia*), published in 1924 but written during World War I, and *Zemlya sannikova (Sannikov Land)* (1926), although he also wrote some notable

Still from the Soviet silent film *Aëlita*, 1924, produced by Y. Protasanov.

Alexei Tolstoi.

short stories. As in Jules Verne's *Journey to the Center of the Earth* (but also reminiscent of Holberg's *Niels Klim*), in *Plutonia* six scientists on a polar expedition happen on an opening leading to the Earth's interior. This turns out to be a complete world with its own sun, Pluto. Further study of the hidden world brings the scientists into confrontation with prehistoric patterns, so that they are in effect researching the Earth's own prehistory. (There is a striking similarity here with Conan Doyle's *Lost World*.) They meet primitive humans, giant insects, dinosaurs, and of course experience countless adventures. By means of their scientific knowledge, they manage to regain the Earth's surface. But during their absence, World War I has broken out and a German warship confiscates all their notes while they look on bewildered.

95

In this way the "proof" of their tale is lost—the usual fate of evidence in such stories.

The strength of this book lies in its mixture of adventure story elements and precise prehistoric factual considerations. The primitive flora and fauna are described in such detail that they are instructional to the young reader to whom the book is aimed. It has been translated into many languages and is still a popular book both inside the Soviet Union and beyond its borders.

Aleksandr Romanovich Belyayev (1884–1942) is widely recognized as an expert in early Soviet science fiction. He is the first Soviet author to turn full time to the writing of science fiction, which he did in 1925. From then until his death he produced more than twenty novels, novellas, and short stories. Some of these rightly belong among the classics of Soviet science fiction—for instance the novels *Golova professora Douelya (The Head of Professor Dowell)* (1925), *Chelovek-amfibiya (The Amphibious Man)* (1926), *Pryshok v nichto (The Leap into the Void)* (1933), *Zvezda KEZ (The Star KEZ)* (1936), and *Ariel* (1942); the short stories "Chudesnoye oko" ("The Wonderful Eye") (1935), and the cycle *Izobreteniya professora Wagnera (The Inventions of Professor Wagner)* in which the best known stories are *Amba* and "Hoity-Toity."

In his first novel, Belyayev chooses an interesting scientific question for his theme. The head of the dead Professor Dowell is kept alive by means of a nutrient solution. The medical and physiological problem of how to keep life systems functioning when the

Another still from *Aëlita*.

96

ored by the South American Indians as a godlike figure. They succeed in installing Balthazar's brother Christo in the doctor's house as a servant. Christo encounters early on in his employment at the doctor's hacienda a six-legged lizard, a two-headed snake, a pig with an ocellus (extra eye), rats joined like Siamese twins, a dog growing a monkey on its chest, and many other monstrosities. (Thus Dr. Salvator joins the ranks of Wells's Dr. Moreau and Renard's Dr. Lerne.) However, he is primarily a man of good intentions who helps the poorest of the poor. He had once, for instance, rescued a fatally ill Indian youth from death by incorporating into his body the gills of a shark, so that his fish-man, or better, amphibious man, or sea devil,[7] is able to live equally on land or in the sea. The novel has two main plots: there is the adventure story, and running parallel to it is a love story. Ichtiander, the amphibious man, rescues Guttiere, Balthazar's

Costume design for the film *Aëlita*.

head is severed from the body is incorporated into a tale full of conflict with interest centering on the moral consequences of the action.

The second novel, *The Amphibious Man*, became popular after World War II in a film version that played far beyond the borders of the Soviet Union itself. The book is again concerned mainly with the social questions surrounding organ transplant. Argentina is plagued by fears of an unknown "sea devil." This monster damages fishing nets, thus releasing the catch, causing all sorts of mischief. But it also rescues drowning persons and washes fish into the boats of poor fisherfolk. Belyayev's narrative gradually discloses, in a very taut structure, how Surita, a pearl trader, uncovers the mystery of the monster with the help of his native assistant, Balthazar. Their investigations lead them to the doors of a Dr. Salvator, hon-

Aleksandr Belyayev.

97

Still from the Soviet film *The Amphibious Man.*

foster daughter, and falls in love with her. But she marries Surita in a bid to help Ichtiander, though she eventually leaves her husband. All the same, there is no happy end to the tale, for Ichtiander has in his adventures upset the balance between his lungs and his gills, and is now able to breathe only under water.

The main theme of the adventure story in the book is that Surita forces the amphibious man to help with the pearl fishing in order to enrich himself. At the end it is made apparent that the fish-man is in fact the son of Balthazar who has been saved by Dr. Salvator. This knowledge is given nearly too late, for Ichtiander and Salvator are sent to jail. The fish-man however, with his friends' help, is able to escape by

means of the sea. But Salvator must sit out his punishment, afterwards carrying on his research.

At the heart of the novel are not the problems attendant upon organ transplants, nor is Salvator made diabolical in the manner of a Frankenstein, but the author concentrates on the possibilities opened up by humanist aid and the social and physical problems that such actions reveal.

Belyayev was to explore such questions again and again, in particular in his book, *The Inventions of Professor Wagner,* the protagonist of which is a second Salvator. In *Amba,* the death of a young German scholar, Ring, in Abyssinia (Ethiopia), is described, and Professor Wagner's experiments in keeping the scholar's brain alive. The professor finds a method of

98

communicating with the brain. By means of the help this autonomous organ suggests, it is possible to discover the trail of Professor Turner, a wanted man, leading to an "amba," (that is, a high Abyssinian plateau, with sheer cliffs all around). Here a link to the story of the elephant "Hoity-Toity" can be drawn, for the reader learns in the latter story that Wagner has now implanted Ring's brain, which grows stronger and stronger, into an elephant. This elephant becomes something of a celebrity, astonishing the public of the "Busch Circus" with its feats of intelligence. A section of the story deals with the elephant's own version of his adventures since his parting from Professor Wagner.

In a letter addressed to Belyayev, H. G. Wells wrote saying how much pleasure he had experienced in reading the former's wonderful books, saying that they, especially *The Head of Professor Dowell* and *The Amphibious Man* differ from such books in the west in the most positive way. Wells even admitted to being not a little envious of Belyayev's success.

Success also attended the Soviet author's subsequent books. The novel *The Leap into the Void* was

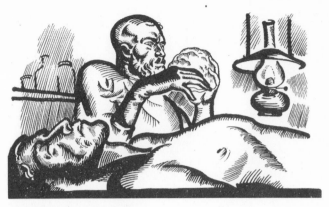

Professor Wagner with Ring's brain, from Belyayev's *Amba*. Illustration by A. Brussilovski.

written in close contact with the great Russian theorist of rocket technology, Konstantin Eduardovich Tsiolkovski. This book anticipates important questions shown to be central during the space missions of recent years—for instance, the details of the rocket's launch, the peculiarities of weightlessness, and also the special training and preparations undergone by astronauts and cosmonauts.

This book is also important for its linking of space travel with an antifascist outlook. One of the major characters of the book is a German research scientist, Leo Zander, who is persecuted on racial grounds. Capitalists in the book are anxious to make use for their own purposes of the time-shift experiences during space flight. A chosen group plans to travel for two years at (nearly) the speed of light before coming home to Earth, where meanwhile a century will have elapsed. Their purpose is to reestablish the power of old. But the author makes his point by having the team land on Venus, owing to a defect in the spaceship caused by sabotage. The elitists are in no position then to survive their new conditions and they revert to their primitive nature, descending to the level of animals. Their radio picks up messages from Earth that a world revolution has been successfully accomplished. Some of the engineers who accompanied the team of researchers to service the machinery then return to Earth, leaving the remains of the outmoded order behind them.

The antifascist nature of these works becomes more and more explicit, in particular in the short story "The Tenth Planet" (published posthumously in

Konstantin Tsiolkovski.

99

Aleksandr Kazantsev.

1945, the action being set in 1956), where human problems of our century are subjected to cold scrutiny. The book describes a tenth planet, revolving around the Sun on our own Earth's path like a doppelgänger, inhabited by barbaric fascist apes. They are exterminated in a conflict with other humanlike beings, who survive to establish a new humanity.

Belyayev remained loyal to the times he lived in and carried on writing in the style he had chosen at the end of the 1920s. He concentrated on technological and scientific fantasy, to which his major contribution was a gift for combining science with elements of social criticism against capitalism and fascism.

Far-reaching changes had meanwhile taken place in Soviet society, in its cultural policy, and in its literature. Now in the foreground stood the urgent need to solve certain essential everyday problems—for example, the creation of an industrial base and a productive socialist agricultural base. It is understandable therefore that major artistic experiments tended to fade in importance and that writers now saw it their duty to wrestle with these situations. At the very time that other countries at the end of the 1920s and the beginning of the 1930s were in the grip of the world-wide economic crisis the USSR instituted its first Five Year Plan, taking concrete steps to reach a solution of its problems. The first World Congress of Revolutionary Literature in 1927, and even more so the second congress in Kharkov in 1930, made it quite clear that the literary life of the Soviet Union and the world communist movement were undergoing decisive changes. The readiness of various literary groups to recognize socialist reform as central to their work became evident. As Gorki had already expressed it in his lecture to the Writers Congress of 1934, this concept was by no means incompatible with the writing of science fiction.[8]

From the middle of the 1930s to the second half of the 1950s, nevertheless, the heights attained by Soviet science fiction in the 1920s was not equalled in imagination, impact, or anticipation. Technological fantasy continued to be written, including even series of science fiction novels such as that published by Detskaya Literatura (a specialist publisher of children's books) under the name "Library of Science Fiction and Adventure." Science fiction stories were still printed in magazines, especially those oriented towards science. Nevertheless, science fiction suffered both quantitatively and qualitatively, largely as a result of the overzealously strict interpretation of the concept of "socialist realism," restricting both content and treatment. As in other countries, science fiction in the Soviet Union came to be thought of as a special branch of lightweight literature for children and young people.

Impressions of America, so strongly depicted in the 1920s, came to be less vehemently expressed. At the time, fiction was an opportunity for giving expression to America as the land you love to hate. On the one hand, an excited approval of the technical, organizing, and financial achievements of the country dominated, and on the other, a repugnance created by the consequences for mankind of the massive concentration of power in the hands of the few was unmistakable. Because of this, portraits of America entered almost every work of science fiction. This situation changed radically in the 1930s and after, one of the major factors being a new sense of pride in achievements at home. In the late 1930s and early 1940s, science fiction was often associated with the spy story.

100

Characteristic of this development is Grigori Adamov's *Taina dvukh okeanov (The Secret of Two Oceans)* (1939). The author takes his main idea from Jules Verne's *Twenty Thousand Leagues under the Sea* and links the action of his story to the war that so obviously threatened. To a certain extent, a changed picture of the enemy is given. A Soviet submarine, furnished with all kinds of fantastic technology, is sent from Leningrad to Vladivostok to accomplish undersea research and eventually to protect the east borders of the Soviet Union from the threat of Japanese aggression. The Japanese secret service learns of the mission and attempts to destroy the submarine. At the heart of this action-packed novel is the industriousness of the crew in their scientific research, and the cleverness and cunning by which they avert a threatened treacherous attack. Enemy agents on the submarine must be sought out and rendered harmless. As in Verne's novel, here too a young stowaway, Pavlik Bunyak, is discovered aboard.

Alongside such full-length works there came an abundance of shorter stories, especially immediately after World War II, which must be seen as a kind of parallel to the factory novel dealing with familiar material—a genre that might be termed fantasy of the immediate future.[9] "Science fiction should restrict itself to descriptions of 'tomorrow,'" which would come about, according to one literary critic, in a matter of a few years, or at most within decades. This theory was the force behind the so-called production fantasy novel, in which fantasy elements were of course present, but only as ideas at the edges of the possible or as reality not yet fully evaluated or implemented.

"Typical books of this kind are *The High Record, The Fireball,* and *Black Gold,* by Vladimir Nemtsov; *Into the Interior of the Earth, The Missing River,* and other stories by Vadim Okhotnikov; *The Mysterious Limousine,* by Viktor Saparin; *Hot Earth,* by Fedor Kandyba; *Conqueror of the Eternal Storms,* by Viktor

Sytin; *The Secret of the Old Castle,* by Yuri Dolgushin; and *The Decline of Kelli Island,* by Aleksandr Morosov."[10]

The grotesque and satirical elements so popular in the 1920s were not totally forgotten in the new climate. In B. L. Lagin's story "Patent AV" (1947), a preparation causing unnatural growth (once again an influence of Wells's *Food of the Gods*) made by criminal powers, is used to transmogrify children into submissive cannon fodder.

Some books included motifs reaching beyond the immediate future, exploring a wider variety of subjects in an attempt to revive the science fiction of the earlier USSR. Such an attempt was Leonid Platov's *The Missing Island,* and an even stronger representative of this trend was Ivan Antonovich Yefremov (1907–72), a short-story writer who was to usher in a new epoch for Soviet science fiction in the 1950s.

This author "was an amazingly multifaceted scientist of encyclopedic knowledge. In his contemplative wisdom, even friendliness, and plucky optimism, he won people's enduring affection. The greatest secret of his life was that he was learning all the time."[11]

Yefremov's early science fiction stories (written from the middle of the 1940s on) contain the fruits of the author's experiences on a number of paleontological expeditions, and his general knowledge of the countryside, its people, and their sayings and legends. But even the story *Kosmicheskie korabli (Starships)* (1948) from early in his career breaks through such limitations, becoming the beginning of the galactic epic of the Great Ring of Worlds.

The caesura in the second half of the 1950s was closed by the political and social repercussions of the defeat of the "cult of personality," the dawning of the cosmic age with the success of the first Sputniks, and—of particular importance to the history of science fiction—the publication of Yefremov's novel *Tumannost' Andromedy (Andromeda Nebula)* (1957).

101

During World War I, the science fiction of all European countries came to a veritable standstill. Only in the US was there no interruption in production. Of course the escalating horrors, the enormous human sacrifice, and the increasingly refined technical means of mass destruction had a permanent effect on the spiritual horizons and world evaluations of American writers, but their own lives were only marginally influenced by the war. The American public of course felt the effects of the war emotionally, but rather from the standpoint of the distant observer or onlooker. America also experienced at the time an upswing in its economy, owing to the production of war goods and food items for Europe.

Science fiction publishing continued to use the major outlet of the pulp magazines as built up before

the war, well interspersed with other stories from the various genres of popular writing, including love stories, horror stories, detective stories, sports stories, and westerns. In an attempt to render the rather technically oriented science fiction more attractive to new readers—especially the rapidly expanding female audience for such fiction—the tradition started by Edgar Rice Burroughs with his first Martian story (1912) and the *Darkness and Dawn* trilogy (1912–13) of George Allan England was developed further. This was to include a tear-jerking love element in the story line, and to set the work in some exotic region. The most favored locations were the planets of Mars and Venus. England's trilogy depicts a pair of lovers waking up in a New York of the future to find it completely destroyed. At this time, a slight change in meaning occurred in the term "scientific romance," which had been in current use since the turn of the century. While this label had heralded a scientific adventure story ever since the time of Wells, now it came to mean literally a scientific story with a large element of romance—thus a fantasy-love story. In the course of this development, the floodgates of sentiment and superficial emotion were opened to inundate the true genre of science fiction.

Though still widely disseminated through the pulps, science fiction now found a new home in scientific and technology-orientated journals and magazines. Sci fi stories were placed in among articles of a popular science nature dealing with general developments in technology, descriptions of new trends in science, and the latest discoveries and curiosities; for the most part the fiction was based on fantasylike suppositions of possible discoveries and their implications.

To systematize the publication of science fiction, and also remuneration of authors, there developed in the United States a pragmatic division of the genre that still forms the basis of subdivision in the award-

Hugo Gernsback founded *Amazing Stories* and *Amazing Stories Quarterly*.

Fall Edition
1929
AMAZING STORIES
QUARTERLY
2/6
IN CANADA SIXTY CENTS
50¢
A. Hyatt Verrill
Edmond Hamilton
David H. Keller

Hugo Gernsback.

feet in America at that time. A very able engineer and businessman, he soon turned his hand to magazine publishing. He founded *Modern Electrics* (in which his own novel *Ralph 124 C 41 Plus* was published in 1911), *Electrical Experimenter, Radio News*, and most noteworthy of all, *Science and Invention*. This last mentioned magazine, more often than the others, carried short technological fantasies, all of which followed the rules of the genre as Gernsback understood them. His idea was that such stories, first and foremost, must act as purveyors of technical information. Thus scientific innovations, fantastic discoveries, descriptions of technological events, and so on, dominated, kept together by means of a (frequently banal) plot and enlivened by bursts of dialogue. A fair example of the type is Gernsback's novel already mentioned.

Gradually Gernsback became convinced that many readers of the magazines bought them primarily for the sake of these make-believe stories. In August 1913, therefore, he carried out an experiment, publishing after the fashion of the specialized western and detective magazines a special number of *Science and Invention* that contained no contributions on popular science but concentrated exclusively on science fiction. This was the first "science fiction" edition to be produced anywhere in the world. At the same time, he invented the name for the genre that it has kept ever since.

Owing to the success of the *Science and Invention* special, plans for a regularly produced publication devoted to science fiction came to fruition. Allowing only a short time for its preparation, Gernsback published the first "pure" periodical for science fiction in the world under the title *Amazing Stories*. On the heels of this came both the *Amazing Annual*, and the *Amazing Stories Quarterly*. These magazines were slightly larger in page format than the pulp magazines of the day, and contained a lot of material (about 130,000 words), thus offering the reader a good amount of reading material for the price. In turn this led to an increasing demand for authors of science fiction short stories and novels. New editions were also prepared of science fiction classics, including the work of Edgar Allan Poe, Jules Verne, and H. G. Wells. To fill any gaps, Gernsback pored

ing of science fiction prices: 7,500 words and under equaled a short story; 7,500 to 17,500 words equaled a novelette; 17,500 to 40,000 words equaled a novella; and over 40,000 words equaled a novel. This so-called division between novelette and novella does not always hold up when these terms are translated into other languages.

Space in these magazines was relatively restricted, and could in normal circumstances be filled many times over. That was the reason the shorter form—which was by far the most popular in US literature generally—encompassed such a vast amount of science fiction literature and why the sci fi short story was a genuinely American form, spreading over the whole world since the 1920s.

At the time of World War I, there entered on the scene the man who actually christened the genre. Hugo Gernsback (1884–1967) was an engineer whose roots reached back to Luxemburg (where his family name was "Gernsbach"). In his home country, Gernsback attended the Ecole Industrielle, and then the technical school in Bingen, on the Rhine. After his emigration, he opened a radio dispatch shop in New York. Radio was just beginning to stand on its own through contemporary publications from other countries and offered his readers novels and stories often in reworked or abridged forms in translation. The lion's share of the contributions were derived from the increasing number of American authors, many of whom came to the field directly from work in practical science and engineering. Gernsback put together teams that could work in harmony to produce a magazine with a unified style and point of view. By careful choice of his closest associates, he was able to avoid recourse to professional writers, preferring practicing scientists who wrote only as a sideline. The German-American chemist, C. A. Brandt, was responsible for the literary and artistic side of the stories and novels; the already graying son-in-law of the famous inventor Thomas A. Edison, Dr. T. O'Conor Sloane, was responsible for the scientific content of the contributions; Frank R. Paul, who came from Austria, produced most of the illustrations and the front covers of the magazine. Gernsback himself held the reins of the production as a whole, and wrote leading articles and editorial commentaries.

The production run of *Amazing Stories* was somewhere in the region of 100,000 per number. Within a very short time, Gernsback and his editorial team were able to woo well-known story writers away from other pulp magazines, even if only for occasional contributions. The list of main authors included E. E. (Edward Elmer) "Doc" Smith (1890–1965). He had graduated in chemistry in 1918, and then worked as a specialist in dough mixtures. This led his sharper-tongued critics to refer to him as "Pancake" Smith.

Working together with the wife of a colleague, Smith had produced his first science fiction novel be-

The changed public taste of twenty years later: serials from 1946 and 1948.

105

fore 1920, even though he was not to find a publisher until it was included in a 1928 edition of *Amazing Stories*. This book, *The Skylark of Space*, escalated the author to instant fame. Some of the reason for this can probably be ascribed to the fact that it was found good editorial policy to proclaim Smith's title of "doctor"—actually "Doc"—on the title page of the magazine. At Sloane's suggestion, Smith wrote a sequel *Skylark Three*, which was published likewise in *Amazing Stories* in 1930.

A number of Gernsback's many other authors also deserve mention. Foremost was Edgar Rice Burroughs, whose appearance on the publishing scene was almost simultaneous with Gernsback's. He was discovered by another publisher—Frank A. Munsey—not Gernsback. Yet his name seems inevitably linked with Gernsback's nevertheless. In actuality, he burst onto the world scene in 1912 with *two* novels published one after the other in the pulp magazine *All-Story*. The first was a serial titled *Under the Moons of Mars* (republished in book form in 1917 as *A Princess of Mars)*; the second was *Tarzan of the Apes*. His biggest success in terms of popularity and monetary reward came from the Tarzan stories and films. However, Burroughs was known from the start, far and wide, for his non-Tarzan books as well. In fact, he started *three* series of novels in the science fiction vein, not just the one Mars line. The first Mars book already mentioned was followed by two sequels: *The God of Mars* (1918) and *The Warlord of Mars* (1919). The hero of this series was John Carter. Carter's birth, like most of Burroughs's heroes, is somewhat shrouded in mystery. But there is no mystery about his ability to stand up to enormous giants on Mars, some green, some yellow, but all ominous. Carter's adventures on Mars hark back to the lusty adventure tales of H. Rider Haggard and the imagination of H. G. Wells. By 1914 Burroughs was hungering for *another* type of adventure, and he came up this time with a *new* lost world—one located within the center of the Earth, right out of Jules Verne. *At the Earth's Core* appeared as an *All-Story* series in 1914, and a new hero was born—David Innes. A new world was also born—not Mars, not Earth, but Pellucidar, that strange place inside the Earth. Hark to the reverberations of Niels Klim, Peter Wilkins, and even Hans

Cover of A. Merritt's lost-tribe novel of fantasy action, set somewhere underneath the Alaskan wilderness.

Pfaall! The "Pellucidar" series continued with many sequels. Yet Burroughs managed to come up with one *more* series in his writing lifetime. The third scene was the planet of Venus, the hero Carson Napier, son of a British army officer and an American girl from Virginia, born in India, brought up by an old Hindu mystic, and taught at an early age—are you ready for this?—telepathy! In 1932 *Argosy* (the magazine that *All-Story* had become after several shifts and mergings) began to serialize this new series, and Burroughs managed several sequels to it before World War II.

106

In the long run, critics agree that the scientific content of Burroughs's "science fiction" is negligible if not nonexistent. But who needs it? It is the *fantasy* that counts! His novels, whether they be the Mars books featuring John Carter, the Venus books starring Carson Napier, or the volumes featuring David Innes in Pellucidar are romantic throwbacks to that earlier English tradition of adventure fiction—works of men like Haggard, Kipling, Wells—and of course Jules Verne. The Burroughs novels, of whatever strain, follow the same ground plan. A love develops between the hero and a female partner—a love never sexually consummated, of course, at least not in Burroughs's mind. In each work Burroughs finds new means of threatening that love, in a story set in the jungle, in the civilized world, on another planet, or even at the center of the Earth. It is usually a scoundrelly heavy who appears and separates the lovers for a time. Nevertheless, there is always a happy ending. The close of each tale sees the triumph of Carter/Innes/Napier, and Burroughs's orderly world is reestablished. These stories, according to many critics, belong to the lowest stratum of literature; however, owing to their huge commercial success, they have found countless imitators and did have a profound effect on the development of the science fiction form in America after World War I. Forgotten by the critics is always that Very Important Person in any literary endeavor—the reader. And the readers gobbled up Burroughs, always seemingly hungry for more!

Contemporary with Burroughs was George Allan England, who also worked in the pulps and for the Munsey chain. Although extremely successful during the period of their publication, his works never attained the overall, lasting popularity of Burroughs's.

Other writers came to Gernsback direct—for example, David Henry Keller (1880–1966) joined the Gernsback team of science fiction writers in 1928 with his story *The Revolt of the Pedestrians*. He had a special success with a string of stories that ran for seven years in *Amazing Stories* under the series title of "Taine of San Francisco." A(braham) Merritt (1884–1943) wrote many successful fantasy stories and novels for *All-Story Weekly*, that were later republished by Gernsback. Merritt produced a number of novels in both the science fiction and the supernatural/horror genres. Four of his science fiction novels, serialized at first and then published as books, are noteworthy: *The Moon Pool* (1919), *The Face in the Abyss* (1931), *Dwellers in the Mirage* (1932), and *The Metal Monster* (1946). Merritt came by his fanciful fictional skills honestly; from 1937 to 1943 he was editor of Hearst's *American Weekly*, a Sunday supplement distributed with all the Hearst newspapers. He wrote quickly and with facility, providing good fast action, brief dialogue, and quick character sketches. His was the pulp formula, but refined; while many revile his prose as "purple," others think of it as popular and "poetic." His work actually is a reversion to the more romantic and airy school of early science fiction, like that of Burroughs and Haggard. *Pool* is the story of a lost race living *underneath* the Pacific in the spot where the Moon was ripped from the Earth at its creation. There the lost tribe of Lemurians continues, with The Shining One an entity of three terrestrials running the tribe. *Abyss* explores another lost race, this one discovered in the remote Andes, living under the subjugation of The Snake Mother. *Mirage* is the story of a mixed tribe of Amerindians, Mongols, and Norsemen located, of all places, in the middle of the Alaskan wilderness. *Monster* involves a form of alien life—metallic, of course!—that reproduces itself with great rapidity somewhere off in the remote Himalayan Mountains.

Stanton Arthur Coblentz made his debut as author of fantasy in 1928 with a reworking of the old Lost Atlantis idea, *The Sunken World*. Other stories and novels, most of them derivative and of little value, followed. Similar histories might be given of the works of Karl Vincent (real name: Harold Vincent Schoepflin, 1893–1968), Miles John Breuer (1889 to 1947, whose first story was *The Man with the Strange Head* in 1927); the series about the International Flying Police (IFP) by Roman F. Starzl, and the first stories by Jack (John Stewart) Williamson, whose first novel *The Metal Man* appeared in 1928.

The Gernsback team also drew on the talents of Murray Leinster (pseudonym for William Fitzgerald Jenkins, 1896–1975), Ray Cummings (Raymond King Cummings, 1887–1957), Otis Adelbert Kline (1891–1946, especially well-known for his Burroughs imitations). These names alone make a good list! Shal-

Gernsback's second peak: *Science Wonder Stories, Air Wonder Stories*, and *Wonder Stories Quarterly*.

low entertainment predominated. Most of the authors were prolific writers, who from the beginning turned their hands to any motif that came to mind, introducing gratuitous violence and horror, propped up their plots by the most banal clichés in the repertoire. An honorable exception to this rule was A. (Alpheus) Hyatt Verrill (1871–1954). An archeologist and anthropologist, he undertook many an expedition to Latin America. Apart from seven books, he was the author of many science fiction stories after the manner of Jules Verne. *Amazing Stories* published his novel *Beyond the Pale* as early as 1926. His stories of giants became best-sellers in this magazine.

The editorial mix of "genuine" mainstream literature, lighter entertainment reading, and some quite ahuman trivia and banalities, became the standard for all science fiction production for many years. It is no-

ticeable that as the reprinting of stories by Poe, Verne, and Wells diminished, so the level of the original contributions sank, and the greater part of science fiction became the repository of the lowest instincts and banalities of dilettante authors.

A favorite form developed during these early formative years was the "space opera," a planetary fairy tale, in which love interest, adventure, horror, the rescue of the heroine and of the world itself from gangs of ne'er-do-wells, detective elements, and western motifs were all brought together in one epic. In place of revolvers, the fearless hero carried new weapons of ever-increasing power and sophistication. His opponent, often a terrifying beast from · outer space, a many-tentacled monster, a BEM (bug-eyed monster), was naturally equipped with equally ferocious hardware. Thus opportunities were offered for scenes of terrible butchery. The cowboy's horse had been superseded by the rocket or spaceship, and the well-established fair daughter of the farmer, always under threat and needing rescuing, was now transformed into a princess from a foreign planet. In the last battle, the hero's superior power still ensured victory, as in the old westerns, and he rode away to his next adventure. This formed the outline for the first serialized stories (after Burroughs's Mars and Venus novels), Starzle's IFP, the Interstellar Patrol series by Edmond Hamilton (who was the author responsible for nearly all the numbers of the serial "Captain Future") and so on ad infinitum.

In 1929, with the crash of the stock market and the beginning of the Great Depression, Hugo Gernsback was obliged to sell all his periodicals, including *Amazing Stories*. They did not however cease production, but simply changed ownership and editor.

Many of his old subscribers supported Gernsback when he made a new start with *Science Wonder Stories*, the first number of which came out in 1929 with a preface in which he firmly established the name of the genre—science fiction.

This new periodical was quickly joined by others, including *Science Wonder Quarterly, Air Wonder Stories*, and *Amazing Detective Tales*. The conception and the mixture of contributions was little changed from the days of *Amazing Stories;* indeed most of the old authors wrote for the new magazines

108

as they had for the old. But the gathering world economic crisis and the amount of competition that had built up since Gernsback's early days did make an impact, and soon *Science Wonder Stories* and *Air Wonder Stories* were combined to make a new single publication called *Wonder Stories,* later changed to *Thrilling Wonder Stories.*

During the 1930s, Gernsback, who had never given up his original conception of technological fantasy literature, was obliged to sell off his magazines one by one. A last attempt to make a comeback, in 1953, with *Science Fiction Plus,* misfired.

Gernsback's unique contribution to the story of American science fiction remains undisputed. It was he who invented the specialist science fiction magazine and who gave a name to the form. At the same time, no one can dispute the "blame" that attaches to his editorial team for allowing science fiction to take the path of uninspired and shallow literary entertainment. These few people worked hard to make science

fiction a mass product of the lowest common denominator. This was the general image that this literature held for a long time, to such effect that as a genre it is still not taken seriously by scientists and theorists but is dismissed as banal at best. The usual assessment has it that this literature is acceptable for young people, but even then with reservations.

An independent branch of this literary development was the American science fiction cartoon strip, later comic book. The precursors of such comics include the illustrated periodical of the street-ballad singers, the world famous series of cartoons by Wilhelm Busch, and Windsor McKay's comic strip fantasy *(Little Nemo).* Although as early as the beginning of the century one of the New York newspaper presses had adapted a four-color process of printing, it took some time for the new possibilities afforded by such technology to be fully explored. One early answer was to print a "comic" strip full color in the

109

Jane Fonda as Barbarella in the French film version of a popular cartoon strip.

paper's Sunday supplement. Competitors soon caught up and gradually such comics became a normal feature of the American press. When, as a form of advertisement, free color comics were given away for a soap manufacturer, and by Gulf Oil, the business of producing color comics became rapidly commercialized.

The first science fiction continuous comic strip was published in 1929, based on Philip Nowlan's novel, *Armageddon—2419 A. D.* from the August 1928 copy of Gernsback's *Amazing Stories* magazine. Buck Rogers thus became the first science fiction hero on the comic scene (if one discounts Jules Verne's Captain Nemo). The Buck Rogers drawings were done by Dick Calkins. In the 1930s, this was followed by such series as *Flash Gordon* (Alex[ander]

Raymond), *Brick Bradford* (Ritt and Gray), and *Mandrake the Magician* (Lee Falk and Phil Davis). These figures are the direct ancestors of the cloaked superheroes around the time of World War II: *The Phantom* (Lee Falk), *Superman* (from 1938, Jerry Siegel and Joe Shuster), *Batman*, and dozens of others out of the same mold. The adventures of these heroes introduced more and more elements of horror, of sex (for example, in the well-known postwar French serial *Barbarella*), black humor, and some aspects drawn from militaristic and fascist ideology. Such comic heroes tended to take on more and more "inhuman" forms. Against this powerful trend, the few stories that retained a humanist outlook paled into insignificance.

Batman, another hero of science fiction cartoon fans.

110

The War
of the Cybernauts

Cover illustrations here und facing page for novelizations of Flash Gordon adventures from Alex Raymond's cartoon strip.

In or around the year 1930, a special form of science fiction adulation came into being when readers of sci fi magazines resolved to form themselves into a "science fiction club," basing themselves on the German "Union for Spaceship Travel," but far outstripping this model, and calling themselves the "International Scientific Association." This "fan" movement quickly gathered momentum and many cities formed their own fan clubs, embodying their love of science fiction in fanciful names. They contributed fan letters to magazines and produced inexpensive newsletters with information for their members. It was

The Witch Queen of Mongo

Since 1961, the business of producing such comics has been concentrated in the hands of the "Marvel Comics Group." Marvel markets a wide variety of monstrous figures, such as "The Man called NOVA," "Guardians of the Galaxy," "The Fantastic Four," "Spiderman," "Ironman and Captain America," as well as the bestselling adaptations of older science fiction titles under the banner of "Marvel Classic Comics."

112

after World War II however that the fan movement became a worldwide phenomenon, and the production of "fanzines" (portmanteau word, fan + magazines = magazines for fans) was carried out in many countries.

This "fandom," as the fan clubs and fanzines might be dubbed, played an important role in the manipulation of public opinion on science fiction, and also helped to discover new authors. Many future science fiction writers recall that their first steps were taken when they became enthusiastic fans of the comics and magazines. Often they produced their own comics, writing much of the copy themselves. This humble beginning was often succeeded by a leap into the world of science fiction magazine writing. Because the professional literary critics left science fiction well alone, it was the fans who did the work of defining and setting critical parameters for the evaluation of science fiction literature. Often critiques became little more than paeans of praise for the work or its author, referring less to established literary or aesthetic criteria than to a subjective declaration of personal taste. Many of today's producers of important science fiction paperback libraries—and indeed the writers as well—come from the ranks of these fans.

Public taste is notoriously fickle, and the financial success of a magazine depends upon its ability to lead, or follow, the fashion of the moment. In order to survive, editors tended to fall back upon the fan movement to keep abreast of readers' opinions of their publications. In most of the magazines of the past (since World War II, many changes have taken place!) readers' letters were published in the magazine, asking questions and expressing opinions as to the quality of the novels and short stories. Also questionnaires were circulated to determine the best stories of the year. Those that received the highest vote were then reprinted in special publications, anthologies of the best stories of that particular magazine. Some publishers repeated this process, drawing on the best stories from a longer period, which would then be published in book form, as "the best of the best of science fiction," or whatever.

Soon individual fan clubs made contact with one another. In the course of time, annual gatherings of all the fan clubs in any particular region became estab-

The Time Trap of Ming XIII

lished and, as an extension of this, in 1939 the first world conference. Since 1953, the participants of the Worldcon (the World Science Fiction convention) have awarded a prize known as the Hugo (for the "Hugo Gernsback Award"), the highest award given on the basis of votes cast by the actual readers of science fiction—that is, the fans.

Shortly after the founding of the first fan club in the United States, the magazine *Astounding Stories* (later renamed *Astounding Science Fiction* and often called *Astounding* for short), set up the most important competitive event ever conceived by Gernsback's

113

A late edition of *Astounding* magazine.

"space opera." As a fan he tried his hand at writing, claiming his first success at the age of twenty with a story published in *Amazing Stories*. The good reception of this story spurred him on to produce others closely modeled on those of his mentor, E. E. Smith, and his "Skylark" stories. Between 1930 and 1932 he wrote novels and stories in the series "Arcot, Morey, and Wade" (first published in book form a quarter of a century later as *The Black Star Passes* [1953], *Island of Space* [1956], and *Invaders from the Infinite* [1961]). These archetypal space operas made Campbell's name so famous that he was invited by Tremaine to join *Astounding*. While there he published *The Mightiest Machine* (1934), in which he outstripped even his own high standards of improbability and the invention of abstruse situations as set by the earlier space operas. At about the same time, he wrote

John W. Campbell, Jr.

publications. Though hardly distinguishable from *Amazing Stories* and *Wonder Stories* in presentation or style at first, changes in this respect were soon under way. The magazine passed into the hands of F. Orlin Tremaine, and by the middle of the 1930s, *Astounding* was a financially successful magazine. It attracted better authors to its ranks, and thus the magazine gained a leading position in the American science fiction market, which it held for many years. This was primarily due to one man, John W. (Wood) Campbell, Jr. (1910–71), whose contribution to the form was unique and virtually unequaled.

Campbell was born in Newark, New Jersey, and completed his education at the Massachusetts Institute of Technology. He was a reader of the short stories in the early Gernsback magazines and was especially enthusiastic about the emerging form of the

114

a story that marked a change from his other achievements. This was "Twilight" (1934), showing a softening of the hard style, the gaudy effects, the cosmic arena of the heroes, and the extremes of conflict with the natives of other worlds. It made way for a description of the end of human civilization—the mood now contemplative and therefore impressive in a different way from his earlier work. Because his own name was so closely associated with his earlier work, he published this and other new science fiction stories under the pseudonym Don A. Stuart (using his wife's maiden name, Dona Stuart).

The year 1937 was decisive in the history of American science fiction literature: Campbell took over the editorship of *Astounding Stories*. Shortly thereafter, he published his most important contribution of all to the genre, *Who Goes There?* (1938). His new duties, about which he was scrupulously conscientious, left him less time for his own writing. Keeping a close eye on public taste, Campbell carried on the publication of space operas in the established pattern, with all their banalities and trivialities, in *Astounding*, but he now devoted some of his efforts to stimulating the interest of new young writers producing material for rival magazines. Of particular importance was the fact that Campbell placed some value on moving away from clichéd situations and old stock of characters. He wanted the people in a story to remain believable as human beings and the situation in which they found themselves to develop, at least sometimes, on lines other than the standard manner. The standard manner usually began in the cosmos, with a meeting on a star or in some galaxy with extraterrestrials, a conflict arising to be resolved only through violence or technological invention, often fantastical superweapons. Campbell demanded that the stories have an inner logic developing naturally from a concrete situation and particular characters. He divided science fiction into three different types: the gadget story (concentrating on technical tricks), the concept story (that developed from an original inspiration or idea), and the character story (in which the story was dominated by the leading personality).

Campbell's ideas had a major impact on a whole group of science fiction writers of the first rank. The

Jarvis's encounter with the Martian Tweel, from G. Weinbaum's *A Martian Odyssey*. Illustration by Werner Ruhner.

team behind *Astounding* during the years 1938–39 and the end of the 1940s produced a large number of works that are now counted among the classic novels of science fiction.

It is of course virtually impossible to do justice to all the authors and their work in a short commentary that must restrict itself to pointing out main trends. This is especially true as even before Campbell's editorial influence there were already some works in *Astounding* that were pushing at the barriers of science fiction as it was then perceived. In this connection it is

115

impossible to ignore the name of G(rauman) Weinbaum (1902–35) and his *A Martian Odyssey*, which was published in *Wonder Stories* in 1934. This story, set as it was outside the then current style of space stories, was one of the most successful ever published in this magazine. *Astounding* soon approached Weinbaum and won him over. Sadly, Weinbaum was able to produce only a very limited amount of writing (five stories in *Wonder Stories* and seven in *Astounding*) before he died of cancer of the throat only eighteen months after the publication of his first story. Some further stories were published posthumously. Nevertheless he earned a permanent place in the history of science fiction and there can be no dispute as to the justice of mentioning his name among the authors of *Astounding* even though their trailblazing work was mainly produced later. The character drawing, stylistic impact, and humanist outlook that raises the level of the writing of some of the *Astounding* authors, are all to be found in at least equal proportion in the writings of Weinbaum, especially in *A Martian Odyssey*. In this book, the meeting with inhabitants of another planet does not lead inevitably towards conflict or war, but comes about by means of an everyday situation, in which help is offered in a case of need, involving humans and Tweel, an inhabitant of Mars.

> The Martian wasn't a bird, really. It wasn't even bird-like, except at first glance. It had a beak all right, and a few feathery appendages, but the beak wasn't really a beak. It was somewhat flexible; I could see the top bend slowly from side to side; it was almost like a cross between a beak and a trunk. It had four-toed feet, and four-fingered things—hands, you'd have to call them, and a little roundish body, and a long neck ending in a tiny head—and that beak. It stood an inch or so taller than I. . . .
>
> We stared at each other. Finally, the creature went into a series of clackings and twitterings and held out its hands toward me, empty. I took that as a gesture of friendship. . . .
> Anyway, I put up my gun . . . and we were pals.[1]

The description of these two friends as they wander over the Martian landscape is very convincing. Tweel

Isaac Asimov.

explains the special nature of the planet to this human friend. The reader cannot help but be impressed by the writer's descriptions of the building of pyramids of a silicate base, the dreadful "dream-beast" (from the clutches of which the two friends rescue one another), the mutual help given in averting the wagon-driving strangers.

This story does not concentrate on a slimy, many-tentacled monster, but presents other life forms as evolved according to certain natural laws that imply that the criteria we use on Earth may not be sufficient to understand them completely. The narrator warns us not to scorn Tweel, who, he feels, would be quite capable of mastering the secrets of the human intellect; although Tweel is clearly no genius, the narrator is acutely aware that Tweel is more able to understand him than vice versa.

This story marks the beginning of a new facet in science fiction, the representation of aliens as having independence. In presenting extraterrestrial intelligence, the English author Eric Frank Russell, another

116

member of the *Astounding* stable, was the nearest to Weinbaum. At the same time as the traditional enemy was being developed into something much more complex, the traditional hero also underwent a major change, being readjusted to conform to everyday standards, reduced, in effect, to life size. This is the case in many of the *Astounding* stories from "the golden age of science fiction" in the 1940s.

One of the most important authors encouraged by Campbell was Isaac Asimov, born in 1920 in a suburb of Smolensk called Petrovich. His parents moved to New York in 1923. The young immigrant lived out his youth in Brooklyn, discovering at the age of nine science fiction magazines for sale in his father's sweetshop. Asimov read chemistry at college, graduating in 1948. He was professor of biochemistry at the University of Boston until 1958. He has published more than two hundred scientific texts and science fiction works. He came to science fiction via the fan movement, making his debut as an author in 1939 in *Amazing Stories.* Campbell immediately summoned him to join *Astounding.* Most of Asimov's books were written for the latter magazine. Campbell was the originator of the basic idea of "Nightfall" (a short story, 1941), which was voted the best science fiction story before 1965. Asimov's robot stories published during the 1940s brought him immense popularity, and these stories were gathered into a book in 1950 under the title *I, Robot,* which took the science fiction world by storm.

Asimov bases each story on a fundamental idea, which he uses to awaken suspense and interest in the opening section of the tale, working the idea through to produce his special effect in the closing pages. This close structure he took from Poe, one of his favorite short story authors. Thus, like Poe's detective Dupin, Asimov has his robot psychologist Susan Calvin (who is seventy-five in the stories, having been born in the year 1982) reach her astounding conclusions with the help of logic in most of the stories.

·The special character in Asimov's work derives from the fact that the robots stand side by side with the humans. "There was a time when humanity faced the universe alone and without a friend. Now he has creatures to help him; stronger creatures than himself, more faithful, more useful, and absolutely devoted to him. Mankind is no longer alone. Have you ever thought of it in that way?"[2]

In the early stories, Asimov's robots look like people; but later, Asimov moves away from this. In "The Inevitable Conflict," the robots have become enormous thinking machines.

It was Asimov who, with the assistance of Campbell, postulated the famous three rules of robotics, which have been adopted by countless later authors. In later stories, conflicts arise from the fact that the robots "overstep" these rules. It is then necessary to reestablish the robot order as it was before. Asimov's three rules were most plainly expressed in his story "Runaround," published in 1942:

Dust jacket illustration for Isaac Asimov's collection of science fiction short stories.

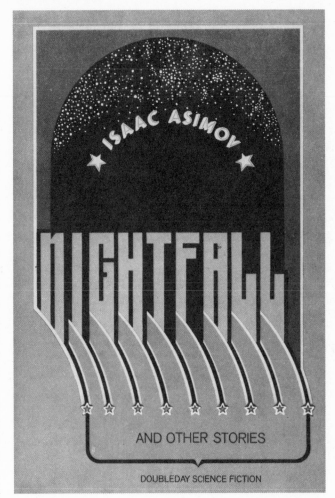

117

"1—A robot may not injure a human being, or, through inaction allow a human being to come to harm; 2—A robot must obey the orders given it by human beings except where such orders would conflict with the First Law; and 3—A robot must protect its own existence as long as such protection does not conflict with the First or Second Laws."[3]

Apart from the robot stories, Asimov wrote many that were later republished in the volumes of the *Foundation* trilogy (*Foundation* [1951]; *Foundation and Empire* [1952]; *Second Foundation* [1953]). This cycle, despite its highly polished style, solid construction, and sense of humanist principle, was in fact little more than a space opera on a particularly large scale. Novels such as *The Stars Like Dust* (1951) and *The Currents of Space,* are not exactly sequels but are nonetheless firmly based in the huge empire of the *Foundation* trilogy.

Asimov experimented with his emphatic style in stories and novels that fall rather into the category of a halfway stage between science fiction and the detective story. These include *The Caves of Steel* (1953) and *The Naked Sun* (1957), and also the short stories in the collection published as *Asimov's Mysteries.*

After World War II, Asimov wrote *C-Chute* (1951), in which he condemned the Korean War. In 1952 he wrote a damning indictment of McCarthyism in his book *The Martian Way,* and in *Silly Asses* (1957) he registered a protest against the manufacture of the hydrogen bomb.

Essentially, Asimov has remained true to his humanist conception of technologically based fantasy, even when forced to make concessions to public taste.

Alfred Bester, born in 1913 in New York, wrote for *Astounding* and *Unknown,* another, albeit short-lived, magazine run by Campbell. He produced some very effective science fiction stories, which later were included, along with others, in a hardback collection. One of the most interesting, and at the same time most characteristic of his outlook, is his "Adam and no Eve." Krane, the hero, is the very last person on the now desolate Earth. Earlier, he had a spacecraft, powered by a fuel of his own invention based on iron, extremely dangerous: the effect of even only a tiny amount of the fuel leaking will lead to the decay of all iron atoms, and turn the Earth into a huge desert. In spite of all warnings, Krane starts his machine. On his return, he is confronted by the consequences of his action. He crawls to the sea, an Adam without an Eve, to die. But, Bester tells us, from the organic substances of the ocean new life will evolve and last for millions of years.

Bester was employed for many years primarily as an author of radio and television dramas, and of comics, before he returned to the field of prose. He made his new start in 1952, returning not to *Astounding,* but to a magazine that had in the intervening years become the leading voice of American science fiction, namely Horace L. Gold's *Galaxy.* The novel *The Demolished Man* was a mixture of science fiction and the detective novel, and was remarkable for its inclusion of stylistic experiments with the spoken form of the language very unusual in the genre. There is one

Alfred Bester.

Robert A. Heinlein.

character in the book, a policeman who has telepathic gifts, that looks forward to the author's next book *The Stars My Destination*, the plot of which centers on parapsychological possibilities. Of far greater importance than the novels are undoubtedly some of Bester's short stories and tales. (This view is supported by the novel *The Computer Connection* published in 1975.) Since the 1950s, Bester has published some short stories that command attention. In "Fondly Fahrenheit" (1954), an android turns into a compulsive murderer when temperatures rise to above 90° Fahrenheit, and is therefore obliged to flee from crime to crime with his master, from planet to planet, until it all but kills its master by fire and is itself destroyed. The master then builds a new cheaper android, into which he builds again the same characteristic. Bester's aim is to point out the schizophrenia

between the android and its owner. Other stories use science fiction motifs (especially time travel and time shifts) in order to offer critical commentary on current American life: for example, in his "Hobson's Choice," or "The Rollercoaster," which interprets our age as the amusement park of the future.

An important, if controversial, author who joined the team of *Astounding* was Robert A. (Anson) Heinlein, born in 1907 in Butler, Missouri. He studied at the Marine Academy of Annapolis and was an officer through and through. After serving as a gun officer for five years on an aircraft carrier, he was invalided out of service owing to unfitness, a heavy blow for Heinlein.

He was, however, not to be enlisted again until World War II, when he spent some years as an engineer in the military. His love of the United States Navy and the military way of life finds expression in some of his novels and stories, which appeared, often under pseudonyms, in *Astounding, Super Science Stories*, and some other magazines.

Heinlein made his debut as a science fiction author in 1939 with his story "Lifeline," which was later incorporated into the cycle *Future History*, along with other novels and stories.

Among Heinlein's work that earned him fame and prizes are *The Puppet Masters* (1951), *The Door into Summer* (1956), *Double Star* (1956), *Starship Troopers* (1959), *Farnham's Freehold* (1964), *The Moon Is a Harsh Mistress* (1965), and the best-seller among the hippies of the 1960s, *Stranger in a Strange Land* (1961), and *The Number of the Beast* (1975).

Without question, Heinlein is one of the most successful of American science fiction authors, although his work is not entirely devoid of ahuman passages. His work contains ideas derived from militaristic and even fascist ideologies (for example, in *Star Wars*). Also, the problem of racial discrimination is estranged even in the future. In *Farnham's Freehold*, war hysteria and terror of the "Russians" are brought together with total nuclear war. Hugh Farnham, the main character, has a theory that the strongest will survive the approaching war, saying that for the first time in history, the cleverest and most able will not be killed, and struggles will follow in which the stronger parties will of necessity come out on top. Because he is in-

119

FARNHAM'S FREEHOLD

a novel by

ROBERT A. HEINLEIN

author of Glory Road, Podkayne of Mars, etc.

Theodore Sturgeon.

cluded in this group, he has built for himself and his loved ones an absolutely safe bunker. It survives three attacks, but there comes a fourth that plunges the bunker through the fourth dimension into a wilderness of the future. The semi-idyllic life, reminiscent of Robinson Crusoe or the frontier pioneers, which Farnham and the others now lead, is ended by strange folk traveling in airships who discover them and rescue them. Some 2103 years have passed since the atomic blasts, and the new society Farnham finds is strictly hierarchic in structure. At the top are the "chosen," all black, and beneath them society is stratified into bulls for production of the necessary workers and servants, women to bear offspring, castrated slaves, and so on. Hugh Farnham is given the job of translating old books and thus comes to understand what has happened in previous ages. The white peo-

Cover illustration for Robert A. Heinlein's novel *Farnham's Freehold.*

ple of the past tore themselves limb from limb, thus leaving an innocent, sympathetic, and grateful black race to inherit the Earth.

The new order established by the blacks is painted in the most dismal manner. The white women must serve as bedwarmers, white men are castrated—and the flesh of the fatted whites is a prized gourmet delicacy. Farnham, his beloved Barbara, and their children are all transported back into the past for their disrespect. They arrive to find that the atomic blasts are just about to occur, see themselves hiding in their own house, and with their special knowledge of what is about to happen, are able to shelter safely in a mountain cave.

Such unappetizing and repugnant scenes as this depiction of the blacks' regime and their cannibalism are also to be found in other stories by Heinlein.

Other authors who wrote for *Astounding* include Fritz Leiber and Lester Del Rey, writers with a light touch who produced mostly shallow entertainment.

One of Campbell's star authors was Theodore Sturgeon, who was born in 1918 and published his first science fiction in 1939. His work stands out today for its unusually low concentration on technological elements. Sturgeon preferred to present a story of the inner feelings, giving more emphasis to the subjective moment, the human psyche (for example, "Microscopic God," 1941). In a certain sense he carried on already established developments that were only to reach full fruition in a later period. This is especially true with his short stories and science fiction tales, but is also true of some of his novels, which can overstep in parts the dividing line between science fiction and poetic fantasy.

Clifford D. (Donald) Simak, born in 1904, had been writing science fiction since 1931, but it was under the editorship of Campbell that this journalist began to concentrate on science fiction. After his novel *Cosmic Engineer* (1938), he published several stories that were later expanded and remodeled into the novel *City* (1952). The stories are set in a time long after mankind has left Earth: robots and clever dogs foregather round the campfire and relate legends of the past, when humans still existed. These tales, written during World War II, reflect Simak's disillusionment with the horrors of war that mankind has

121

Clifford D. Simak.

imaginative power. But he did have at least one new idea. He developed a doctrine of salvation called Dianetics, which he made the basis of a "church," and by the end of the 1970s numbered more than six million members in the United States and other countries. Called "the Church of Scientology," it afforded, financially, an almost inexhaustible living for its originator.

The underlying bases for Hubbard's teachings were published in *Astounding* in 1950. Campbell's inclination towards Hubbard's "dianetics" and other pseudotheories brought forth a shower of criticism

Cover of Simak's *City*.

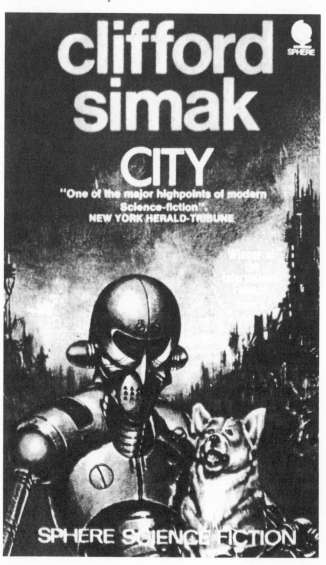

brought into play. Overall, his stories are characterized by their sensitivity, which sometimes verges on sentimentality. Sometimes the style is rather overexpansive. During the 1950s Simak, like Bester, moved to *Galaxy* magazine and published more stories, finally turning to concentrate on novels in the 1960s.

The Canadian writer A. E. (Alfred Elton) van Vogt joined *Astounding* during Campbell's reign, and with his novel *Slan* (1940), a tale of superhuman mutants, became a popular success. He is one of the many prolific writers who delight in describing the antics of "supermen." Much of his work includes self-borrowings: he drew on his earlier publications, which had nothing in common in content or theme, and made them into novels. He uses current clichés and motifs in his plots, which tend to be built along well-established lines offering his supermen a wide variety of opportunities to make use of their "talents."

A personal friend of van Vogt was L. (Lafayette) Ron Hubbard, born in 1911. Hubbard had been writing science fiction since 1938, though it must be said his stories do not stand out for their originality or

122

from the science fiction camp. Alongside the magazine's reactionary political point of view, it was one of the main reasons for *Astounding*'s decline in importance. Campbell renamed the magazine *Analog—Science Fact and Fiction* in 1960. The first part of the title was meant to imply that the magazine was also going to contain theoretical contributions on science fiction. Campbell continued to edit the magazine until his death in 1971. But the golden years of his editorship had drawn to a close some two decades before, and the leading light of the science fiction magazine world was now *Galaxy Science Fiction*, founded in 1950 by a Canadian, H. L. (Horace Leonard) Gold. Gold had himself written and published in magazines, including *Astounding*, but his importance in the history of science fiction lies much more in his editorial activities than in his writings.

Apart from these two, there were of course other magazines. In the wake of World War II there was a considerable increase in titles that lasted for several years, but competition was rife.

Some of the important authors of the 1940s were unable to work with Campbell. This was the case especially of one of the most important science fiction writers of them all—Ray (Douglas) Bradbury. Since Campbell would not print his stories, they came out in *Thrilling Wonder Stories*, *Planet Stories*, and also (and this is indeed something unique) in magazines outside of the world of science fiction. Possibly this was due to their exceptionally high literary quality.

Ray Bradbury began his life with science fiction in the fan movement, publishing his first attempts in *Futuria Fantasia*, a magazine he edited himself and for which he wrote almost all the contents. In the 1940s he produced a number of stories set on Mars. These were brought together in 1951 in book form under the title *The Martian Chronicles*, and form one of the classics of science fiction literature. The stories are set in the years between the "rocket summer" of January 1999, and the "eternal picnic" of October 2026, and together tell the history of the colonization of Mars. The first three expeditions from Earth fail because Mars is trying to protect itself against a threatening cultural collapse and barbarism. Delightful humor informs the portraits of the Earth men, as they are shown expecting to be welcomed with open arms by

In 1960, *Astounding* was renamed *Analog—Science Fact and Fiction.*

thousands of Martians. What they encounter is complete indifference; everyone is occupied with their workaday duties. Then they land in a lunatic asylum, where they are greeted with the expected jubilation. But—and here Bradbury takes up a motif of H. G. Wells—when the fourth expedition lands, the whole population of Mars has fallen victim to an epidemic of chickenpox, against which they have no protection. Rocket after rocket can now land freely. For Bradbury, the ancient Martian culture and its relics, including buildings und books, pottery, and so on, obviously humanist in character, is destroyed by the besieging "pioneers." He repeatedly suggests parallels between the events of his story and the colonization methods used by nations; the glorification of the first settlers, which lies at the core of the western, is sub-

123

Oscar Werner in the François Truffaut film of Ray Bradbury's *Fahrenheit 451*.

ject to special scrutiny. Instead of the old harmony grown up on Mars over millions of years, there now comes to that planet what Bradbury particularly was critical of in American society: greed for money, struggles for power, and a social order of rigid hierarchy.

Bradbury makes reference to many literary motifs and themes, weaves them into new variations and uses them to highlight his own interpretations. In "Usher II," for instance, he looks back at Poe's famous tale of "The Fall of the House of Usher." A symbol of the modern pseudocivilization is Sam Parkhill's Hot Dog Restaurant in *The Martian Chronicles*, the glass of which has been broken from the old Martian buildings in the hills.[4] In November 2005, the settlers of Mars experience from their great distance fiery explosions on Earth, receiving the message flashing by Morse code that:

> AUSTRALIAN CONTINENT ATOMIZED IN PREMATURE
> EXPLOSION OF ATOMIC STOCKPILE. LOS ANGELES,
> LONDON BOMBED. WAR. COME HOME. COME HOME.
> COME HOME. COME HOME.[5]

Most of the settlers on Mars leave and return to Earth to play their part in an atomic war, and are lost in the general destruction. In the twentieth year after the

war, Mars is a dead planet, and Earth is also dead. A small handful of people use the last rocket to fly to Mars, in order to make a fresh start there. "Life on Earth never settled down to doing anything very good. Science ran too far ahead of us too quickly, and the people got lost in a mechanical wilderness. . . . Wars got bigger and bigger and finally killed Earth. . . . Now we're alone. We and a handful of others who'll land in a few days. Enough to start over. Enough to turn away from all that back on Earth and strike out on a new line."[6]

This is at once Bradbury's humanist message and his warning. This aspect of his work is even more pointedly marked in his dystopia *Fahrenheit 451*. When this novel was first published in 1953, McCarthyism in the US was reaching its climax. The anticommunist hysteria had affected almost every area of American society. Anxiety shut the mouths of many writers, including some science fiction writers. Ray Bradbury found a successful way of tackling the problem through fantasy. In the social system depicted in *Fahrenheit 451*, it is not difficult to see the relation it bears to a country terrorized by a type of McCarthyism or Hitlerism. The title hints at the central symbol of Bradbury's theme: "Fahrenheit 451: the temperature at which book-paper catches fire and burns."[7] The book burning is a symbol of the rooting out of

Illustration for one of Ray Bradbury's short stories, drawn by Joe Mugnaini.

any remaining humanity in this inhuman social system, a symbol that of course refers to much more than simply McCarthyism. The society is blessed with much luxury and technology, but there exists an absolute prohibition against the reading of books. The main character, Guy Montag, works in the fire service, which has meanwhile totally reversed its functions, with Montag's duty to oversee not the saving but the burning of books. The rationale for this is given by Beatty, the fire captain: "A book is a loaded gun in the house next door."[8]

The first part of the novel, "It Was a Pleasure to Burn," tells of Guy trying to hide books away despite the fact that punishment for this is imprisonment. At last he and his wife begin to read the twenty or so books they have collected. The second part of the book shows the first effects of his new experience ("The Sieve and the Sand"): Guy makes contact with a Professor Faber. He develops a plan to print books secretly and smuggle them into the houses of the firemen, with the aim of striking a death blow to those in power—a kind of partisan scheme to preserve culture. But then the unexpected happens: the fire engine stops before his own house, led there by information given by Guy's wife, Mildred.

The third part of the book, "Burning Bright," sees Guy forced to burn down his own house. He kills the captain, two fire officers, and destroys the "mechanical hound" that terrorizes them all. Now Guy must flee. Eventually he reaches a group of "outsiders," former intellectuals who preserve the great books of world literature in their memories for posterity. These people are Bradbury's hope for the future. The television screens show someone referred to as "Guy Montag" captured and killed. It is a fake news report. The powers that be think they have avenged Guy's crime. But there are in fact thousands of outsiders: looking no more than tramps they are in fact a library of culture. After the war, they will each commit the book they carry in their memories to paper, and the volumes will then be printed and circulated. They already see the airplanes coming and the city razed in seconds. They start their journey back to the totally flattened world, to bring the spirit back into it.

Bradbury's vision is a warning of the possible future of any country upon which McCarthyism or any

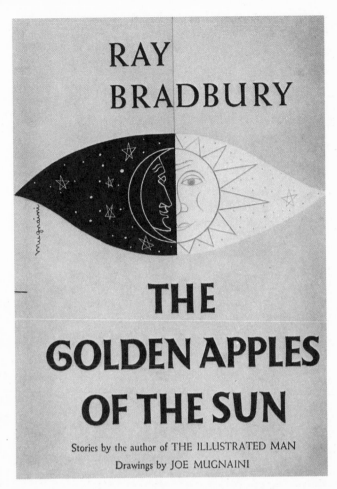

RAY BRADBURY

THE GOLDEN APPLES OF THE SUN

Stories by the author of THE ILLUSTRATED MAN
Drawings by JOE MUGNAINI

Illustration for dust jacket of Ray Bradbury's short story collection, *The Golden Apples of the Sun.*

similar book-burning terror is unleashed. The vision derives some of its detail from the book burnings experienced during the Nazi regime and during World War II. Bradbury also demonstrates how such a society contains within it the seeds of war. Thus he makes his contribution to the preservation of peace. Bradbury's humanism is equally apparent in his episodic novel, *The Illustrated Man* (1951).

Writers in the mainstream during this period of the burgeoning of science fiction sometimes were tempted to try their hand at scientific fantasy—using it as a fictional entity or using elements of the genre to enhance their own work. One of these men was Philip (Gordon) Wylie (1902–71), born in Beverly, Massachusetts. The brother of the more famous novelist Eli-

WHEN WORLDS COLLIDE

By

EDWIN BALMER

and

PHILIP WYLIE

A STOKES BOOK

J. B. LIPPINCOTT COMPANY
PHILADELPHIA NEW YORK

Title page from the Philip Wylie-Edwin Balmer novel *When Worlds Collide.*

several thrillers in the crime vein, and other pure romances—Wylie returned to science fiction with *The Disappearance* (1951), a fantasy in which the world splits into two entities—one populated exclusively by women, the other by men. No advocate of women's liberation, Wylie lets the satire reduce *both* groups to their helpless levels of inadequacy before bringing the two worlds together again. Always a militant preacher against human stupidity—his father was a minister—Wylie used *Tomorrow!* (1953) as a diatribe against the evils of civil-defense unpreparedness for nuclear attack. *Triumph* (1963) goes further, depicting the destruction of the Earth with only fourteen people left in a bomb shelter built by an egocentric millionaire for his own private use. *The End of the Dream* (1972) is Wylie's final pessimistic denunciation of human stupidity—the end of life on Earth through air pollution and the mutation of an ocean leech that takes over largely through human default.

More critically accepted by the literary establishment than Wylie, (Eugene Luther) Gore Vidal would turn to science fiction fantasy whenever it suited his purposes. Born at West Point, New York, in 1925, he first wrote in the science fiction genre in 1954, when *Messiah* appeared. The story concerns Eugene Luther—note the two names are Vidal's own—and the "messiah," a man named John Cave, whose preachments are that death is *good*! To point up the ironic Christ allegory, Clarissa, the female protagonist, be-

Rocket is ready to send select few into interplanetary space for survival after Earth and errant planet have collided in film *When Worlds Collide.*

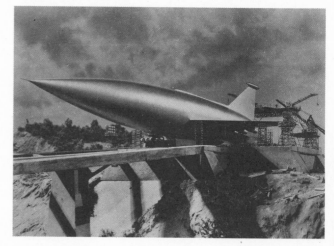

nor Wylie, he broke into the writing business with the sale of his novel *Gladiator* (1930), a science fiction tale, pure and simple. Because of the exigencies of the publishing business, he was required to write two mainstream novels before its publication. Three years later, in collaboration with Edwin Balmer, Wylie produced *When Worlds Collide* (1933), which was an immediate success, followed by its sequel, *After Worlds Collide* (1934). Although quite routine in its science fiction structuring, the 1933 novel was used as the basis for a popular motion picture. After a number of successful mainstream novels—plus

126

comes the Virgin Mary, and Paul Hummil, St. Paul; Hummil is a publicist who spreads the story of Cave/Christ. In the end Cave is killed—as in the biblical story—and Eugene flees, realizing that *he* should have been the messiah. Later on, in the 1960s, *Myra Breckinridge* (1968) appeared, a recasting of the Frankenstein tale—with Myron undergoing a sex change to become Myra, and, in the end, subjected to a reverse change to become Myron once again—or as near to him as he can possibly get, given the physical problems. *Myron* (1974) is a sequel in which another staple of science fiction is exploited—the alternate utopia/dystopia universe. Vidal uses the modern de-

Cover illustration for Philip Wylie's fantasy novel
The Disappearance.

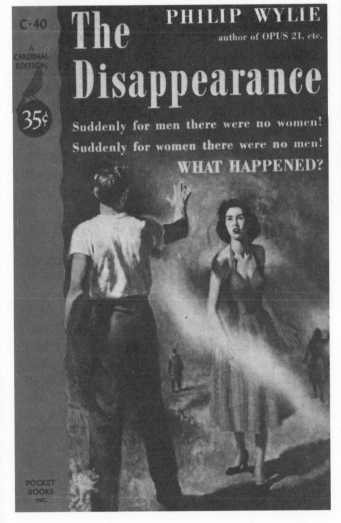

Typical "bug-eyed monsters," known as BEMs, from thirties pulp cover—this one illustrated by Howard V. Brown.

vice of the television set to let his characters enter this other world—a kind of sendup of *Alice through the Looking Glass. Kalki* (1978) is a dystopian novel in which the Hindu god Kalki conquers the world with four chosen followers. As in most dystopian novels, this one preaches social causes and makes statements on the real world through the medium of the fictional story. Back in 1955 Vidal wrote a television script called *Visit to a Small Planet*, later expanded into a Broadway play, and made into a film. In the true science fiction formula, this play stars Kreton, who has been sent from a Greater Solar System to warn Earthlings to cool it or be destroyed as a nuclear danger to the entire universe. Kreton develops a god

127

speak of the start of a new era. The break between the older and newer phases is chiefly marked by the opening of the cosmic age heralded by the Sputnik missions and the advent of manned space flight, and the fact that the US version of the genre became established worldwide. A third factor was the demise of magazine publication of science fiction during the new age of the paperback book.

Although *Weird Tales* ran mostly fantasy and sometimes horror, it used science fiction as well. Illustration by Margaret Brundage.

A potpourri of "hero" sci-fi pulps, mostly in the vein of early Edgar Rice Burroughs or Hugo Gernsback himself.

complex, almost causes Russia and America to go to war through his ability to use telekinesis—and is eventually checkmated by *another* deus ex machina, Delton 4, who sets things to rights again.

These various writings during the years up to 1960 proved that science fiction was not standing still. At the end of that decade, science fiction underwent such marked new developments that one can honestly

ROBOTS, WARNINGS, AND ROCKETS:
EUROPEAN SCIENCE FICTION BETWEEN 1918 AND 1955

After World War I, hardly any European country witnessed any drastic alteration in publishing practice. Book production or serialized novels in newspapers or periodicals continued to dominate as they had before. In these years, there was nothing to compare with the American science fiction magazine. In addition, most books of popular literature were simply carrying on the fashion. Some of the better known—for example, those of Robert Kraft, were even republished. Of this ilk were such series as "Sun Koh, the Heir to Atlantis" (some 150 titles) and "Jan Mayen" (120 titles dealing with the heirs of Thule) published in Germany between 1933 and 1936. They were all the work of Paul Alfred Müller under his pseudonym Freder van Holk.

There was also little noticeable change in content or thematic direction. The main type was the novel of the future, which speculated on technological, scientific, or medical possibilities; also still popular were variations of the social utopian novel. Most of these books were of national significance only, few were translated or even known abroad, and even fewer of them are of interest today.

Among the exceptions to this generalization are the scientific fantasies of the Czech author Karel Čapek (1890–1938). After attending the university and attaining his PhD, he worked as a writer and journalist. Between 1908 and 1910, he wrote short prose pieces together with his brother Josef (who was to die during World War II in Bergen-Belsen, the Nazi concentration camp). Karel Čapek was a highly gifted writer who experimented with many forms and genres. He wrote travel literature, novels, short stories, novellas, plays; fantastical motifs are to be found even in his earliest work. In the story *System* (1908), workers are subjected to absolute standardization. This grotesque story of modern methods of increasing industrial productivity gives a clue to the kind of interest Čapek was to show in his later work.

World War I marked a progression in the inner development of this author. After 1918, Čapek passionately defended the new Czechoslovak state and the principle of bourgeois democracy, as Tomas Masaryk was at the time trying to realize it. Čapek's journalism was a factor in the formation of an intellectual and cultural climate in his homeland, especially in the pieces he wrote for its leading paper *Lidove noviny* from 1921 onward. But despite his commitment to the new in Czechoslovakia, Čapek was also a critical observer of certain manifestations of the time. In his travels in numerous countries throughout the world, and in his own country, he recognized an increase in violence, and saw the dangers inherent in manipulating people and subjecting them to faceless power.

In these circumstances, it is perfectly understandable that Čapek, an important humanist author, should choose to estrange himself from individual and social trends by means of science fiction at the beginning of the 1920s. In rapid succession he published a series of works that are of equal interest in terms of the history of mainstream literature and in terms of the history of science fiction literature. These products included the play *R.U.R.* (1920); *The Insect Play* (1921, written in collaboration with his brother Josef); *The Makropulos Case* (1922, set to music by Leos Janacek in his penultimate opera in 1926); *Tovarna na absolutno* (*The Absolute at Large* [1922]), and *Krakatit* (1924). In the years succeeding this burst of literary fantasy, Čapek turned his attention to the small everyday things in life. Only in 1936 did he revert to the metaphorical mode of science fiction in his book *Valka s Mloky (The War with the Newts)*.

In all these works, Čapek shows his main concern to be for the danger to mankind arising from contradictions between the almost incomprehensible advances in technology and the stagnation in human ethical maturation. The discrepancy between the distortions of our moral, spiritual, and intellectual life and the potential of scientific and technological progress is the main theme of the world-famous *R.U.R.* Čapek here invents a new kind of conflict for world literature, which grew to become an important theme for science fiction literature. *R.U.R.* is the abbreviation of "Rossum's Universal Robots": Čapek also in-

Karel Čapek.

vented here a term that turns up not only in science fiction, but also in scenarios common to everyday life. Čapek's term is of course robot.

Although the term is now generally understood to mean something made of inorganic material, for Čapek a robot was a being produced from a "substance that behaved exactly like living matter, although its chemical composition was different."[1] Robots were made, according to Čapek, by machinery in factories. "What sort of worker do you think is the best from a practical point of view? . . . the cheapest. The one whose needs are the smallest. Young Rossum invented a

worker with the minimum amount of requirements. He had to simplify him. He rejected everything that did not contribute directly to the progress of work. In this way he rejected everything that makes man more expensive. In fact, he rejected man and made the Robot. . . . Robots are not people. Mechanically they are more perfect than we are, they have an enormously developed intelligence, but they have no soul. . . . The product of an engineer is technically at a higher pitch of perfection than a product of nature."[2]

Čapek's *R.U.R.* is at once a warning and a parable. The owners of the robot factory are interested only in the fact that robots work hard for little input of energy, and therefore represent a cheap source of income. In the play, the robots take over the position of human workers to an ever-greater extent. When the workers revolt and begin to smash the robots, the factory heads hand out weapons to the robots and teach them to kill. Because there is now a near-inexhaustible source of soldiers, more and more wars are fought. At the end, the robots rise and kill all the humans, with just one exception, and establish their own rule. But very soon they are obliged to recognize that the production of further robots is impossible, for the secret of their construction has been lost with the death of humanity. The mechanical beings see their end coming. But at the end of the play, two robots, Primus and Helena, discover the sublime human emotion of love, and one is ready to sacrifice itself for the other. In this act lies hope for a new beginning.

Čapek further developed the theme of the polarity between humanity and soulless inhumanity. The opera singer Emilia Marty, in *The Makropulos Case*, is the daughter of the alchemist Hieronymous Makropulos, who has been medical doctor to the Kaiser Rudolph. On the orders of the kaiser, an elixir of eternal life is discovered by this dabbler in black magic and must be tried out on his daughter. Thus she lives on to our present age. In her life, spanning centuries, she loses the human emotions of love, hate, anxiety, and sympathy. This is Čapek's response to the question of the meaning of life: without those emotions that differentiate humanity from animal and plant life, existence becomes a curse, ultimately futile. Human existence has meaning only when individuals can make best use of their time on Earth and fully cherish their feelings.

130

At the close of the drama an aspiring young singer Krista gives her response to the artificial longevity of people like Emilia Marty. She sets on fire the parchment on which is written the recipe for the elixir of life. Human dignity is only preserved by actively attending to the realities of living.

The story *The Absolute at Large* is the weakest of Čapek's writings in the science fiction vein. The first twelve chapters were written in a sudden rush of creativity during a holiday. They were serialized in *Lidove noviny*. Chapters 13 through 30, the rest of the book, are lacking in unity and logic. Čapek's main aim is to examine the problem of whether mankind's great aspirations can come to fruition when nature is all but overwhelmed by technology. The technological basis of this conquest of nature is made possible as the novel's central character, Rudi Marek, explains, by the perfect exploitation of atomic energy.[3] Čapek again has devised a plot that discusses the contradiction between technological possibilities and the moral quality of the people who are most likely to gain from the application of that technology—especially when only harm, even "the greatest war,"[4] starts, which ultimately leads to a "general and indescribable collapse."[5]

Krakatit presents a similar thematic case. The title alone gives an immediate hint of what is to come by recalling the devastating aftermath of the famous 1883 eruption of the volcano Krakatoa. The book "presents Čapek's splendid and perhaps unique attempt to mix together elements of the realistic novel,

Set design from the original production of *R.U.R.* in the Prague National Theater of January 21, 1921.

131

Karel Čapek's novel *The Absolute at Large.*

the futuristic novel, and even the dime novel to produce a richly plotted, inventive, profound and poetic science fiction novel, a novel about the fundamental questions of modern life, a novel which speaks to a wide readership."[6]

A strictly organized militaristic state, Baltlin—note that the references to Germany are unmistakable—wants unlimited supplies of "krakatit," a superexplosive atomic substance discovered by a man named Prokop, in order to conquer the world. Instead, "krakatit" destroys those who try to misuse it.

In addition, at the end, Prokop has forgotten the formula for the superexplosive, and so no one can ever again misapply the terrible power of this material. The true significance of life is summed up at the end of the novel by one character in it: "Dear, dear—for this you will serve them."[7]

Such strong and convincing humanism is especially pervasive in *The War with the Newts*, one of the masterworks of science fiction. A sea captain makes an unusual discovery on an island near Sumatra—a special kind of salamander that can be trained to fish for pearls, build dams, and so on. Businessmen form a "Salamander Syndicate" and begin to publicize and sell these "slaves." The mass media laps up the story of this wonderful species, which can even be taught to speak. Very soon England, France, and Italy are employing large numbers of this cheap labor; they also establish a standing army of salamanders against the possibility of war. Germany—and here the satire is especially sharp—demands living space for her "aristocratic" salamanders, which have the elongated Nordic skull and are of special "Prussian" discipline. Very soon the salamander population has grown so large and powerful that it turns against man. These newcomers remove portions of land and create new coastlines, in the quest for new space (lebensraum) for themselves. This is "the end for us," sighs a character at the end of the story.[8]

In the closing chapter, the author argues with himself; here the parablelike aspect of the work becomes especially evident. The novel closes thus: "It is simply the logic of events; how can I interfere with it? I did what I could; I warned people in good time; that X, that was partly me. I preached: don't give the Newts [salamanders] weapons or high explosives, stop that hideous trade in salamanders, and so on—you know what happened. Everybody always had a thousand perfectly sound economic and political arguments why this wasn't possible. I'm not a politician nor an economist; how could I convince them? So what's to be done? The world will probably disintegrate and become inundated—but at least it will do so for universally accepted political and economic reasons, at least it will do so with the aid of science, engineering and public opinion, with the application of all human ingenuity!"[9]

The fantastical story of the salamanders is an amusing and at the same time a most meaningful satire on the ramifications of both the colonial system and the barbarism of fascism. Above all the novel is an appeal to the powers of humanism the world over to continue the struggle against the abuse of power.

132

In this respect Čapek's work is not unique. Other European authors also wrote equally convincing literary warnings. It seems characteristic of the twentieth century that it seldom produced novels describing desirable utopian societies, turning its attention instead to pictures warning of threatening horrors, in effect, to dystopias rather than utopias.

Utopian sketches are however to be found among the authors of the so-called higher literature—for example, in Gerhart Hauptmann's *Insel der grossen Mutter (Big Mother's Island)*; in Franz Werfel's *Stern der Ungeborenen (Star of the Unborn)*, and similar works, which hardly belong to the genre of the science fiction elite utopia any more than, say, Hermann Hesse's *Das Glasperlenspiel (The Glass Bead Game)*. The 1930 *Utopolis* of Werner Illing, which follows the well-established form of a shipwreck adventure and includes descriptions of a free workers' society, is simply a late addition to the early great utopian tradition and is a parablelike warning of the ending of the Weimar Republic.

The dystopian mode of science fiction writing was first encountered in H. G. Wells, with its streak of disillusion concerning the plight of humanity. The swapping of utopian optimism for dystopian pessimism is characteristic of several other works predating World War I. For example, *Zemnaja os (Earth's Axis)*, a book of short stories published in 1907, contains the story "Respublika Yuzhnogo kresta" ("The Republic of the Southern Cross"), by Valeri Yakovlevich Bryusov (written in 1904–05). This story of the future starts with the premise that the southern polar region has been transformed some forty years previously from a trust of steel foundries into the Republic of the Southern Cross, with Star Town—sited right at the South Pole itself—a brand new metropolis. Steel workshops are nationally owned; the individual has a short working day: "The education and upbringing of children, the legal and medical services, religious services according to several different faiths—all are provided by the state."[10] After this highly utopian beginning, however, dystopian ideas begin to dominate in Bryusov's depiction of the power structure of the state: "The Council had kept power in its own hands, thanks mainly to the merciless regimentation of all life within the country. The apparent freedom afforded the citizens meant in fact that their lives were regulated down to the last detail. In all towns the buildings were built according to one and the same plan laid down by law. The furnishing of the workers' rooms was uniform in luxury. All ate the same food at the same hour. The clothes were provided centrally, and cut from the same pattern year in year out. At a certain hour a curfew was called by the City Hall and thereafter nobody was allowed to leave their house. All the press of the land was subject to severe censorship."[11]

When an "epidemic of contradictions" breaks out, catastrophic events are set in motion that lead to the

A paperback edition of Yevgeni Zamyatin's antiutopia *We* in German, Munich, 1982.

133

total collapse of the hitherto blossoming system. What Bryusov's critique emphasizes in this story was later adopted by other important antiutopian authors, who expanded this idea and filled in the details.

These early antiutopias (among which E. M. Forster's story *The Machine Stops* [1909], directed against H. G. Wells's early utopian writings deserves mention) confirmed a growing public consciousness through artists and intellectuals of a breakdown of interpersonal relationships in society. The key word here was fin de siècle—literally, "end of the century," but meaning rather "end of the era." The French poet Paul Verlaine gave expression to this when he spoke of his contemporaries as poets in an age of decline, twilight, and decadence.

This mood of the closing of an era was very evident after World War I in all science fiction literature, but most especially so in the literature of social utopia. Now science fiction was giving utterance to a somewhat different—and ambivalent—message. Apart from the opaque, anonymous imperialist powers under which writers felt themselves to be in a position of helpless subjection, apart from this type of Kafkaesque nightmare, there had meanwhile come about a new social system after the 1917 Revolution in Russia. This system was viewed by dystopian authors with a rather mixed outlook. On the one hand they felt drawn to the optimistic future the Revolution promised mankind, and cheered the victory it represented over human exploitation; but on the other hand they felt resistance fueled by their own prejudices that had been expressed by bourgeois powers ever since the inception of the socialist workers' movement. This ambivalence is the main thread of the modern dystopia, in which anticommunist prejudices became increasingly crystalized.

Yevgeni Ivanovich Zamyatin, born in 1884 in Lebedyan, a small mid-Russian town on the Don, came from a middle-class bourgeois background. As a student he became receptive to the ideas of the revolutionary movement. He decided to join the Bolshevik faction from an ethical and morally based socialist conviction. After the 1917 Revolution, he collaborated with several institutions in Moscow concerned with cultural policy. However, the realities of revolutionary change and the consequences of the necessary struggles made him to lose sympathy with the cause. He came increasingly to fear a threatening collectivization of the people, and a consequent loss of individuality. Thus he came to write in 1920 his own warning novel, *We*. One must remember that at this date only the very first steps had been taken in forming a socialist society, that endless experimentation was necessary, that opposing forces were trying their hardest to destroy the revolution, and that the whole land was undergoing a radical change.

Both the plot and the details of Zamyatin's antiutopia were shaped by his limited scientific insight into the laws of the developments around him. The fable is relatively easy to comprehend. D-503 (names no longer exist) who is the designer of the spaceship *Integral*, writes forty entries in his diary. He lives in "the single state," which at this time has reached its millennium, and which is run by an unidentified "benefactor." The inhabitants are not told that outside "the Green Wall" there exists another world, a wilderness all but undisturbed, where there live survivors of a two-hundred-year war who have evolved naturally to a new stage of development. Within the home state, everything is regimented. In contrast to the major social utopias of the past, however, the author here says nothing about the economic basis of the society, or of the relation of people to the means of production. Also, the power structure is outlined only insofar as to mention the symbolic "benefactor," with his "guardians" preserving the existing power. Who is in fact in control remains unclear. Zamyatin explains only the apparent state of affairs, which plays along with the inhabitants' fears of a total loss of identity: "Every morning millions of us get up as one, at the exact same moment of the exact same hour. At the exact same time we, an army of millions, take up our work, and at the same moment, we lay it down again. And, melted together into one body with millions of hands, we raise the spoon to our mouths at the precise moment as laid down in statute; at the same moment we take our constitutional, and foregather for our Taylor-exercises in the auditoria, and then lie down to go to sleep."[12] There are two hours of personal time per day, but they too are subject to order by decree, so that "the law enters each and every one of the 86,400 seconds of the day."[13]

75¢ • SC206 • A BANTAM CLASSIC

brave new world by aldous huxley

33rd printing. Over 2,750,000 copies in print

Aldous Huxley's famous novel.

Zamyatin's people are totally ordered and manipulated, the whole of life directed by mathematics and formal logic. Thus the railway timetable comes to be "the greatest of all monuments of old literature to be handed down to us."[14] Into this totally regimented world Zamyatin places a group of revolutionaries whose aim it is to alter the system for a more humane one. The implied utopian aim of a meeting on the other side of the Green Wall—reminiscent of a religious rite—is to pull down the wall and reintroduce "nature" to the sterile, rationalized world.

The spaceship *Integral* must, according to the state leaders, spread the principle of the "single state" throughout the cosmos, and thus the wonderwork must come into the hands of the malcontents! Number I-330 is assigned to subvert the designer, and she successfully persuades him to join the insurgents. Prologued cogitation produces in him a "soul," an individual identity. But at the end, it is the established order that triumphs. Designer D-503, along with many others, is lobotomized to remove his imagination, the last obstacle to his perfect happiness. He is thus once again fully part of the system, and once again marches in perfect time. The insurgents are brought to compliance when they are subjected to the gas-belljar, and are sentenced to suffer the "machine of the benefactor."

An important motif of most modern antiutopias is sexuality. In the "single state," there is of course no marriage and no family. Each person lives behind glass walls alone and in full view of everyone else. To conceive unplanned children is against the law and punishable by a grizzly death. Anyone feeling a sexual urge sends a ticket to the desired being. After forwarding this paper to the administrator of the house, one is permitted to close the curtains for a short while to be alone with the particular chosen sex object. One characteristic of all literary antiutopias is that the temporary selection of the hero is possible only via sexuality, the deepest human drive. Here too expression is given in the end to bourgeois anxieties and secret desires.

In many passages, Zamyatin can be perceived to be harking back to the capitalist system of normative work, developed by the American engineer and manager Frederick Winslow Taylor, the "father of scientific management," as the supreme step towards rationalization, but also of worker exploitation. It was Taylor who had in the 1880s measured with a stopwatch all activities of his workers, differentiated them into the smallest units of activity, and tried to order material, machines, and tolls to produce optimum production. Taylor's studies had the effect of ensuring that no machine was ever left idle at any time. Zamyatin carries this into all his pronouncements on life, and his antiutopia thus demonstrates him as critical of the obviously negative tendencies of Taylorism.

135

Aldous Huxley.

is contained in this book, and is a contradiction that was to be used with ever greater effect in the subsequent history of science fiction.

Zamyatin's dystopia was not published in the USSR. Translations appeared in English, Czech, and French in 1924–25, and in 1927 a shortened Russian version (not authorized by Zamyatin) appeared in a Prague emigrant newspaper. The complete original was published in New York only fifteen years after the death of the author.

Eventually Zamyatin renounced communism, and in 1931 submitted a request to leave the Soviet Union. He lived in Paris until his death in 1937.

At the time that Zamyatin left the Soviet Union, in England Aldous Leonard Huxley (1894–1963), the grandson of the famous biologist and tutor of H. G. Wells, was writing an antiutopian novel. Huxley has made it clear that Zamyatin's book was quite unknown to him, but despite some differences there are basic similarities that imply that the British writer may have at least heard rumors concerning *We.* In Huxley's book, one finds parallels to the "single state" and the "benefactor," with a state run by a council. Natural life is presented as on the other side of the reservation; wild creatures live there. Thus Huxley continues the great English tradition of the "noble savage," as in *Robinson Crusoe.*

Brave New World was published in 1932, its title making reference to Shakespeare as a moral standard against which the "perfected" world of the future must be evaluated. In *The Tempest*, Miranda exclaims:

> How many goodly creatures are there here!
> How beauteous mankind is! O brave new world,
> That has such people in 't!   (V i 182–84)

Huxley presents his world of the future with scientific exactness. In this he is at the same time polemicizing against H. G. Wells's utopian pictures, especially his *Men Like Gods* (a superficial, smoothly polished presentation of a beautiful future, for which—and this is quite different from most of Wells's other work— optimism as regards technology was a kind of overriding force).

Huxley incorporates into his book aspects drawn from the imperialist economic and social structure,

The main problem with Zamyatin's dystopia is his avoidance of any analysis of social processes and their inherent contradictions. The role of the masses is totally ignored: they appear merely as manipulated objects, to be used and positioned according to the whim of the anonymous "powers-that-be." The unity of optimism in progress (all conflicts may be resolved by advanced technology, so that in the static "single state," where development has reached a standstill, there is no possibility of further evolution) and pessimism in civilization (epitomized as the reverse side of technological development—that is, the loss of humanness, here described as "soul," or "imagination")

136

which were even more strongly pronounced in the 1920s, after World War I, than beforehand. The people are good-looking and proud. This perfection is reached, according to Huxley, not by means of bourgeois democracy nor by socialist revolution but by rigorously planned breeding of human beings that excludes the workings of chance. Biology, chemistry, and physics afford the sole means by which social problems are eugenically solved. Division into various classes is effected when new lives are still at the test-tube stage, being classified from Alpha to Epsilon (from the leading elite to the lowest workers). Each is developed solely for future position, and appears to welcome such a position with perfect happiness: "And that . . . is the secret of happiness and virtue—

George Orwell.

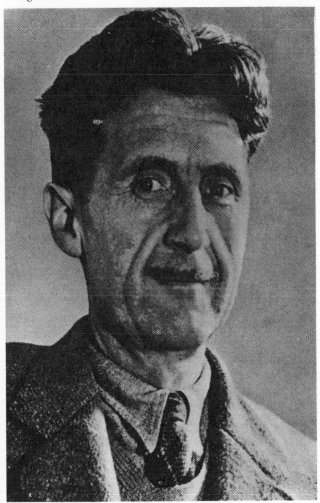

liking what you've *got* to do. All conditioning aims at that: making people like their unescapable social destiny." [15] By utilizing the names of historical figures symbolically, Huxley makes clear the direction in which he is aiming his dystopia, especially, for the time scheme of the book, where the years are reckoned as "Anno Ford." Each of the ten "world controlers" is referred to as "His Fordship." This gives rise to ironic juxtapositions—for example, "Our Ford—or Our Freud" [16]—which underpin the new regime's loosening of family ties and close family relationships. As in Zamyatin, anyone may sleep with anyone. Sexuality is also turned on its head to form an important instrument by which the author can criticize this inhuman world.

Here Huxley gives particular figures significance through their names, borrowed from famous philosophers and economists, psychologists, politicians, and industrial bosses, and other eminent authorities in other fields. This device serves to strengthen the satirical criticism of certain trends: against the ever harder drive for profits that result from the American social system; against a tendency among scientific circles in the 1920s to profess helplessness; and in particular to take no responsibility (a case of "not thinking of the consequences"); and also against Marxism-Leninism and its social prognoses. This "mixture" of targets made it possible to interpret the novel's meaning as emphasizing the antisocialist elements and regarding it as a prototype of anticommunist literature. In the last twenty or thirty years many of Huxley's denunciations have become so evident in modern bourgeois society that *Brave New World* can be argued to be a sarcastic putdown of this system as well.

Since all individuals of this future society are preprogrammed eugenically, there is not much room for natural selection. But Huxley's system does experience hitches. For example, to the embryo of the later Bernard Marx, destined to be a bourgeois-liberal intellectual, more alcohol than necessary has been added—and thus is established the basis of his deviant behavior. Huxley makes him a talker, an intellectual who thinks much and does little. (Huxley here shows some dependence upon Carl Gustav Jung's psychoanalytical system.) He can think clearly and wittily, but is so introverted that he cannot strive for

137

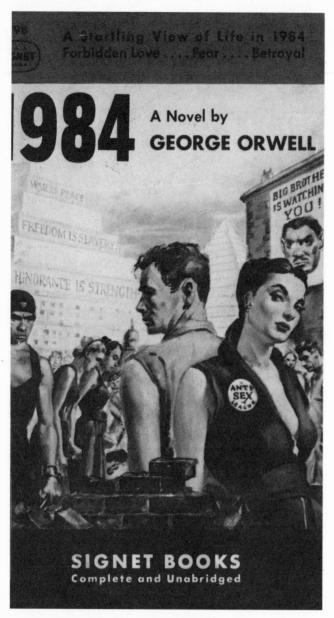

Cover of George Orwell's famous novel.

Huxley's joke here makes a double point: the founder of behaviorism was John B. Watson. This character is an advocate of an intellectual elite that wishes to triumph without any reference to others, least of all people at large. (Such persons Huxley included in other works, portraying in them one facet of the character of fascists.)

Logically, the outsiders, Bernard Marx and Helmholtz Holmes-Watson, must fail. They are brought to this by Mustapha Mond, whose character contains an amalgam of elements of theirs—intellectually reflective and also impetuous in action. They are set upon an island where they and others like them can continue to live without endangering the perfect society.

The third main figure, who opposes all that the "brave new world" stands for, is "the Savage." In chapter 17, Huxley presents a basic opposition in a conversation between him and Mond, always bearing in mind the reference to the worth given the world in the great humanist plays of Shakespeare:

> "But I like the inconveniences."
> "We don't," said the Controller. "We prefer to do things comfortably."
> "But I don't want comfort. I want God, I want poetry, I want real danger, I want freedom, I want goodness. I want sin."
> "In fact," said Mustapha Mond, "you're claiming the right to be unhappy."
> "All right, then," said the Savage defiantly, "I'm claiming the right to be unhappy."
> "Not to mention the right to grow old and ugly and impotent; the right to have syphilis and cancer; the right to have too little to eat; the right to be lousy; the right to live in constant apprehension of what may happen tomorrow; the right to catch typhoid; the right to be tortured by unspeakable pains of every kind."
> There was a long silence.
> "I claim them all," said the Savage at last."[17]

The opposition postulated here corresponds with the analysis of Zamyatin, who finds room for the old biblical story of paradise in a passage similar to the above: "It is the old legend of paradise . . . brought forward, naturally, to us, to the present. Those two

social change. His eugenic classification is of course Alpha-plus; among the other classes in the brave new world such a personality type is unthinkable.

Another member of this elite group is an outsider—Helmholtz Holmes-Watson. This time Huxley appropriates the name of a famous scientist, and couples it with the names of Conan Doyle's literary detective Sherlock Holmes and his naive narrator-partner.

138

people in paradise had to choose either happiness without freedom, or freedom without happiness. And those fools chose freedom—how could it have been otherwise?"[18]

In Huxley's novel, the world, so harmonic, so eugenically regulated, so cleansed of the unusual, is presented through the eyes of the Savage, and from this view it appears more and more repulsive. This is the aim of the antiutopia, Huxley's answer to the contradictions of civilization—the natural is so weak that it fails to convince. Thus Huxley's logic again determines the downfall of the Savage, the embodiment of the positive.

Both these dystopias influenced George Orwell's novel *Nineteen Eighty-Four*, written in 1948 and published in 1949. Orwell makes use of many existing motifs, and his novel stands out mainly for the totally pessimistic future it paints, and for the more adroit managing of the plot. Also to be considered is that Orwell was incorporating negative sociopolitical developments of the 1930s and after.

Orwell's book is only fully to be understood with reference to the inner development of the writer. Eric Arthur Blair (Orwell's real name) was born in 1903 in Motihari, Bengal, and educated at Eton. He served for five years from 1922 to 1928 in Burma in the Indian Imperial Police. He turned against the methods of the colonial service, and left his position. For some years he led a varied life in different professions. He eventually found his way into journalism.

At this period, Orwell became interested in and joined in the general democratic-socialist movement of the era, with its anarchist-trotskyite overtones, and fought in the International Brigade in the Spanish Civil War in the mid-1930s. When reports began coming in of the personality cult of Stalin, and violations of the Leninist norms in Soviet life grew in frequency, Orwell gave up his communist ideas. He later came to adopt the position of the British Labour Party. He joined the regular staffs of various London newspapers, and was on the staff of the BBC during World War II. In 1945, he published his first dystopian satirical novel, *Animal Farm*, in which he campaigned against dictatorial power structures by means of a parable. In 1949, Orwell published the book that ensured his worldwide fame and that became a supreme example of science fiction literature that dealt with society and politics. Orwell died in 1950. Six years later, a film version of *Nineteen Eighty-Four* produced by Michael Anderson introduced it to further millions.

While Zamyatin had laid his story in a nebulous far-distant future, and Huxley his in an imaginary "seventh century After Ford," Orwell sets his fiction in the near future, the date determined simply by swapping the numbers in the date of composition (48 and 84). He thus produced a utopia of the near future, distanced by a mere thirty-six years. This time has now passed, and it is easy to make carping indictments of the work by pointing to the many details and the main idea itself by arguing that what Orwell prophesied has not in fact come to pass. But it is important to remember that science fiction is not in the business of foretelling the future, nor is it obliged to paint a literal picture of what is to come; its premises are based in the present, and though the problems it probes may be estranged by being set in the future, its arena is the present.

Orwell saw three important problems. First was the modern level of development reached by imperialism. Important trends in capitalist development were clear after World War I and even more unavoidable after World War II, and the speed of development was accelerating. Part of this trend was the further nationalization of the means of production, the imperialist endeavors of the gigantic multinationals and the world powers, the increasingly smoothly organized administrative methods of nearly all aspects of life, the ever-growing militarization, and the suppression of other aims to rearmament, the "opinion-building" and manipulation of the public by means of ever-larger propaganda machines (especially with the help of electronic mass media) and so on.

The second important problem for Orwell was the then still fresh impression made by the gruesome fascist apparatus of violence in action. The world, after the defeat of Hitler's Germany, learned the full extent of the ahuman horrors perpetrated by an absolute authoritarian structure. Important sections of Orwell's novel are an embodiment of his response to such newfound knowledge.

And Orwell's third main problem was his impression of the wrongs committed under Stalin (for exam-

139

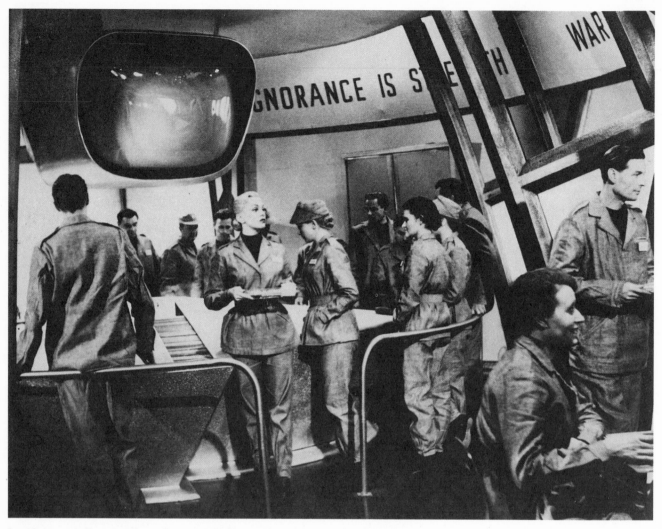

Lunch is a mindless, tasteless affair in 1956 film version of George Orwell's *1984*.

ple, the Show Trials and the extorted public confessions); these also play a part in his book.

Orwell's novel differs from its predecessors in having no refuge outside the world of oppression described: there is no area the other side of the "green wall," no reservation for Savages. From his understanding of the world about him he develops the idea that three huge power blocks will have arisen by 1984:

> Eurasia comprises the whole of the northern
> part of the European and Asiatic land-mass, from
> Portugal to the Bering Strait. Oceania comprises

the Americas, the Atlantic islands including the British Isles, Australasia, and the southern portion of Africa. Eastasia, smaller than the others and with a less definite western frontier, comprises China and the countries to the south of it, the Japanese islands and a large but fluctuating portion of Manchuria, Mongolia, and Tibet.

In one combination or another, these three super-states are permanently at war, and have been so for the past twenty-five years. War, however, is no longer the desperate, annihilating struggle that it was in the early decades of the twentieth century. It is a warfare of limited aims

140

between combatants who are unable to destroy one another, have no material cause for fighting and are not divided by any genuine ideological difference.[19]

War is waged by each of the three states for the sole purpose of upholding its particular idea of what is in fact the identical order the world over, and they continually fight over the few countries not allied to any one of the three states. Thus the alliances are in continual flux.

The propaganda magnifies and distorts the "external" enemy to such an extent that it forms a screen behind which it can preserve a perfect system of internal oppression. The individual in all three states is governed totally—that is, the 15 percent or so that are important for the system. There is at the top of the pyramid the ever-present, symbolic "Big Brother" (who probably does not even exist). The true apparatus of power hides behind this figure. "Big Brother is the guise in which the Party chooses to exhibit itself to the world. His function is to act as a focussing point for love, fear, and reverence, emotions which are more easily felt towards an individual than towards an organization."[20]

Two percent of the population belongs to the Inner Party. These members form the "brain of the state; and some thirteen percent form the 'Outer Party,' the state's 'hands.'"

Zamyatin's "protectors" are transformed into the organs of the "Thought Police"; the glass walls of the Russian writer are replaced in Orwell's dystopia by the ever-present spy and snoop—the telescreen. An army of workers is engaged in historical misrepresentation, for the picture of the past must be continually amended to fall into line with present policy through the falsification of historical evidence. Orwell describes the enormous propaganda machine and places the three party slogans (each embodying an apparent contradiction) in the center of the fictional Goldstein history (which has in fact been produced by the party itself): "The Theory and Practice of Oligarchical Collectivism".[21]

WAR IS PEACE
FREEDOM IS SLAVERY
IGNORANCE IS STRENGTH[22]

Apart from the dissection of demagogy, physical and psychological torture are given a great deal of attention in the book, especially in the closing section. Here the author demonstrates how deviants, broken by unlimited violence, are brought back into line.

Orwell uses a bourgeois intellectual, Winston Smith, a worker in the Records Department at the Ministry of Truth (where his job is to falsify history), as his rebel against this totally seamless system. Because genuine love and individual education are seen as dangerous to state power and are not tolerated, the hero and his lover, Julia, seize a few moments of personal happiness through clandestine sexual encounters. This is their rebellion against the all-powerful system. Of course they are discovered in the corner in which they have taken refuge. Under torture each betrays the other. Their spirits broken and rendered malleable, they return to society. Winston Smith is, after all, just another puppet invented by that gifted thinker but inactive member of society, Huxley's Bernard Marx.

These three major dystopias, finally, may be said to articulate the fear of loss of identity that wracked the petit bourgeois. Because of this, the only alternative (that is, the total liberation of society, which of course implies and includes the true liberation of the individual) is not recognized. This fact adds to the impact of Orwell's novel, in which 85 percent of the population is composed of "proles"—workers. But these "dumb masses"[23] are so insignificant it is unnecessary to draw them into state regulation. They seem simply to allow themselves to be arbitrarily manipulated. And it never enters the heads of the rebels, who stem from the upper stratum of society in Orwell's novel as in previous dystopias, to appeal for their help in changing the situation; they simply exhibit class prejudice and dismiss the laboring class.

The dystopian elements described in these three novels reappear time and again in modern science fiction, though most of their successors avoid the creation of new worlds. Mostly the creators restrict themselves to small parts of the social landscape or to the dystopian future of their own country alone. Also, antiutopian elements tend to form simply a roughly sketched background for the particular plot or action of the book in hand.

141

Beside such works, important mainly for their literary quality and their social utopian warning, the everyday science fiction works of the various countries of Europe that deal mainly with technological and scientific problems appear somewhat banal. They do frequently attend to political and social questions, but only peripherally, and offer somewhat shallow responses that are for the most part colored by the prevailing ideology. Precisely because they reflect the longings and fears of the broad masses, and because they express the so-called public opinion (strongly manipulated), such products are secured at least a place of the bookshelves or even encouragement via the state organs. An obvious example of such a product between the two world wars, is the output of Hans Dominik (1872–1945). His books cast a spell over a generation of readers, and even today older science fiction readers come all over nostalgic when they are reminded of his works. Reading these books again after a gap of some decades, one feels a bitter disappointment. Time has overtaken Dominik and his fantasies have no living form, despite the fact that they have been reprinted and read by many younger readers.

Dominik studied mechanical engineering, concentrating on railway engineering, though electrical engineering was far more to his taste. In his day, however, there was no such subject in the curriculum. Visits to America in 1895 and 1897, where he worked as an electrical engineer, extended his expertise and his knowledge of the English language, so that after his return he was in demand both as an engineer and as a writer of popular scientific literature. He spent some time working at Siemens & Halske in Berlin. From 1901 he worked as a free-lance author. It was at this time that he published *Technical Tales* through the *Berliner Tageblatt*. These books carried on the idea started by Lasswitz, his erstwhile tutor, in *Modern Fairy Tales*, adopting both their strengths and their weaknesses (for example, the personalization of scientific objects).

In 1903 Dominik and two associates—Rumpler (who had taken over Etrich's license for Germany and developed the airplane "Rumpler-Taube," or "Rumpler Dove"), and Count von Arco (who had established his position as the leader of the Telefunken-Gesellschaft, or wireless company)—founded the Automobiltechnische Gesellschaft. Dominik became technical correspondent of a local Berlin paper in 1905, and in 1907 published his first short stories orientated wholly towards technical detail in *Neues Universum (The New Universe)*.

During World War I, Dominik rejoined Siemens & Halske. Later he concentrated almost wholly on writing technological fantasies. His first serialized novel, *Die Macht der Drei (The Power of Three)*, was published in a national paper in 1922 with great success. During the period of high inflation, Dominik once again took up employment as an engineer, but carried on his writing, producing another serialized novel, *Die Spur des Dschingis-Khan (The Trail of Genghis Khan)* which appeared in the same national newspaper in 1923. From 1924 Dominik was again able to support himself from his writings alone. He produced book after book, all eagerly snatched up by the market:

Dominik's novels appeared in the *Berliner Illustrierte*. One of these was *Lebensstrahlen (Life Forces)* (1938), in which life enters dead material through a process called "abiogenesis," and lead can be turned into gold. The dreams of alchemists, economists, and politicians all come true when an element with the *Atomgewicht 500 (Atomic Weight 500)* (1935), a *Treibstoff SR (Propellant SR)* (1940), or *Himmelskraft (Skycraft)* (1937), or a seabed gasoline fuel is discovered in an ocean tunnel shaft in *Stählernes Geheimnis (Steely Secret)* (1934), forming a new source of energy; when technological telepathy (*Befehl aus dem Dunkel [Command from the Dark]* [1925]), or the opening up of new continents provides new living space for expanding world populations is envisaged (*Atlantis* [1925]). There are tales of strange beams that can render people invisible (*König Laurins Mantel [King Laurin's Cloak]* [1928]), an atomic inferno threatening to destroy the Earth (*Das Erbe der Uraniden [The Legacy of the Uranides]* [1927]; *Der Brand der Cheopspyramide [The Fire in the Great Pyramid]* [1926]), a German wins the *Wettflug der Nationen (The Nations' Compe-*

tition) (1934) in the flight through the stratosphere, and *John Workman der Zeitungsboy (John Workman the Newspaper Boy)* (1925) becomes a millionaire and thus mimics his creator, Dominik, himself, who made the transition *Vom Schraubstock zum Schreibtisch (From Workbench to Writing Desk)* (1942), from mechanical and electrical engineer to successful author.[24]

All Dominik's writings, including those left out of Hasselblatt's short account quoted above, center upon gifted inventors, explorers, and researchers—mainly German in origin. The ethical reference system of the fairy tale, the division into good and evil, informs the work of this author. Development of character hardly takes place, the figures in the books are presented

Hans Dominik.

more as types who act totally in accordance with stereotyped notions. The style Dominik cultivates is somewhat staccato and prevents the books from being easy to read today.

But two fundamental, contradictory questions enter into all Dominik's work. At the heart of his writing, is, without question, the force of technology. Dominik concentrates on problems from technology and physics that appeared to him as possible (development of air travel, airplanes driven by radiation, atomic power, sources of energy in space, or at the bottom of the ocean). He sets his problems in the future and works them out logically. His favorite area is electrical engineering and the possibilities it opens up—his original training ground. But he also has a tendency to explore other scientific disciplines in which his understanding is far less developed.

His second, and more dangerous tendency, is to interpret progress as merely further development of technology in unchanging social circumstances that he personally found quite comfortable. As Manfred Nagl reasons in general terms in his convincing academic analysis, this is especially true of Dominik's most widely read books:

> Thus German science fiction created, between the two world wars, legions of inspired Faustian inventors and engineers, who—surrounded by racially "inferior" traitors and foreign spies—work in secret laboratories to roll back the wheel of history, to divide the world anew under German authority, "to protect our nation and give it back the power it used to enjoy" . . . in short, (as the fascist technocrat Hans Dominik put it) "to combine the political consequences of the greatest dimension with technological work undertaken apparently in the interests of science only."[25]

Dominik's works are patterns of trivial entertainment in the field of science fantasy, which is heavily imbued with nationalist, racist, or "occidental" accents. In his works there is no lack of clichés concerning the "yellow peril" *(The Trail of Genghis Khan)* or the threat to European whites posed by the African blacks *(The Fire in the Great Pyramid).*

143

Other writers could be named who fit the Dominik mold, including Joseph Delmont (1873–1935). Delmont was the pseudonym adopted by Karl Pick, the author of *Der Ritt auf dem Funken (The Ride on the Spark)* (1928), and before that, *Die Stadt unter dem Meer (The City beneath the Sea)* (1925). In this latter book, a German submarine crew refuses to accept the "ignominious peace" (the Versailles Treaty of 1918 as it was called later by nationalist propaganda), and flees to a cave reachable only by means of underwater canals. Here Delmont showed how assiduously he had researched the pages of Jules Verne! In this seclusion the submarines turn into a group of enthusiastic and experienced explorers. Then comes the turnabout, for they discover a radiation that can destroy projectiles of all calibers without conventional power. This puts them in a position to reappear in the world with a German-based ultimatum, turn the tide of events back to the reactionary, and resurrect World War I, this time ensuring Germany's victory. With fantasies like this, the bourgeois reader was offered some "ersatz" amusement, the call for "strong men" being given fresh resonance and the dreadful decline into fascism an extra impetus.

Other works can be cited that are not so extreme in their chauvinism, but which are nevertheless tainted by nationalistic elements. Otto Willi Gail published three books about space travel, of which two, *Der Schuss ins All (Shot into Space)* (1925) and *Der Stein vom Mond (The Stone from the Moon)* (1926) form a pair, while the third, *Hans Hardts Mondfahrt (Hans Hardt's Moon Journey)* (1928) stands structurally alone. Technological precision is most evident in *Shot into Space*, especially in the way future blast-offs are anticipated, in which Gail puts all other crystal gazers to shame. Gail consulted Max Valier, a German rocket pioneer and propagandist, and to him science fiction was primarily a means of propagandizing popular science. In order to further the plan to build a rocket in postwar Germany, some ideas were adopted from the 1912 campaign in favor of the zeppelin (still alive in people's memories ten years later). Thus a refined ruse was developed for involving the mass of the nation in the heroic adventure of flying, and the joy at technical progress and fear of French competition were advanced as reasons for enticing

some seven million gold marks from the pockets of the populace. This campaign in fact was directed at the development of military capability in the years immediately preceding World War I. Gail's fiction contains a comparable national campaign of unprecedented proportions to support the project. The campaign ensures that the furious competitions between the Germans and the Russians to reach the Moon was won of course by the Germans. The sequel contains much that was accepted as fact at the time according to the legendary islands Atlantis and Thule.

Gail's novels conform, in their basic layout, to Gernsback's conception of science fiction, and belong to the small number of novels that Gernsback included in translation in his magazine *Science Wonder Quarterly*. For comparison, it is worthwhile noting

The magazine *Film-Kurier* advertising Fritz Lang's film *Metropolis*.

that Dominik's writings were never translated into English, with the exception of one short story. On its own, however, being translated is no guarantee of high quality: books that enjoyed the same honor as Gail's included novels of the lowest literary order such as those by the prolific Otfried von Hanstein (1869–1959). Hanstein's *Electropolis* (1927) is a tomfool morass of truly pubescent fantasy of robotics and much else. In the end, the secret city of Electropolis, in the desert of Australia, by means of its three "servants" (technology, electricity, and radium) achieves victory over Australia and its air force. After the fighting is over, Electropolis becomes the "New Germany," and offers the impoverished and those without hope among their fellow citizens in Europe a new home, in order that the old country may be helped to become once again a famous world power.

Curt Siodmak, born in Dresden in 1902, had a major success with his science fiction novel *F.P.1 antwortet nicht (FP1 Is Not Answering)* (1931), which tells the story of sabotage and mutiny on the artificial island *F.P.1 = Flugplattform 1* (Airstrip 1) in the ocean, and the intervention of the pilot hero who has the "Hang on! I'm coming!" manner. A film of this book was made in 1933, with Hans Albers scoring a success in the main role. Siodmak then turned to writing detective novels, using some elements of science fiction. After he had left fascist Germany for political reasons in 1933, he began a new and very successful career as a scriptwriter of science fiction and horror films in Hollywood. But he did not stop writing; his *Der Zauberlehrling (Donovan's Brain)* (1943) and *Das dritte Ohr (The Third Ear)* (1973) proved very popular in the science fiction-horror vein.

The most famous science fiction work to come out of Germany in the 1920s was the novel *Metropolis* by Thea von Harbou (1888–1954), which achieved world renown in a contemporary film version. Preceding this there were other books in the entertainment genre, including some with science fiction subjects (*Frau im Mond [The Woman in the Moon]* and *Die Insel der Unsterblichen [The Island of the Immortals]*). The motto of *Metropolis* (1926) clearly gives the direction of Thea von Harbou's thoughts: "This book does not promote any trend, class, or party. This book is an event which has grown up around this knowledge: that the mediator between the head and the hands must be the heart." [26]

At the beginning of her book Thea von Harbou describes the extreme contrast between the world of the wealthy idlers and the misery of the working masses. Maria, a "workers' leader" with a deep sense of humility and Christian neighborly love, is looking after a crowd of proletarian children at a party when she chances upon a gathering of parasites from the upper echelons. Her glance falls like a flash of lightning into the soul of Freder Fredersen. This playboy, the son of John Fredersen, the ruler of the gigantic city, then steps down into the milieu of the workers out of love for Maria. He is deeply impressed, and infuriated. His father, in order to cure him of his love, constructs an artificial double of Maria. This creature is given the job of stirring the workers to strike and rebellion, in which it is totally successful. The revolt of course proceeds in the wrong direction, turning first upon the great machinery that lies at the heart of Metropolis. With the failure of the life-preserving center, the gigantic city starts to disintegrate, taking with it all the workers. (This motif, that the proletariat sever its own lifeline during rebellion, corresponds with the motto printed in the preface.) Even the innocent children are threatened with drowning as the tide rises. At the last moment, they are rescued by the real Maria, and the now-purged Freder. In the end they find their way to each other, and Fredersen senior's objection to their marriage melts away. Metropolis will be built again, but along happier and better lines. The harmony between the classes, which levels no threat against the existing social system and lets everything remain as it was, enlightens everything.

It is no wonder, then, that Hitler thought the film version, with its irrational fairy-tale structure and the closing promises of community of the classes (that is, a national sense of community), the best film of all time. Thea von Harbou's husband, the director Fritz Lang, was told by the Nazi propaganda minister Josef Goebbels, that the Führer "had selected him many years ago, to be the one who would one day present the film of the Third Reich." [27]

Between 1937 and 1940 another author came to notice who clearly trod the path mapped out by Dominik in technological fantasy. He was Rudolph

145

Stills from the film version of Thea von Harbou's novel. The false Maria is constructed as an automaton.

H. (Heinrich) Daumann (1896–1957). In this author's best work *Dünn wie eine Eierschale (As Thin as Eggshell)* (1937); *Macht aus der Sonne (Power from the Sun)* (1937); *Gefahr aus dem Weltall (Danger from Space)* (1939); *Abenteuer mit der Venus (Adventure with Venus)* (1940); *Protuberanzen (Protuberances)* (1940), he avoids overweening nationalism that is such a characteristic of Dominik. Daumann had lost his profession as a teacher in 1933, and writing represented to him the possibility of earning a living. In the closing years of the war he joined the antifascist resistance as a member of the outlawed Austrian Communist Party. After the war, he returned to Potsdam, and had great success in the German Democratic Republic (East Germany), especially with his novels of American Indians *Tatanka-Yotanka* and *Der Unter-*

146

gang der Dakota (The Decline of the Dakotas). After the war, Daumann wrote no more science fiction.

The features peculiar to German science fiction between the two world wars are to be traced in origin back to the singular position of the country after its defeat in World War I and the unchanged power structure after the abortive 1918 November Revolution. In the science fiction of other countries similar restless, Faustian-minded, and creative explorers and inventors are met; they are of course nationals of the home-country of the author. Hardly ever is such chauvinism found as in German writings. Tremendous heroes and the well-established motifs that are constantly found in science fiction abound in the work of the Italian writers Emilio Salgari, Luigi Motta, and Giorgio Scerbanenco; the Spaniards Capitan Sirius (the pseudonym of Jésus di Aragon y Soldado), José de Elola, and Ramon Gomez de la Serna; the Czechs Jiři Haussmann, Emil Vachek, Tomaš Hruby, Jan Weiss, and J. M. Troska (who was often called the Czech Jules Verne and who wrote further adventures for Verne's Captain Nemo); and the French writers Jean de la Hire and Jacques Spitz—to mention only a few of the many, many European authors. However, most of the books by these authors are known only to readers of their native language, or have been translated to such a limited extent that they have no international recognition in science fiction circles.

The workers at the great mechanical complex that runs the city.

147

Metropolis.

In French science fiction, there were, besides la Hire and Spitz, Joseph-Henri Rosny the Elder and Maurice Renard. These two had established reputations even before World War I. Owing to the slow historical development of French publishing houses, publishers at this time were not yet forced to produce only "sure sellers." The great divide between "higher" and mass literature was thus much less evident in Paris than in New York. The traditions of the social utopia stemming from the seventeenth and eighteenth centuries, and the fantastic literature of the past (for example, Jean Marie Mathias Philippe Auguste, Comte de Villiers de l'Isle-Adam), were just as effective as the influences of the surrealism of the 1920s. Already at this early date national differences were clearly recognizable between the majority of French

science fiction stories and the mostly "harder" stories coming out of England and America: in the former a stronger apprehension of the human psyche, a more poetic and unobtrusive humor, a more consciously inventive use of language and wordplay—a touch of eroticism here and there—in other words a more appealing, more human, and more emotional tone. Information about the development of science fiction literature within the boundaries of the French-speaking world between the two world wars has been collated by Jacques Sadoul, a committed fan of the genre, in the second volume of his *Histoire de la science-fiction moderne (History of Modern Science Fiction).*[28]

One of the most important talents of international significance during the last phase of development since World War II is René Barjavel. His work forms the bond between the older generation centered on Renard and the new generation that has come onto the scene mainly since 1953. (That particular year is crucial because it saw the first French science fiction magazines, *Fiction* and *Galaxie*, published following the example set by America. This served to emphasize the growing differences.) Barjavel's first book, *Ravage*, was written during the war, and deals with the story of a world catastrophe. This work makes it clear that the author is sceptical about the new scientific knowledge. Like Čapek (and also, in a certain sense, like Huxley) he presents the consequences of an overtechnological and rationally organized development, which necessarily lead to chaos and destruction. In *Ravage*, the cut in supply of electricity renders Paris wholly at a loss and causes a terrible war, which is survived only by the peasants. In such harking back to a nature-based life-style, a Rousseauesque "retour à la nature," Barjavel saw the only way out of the misery of the present. In 1944 he wrote *Le Voyageur Imprudent (The Imprudent Voyager)*, a novel based on a tale of time travel, and in 1948 this was followed by *Le Diable l'Importe (The Imported Devil)*. In these further novels of catastrophe life on Earth is destroyed by new horrific weapons. Of importance here is obviously the awful experience of the bombing of Hiroshima and Nagasaki, which mankind has had to learn to bear. Barjavel's crumb of comfort is the survival of one human pair, who had been shot into space. The finale is this signal of hope for a new

148

and better beginning. During the 1950s, Barjavel wrote no science fiction literature. When he returned to the form in 1960, the scene had altered and a new phase of development been introduced.

In England, unlike France, the divergence of literature into the "meaningful" and the "trivial" became obvious between the wars. Mainstream literature tended to encourage antiutopian themes and continued the tradition started by Thomas More. Important writers of the more trivial literature tended on the contrary to seek, with success, the openings offered by the American magazine market. This was the beginning of the phenomenon of mutual influence and exchange between the science fiction of Great Britain and that of the United States, which became increasingly noticeable during the 1950s. This process was of course made simple by the lack of a language barrier. An English "fanzine" after the American model had

Arthur C. Clarke.

been successfully published in Leicester in 1936 under the title *Novae Terrae*, and in the succeeding year, the Science Fiction Association was founded, adopting the fan magazine as a journal, which soon became however *New Worlds*. The three editions published up to 1939 were edited by John Carnell. World War II interrupted this development.

Among the first writers blazing the trail in the close relationship that developed between English and American science fiction were Chandler, Clarke, Russell, and Wyndham. A. (Arthur) Bertram Chandler, an English naval officer, was born in 1912, and had already had his first successes in the American science fiction market in the 1930s. During a period spent in New York during the war, Chandler made contact with Campbell. The result of this was that some of his stories were accepted for publication in *Astounding* from 1944 on. In almost all his stories adventurers on the sea are transported into space. Among the best known of these are the stories of Commodore Grimes, who appears in the "Rimworld" series, and travels at the outskirts of the galaxy, racing from adventure to adventure. The literature of Chandler is, essentially, lightweight entertainment, in which standard plots, clichés, and stereotype figures abound.

Arthur C. (Charles) Clarke was born in Minehead, Somerset, in 1917, and his writings take him into quite another league. He participated in radar experiments as technical officer in the Royal Air Force, and after the war studied physics and mathematics, working later as editor-in-chief of the specialist journal *Science Abstracts*. He has been free-lance since 1950, apart from his tourist enterprise in Sri Lanka (Ceylon). He came to know this island, on which he has spent much time, through his interest in underwater photography.

Clarke, a multifaceted writer, published his first science fiction stories in the short-lived English magazine *Fantasy*. After the war however, he turned to *Astounding*, and other American publications. Classics of his early phase include *The Deep Hangs* (1954, 1957 in book form). In this novel a futuristic cowboy romance is lived out in tiny submarines in the ocean, a kind of pasture for "domesticated" deep-sea mammals. The "cowboys" must protect the herds from predators like sharks and human thieves. A wealth of

149

effects keeps the reader of these adventures on tenterhooks till the final paragraph. Several other of Arthur C. Clarke's books have found great favor with the science fiction reading public, for instance *The City and the Stars* (a reworked version of *Against the Fall of Night*), *Childhood's End* (1951), *Prelude to Space* (1951), *Sands of Mars* (1951), *Earthlight* (1951, in book form 1955). *Islands in the Sky*, written especially for the young in 1952, has even more than the average share of adventure, as has *A Fall of Moondust* (1961). In this latter novel, a group of tourists visiting the Moon find themselves sinking into the dust of a moon crater owing to a defect in their vehicle, and are rescued.

Most of Clarke's early books continue the well-established line of the novel of the future dealing with technological and scientific developments. These books stand out for their meticulous description of technical details and their understandability—both of which attributes evidence the breadth of knowledge mastered by Clarke as physicist and mathematician. These books established Clarke as a well-respected science fiction novelist, but he only reached a worldwide audience with a later work that was written in a succeeding phase of science fiction, a short story called "The Sentinel." This was the work on which

Stanley Kubrick based his film *2001: A Space Odyssey* (1968). Clarke used the fame of the film and its success to expand the story into a novel. Arthur C. Clarke has been a most influential voice in shaping Anglo-American science fiction in the epoch of the recent and continuing scientific and technological revolution.

Under his pseudonym of John Wyndham, the English writer John Beynon Harris (1903–69, born in Warwickshire) became well known. His first publications appeared in *Wonder Stories* from 1931, and were followed by numerous stories and novels. Only a limited amount of his work reveals any originality; for the most part he writes variations on clichéd situations and well-known motifs. His gift is for setting these motifs into such readable adventures that they have proved popular with the general reading public. His best-known novel is *The Day of the Triffids* (1951), in which the majority of the world population has been catastrophically blinded, and is threatened by a new mutant fauna that can lift its own roots and walk. In *The Kraken Wakes* (1953), the plot revolves around the old science fiction motif of invasion.

In Wyndham's earlier work there is some residual racial arrogance, which gradually receded in the course of his writing. In this connection, special men-

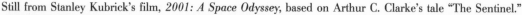

Still from Stanley Kubrick's film, *2001: A Space Odyssey*, based on Arthur C. Clarke's tale "The Sentinel."

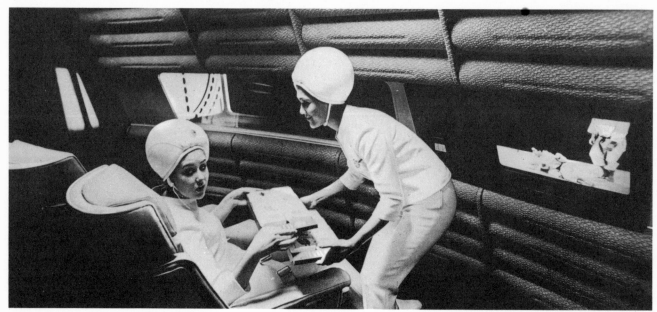

150

tion must be made of his story "Dumb Martian," which often finds its way into anthologies, and which is especially clear in its antiracist accent. The story concerns the purchase of a Martian wife, Lellie, by Duncan Weaver, who is posted out to the lonely reaches of space for five years. He treats her like a colonial master would treat a slave, considering her of little value. A geologist comes to join Weaver, and in contrast treats her in a humane manner. Duncan murders the geologist. Shortly before the posting is finished, Lellie takes revenge for her humiliation and for the murder. She bans Duncan from the space station, so that he must die. The way the story is told ensures that the reader's sympathies are with Lellie, and that the finale of the story is felt as justified and liberating.

Another British author who came to science fiction via the American magazine circuit is Eric Frank Russell (1905–78). He was the author of popular entertainment fiction. His best-known works are *Sinister Barrier* (1939) and *Sentinels of Space* (1953). His series about the humanlike robot Jay Score, which were published from 1941 on, were later collected and published in book form as *Men, Martians, and Machines* in 1956.

In Russell's postwar works interaction of mankind with other races is of considerable importance, as can be seen from *Wasp* (1957) and *The Space Willies* (1956). Once more Russell proves to be one of the science fiction authors who credibly depict extraterrestrial intelligent beings and do not show them as nothing but monsters.

A unique place in the history of science fiction is occupied by the English philosopher Olaf Stapledon (1886–1950). He began writing as a follower of his beloved H. G. Wells, creating pictures of the future with mankind's position in cosmic events. His *Last and First Men* (1930) comprehends the whole of human history. *Star Maker* (1937), *Darkness and the Light* (1942), and *Death into Life* (1946) belong to a group of works in which Stapledon concentrates on transforming his philosophical conceptions into belletristic literature. Books like *Last Men in London* (1934) have been called science fiction tragedies, owing to their thread of pessimism. Others in this vein are *Odd John* (1936) in which mutants are destroyed

A SIGNET BOOK • Q3580 • 95c

2001 a space odyssey

A NOVEL BY **ARTHUR C. CLARKE**
BASED ON THE SCREENPLAY OF THE **MGM** FILM BY
STANLEY KUBRICK and ARTHUR C. CLARKE

2001 a space odyssey
is the history-making motion picture
produced and directed by Stanley Kubrick.
In Cinerama®

Cover illustration for Arthur C. Clarke's novelization of his famous screenplay.

by humans, the sorrowful plight of an intelligent dog in *Sirius* (1944), or *A Man Divided* (1950), which charts the case of a man controlled in turn by two different brains.

This short examination of developments and trends in science fiction between the wars cannot be closed without a mention of a work that has been discovered internationally only in recent years. The author does not in fact belong among the ranks of regular science fiction authors. Karin Boye was born in 1900 in Sweden, and took her own life in 1941. She

151

wrote mainly short stories and lyrics, but published her novel *Kallocain* in 1940 as a result of her response to the dreadful and violent fascist regime. In the book she paints her gloomy forecast of the future. A scientist in a wholly militarized country (this looks forward somewhat to Orwell), develops a "truth drug," under the influence of which anyone will reveal his or her most secret thoughts and feelings. But instead of becoming an even more effective method of controlling the people, use of this drug makes clear the internal weaknesses of the system itself—that it is built on lies and cannot survive.

152

SCIENCE FICTION
IN THE SECOND HALF
OF THE TWENTIETH CENTURY

THE INCREASING INTERNATIONALIZATION
OF MODERN SCIENCE FICTION

In the second half of the twentieth century, a new qualitative development in scientific and technological progress allowed automatic regulation of machines to free human beings from the task, and to transfer the work to technical and mechanical regulators. The basis of this change was widespread automatization and new systems such as data processing. Distinct evidence of this new qualitative level was the technical and scientific control of information processing (for example, the linking of information, its storage, the programmed determination of optimal values, the adaptation of reactions owing to the ability to update knowledge, and so on). Through these means the automatization of so-called intellectual work became possible, quite outside the realms of material production. Complex systems for information processing were being used to an ever-increasing extent in production, in planning, in management, in research, in construction, in communications, in public administrations, and in the use of credit facilities. Thus there was a huge growth in the significance of science as an immediate factor in production.

Such developments necessitated an alteration in the relationship of the individual to the work process—a change more fundamental than during any technological change in the past. The workers now worked alongside the entire production process, and their task of programming the work constituted a complete qualitative change.

This development has had enormous consequences that reverberate beyond the technological or economic field. Some of these consequences have become clear over the last few years—for example the termination of millions of laborers in countless countries. The technological revolution is even now making demands on the social systems of many countries for an adequate response to these developments.

An eloquent expression of the fact that a new qualitative step was reached in technological progress at the middle of this century was the blossoming of the cosmic age with the launching of Sputnik, the first artificial satellite.

This leap forward in science and technology had of course a major impact on the writers of science fiction literature: the material, themes, and objects encountered in earlier epochs were overtaken and rendered obsolete. Though Verne could dream of a cannon blasting a human being to the Moon, and Wells could paint rich fantasies of the Selenites at home on the Moon, though other authors could postulate all kinds of humanlike life forms living on Mars and Venus, mankind now possessed, with the launch into space and the use of space probes, information that showed such fantasies to be completely without foundation. Robots have become a common feature of factory production, and the old idea of such a machine has been replaced by the real thing in a new image. Informational systems now record data not only

153

concerning the work process, but concerning people as well. On the one hand, this last development has proved some of the warnings of the early twentieth-century dystopias; on the other hand, new kinds of manipulation and new possibilities in this area have been established next to which anything Huxley or Orwell described pales to insignificance.

Scientific fantasy is so altered in its basics that one must now speak not only of a new period of development, but even of a changed quality and standard. What factors lie behind such a claim?

Science fiction has broken down the barriers that largely confined literature to national or at least language borders. The triumph of the classic American works of science fiction led in the important western countries to the demise of the hitherto dominant technological, futuristic novel. Thematic and motivic content within the genre broadened, and authors, unable to challenge the precedence of the Anglo-American writers, nonetheless introduced new ideas and were able to make creative use of the interaction between their own national tradition and the patterns being developed in England and America. They actively contributed to the genre's recent development.

In the socialist countries, science fiction experienced a revival and upswing as the "cult of the personality" was rejected and the various national groups formed closer cultural and intellectual ties. These countries did not however have particular formats in science fiction that dominated the genre, as was the case in the western countries; in addition, the obviously ahuman products of the lowest popular literature were allowed no place.

Very early on, authors and readers in Poland, the USSR, Hungary, and other countries, were taking account of the best productions of Anglo-American science fiction, noting the stimulation they aroused in their motifs and subject matter. These works were introduced to the public both in collections and in book form. The reverse process began about fifteen years ago with the works of Stanislaw Lem, the brothers Arkadi and Boris Strugatsky, not to mention the theoretical works of Yevgeni Brandis and Yuli Kagarlitski, which have exerted an influence on science fiction in western countries and on the questions raised by science fiction studies.

Problems and consequences following the scientific and technological revolution manifest themselves similarly in the western industrial countries and in the socialist countries. Ever more areas of life come under the influence of electronic data processing, microelectronics, overexploitation of raw materials and their threatened disappearance, environmental problems—to name but a few. The increasing internationalization of science fiction means that it has become a forum for the exposure of the general underlying problems that have appeared despite differences in national developments and national sociopolitical systems. The questions, explored mostly in disguised or alienated forms, and the answers, offered by authors, are of interest to an international public.

Another relevant point is that science fiction at the middle of the twentieth century shook off its "ghetto" image of the trivial genre with a small hoard of enthusiastic fans, or a form of literature acceptable only for the young, and established itself as worthy of a new and wider audience. The wide gap between "entertainment" and "true" literature began to close a bit. In the best of the new works, science fiction joined the ranks of "mainstream" literature by raising its literary quality, its artistic and aesthetic level through the creation of more convincing characters, the study of concerns fundamental to the individual and humanity at large, and new experiments in form and imaginative creation. The better works of science fiction now commanded attention beyond the frontiers of the genre and its established readership. Authors of "recognized" literature began more and more to write in the science fiction genre, or at least developed a tendency to adopt some of its elements and motifs.

The original fan movement began to encompass new countries, in a somewhat altered character. Since the 1950s, prizes have been awarded to the best science fiction works, thus ensuring their international recognition. The highest such prize is the "Hugo," awarded by the participants of the annual World Science Fiction Convention, or Worldcon. These conventions are attended by writers, editors, publishers, literary agents, artists, and of course, the fans themselves. The majority of participants—as the majority of science fiction works—come from the US.

154

The first association to bring science fiction authors together was formed in the 1960s, and was called the Science Fiction Writers of America, or SFWA. Since 1965 this body has awarded its own prize, the Nebula Award. In contrast to the Hugo, the Nebula Award is selected by professional members of the Association.

Since the 1970s, the Worldcon has also awarded the John W. Campbell prize to promote young science fiction writers.

Following the example set by the Worldcon, the Center Culturi Science-Fiction in Triest convened its first European convention, or Eurocon, in 1972. The third meeting, held in Poznan, Poland, in 1976, was attended by 250 authors, sculptors, painters, film producers, publishers, and journalists. A testament to the increasingly international flavor of science fiction is the fact that a venue in a socialist country was chosen for this third meeting. There has been no further meeting of the Eurocon after 1976 as the organizational form similar to the Worldcon didn't prove well for Europe. The established contacts between authors and other people concerned with science fiction are maintained although in altered forms. Apart from this, it was "a non-contentious gathering of science fiction authors from all over Europe, from the Atlantic to the Urals."[1] The seat of the organization is in Geneva, and its president is the French author Claude Avice. The European Science Fiction Committee is divided into the Eastern Committee (whose president is the Soviet author Alim Keshokov) and the Western Committee (whose president is the British author John Brunner). This organization holds a congress every two years: in 1978 in Poland, in 1980 in Italy, in 1982 in Switzerland. These meetings likewise award prizes for national and international recognition.

The USSR inaugurated its own annual prize for science fiction literature in 1981. It has been named the "Aëlita," in memory of the Soviet's most important science fiction novel by Alexei Tolstoi. Among the first to be honored for their outstanding works with this award were the brothers Arkadi and Boris Strugatsky, and Aleksandr Kazantsev.

Another new development is the organization of science fiction painting and graphics exhibitions, independent events held in association with the Worldcon or European meetings.

Such conventions and prizes are not important simply in their own right, but serve to encourage authors, illustrators, film, and television producers, to produce more original work. This in itself has given science fiction a stimulus and has helped raise the standards of science fiction.

The internationalization of science fiction as well as the increasing interest aroused by science fiction in new readers, the growing number of science fiction films and television series, and various other factors, have brought about a growth in science fiction the world over. It is now practically impossible to approach a full description of developments in the most important authors and works in the genre and the historical significance in one book. Every year countless numbers of new titles appear. In order to try to master such difficulties, the latest and current phase in the history of science fiction must be presented in a slightly different manner from that used to describe earlier developments.

A summary will first be offered to sketch out trends. As far as possible, authors will be grouped together according to age and aims in writing science fiction. A few of the outstanding books and some that are the best examples of certain tendencies will be discussed in greater detail.

After this short overview of developments, there will be comparative discussions of main themes, subjects, and motifs. The possibilities and the boundaries of science fiction will be illustrated by reference to important examples, though without any pretense at comprehensiveness of scope. Science fiction extends over "a practically limitless field,"[2] as the Soviet science fiction author and commentator Ivan Yefremov put it. In contrast to other science fiction histories, the chapter dealing with the "topics of science fiction"[3] and basic structures will attempt to examine such features as they relate to mankind[4] in terms of the relationship between the individual and society.

155

The science fiction of the European socialist countries has undergone a vast and stormy development since the middle 1950s. These countries were among those most affected by the ravages of World War II. The first problem was to restore the damage and rebuild the ruins, and literature immediately after 1945 formulated the main problem thus: what could be done to prevent such a barbaric step backward from happening again? Most of the epic works were set in the most recent past and sought to clarify the problems of fascism and World War II in terms of the fates of their heroes. Alternatively, authors concentrated on the problems of the present—the arduous task of reconstruction. Here the main concern was not to sound the depths of the human psyche, but to detail the external factors that appeared to change from day to day. This point of view, along with its narrow interpretation of the concept of realism, was the main reason behind the flood of novels dealing with production, industry, and the workplace.

In such conditions, science fiction found it difficult to assert its claims against other works with contemporary or historical themes. The old novel of the future was not longer acceptable by reason of the penetrating nationalism and social structures it envisioned, especially in the German-speaking territories. Technological forecasting could not compensate for these weaknesses; they had for the most part proved banal or were overtaken by developments during the changing war-wracked 1940s.

Science fiction thus turned back to the proven classics of the past. Reworked editions of Jules Verne and translations of the most recent Soviet literature appeared. The new beginnings of science fiction in the socialist countries are various, but one general feature seems to be common to them all. First there was the aim of combining technological factors and the new social conditions. Some authors were even trying to incorporate the fundamental structure of the industrial novels that concentrated on contemporary life into their science fiction. Works similar to the Soviet novel of the near future, as mentioned, are common

in the socialist countries up to the 1960s. A typical example of this is the science fiction of the German Democratic Republic (East Germany) author Eberhardt del'Antonio, born in 1926, in which he attempts to portray the wealth of opportunity inherent in science and technology and the problems he feels will be confronting mankind in the next few decades. *Gigantum* (1957) deals with problems of automatization, and *Titanus* (1959) and its sequel *Heimkehr der Vorfahren (The Ancestors' Return)* (1966) are del'Antonio's contribution to the discussion of the atomic-bomb threat, estranged by being set in space. A photon spaceship of the combined socialist states of Europe, Africa, and Asia is launched in 1990 to the constellation Pleiades. A guest from the capitalist countries accompanies the mission—the physicist Stafford, who has previously been obliged to work in an underground bomb factory in Australia. He is oppressed by guilt associated with this work.

A planet with intelligent life is discovered in the Pleiades; they name it Titan. It turns out that the inhabitants came originally from another planet, being the exiled exploiting classes who are planning atomic warfare against their old home. Anxious to learn the secret of photon power, the inhabitants of Titan capture the Earth scientists. At the point of greatest danger, three spaceships from Titan II, a companion planet, appear. When Titan I launches hundreds of atomic weapons, those on board the three Titan II spaceships reply effectively. They are able to render the weapons' motors inactive. Drawn back by the gravity of Titan I, the weapons fall and destroy the planet.

On Titan II, the cosmonauts learn the nature of a fully developed communist society. In this section, del'Antonio incorporates some of the old science fiction gags—for example, the Titan inhabitants have visited our solar system in the past (one of their damaged spaceships was the meteorite that fell in Siberia in 1908). Stafford, having learned from this terrible example what atomic war involves, sends a warning home to Earth.

The second volume narrates the journey home and the problems that arise from the confrontation of the "ancestors" with the wonderfully unified humanity-serving world of the twenty-third century.

The world situation is simplified in many novels. Didactic elements such as the authors' aim to impart their vision so dominate them that even the use of traditional science fiction motifs and the tricks of adventure literature cannot create much excitement.

At the time of the publication of this and similar works, the process of change in science fiction had already begun. In Poland, the first science fiction books of Stanislaw Lem were coming out. These were only a short while later to take the international scene by storm. His novel *Oblok Magellana (Guest in Space)* (1955) was translated into German in the GDR only twelve months after its first appearance. The first three Lem books are not in his mature style; they use, for instance, a lot of old motifs, but they stand out nevertheless for their convincing characterizations, the inner logic of the plotting, and the aesthetic quality of the narration. The fantasy roams freely throughout space, and the reader is invited to participate through the many special features of the books.

In Poland as Lem was conducting his early experiments in science fiction, from *Astronauci (The Astronauts)* in 1951 to *Eden* in 1959, in the USSR Ivan Antonovich Yefremov (1907–72) was writing *The Andromeda Nebula.* This work comes from an era in the USSR when science fiction in general was undergoing a deep and qualitative transformation.

An important Soviet Russian paleontologist, Yefremov began his writing career with tales of fantasy, based on his knowledge of folk tales, geology, and of course paleontology. Examples of his work from the 1940s include *Rasskazy o neobyknovennom (Tales of the Unfamiliar)*, and above all, *Olgoi-Khorokhoi (Death in the Desert)* (1944), in which Yefremov uses a Mongolian legend of wormlike creatures "olgoi-khorokhoi," which are able to inflict death from afar.

By the end of the 1940s, this author was moving away from his hitherto relatively confined area of fantasy. He began to conceive a cycle in which he would break through the barriers of the familiar fantasy of the immediate future, setting his story in a wider cosmic context. The introduction to this cycle was the tale *Starships* (1948). According to Yefremov's biographers, Yevgeni Brandis and Vladimir Dmitrievski, this story is "an overture to the gripping hypothesis of the Great Ring of Worlds, in which the writer is a committed champion of an anthropocentric view of the development of intelligent life in the cosmos. Based in a logical chain of premises, he comes to the conclusion that the biological processes of development are relatively unchanging under relatively similar conditions. This necessarily leads him to believe that humans will have evolved as the highest form of thinking creation on several planets."[1]

This conviction informs the whole oeuvre of the scientist and writer Yefremov. It is not by chance that the Earthly cosmonauts in his works always meet intelligent life in human form.

The publishing of his most important work, the novel *The Andromeda Nebula*, coincided almost exactly with the opening of the cosmic age and the

Ivan Antonovich Yefremov.

launch of the Soviet Sputnik. At this time too, gates that had been impregnable during the previous decades were stormed in the cultural and political field. The enthusiasm of the public for all things to do with space, the euphoria at the great success of the venture, together with the increasing strength of the social system and the worldwide movement away from confrontation that had been so pronounced in the Cold War of the 1950s, the appeals for understanding—all these created a climate in the 1960s in which Soviet science fiction flourished and grew.

> From the end of the 1950s and the beginning
> of the 1960s, Soviet utopian literature made an
> energetic leap forward both quantitatively and,
> which is far more significant, qualitatively.
> In the course of a few years the situation
> altered fundamentally: today there are some fifty
> writers active in the field of scientific utopia,
> as opposed to the four or five in the 1940s and
> 1950s.[2]

Yefremov with *The Andromeda Nebula* was the first author to create a complex fantasy of a highly developed society of the future. He paints a relatively wide picture of the mental, spiritual, and emotional world of the humans of that era. It is apparent that Yefremov is carrying on the traditions of the great utopias, and that his book should be seen as a kind of opposite pole to the western European dystopias of the twentieth century. He examines all important areas of human existence, from the upbringing of children to love and sexual relations, and voluntary creative work. New scientific disciplines are adumbrated just as are the problems of grammar and morality of a future time.

Yefremov's conviction regarding the consistency of the laws concerning the evolution of intelligent species takes him well beyond Earthly concerns. The contact of future generations of Earth dwellers with gifted representatives of other worlds is, with this author, effected not through war or violence, but through a fraternal bond of all inhabitants of the universe, in a "Great Ring of the Galaxy," which is only to be achieved through general exchange of information concerning all aspects of life.

An impressive cover illustration for Stanislaw Lem's *The Chain of Chance* in a German-language edition. Illustration by Carl Hoffmann.

158

Cor Serpentis; Serdze Smei (The Heart of the Serpent) (1959) does not carry the plot forward directly. It documents however the next stage—that is, the attempt of two intelligent life forms to make direct contact. Although attempted, contact fails, owing to a fundamental difference in the basis of metabolism: here it is carbon, there fluorine.

Yefremov's belief in the humanizing function of literature shines through all his books from *Starships*, *The Andromeda Nebula*, and *The Heart of the Serpent* to the next books in the series, *Lezvie Britvy (On the Knife Edge)* (1963) and *Chas Byka (The Hour of the Bull)* (1968), which develops the thematic thread established in the earlier books.

Without doubt the novel *The Andromeda Nebula* is at the heart of his oeuvre. This book has been published in editions of millions in the Soviet Union and abroad, and has been translated into nearly forty languages. The author is a classic of world science fiction and has many imitators, as is nearly always the case in such situations, but they do not maintain the quality of Yefremov's own work.

The most important change in the character of Soviet science fiction, initiated by Yefremov, is the new thematic content. The problems of technology, which so dominated the genre in earlier years, have given way to philosophical, moral and ethical, psychological, and social problems. At the center is always the relationship between humanity and nature, technology and society.

A great number of young authors were turning to science fiction making their mark on the genre and having a decisive impact on its character in the 1960s and 1970s. In contrast to the western countries, where the Americanization of the genre was all pervasive, the science fiction of each of the socialist countries reflects a national literature, as built up through traditions, through historical cultural development, and through the variety of experience of each country and its developmental trends. The cultural and publishing policy of these countries is aimed in the first place at making available works of their own indigenous authors, including writers of science fiction. At the same time a flourishing cultural exchange exists among these states, so that the work of the best authors, in good translations, soon finds a second home in the fraternal countries. Western science fiction is also well represented. The classic works of science fiction and its most important authors are not unfamiliar to readers of science fiction in the socialist countries. But there is one significant exception: the selection made excludes any and every book with the presentation of barbaric deeds or terror, as are those based on unrelieved pessimism, contempt for humanity, or racism.

Certain aspects of science fiction in socialist countries have become characteristic: a sense of optimism dominates the pictures given of the future, even where the author aims to give the readership a warning; in other words, there is always a belief in the eventual winning through of reason.

These pictures of the future are not without conflicts; they offer some ideas of how problems of all different kinds may be solved for the good of all. The war of total destruction, a mainstay of current western science fiction, is hardly ever found among eastern science fiction. If it does occur, it will probably be out in space where cosmonauts from Earth might be confronted with the consequences of such an event.

The heroes and the central figures in the plots are not "supermen," but are socially active people, whose humanity is likely to be put to the test in the strange situations in which they find themselves.

A very important trait of socialist science fiction is the moral rigorousness that pervades every page. Solutions to problems, or at least the direction in which a solution is to be found, are offered where the overriding factor is the humane.

From these few basic principles, it is clear that there is much in common between the science fiction of the socialist countries and that of the western countries.

The latter includes of course many works that eloquently express responsibility towards humanity. "This is yet another proof of the fact that the best writers of all countries and peoples are international and united in their love of mankind and regard with hatred all that which darkens its future prospects. As far as the artistic divergence in the science fiction literature of the world is concerned, it is splendid that it exists: it would be boring if in all the pans in the world there were produced identical pancakes."[3]

159

The closeness of the socialist and the nonsocialist authors is made evident by the similarity of their chosen motifs, themes, and subjects. There has been a parallel development over the last twenty-five years away from the purely technological fantasies to the problems of coexistence among peoples.

The uncontested master of science fiction writing in the socialist countries is Stanislaw Lem, born in Poland in 1921. Like many other science fiction authors, he started as a scientist. After completing school, he studied medicine until 1941, but then switched to motor mechanics and electrical engineering, owing to the changed circumstances under the occupation of Poland by Germany. After the war he reverted to medicine, completed his studies, and practiced as a doctor. Lem started writing at an early age (his first story was

"The Man from Mars"). He soon turned to writing full-length novels. In his first book *Czas nieutracony (The Errors of Stefan T.)*, written in 1948 but not published until 1955, he addressed the problem of the responsibility of the scientist in the tragic conflict of the occupation of Poland by Hitler's Germany. From the end of the 1940s, Lem has concentrated almost exclusively on science fiction. Even his very earliest books showed, as already mentioned, an unusual talent. These books center on adventure and action, and the questions posed are solved with simplistic responses, but nevertheless in his early books as in his mature work, Lem's concern is the existential problems of mankind. Lem has often spoken and written on his artistic credo in response to the questions of interested readers and critics: "As a reader,

The Silent Star, a German film version of Stanislaw Lem's novel *The Astronauts*.

160

I want to find in this literature new conceptions, new thoughts and possibilities that can give it the role of intellectual force. In physics there is the so-called 'thought experiment.' I would like to borrow that term for literature, which in fact should undertake such experiments, for example in the question of relations between civilizations."[4]

Lem introduces new ideas into nearly all his books, he excites the imagination of the reader and forces him or her to think through and beyond the original problems. Among his most important and most often translated books are *Solaris* (1961), *Dzienniki gwiazdowe (The Star Diaries)* (1957, expanded edition 1971), *Bajki robotow (Robot Tales)* (1964), *Niezwyciezony (The Invincible)* (1964), *Opowiesci o pilocie Pirxie (Tales of Pirx the Pilot)* (1968), *Glos pana (His Master's Voice)* (1969), *Maska (Masks)* (1967), and *Katar (The Chain of Chance)* (1976).

In the early works, the action concentrates on the adventure of space travel itself, whereas in *The Astronauts*, Lem's concern is to confront important and concrete considerations of the consciousness of atomic power, which goes out of control. The adventures of Lem's astronauts teach that the power of atomic energy should be valued even at the time people are warned against its misuse. The story of the venturing of the spaceship *Gea* in *Guest in Space* outside the solar system, in the thirty-second century, is used by Lem to examine problems of the cohabitation of humans in the most confined of spaces for long periods of time, and the way in which these problems may be overcome until such time as a planet can be found that has intelligent life where contact can be made.

Already in *Eden* Lem shows he can create new permutations on the old motifs of traditional space travel; he tells here of a group of space travelers forced to make an emergency landing on the planet Eden. They stumble upon a factory that makes, and then destroys, complicated machinery. They meet the "dopplers," the planet's inhabitants, and find themselves in inexplicable situations, believing themselves to be under attack. They then learn from one doppler something of the history of the civilization of Eden. Lem probes at a distance some of the contemporary

Stanislaw Lem.

problems facing Earth. Fascist elements exist, most obviously in the racist ideology and in the euthanasia program. The actual power structure is veiled. The problem facing the space travelers is whether to intervene or not. (There are distinct parallels here to *Hard to Be a God*, by the brothers Strugatsky.)

The civilization on Eden appears to exclude human capacity for knowledge and ability. This problematic situation is explored again in *Solaris*, and *The Invincible*. On the planet Solaris, there is a giant colloidal organism. All attempts to make contact with it fail. Only the psychologist, Dr. Kelvin, is able to observe the situation at all objectively, and then only with extreme difficulty and strain. He is enabled to regain control of himself and the situation, though without achieving any key to the phenomenon. A whole gallery of fantastic episodes and details, including for instance the strange appearance of artificial "visitors," make this an intellectually satisfying novel. It is popular even among readers who are not particular fans of science fiction. This is equally true of the later works of Lem, which have an even larger readership.

The novel *The Invincible* uses a multitude of motifs of science fiction in the course of a thought experiment into the creative potential of mankind and the outer reaches of human productivity. There is the au-

161

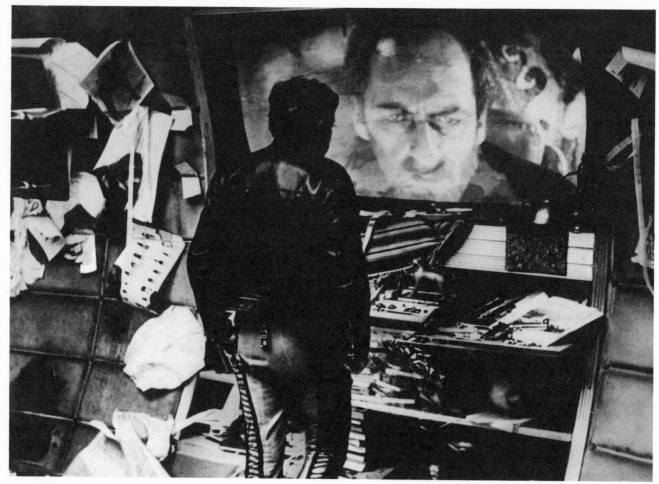

The film *Solaris* after Stanislaw Lem's book of the same title.

tomatic flight of a space cruiser, the survival of the crew after refrigerated sleep and thaw before landing, the search for a damaged spaceship, the puzzle over the fate of the crew found dead—and much else besides.

But at the forefront of the novel are the peculiar events in the space cruiser *The Invincible* itself. Mysterious "flies" have the power to buzz around like clouds and extinguish the mental impressions of humans. At the end, Lem solves this riddle. Millions of years before, intelligent inhabitants of another star had to send out exploratory spaceships in the face of a cosmic threat. One was allowed to land on the star. In all probability, the "humans" were, owing to certain events, already dead. Only machines—highly special-

ized machines—arrived and were able to survive under the most difficult conditions. Thus began a still-born evolution: the evolution of the machines. The only system that could prevail was one that had the highest degree of miniaturization and flexibility. This system, even including the "flies," had the capability of joining together at any time and for any period. The astronauts gradually learn that not everything in space is fit for mankind. Lem continually experiments with the dialectic of possibility and reality—that is, the real problems as he sees them: "Artificial problems I find uninteresting. I think up nothing. . . . I have to work with what exists in reality for me."[5]

Lem's books have fulfilled high literary expectations since the end of the 1960s. They demand read-

162

ers who are willing to play along, interested in the intellectual games Lem devises, and they therefore have had somewhat less impact on the usual wide science fiction audience than previous great novels in the genre. One such novel is *His Master's Voice* (1969). In this story, Lem develops the situation where an unknown ray of neutrinos from space has the effect of promoting life. Is this to be understood as a message of a hitherto unknown civilization? A large select team is set to work on the American "Master's Voice" project, strictly isolated from their surroundings. With the history of this secret project Lem discusses the problems of scientific responsibility for the survival of mankind. Even more unconventionally, he published in 1973 a volume, *Wielkosc urojona (Imaginary Magnitude)*, which contained a number of prefaces to books from the twenty-first century. The collection is introduced by Lem's foreword. The individual pieces abound in ideas and comic effects that reach a high point in the preface to *Golem XIV*. This book, Lem says, tells of an aggregate of computers, designed for specific strategic purposes, rebelling against their own misuse. This aggregate gives a lecture on mankind, in which it abolishes mankind's "imaginary magnitude."

In the novel *The Chain of Chance*, Lem makes use of the compositional principles of the traditional detective novel. Eleven Americans, all around fifty years of age, die over a period of two years in mysterious circumstances. All of them had been patients at a health spa in Naples. A former astronaut is given the task of solving the case. Step by step the reader observes the investigations of this "detective." What does Lem mean to say by such a narrative?

> The susceptibility of our technological civilization in connection with its unexpected setbacks is, for me, the major problem of our age. . . . Taking, at the very beginning of the industrial revolution, the smoke from the chimney stacks as an unfortunate but necessary by-product of development, we now see that the dimensions of this problem are very much larger. These unfortunate by-products have become dangers to our very environment. But, as an extension of this we have now in the meantime reached yet another stage, in which it is possible and indeed probable that the complexity of technological perfection leads to situations in which individual factors begin to react together in new and unknown ways, triggering off atavistic reversions of all sizes. . . . In my book . . . I relate the story of such a possible situation.[6]

It is striking that in his most recent books, Stanislaw Lem lays his plots nearer to our own time, while in his early work he spread himself to the thirtieth century and throughout the universe. This alteration has to do not only with the fact that in the meantime new scientific disciplines have grown up and established new knowledge, which cannot be ignored even in the free play of imagination, but also with the author's new standpoint: "However, I am also convinced that people are what interests us most, and what can come to pass in our own lifetimes. Thus I now avoid striding over thousands of years."[7]

Of equal value to the history of science fiction are Lem's stories. In *Star Diaries*, Ijon Tichy, the space and time traveler, writes his memoires and observations. For Lem, the first object of the book is to play through the problems, questions, and situations thrown up in contemporary human life as a sort of mental game or grotesque exaggeration. Often the author takes the well-known motifs of science fiction and offers his own belletristic commentary. Thus the seventh journey of Ijon Tichy recalls stories by the American author Robert Heinlein (*By His Bootstraps*, and *All You Zombies*), in which time paradoxes are carried to the absurd. In the fourth section, he reviews the illogic of time travel.

Whereas the deep symbolism and ironic criticism of *Star Diaries* are not easily unraveled, the later stories telling of space-travel cadet, and later cosmonaut, Pirx, are immediate in their effect. Pirx is a figure through which Lem makes it convincingly clear that technology will continue to play a major role in the future, that the creativity of humans makes the future, and that it is mankind who consciously shapes the future and is responsible for it. The courage, self-sacrifice, and above all the ability to overcome one's fears and doubts, becomes even more essential in the highly technological world of the future. Pirx is no

163

standard hero of the science fiction serial, no superman, but a human being like all of us. In extraordinary situations, he is able to respond with extraordinary strength. He uses his common sense, thinks independently, and has the courage to make his own decisions. Lem confronts him with antagonists, illustrious and dazzling, such as Boerst, in "The Test." In the moment of truth however, the true qualities of mankind shine through and it becomes clear who is defeated by the situation and who can grow to meet it.

Lem has tried his hand at radio and television plays but he is primarily one of the few scientists who has applied himself to science fiction. For some years, beginning in 1973, he held lectures at Kraków University on "The Problems of Contemporary Science Fantasy Literature." In a number of books, he has offered an important foundation for a theory of science fiction that no one can today afford to ignore, and that seriously sets out and dissects the problem. In 1964 Lem published *Summa Technologiae*, a work in which he outlines the possible outlook for the world after the scientific and technological revolution. This was followed in 1968 by *Filozofia przypadku (The Philosophy of Chance)*, and then in 1970 with the two-volume *Fantastyka i futurologia (Fantasy and Futurology)*. In this last he interprets a multitude of books and tales of science fiction and develops, from his critical analysis, demands that science fiction literature must satisfy, and that form the credo of Lem the author.

Fiasco (1987) was begun back in 1977, according to Lem. The story concerns a space flight to the planet Quinta, where there is evidence of life. On the spaceship *Hermes* is a group of people who are trying to establish communication with Quinta. As yet none has been effected. Why is Quinta silent? How can the expedition set up contact? The spaceship seems to be attacked as it approaches Quinta in a friendly manner—but why? Has the planet's security system gone ape and is it attacking for no reason? Or, to put it in Lem's words, has the population of Quinta become "nonbiological automata: the heirs of an extinct civilization"? In other words, have cyborgs taken over for a dead people to carry on? The two main characters aboard the *Hermes* are a papal nuncio, the priest Arago, and a space pilot, Mark Tempe, who has died on

another expedition, was frozen, and has been resurrected out of parts of two different bodies—clearly a new look at the Frankenstein motif. Lem has created Arago and Tempe to symbolize the survival of the sacred and the archaic in the world of the future. In subsequent dealings with Quinta, the crew of *Hermes* shows how deeply the idea of aggression is rooted in man's interpretations of the moves of strangers. *Fiasco* thus becomes a warning tale about the future of the human race.

One of Lem's most dearly held beliefs is that science fiction must first and foremost come up to a high literary standard—precisely because the vast number of books he has assessed give so often a negative impression in terms of their artistic quality: "Yes, I am fighting to make this form of literature into good literature with a cultural value."[8] With such views, it is not surprising that Stanislaw Lem, who had long been an honorary member of the Science Fiction Writers Association in America, was expelled from this body because he had publicly criticized the fact that "this genre in the USA has gone to the dogs through sheer commercial pressure; because . . . [he] . . . demanded that his colleagues should actively resist and not obey Mammon."[9]

In addition, Lem would like to see science fiction literature "take seriously its connection with science, and acknowledge itself, according to the number of tasks allotted to science in today's world, its special responsibility."[10]

Science fiction is for Lem equally poetic fantasy and a preview of an as yet only guessed-at future: "Even if we can present no exact detailed picture of future ages, it is still possible, building on the developmental trends of science and technology, to sketch such a picture in its essentials."[11]

Thus Lem regards science fiction as a method of expressing "in the form of similes"[12] the moral problems of our age.

The realization of these basic principles is at the core of all Lem's publications. To date even the breadth of ground his interests cover—including engineering, medicine, biology, electronics, astronomy, cybernetics—is not easily comprehensible. But Lem remains, essentially, a "moralist, who . . . wishes to hold a mirror to his age, a doubter who poses

164

questions where everything seems clear already; he is a world improver, even though this may not be admitted."[13]

Stanislaw Lem was soon emulated by other authors in his home country who devoted themselves to the writing of science fiction. In 1977, Lem wrote: "In the following years scientists in my homeland began to write, as did young people too. Some of the younger ones, unfortunately, are still of the opinion that for fantasy all you need are paper, pencil, and an idea, and they regard the idea of mixing the utopian with the scientific as mitigating much."[14]

Nevertheless, among contemporary Polish writers there are some undoubted talents. One of them is Konrad Fialkovski, born in Lublin in 1939, and Professor at the Warsaw Polytechnic. He has published more than sixty science fiction tales since 1956, including "Wroble galaktyki" ("Galactic Sparrows") (1963) and "Proprzez piaty wymiar" ("The Fifth Dimension") (1971). In 1979 he published his first novel, *Homo diversus*. Janusz A. Zajdel, born in 1938, is another author whose main line of work is nuclear physics, his particular field being radiation protection. He has written more than fifty science fiction stories (including "Journey to the Cold Star" and "Near the Sun") and the novel *Lalande 21 185*. A list of authors better known for their stories, many of which have been anthologized in collections beyond Poland's borders, might include Krzysztof Broun, science journalist, born in 1923; the journalists Ireneusz Choroszucha, born in 1943; Czeslav Chruszczdwski, born in 1922; and Witold Zegalski (1928–74); Andrzey Czechowdki, born in 1947, and Krzysztof Malinowski, born in 1946, both scientists; the engineers Ryszard Sawwa, born in 1937; Stefan Weinfeld, born in 1920, and Maciej Misiewicz, born in 1935. Adam Wisniewski-Snerg and Viktor Zwikiewicz likewise belong to the great number of Polish science fiction authors.

In the Soviet Union, science fiction has proliferated since the days of Yefremov's *The Andromeda Nebula*. Nowhere in the world do books achieve such high print runs in such short times as in the USSR. Darko Suvin has said, after careful calculation, that the first editions of anthologies run on the average to some 150,000 copies and books by single authors to some 90,000.[15] Where authors already have a following or are great favorites, or where a book is in great demand, subsequent editions follow quickly, as well as very cheap paperback editions. Thus millions of copies can be made available quite soon. This still is often not enough—the Soviet Union's thirst for reading is hardly quenchable. Science fiction books are produced centrally in Moscow, Leningrad, and Baku. In addition, science fiction books are published in all republics of the union in the languages of the various peoples. Apart from in the oldest Russian language magazine, *Vokrug Sveta*, founded in 1861, science fiction stories are printed regularly in *Tekhnika-Molodezhi, Avrora, Znanie Sila, Yuny Tekhnik, Nauka i Zhizn, Sel'skaya Molodezh, Khimiya i Zhizn, Modelist-Konstruktor*, and *Zemlya i Vselennaya*, for instance, as well as in many other popular science magazines and literary journals of the USSR or of the individual republics.

This widespread distribution of science fiction literature and its enthusiastic reception, as well as the passion for all things to do with science and space in the 1960s and 1970s, have led to a situation where the Soviet Union now has a whole stable of interesting science fiction authors. Many of them are scientists who write science fiction only in their free time; a few have become full-time free-lance writers. Exact numbers are hard to come by as there are so many regional publications in the many minority languages. But while in 1968 Brandis and Dmitrievski wrote that the number of authors of fantasy had risen from four or five in the 1940s and 1950s to about fifty,[16] it can now be justly claimed, bearing in mind the number of Soviet authors who now have an international reputation, that there are today more than a hundred full or part-time authors of science fiction.

The work of the brothers Strugatsky has become so well known over the last twenty-five years outside the Soviet Union that it has almost become a symbol of what the rest of the world understands by Soviet science fiction.

Arkadi Natanovich Strugatsky was born in 1925. He took part in World War II and was wounded. After 1945, he enrolled for English studies and Japanese studies in Moscow, after which he worked as foreign language assistant in a publishing house, trans-

165

ISSN—0202—1889

SL
1982

MODERNE
SCIENCE-FICTION

lating books from English and Japanese into Russian. One of his duties involved him in the editorial board of the twenty-five-volume *Library of Modern Fantasy*. His brother Boris Natanovich, born in Leningrad in 1933, studied at the mathematics and technology faculty at Leningrad University and worked as astronomer at the Pulkovo Observatory. He entered the Leningrad writers' circle, where he gave particular help to young authors in the section concerned with fantastic literature.

Since 1957 the brothers have collaborated on science fiction literature. The list of their work consists of some fifteen novels or long tales, two collections of shorter texts, and, very characteristic of their work as a whole, a cycle of stories under the general title *Polden', XXII Vek (Noon: Twenty-Second Century)* with its many associations. They view the novel and the novella as the best forms in which to realize their literary aims.

It is particularly striking that the Strugatskys published no short prose pieces during the 1970s. Actually, they favor the characteristic Russian length of the *povest'*, which, while called "novella" for lack of a better word, in reality falls between the length of the novel, the novella, and the short story. It has, as a rule, "just one main focus, and in most cases [concentrates] on the presentation of the character of one literary figure, or [places] the spotlight on very particular circumstances."[17]

The works of the brothers Strugatsky have, in the last ten years, moved increasingly away from traditional science fiction to develop forms in which the great traditions of Russian fantasy as in Gogol and elements of the nightmarish world of Kafka are melded together and developed in new ways.

In the works to date of the brothers Strugatsky, a cyclical development can be clearly traced. There is the first group, the plots of which take place not very far into the future, quite reminiscent of traditional science fiction. In *Strana bagrovykh tuch (The Country of Crimson Clouds)* (1959), the reader is introduced to space travelers engaged in research on the planet Venus. In its basics, the book resembles the

Today's most important Soviet authors of science fiction: Arkadi and Boris Strugatsky.

science fiction industrial book of the 1950s, or the "fantasy of the near future." The point of the story is the proving of the individual in a complicated situation.

The most important characters in the early books reappear in the later books. In *Put' na Amal'teyu (Destination: Amaltheia)* (1960), a photon spaceship is having enormous difficulty in landing on Amaltheia, a moon of Jupiter. The ship is carrying fresh supplies for the people on the moon station, without which they will perish. In the episodic novel, *Stazhery (The Apprentices)* (1962), the heroes travel to manned space stations.

The fourth book differs from its fellows somewhat in that its action takes place in an imaginary country that, although it offers everything material, has sunk into moral decline. In this fictional world of unadulterated consumerism, *Khishchnye veshchi veka (Predatory Things of Our Times)* (1965), alone control mankind. But the most important thing, humanity, has been lost, degraded to mere hedonism. Culture is replaced by a false surrogate, genuine feeling by illusion. In this book, a change in direction of the Strugatskys is visible: here they began to move increasingly to parablelike formulations of the social problems of our own day.

A second cyclic group in the work of the brothers may be seen in their short stories. In terms of fantasy, these go further than the books discussed above.

167

The third and, for the Strugatskys, the most characteristic cyclic group, is set around the people of "Noon" in the twenty-second century. The works in this cycle present a world that is the ideal dream world of the authors. In their own comment on the book they write that they find it uncongenial to say exactly how the future will be, and that they have therefore described a world about which they dream and in which they would happily live and work—a world they are even now aspiring to in order to live

A world in which it is objects that dominate man. Cover illustration for a German edition of the Strugatsky novel *Predatory Things of Our Times* by Jörg Hennig, Berlin, 1981.

ARKADI UND BORIS STRUGAZKI

Die gierigen Dinge des Jahrhunderts

PHANTASTISCHER ROMAN

and work in it. It is a world that offers mankind unlimited opportunity to develop spiritually and mentally all its creative potential. They have peopled their world with citizens who exist in our world, people the brothers know and love; they admit there are not yet so many of these as they would like, but nevertheless the core is there and the numbers grow year by year. In the world of their fantasy, such people are in the absolute majority.

This conception is the unifying thread running through all these tales about the world of "Noon." As in the Strugatskys' other novels, the main concern of the authors here is the quality of the individual and of the society. Whereas in the first cycle, the deeds and activities of the hero lay at the center of importance, now the hero's motives and aims are highlighted.

In the book *Popytka k begstvu (An Attempted Escape)* (1962), Saul Repnin, an erstwhile inmate of one of our century's concentration camps, lands through an unspecific time leap in the world of Noon. There he flies to EN 7031, a hitherto unknown heavenly body, and, together with two people from the world of the future, conducts experiments. They come across a barbaric society on this planet that treats most of its citizens as servants in the most miserable conditions. Saul gets to know the people of the future very quickly, and, in observing this distant and violent society, comes to acknowledge a moral responsibility. He returns to his own time and, at the end of the book, is shot down while making a new bid for freedom from the concentration camp.

In other books the problem of encounters between the people of the future and the "medieval" societies on other planets forms the thematic background. In *Trudno byt' bogom (Hard to Be a God)* (1966), scientists from the communist Earth are shown studying the life forms found on the distant planet Arkanar. They have at their disposal the most modern weapons and knowledge, but they are nevertheless forced to stand back and observe the medieval society of Arkanar developing into a kind of fascist dictatorship. They are in fact barred from interfering, and must let the development proceed according to its own logic. The main figure, Anton-Don Rumata is, in his internal struggles, one of the most moving and impressive of the Strugatskys' creations, and at

168

the same time a continuation of the same character in *An Attempted Escape*.

The character Maxim, in *Obitaemy ostrov (The Inhabited Island)* (1971), whom the reader will again meet in *Zhuk v muraveynike (A Beetle in an Anthill)* (1980), is similarly impressive. He, however, though likewise an observer sent by Earth, actively resists the barbaric system he chances upon. He thus learns that spontaneous action and revolutionary impatience are no substitute for deeply considered political moves based on a thorough understanding of existing historical conditions. The historical process may not be directed from outside by violence if the community is not yet ready for certain activities.

An equivalent encounter, this time set even further in the future, between space travelers from the communist world and antagonistic social-class structures on other planets and stars, is also the basis for the tale "Mal'chik iz ada" ("The Child from Hell") (1974).

In *Dalekaya Raduga (Far Rainbow)* (1964), the Strugatskys turn their attention to another problem that challenges the mental and moral horizons of the people of Noon. A couple of hundred scientists have transformed the far planet of Rainbow into a huge laboratory. They are on the trail of the phenomenon of telekinesis, and are indeed having some success in moving a small piece of material by mental effort. But in their enthusiasm for their work, the scientists overlook the deadly side effects of the process. They are forced to evacuate their rapidly deteriorating planet as fast as possible. Only one spaceship is available, and thus the decision must be made as to who can be saved and who cannot. Should it be the trailblazing results of their research, or the children? The planet's inhabitants take the humane course. Thus, the planet's enormous cultural and intellectual heritage is lost, and the majority of the inhabitants are condemned to die; there grows out of this story the confidence that the perfection of the human spirit serves first and foremost the perfection of human beings and their humanism.

In the story "Malysh" ("The Third Civilization") (1973), working groups transform the nature of a planet in order to provide for a humanlike civilization, with very strange results. At the end the origina-

tor of the puzzle himself appears, one "Midget" (the original Russian-language title of the book). Midget is a human child, the sole survivor of an Earth spaceship that crashed years before; somehow he had been brought up by unknown beings. His body grotesquely altered, Midget was blessed with certain abilities he shared with no other Earthly human. The working group wishes to force contact with this "secret" civilization, but without success.

Again and again in these books of the third cyclic group, there is mention of mysterious "wanderers." This is the Strugatskys' way of indicating the key function of the episodic novel based on four characters: *Noon: Twenty-Second Century* (1967) (first version *Vozvrashchenie—[Return Journey]* [1962]), and the key position in this volume of the short story "Pilgrims and Wayfarers." In this work the scientist Stanislav Ivanov is trying to trace the wanderings of strange alien beings. He and his daughter are joined by the astroarchaeologist Leonid Andreevich Gorbovski, whose job it is to seek out traces of intelligent life in space. He confesses: "I have to search for evidence of intelligence in the universe, and I don't even know what intelligence is. . . . But there is intelligent life in the universe. That's beyond doubt. But it isn't the way we think. It's not what we're expecting." [18]

The point of the story is this: the radio receiver picks up signals, not from Septopodes, but from Gorbovski, who is obviously being tracked by some *other* researcher in an analogous situation somewhere else in space by an unknown and more advanced civilization. These "wayfarers" appear time and again in the work of the Strugatskys, as people projected into space, finding traces of the "pilgrims," of civilizations that are so completely different from anything hitherto known that mutual communication seems impossible. It is noteworthy that the Strugatskys share their basic position here with Lem—for example, in the latter's *Solaris*.

The Strugatskys have written books other than those that form their cycles. In their novel *Ponedel'nik nachinaetsya v subbotu (Monday Begins on Saturday)*, published in 1965, three relatively independent parts are loosely connected, the plots concerning the same people in the same setting, the "Institute for Magic and Conjuring." This institute is de-

169

dicated to the use of magic and scientific knowledge in solving existing problems—including time travel.

Ulitka na sklone (The Snail on the Slope) (1966–68) consists of two semirelated parts. A very complicated symbolism of the part *The Forest* is particularly difficult to decode. In this book again "contact between humanoid and nonhumanoid intelligence is impossible."[19]

Even in repeated readings the meaning of the book is not easily understood. The story crosses the boundary between science fiction and "normal" fantasy, more so even than *Monday Begins on Saturday*.

The fantasy tale *Vtoroe nashestvie marsian (The Second Martian Invasion)* (1968) is based on the idea of extending H. G. Wells's *War of the Worlds* and the events surrounding the radio version that was broadcast in 1938. The methods of the Martians are this time quite altered from their previous invasion with superpowerful weapons that Wells dates at 1898. Now the Martians are no longer concerned with living space for their excess population but are seeking to subdue mankind slowly, to provide them with a continuous supply of gastric juices they have about exhausted. The Strugatskys report, satirically, how a bourgeois society reacts to such a plan for its future. There is no fighting or struggle, just a pathetic compliance, offering aimless opposition or lethargically awaiting the end. Very quickly the majority of people become accustomed to the idea and resume their everyday lives as if nothing untoward is happening. In this work the Strugatskys repudiate all forms of egoism, narrow-mindedness, careerism, and limitedness.

The aim of the book *Za milliard let do kontsa sveta (A Billion Years before the End of the World)* (1977), purporting to be a manuscript found in unusual circumstances, is of a similar nature. In this tale fantasy elements are used to illuminate the telling contradictions and conflicts of life today in allegorical form. The authors choose as their starting point a quite crazy situation: a biologist is being pressured by a red-headed dwarf, a visitor from an extraterrestrial civilization, to break off his experiments without delay and destroy his collected data.

Fantasy is likewise a major element in the science fiction detective novel *Otel' "U pogibshego al'pinista"* *(Hotel "To the Lost Climber")* (1971) and *Piknik na obochine (Roadside Picnic)* (1972), freely adapted by Andrei Tarkovski for his film *Stalker*. This story tells of contact being made by extraterrestrial beings with our planet towards the end of the twentieth century. They then leave behind them inexplicable things at six sites on Earth. Scientists must try and work out what it all means, all the while being aware that the objects can be potentially harmful to mankind. Research is undertaken not only by the "International Institute for Extraterrestrial Cultures," but by private individuals as well, who see in the objects means of extending their own personal power. A new and dangerous activity emerges: that is, seeking the treasure and smuggling it away for the sake of whatever gains it may represent. The fate of the people involved, particularly that of Roderick Shukhart, demonstrates that such selfish moral actions bring danger not only to the individual but to society as well.

In *The Time Wanderers* (1987), the Strugatskys once again turn to the theme of the incomprehensible alien, as they did in the short novel *Roadside Picnic*. *Wanderers* concerns scientific experiments about unusual human responses to new techniques of brain-and-body-strengthening and the artificial construction of living organisms. Why, for example, do some, *but not all*, inhabitants of a resort village react with panic when confronted by ugly, menacing, alien monsters? The novel is in the form of a series of excerpts from official documents selected by Maxim Kammerer, head of the "Department of Unusual Events of the Commission on Control." The action focuses on Toivo Glumov, one of his team, whose intuitive reactions initiate most of the action as the Strugatskys delve deeply into the mysteries of human cultural and physical evolution.

Nearly all the work of the brothers Strugatsky avoids the neat solutions, and for the most part they equally avoid repetition of the cliché situations of early science fiction. "Not only the Strugatskys' heroes but the authors themselves are tireless in their neverending searchings. In each new book they reveal new facets of their great talent."[20]

Apart from this exceptional talent, the USSR has also produced a number of writers who have introduced new themes, varied the standard motifs in interesting ways, or, like the Strugatskys, have inspired readers to ponder the question and dangers of modern civilization.

For over forty years Aleksandr Petrovich Kazantsev (born in 1906) has been revered as a sage. He was awarded the Aëlita Prize in 1981 for his collective works, which consist of traditional science fiction stories and novels. His books, along with a great number of others in the Soviet Union in the 1960s, developed themes related to the testing of humanity in the age of space research. This theme remained a favorite in his later years, but gradually the extraordinarily quick developments in many scientific disciplines forced science fiction to consider new questions; the turn toward considerations of "inner space" became more pronounced.

Anatoli Petrovich Dneprov (born Mickiewicz, 1919–75), a physicist who wrote works of scientific fantasy after 1958, came to be especially well known through the investigation of problems of cybernetics in his story "Kraby idut po ostrovu" ("The Invasion of the Crabs") (1959), in which an inventor sets up on an island the artificial evolution of metal crablike robots to be used in war. Dneprov gives the inventor the name of Cookling, and thus points the direction of his satire: the robots get bigger and bigger through a process of "selection." At the end this artificial monster revolution—true to the old sorcerer's apprentice theme—redounds back on the originator, exterminating Cookling. The story is a parable of uncontrolled arms buildup.

Andrei Tarkovski made his film *Stalker* based on motifs from the book *Roadside Picnic*.

171

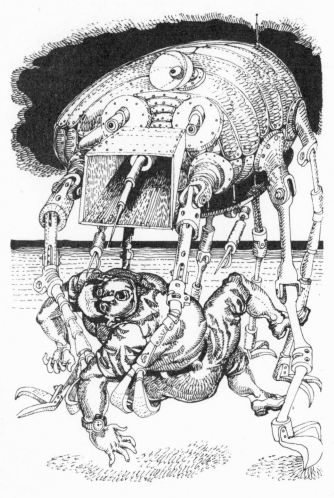

Cookling falls victim to his creation. Illustration by A. Brussilovski.

At the end of the 1950s and the beginning of the 1960s the writer Sever Feliksovich Gansovski (born in 1918) began writing science fiction. His story "Vincent van Gogh" is not merely the story of a new version of time travel, but in it the author also makes his readers wish to renew their acquaintance with the life and work of the great painter. In other stories too, many of them translated and issued abroad in anthologies, he demonstrates that even the most traditional themes have unexpected possibilities. Above all, he has continued the tradition started by H. G. Wells. For instance, his "Step into the Uncertain," dealing with the changing of human biorhythms, is a variation on Wells's "The New Accelerator." In other stories,

such as "Electrical Inspiration," the influence of Wells is obvious.

The engineer and inventor Genrich Altov, born in 1926 and a resident of Baku, has written short stories and tales that have been published in various collections since 1957. Like Gansovski, he mixes the old well-known ideas of science fiction—such as flights to distant planets, thinking machines, and encounters with aliens—with new and surprising elements. In "The Harbor of the Stony Storms" (from the book *Sozdan dlya buri [Created for the Storm]* [1970]) he blends cosmological hypothesis with thoughts on the attitude to possible civilizations and our own place in the universe.

His almost lyrical or hymnlike novella (actually a *povest'*) *Stone from the Stars* was written in collaboration with Valentina Zhuravleva (born in 1933). This latter author has become known in science fiction circles since she began writing in 1958 with her stories issued in collections such as *Through Time* (1960), *The Man Who Made Atlantis* (1963), and *The Bridge of Snow over the Crevice* (1971).

Ilya Yossifovich Varshavski (1909–74) wrote from 1962 until his death a wealth of science fiction short stories. He manipulates small, apparently unimportant daily irritations into scenes of high comedy. He also wrote several dystopian novels with the usual warning social comments. Important collections of his work include *Molekulyarnoe kafe (The Molecular Café)* (1964), and *Lavka snovideniyu (The Dream Shop)* (1970).

Other Soviet authors of the 1960s are Yeremei Parnov and Mikhail Yemtsev (collaboration: *Black Sign the Sphere*); Yevgeni Voiskunski and Ossai Lukodyanov (*Pandit's Knife*, published by both!); Gleb Golubev; and Sinovi Yurev (the grotesque *Mr. Gropper's Peculiar Death*).

A trilogy by Sergei Snegov was greedily devoured by fans of traditional science fiction. The first book, *Lyudi kak bogi (Men Like Gods)* was published in 1966; the second, *Vtorzheniya v Persei (The Invasion of Perseus)* in 1968; and the last, *Koltso obratnogo vremeni (The Ring of Anti-Time)* in 1976. As can already be appreciated from the titles, this trilogy closely resembles in breadth (and in the fact that it could be continued at will) the space

172

opera of western science fiction. Eli, the manufacturer of artificial suns, tells the tales of three interstellar expeditions that he has accompanied as space secretary, galactic fleet chief, and lastly as scientific consultant. The Earthly cosmonauts come across an artificial planet where they learn about a gigantic planetary war in the constellation of Pleiades; they decide to help those under threat. At first they are chased off, but eventually they stand between the galaxies and the "destroyers" (a combination of human and machine). Every possible cliché and motif of the space opera is incorporated in these books. After the resolution of this conflict, there follow even greater adventures in the search for a legendary, very highly developed, star people.

Sever Gansovski.

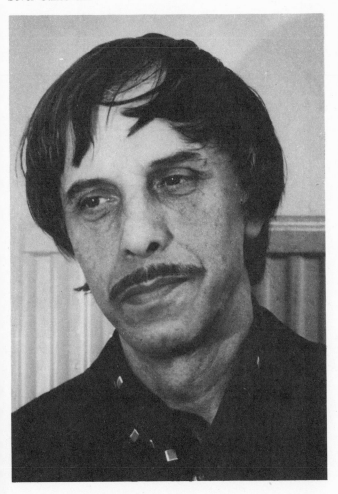

Equally popular and frequently reissued in the Soviet Union, and of higher literary quality than the Snegov books, are the books of former chemist Aleksandr Meyerov (1915–75), *Sirenevyi kristall (The Lilac Crystal)* (1965) and *Pravo veto (Power of Veto)* (1971).

Some of the writers of the Soviet Union who began writing in the 1960s were later on to have a decisive effect on the direction in which the genre would develop in the USSR. The geochemist Dmitri Aleksandrovich Bilenkin, also known for his work as editor of specialist texts, wrote his first story in 1958, but only in the following years he concentrated on writing fantasy tales. Since 1979 he has lived as a free-lance writer. His best-known work revolves around the confrontation between human intellect and various fantasy happenings on Earth and in the cosmos. He develops these conflicts into interesting resolutions, calling upon the reader to reconsider the meaning of life. In stories suitable for children he blurs the boundaries of the fairy tale, for example in "Dognat' orla" ("Eagle Hunting") and "Gorod i volk" ("The City and the Wolf").

Vladimir Grigorev (born in 1935) is known widely for his collection of stories *Axioms of the Magic Wand* (1968); Yevgeni Veltistov and Viktor Kolupaev (authors of the *Swing of Emeritus*) also belong to this newer group of Soviet science fiction authors, as do Petr Voronin, Vladimir Firsov and a number of others.

One of the most important authors of fantasy in the Soviet Union is an orientalist from Moscow who writes children's books under the pseudonym Kirill Bulychov. His books include *A Token for the Children of Earth* and *The Mars Elixir, or, the Warriors at the Crossroads* (1971).

The respective developments of the physicist Olga Nikolaevna Larionova (born in 1935) and Gennadi Gor (1907–81) show that in the last fifteen years the boundaries between scientific fantasy and nonscientific fantasy, and between science fiction and "normal" fiction, have become ever more fluid. "There is also a quasiscientific milieu in fantastic fairy tales, while traditional science fiction has less and less to do with the motivation of scientific ideas and prognoses," is Jevgeni Brandis's comment.

173

While Larionova's novel *The Kilimanjaro Leopard* (1965) is clearly a work of science fiction, it is far less easy to classify her later books, for instance *Sonata usha (Snake Sonata)*, even though the hero Tarumov is a space pilot through and through. He is transported to another planet by a secret force as the object of scientific investigation of cold research to join other imprisoned and intelligent life forms. He rescues the others by sacrificing himself, dying voluntarily in this "terrarium." The poetic language, with many images, and the deep symbolism place these stories in the realm of fantasy. Similar conclusions may be drawn in connection with some of Gor's works in particular the novel *The Statue* and the tales of younger authors.

In a change of pace, *Moscow 2042*, by Vladimir Voinovich, appeared in 1987—a satire in science fiction format aimed at the Soviet Union. Written by Voinovich in exile in Stockdorf, near Munich, Germany, in the Federal Republic of Germany (West Germany), the book details a futuristic dystopian view of Moscow, called Moscowrep, where all things, air, water, food, and clothing are satisfied by the state—even masturbation. In typical science fiction manner, Voinovich's hero, Vitali Nikitich Kartsev, an exiled Russian writer, is invited to take a Lufthansa flight to Moscow sixty years in the future (flights for fifty years in the future are *already* booked). In Moscowrep, Kartsev meets the country's leader, called the "Genialissimo," who is a literary and scientific genius, and who orbits the space over the city. In Moscowrep there is no death or illness—the ill and dying are very simply exiled elsewhere! Kartsev is given a book of his adventures to read, and is asked to correct it; of course, sixty years in the future he has not yet written it. Kartsev refuses, pointing out that if he could have corrected his novels back then he would have had no reason to move into exile. Here are amusing and telling shades of the more stinging criticism of totalitarianism in Orwell's *Nineteen Eighty-Four*.

Apart from the Russians, there are many writers of national minority languages in the Soviet Union, including the Estonians Boris Kabur and Friedebert Tuglas, the Azerbaijan Maksud Ibrahimbek, and the Ukrainians Vadim Vladko and Igor Markovich Rossokhovatski.

Another non-Russian author of the Soviet Union is the Ukrainian electrical engineer Vladimir Zavchenko, born in 1933. He is chiefly known for his novel *Otkrytie sebya (The Triple I)* (1971), in which

Vladimir Zavchenko.

Dmitri Bilenkin.

Aleksandr Meyerov.

A German-Soviet joint production. Design by Gerhard Medoch.

he poses questions on the subject of cloning and the biological existence of humankind.

That science fiction in the USSR also permeates other fields of interest is demonstrated by the novel *The Day Outlasts the Century* by the Kirgiz poet Chingis Aitmatov, recognized as one of the high achievements of literature. A science fiction theme is developed in connection with an old Kazakh legend, a process that throws up the question of whether humanity today is ripe for an attempt at contact with other, more highly developed civilizations from another solar system.

Such trends whereby mainstream literature is being imbued with science fiction motifs and problems (for example, in Yevgeni Yevtushenko's fantasy novel *Ardabiola*) and science fiction is being opened up into hitherto rare, nonpseudoscientific elements, are characteristic in the latest stages of the development of the genre not only in the Soviet Union but also in other countries.

In the science fiction literature of the smaller socialist countries, there is today neither such depth of

Examining the possibilities and problems of cloning. Cover illustration for Vladimir Zavchenko's *The Triple I*, by Stefan Duda, Berlin, 1979.

175

thought, or such above-average books as those of Stanislaw Lem or the brothers Strugatsky, nor the vast breadth among science fiction writers and readers as there is in the multinational Soviet Union. Science fiction is just one of the many colors in the great palette of literature as a whole. In addition to this, science fiction literature is still regarded by the majority of "serious" writers with the odium of a somewhat primitive genre oriented towards the scientific rather than the artistic. To preserve their reputations authors prefer not to dabble in science fiction, and thus—despite specific encouragement—even today science fiction in these countries is counted as a playground for scientists and engineers who see themselves as dilettante writers. The current stereotypes of photonpowered spaceships, deep freezing of astro-

Lyuben Dilov.

Tales by the Bulgarian author Lyuben Dilov in German.

nauts, time travel (particularly into past ages) and twin paradoxes, and mutants, robots, genetic manipulation, and even the arsenal of von Däniken's fantasies, seem to be the standard bill of fare. In the last twenty-five years, changes have come about slowly, and some authors have achieved recognition even beyond their own countries' borders.

In Bulgaria, modern science fiction is mostly thought of in connection with the name of Lyuben Dilov. Born in 1927, this author studied philology and then worked as a magazine editor. He has made a name for himself as an author in several different genres. His science fiction works include the novels *The Atom Man* (1958, new version 1979), *Fear Has Many Names* (1974), *The Burden of Skaphander* (1969), and *The "Icarus" Way* (1974). His stories have been collected and published in *My Curious Friend the Astronomer* (1971); *Feeding the Eagle* (1977); *The Double Star* (1979); *The Lost Chance— from the Works of My Computer* (1981). In addition, Dilov has published a children's fantasy book, *The Star Adventures of Numi and Niki* (1980) and its sequel *To Paradise Planet and Back Again* (1983).

Dilov sees himself as treading in the footsteps of Lem. It is from this source that he gets his great sense of moral responsibility as an author: "Fantasy is the fairy tale of our century. While fantastic fairy tales used to take their themes and subjects from the myths, now our current fantasy derives from the 'myths' of science and technology, in order to say something to contemporary readers. Above all, the message is that our world really is in danger of being destroyed, unless we all work for peace, for our continued existence."[21]

Other Bulgarian authors include Petyr Stypov *(Myon Calls Earth)* and Peter Bobev *(Shark Bay)*, who specialize in writing action-packed novels for a younger audience. Doctor of Criminology Dimiter Peev, born in 1919, and author of the short story "A Hair from Mohammed's Beard," and the novel *The Photon Spaceship* (1964), and the physicist Nedialka Michova *(The Stars Approach*, 1969), the lawyer and cultural functionary Anton Donchev (born in 1930),

176

Ljuben Dilow
DER DOPPELSTERN
Phantastische Erzählungen

and the doctor Svetoslav Slavchev (born in 1926), together form the core of the writers of science fiction in Bulgaria, although they are mostly engaged in writing works in other genres. This is also true of Pavel Veshinov (pseudonym for Nikola Gugov, born in 1914), whose short stories include "The Blue Butterflies," and novels like *The Decline of Ajax* (1973), and Atanas Nakovski (pseudonym Nakov, born in 1925), whose collection of fantastic novellas has the title *No Shadows* (1972).

According to Lyuben Dilov, science fiction in his homeland has in the last ten years developed at a faster rate than ever before, and now some seventeen new titles are published each year. "It has even overtaken detective literature. Editions of a hundred thousand are today nothing exceptional in Bulgaria."[22]

Young authors can publish their work in such magazines as *Cosmos, Science and Technology*, and in the weekly *Orbita*, which holds an annual competition for short prose pieces. Since 1976 fantasy yearbooks have also appeared.

In neighboring Rumania, the chief representative of science fiction literature is Vladimir Colin, born in 1921 in Bucharest. After studying philosophy, he became a journalist and main editor of the cultural magazine *Viaţa romaneasca*. Since 1947, he has been recognized as a poet, adapter of literature, and children's author; he first tried his hand at science fiction in 1966. His first concern here was not excitement and action, but the exposition of philosophical and moral questions, giving the reader provocation to think. For example: "The Second Future," short story, 1966; "Timefalls," short story, 1972; *The Teeth of Chronos*, short stories, 1975; and *Planet Babel*, novel, 1977.

Ion Hobana, born in 1931, worked as a foreign language assistant in Bucharest after studying philology. Since 1955 he has set himself the task of propagating and developing the science fiction literature of Rumania. His philological knowledge of course helps him with his work as a translator (mainly the works of Jules Verne). Through his commentaries, which are also read abroad[23], he has broadcast to a wider audience the very little-known developments of the genre in his homeland, if only in summaries. He has also written some original tales.

A German-language paperback edition of the Rumanian science fiction novel *Planet Babel*. Illustration by Peter Nagengast.

As in Bulgaria, in Rumania magazines are the ready-made platform for science fiction tales (for example, *Viaţa romaneasca*, already mentioned), and it is through this medium that authors such as Gheorghe Sasarman (born in 1941) and Sergiu Farcasan (born in 1924) have become known in the field of science fiction.

During the 1950s the technologically orientated fantasy and the science fiction of the near future was dominant in Hungary. Science fiction at this time was largely regarded as children's literature with a large dose of adventure, or as belletristic popular science. From the mass of the justifiably forgotten books then written, one stands out for mention: the children's book *The Violet-Blue Light* by Peter Földes, for its well-constructed, exciting plot and some original ideas.

An upswing came only with the end of the 1950s and the beginning of the 1960s. The translation of new Soviet science fiction and the classic works of western science fiction, together with critical and theoretical works, fundamentally changed the picture. Magazines began to publish science fiction stories, and anthologies, serials, and monographs were published. A commission for scientific fantasy was founded in the national association of authors, to which belonged not only writers but also artists, filmmakers, and musicians. The fan movement widened. Now conditions were ripe for the rapid development of "sci-fi," as science fiction is known in Hungary.

In an article outlining the situation, Peter Kuczka wrote that the important science fiction authors can be grouped largely according to age. Some writers view sci-fi as just one of many genres they contribute to, testing themselves now and again but writing mainly in other forms. Some authors have turned to science fiction in the course of their main work as scientists or journalists. The situation is therefore very similar to that obtaining in other countries.

According to Kuczka, Hungarian science fiction can be conveniently divided into the following four groups:

The first group includes experienced authors already considered among Hungarian national classics, such as Jenö Szentivanyi *(The Man with the Stone Axe)* and Maria Szepes *(Looking Glass Door to the Sea)*, and other psychologically based novels.

The second such group is made up of authors all born between 1913 and 1930, among them György Botond-Bolics, Lajos Mesterhazi, Gyula Fekete, Ervin Gyertyan, Gyula Hernadi, Peter Zsoldos, Zoltan Csernai, Miklos Rosaszegi, Laszlo Nemes, Klara Feher, and Deszö Kemeny. This group is defined solely in terms of age, and represents a wide variety of styles. "Fekete is a moralist; Hernadi experiments with modern forms and paradoxical ideas, Mesterhazi reacts to the general problems facing mankind as sensitively as

to the particular cares of our native lands, Csernai wrote his trilogy of novels on the unknown secrets of our Earth in the leisurely tempo of the classic storytellers; Gyertyan uses robots to hit out at manifestations of late capitalism, Zsoldos writes very original tales about the adventures of future space explorers and the histories of distant planets; Kemeny is a master of the science fiction detective story; Feher writes instructive allegories like *The Island of Earthquakes*, or the extraordinary society of *Oxygenien*, mainly for young people; Rosaszegi's books concern mysterious discoveries, his scientists send out from their laboratories strange chemical compounds or dreadful beetles into the outside world; Nemes's imagination draws on hibernation."[24]

Younger authors have loosened the old ties with traditional developments even more than the foregoing group, and have turned to searching out new directions. They prefer to experiment with shorter literary forms, in concise and concentrated style. Authors in this group include Peter Szentmihalyi Szabo, Kalman Papay, Bela Balazs, and Istvan Kazas, all born between 1930 and 1950, and all published already and known as science fiction authors.

The fourth of Kuczka's groups is made up of the very young authors at present between twenty and thirty years of age—for example, Gabor Haller, Gabor Rubin, and György Selmeci. These authors have all come before the spotlight of publicity "with their poetical and satirical stories, in which they often make fun of science fiction by irony and by self-mockery. They do not write novels, they choose rather to interpret the world and mankind in works of two or three sides, selfless, naive and clean, however mocking."[25]

Such a classification is useful as a starting point, but the scene changes very quickly and is anyway subject to influence by the introduction of new ideas by translations from other languages.

Science fiction in Czechoslovakia shows no differences from that of other countries either in thematic breadth or in the decisive changes that have taken place in the last thirty years. The most important personality in Czech science fiction is the writer-psychotherapist Josef Nesvadba (born in 1926), who also writes in other genres. His short stories have been published in numerous anthologies and collections, and include "Tarzan's Death" (1958), "Einstein's Brain" (1962), "The Discovery Against Itself" (1964), "Captain Nemo's Last Journey" (1965), and "Driving License for Parents" (1979). At the outskirts of science fiction is his story "The Mistakes of Eric N." (1974), which is a parody of the books of Erich von Däniken.

Nesvadba likes to challenge previous major writers and also likes to carry on their work: "Tarzan's Death" derives from Burroughs's popular books; "The Second Island of Dr. Moreau," and "The Trust for Destroying World History," take on ideas from H. G. Wells; "Captain Nemo's Last Journey" and "How Captain Nemo Died," refer to Jules Verne.

Josef Nesvadba's *The Secret Message from Prague.*

A classic of Hungarian sci-fi, Frigyes Karinthy's *The New Journeys of Lemuel Gulliver* in a German edition.

Nesvadba is an intellectual storyteller, each of whose tales concentrates on making one single point through wit or irony or both. His experience as a psychotherapist is often in evidence and he prefers to probe the basic questions facing humanity—such as love, hate, fortune, the meaning of life, and so on. Both of these aspects of his work mark him out. In his work too, as in that of many of his fellow writers, the national traditions of Czech fantasy (as per Čapek) are discernable.

Other Czechoslovakian writers who deserve mention are the army doctor Ludvik Soucek (1926–78),

180

mainly for children's books; Frantisek Behounek for the novel *Stranded in Space*; Vaclav Kajdoa (born in 1922), for *Invasion from Space* (1970); Jaroslav Veis (born in 1946), for *Experiment for the Third Planet* and *Pandora's Box*; Adenek Volny (born in 1946); and Jiri Brabenec and Zdenek Vesely.

There are also academics who have written occasional pieces of science fiction—for instance, the professor of film and television arts Oldrich Zelezny, professor of chemistry Jaroslav Zyka, and teacher Ludmila Freiova.

In the German Democratic Republic (East Germany), scientific fantasy was rediscovered in the late 1950s when the genre had new life breathed into it. Early on, of course it was the general objective to put a stop to the negative traditions which had grown up during the fascist period. The desire to break away from the technological fantasy of Dominik and Delmont was the background that inspired the first attempts in the genre. The trailblazers were those authors who adopted the adventure of space or technology but were at the same time able to incorporate the issues of the time, even though this often involved deploying the current clichés, especially the simplified moral coordinates of good (that is, socialist) and bad (that is, imperialist). Among the early significant works are those of authors Eberhardt del'Antonio (born in 1926), for *Gigantum* (1957), *Titanus* (1959), and *The Ancestors' Return* (1966); Richard Gross, for the *Der Mann aus dem anderen Jahrtausend (The Man from the Other Millennium)* (1966); Heinz Vieweg for *Ultrasymet bleibt geheim (Ultrasymet Stays a Secret)* (1955), *Die zweite Sonne (The Second Sun)* (1958); and Lothar Weise, for *Das Geheimnis des Transpluto (The Secret of Transpluto)* (1962), and *Unternehmen Marsgibberellin (Project Marsgibberellin)* (1964). Some of the publications in the series *Das Neue Abenteuer (The New Adventure)* were written by Weise in collaboration with Kurt Herwarth Ball.

Carlos Rasch (born in 1932) has been writing science fantasy work for the last quarter century, and, according to the number of publications is the most published author of science fiction in East Germany. His books include *Asteroidenjäger (Asteroid Hunters)* (1961), *Der blaue Planet (The Blue Planet)* (1963),

Im Schatten der Tiefsee (In the Shadows of the Deep Sea) (1965), *Magma am Himmel (Magma in the Sky)* (1975), besides many stories mainly known through the collection *Krakentang (Kraken Weed)* (originally published 1968, republished with the order altered in 1972). He is an author who tries to create an exciting entertainment aimed mostly at younger audiences, and has remained loyal to the technologically orientated mode of science fiction even though it must be said that his early one-sidedness has given way to deeper characterization.

The doyen of GDR science fiction is Günther Krupkat, born in 1905, who came to prominence mainly in the 1960s with several novels and short stories, especially *Die grosse Grenze (The Great Frontier)* (1960), *Als die Götter starben (When the Gods Died)* (1963), and *Nabou* (1968). He has also added nuances to enrich the thematics of outer space and the oceans' depths.

At the end of the 1960s, new authors joined the ranks of science fiction, whose first concern was no longer to portray scientific or technological experience, but whose interests were more firmly rooted in social, moral, ethical, psychological, and philosophical questions. Their individual styles are thereby unmistakable.

Members of this group include Hubert Horstmann with *Die Stimme der Unendlichkeit (The Voice of Infinity)* (1965) and *Das Rätsel des Silbermondes (The Mystery of the Silver Moon)* (1971); Curt Letsche with *Der Mann aus dem Eis (The Man from the Ice)* (1970) and *Raumstation Anakonda (Space Station Anaconda)* (1974); Heiner Rank with *Die Ohnmacht der Allmächtigen (The Impotence of the All-Powerful)* (1973); Herbert Ziergiebel with *Die andere Welt (The Other World)* (1966) and *Die Zeit der Sternschnuppen (Stellar Influenza)* (1972).

Of a higher literary quality are the few science fiction works published by the well-known author Werner Steinberg: *Die Augen der Blinden (The Eyes of the Blind)* (1973) and *Zwischen Sarg und Ararat (Between the Coffin and Ararat)* (1978). Günter Teske (*Telepatis* [1981]) mingles science fantasy with sports problems.

Gerhard Branstner (born in 1927) had no need to prove his many-sided literary talents when he published his first work of fantasy. In the "unreal events" he wrote of in his book *Zu Besuch auf der Erde (Visit to the Earth)* (1961), he gave incontrovertible proof of his ability to present a comedy on the problems of our age with the aid of motifs from scientific fantasy. He continued this line, writing usually in the short story form, as is shown by quoting some of his titles: "Reise zum Stern der Beschwingten" ("Journey to the Star of the Elated") (1968); "Der falsche Mann im Mond" ("The False Man in the Moon") (1970); "Der astronomische Dieb" ("The Astronomical Thief") (1973); "Vom Himmel hoch oder Kosmisches Allzukomisches" ("From on High; or All Too Comic Com-

edy") (1974); "Der Sternenkavalier oder die Irrfahrten des ein wenig verstiegenen Grossmeisters der galaktischen Wissenschaften Eto Schik und seines treuen Gefährten As Nap" ("The Star Cavalier; or, the Wanderings of the Slightly Eccentric Master of the Galactic Sciences Eto Schik and his Loyal Companion, As Nap") (1976). Gerhard Branstner's prose is for the most part free of the usual science fiction clichés. His main aim is to infuse the issues of science and technology with interesting and especially comic social prognoses. For his achievements he was awarded a national prize at the Third Eurocon in Poznan in 1976.

The green medallions, before Mittelzwerck disturbs the balance of nature. Illustration by Erhard Grüttner.

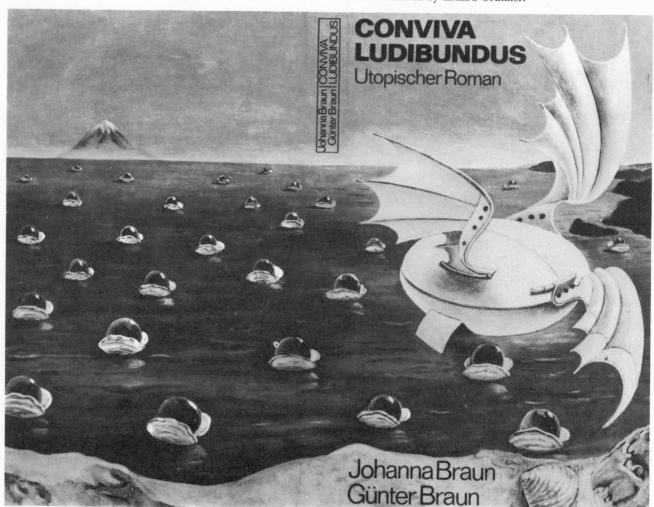

182

Gerhard Branstner.

Carlos Rasch.

Branstner's conception of science fiction corresponds strongly with that of the husband and wife team Günter (born in 1928) and Johanna (born in 1929) Braun. In their books, the Brauns show concern with the social behavior of people, with the despoiling of the environment, with sterile and narrow-minded scientific thought, with love and pleasure, with the degeneration of the mass media, and even with science fiction itself in terms of the do-it-yourself movement. In their hands language becomes a handy and efficient tool that illumines the text with added significance, giving it an underlayment of symbolic meaning. Most of their works break through the ghetto existence of those who confine themselves to science fiction and nothing else, helping science fiction to enter the ranks of mainstream literature. Among their works are the 1968 short stories "Die Nase des Neandertalers" ("The Nose of the Neander-

thal"), "Der Irrtum des Grossen Zauberers" ("The Mistake of the Great Magician") (1972), "Unheimliche Erscheinungsformen auf Omega XI" ("Mysterious Apparitions on Omega XI") (1974), "Der Fehlfaktor" ("The Failure Factor") (tales written in 1975), the novels *Conviva ludibundus* (1978), and *Der Utofant—In der Zukunft aufgefundenes Journal aus dem Jahrtausend III (The Utofant—A Journal Found in the Future from the Third Millennium)* (1981).

Apart from these attempts at renewing the genre, traditional science fantasy adventure has not been neglected, especially in the field of books for children, for example in the series *Spannend erzählt (Excitingly Told)*, and *Kompass Bücherei (Compass Library)*. Popular authors include Klaus Frühauf with *Mutanten auf Andromeda (Mutants on Andromeda)* (1974), *Am Rande wohnen die Wilden (Savages Live at the Edge)* (1976), *Das Wasser des Mars (The Water of*

183

Mars) (1977), *Stern auf Nullkurs (Star on Course Zero)* (1979), *Das fremde Hirn (The Alien Brain)* (1982) and *Die Bäume von Eden (The Trees from Eden)* (1983); Alexander Kröger with *Sieben fielen vom Himmel (Seven Fell from Heaven)* (1969), *Antarktis 2020 (Antarctis 2020)* (1973), *Expedition Micro* (1976), *Die Kristallwelt der Robina Crux (The Crystal World of Robina Crux)* (a kind of Robinson Crusoe set in space) (1977), and *Energie für Centaur (Energy for Centaur)* (1983); Karl-Heinz Tuschel, whose works include *Ein Stern fliegt vorbei (A Star*

Günter and Johanna Braun.

Paperback editions from the series "SF-Utopia" from the German Democratic Republic (East Germany).

Flies By) (1967), *Der purpurne Planet (The Crimson Planet)* (1971), and *Die Insel der Roboter (The Island of Robots)* (1973); and Michael Szameit with *Alarm im Tunnel Transterra (Alarm in Tunnel Transterra)* (1982) and *Im Glanz der Sonne Zaurak (In the Radiance of the Sun Zaurak)* (1983). Even elements of space opera are used, as Arne Sjöberg (pseudonym of Jürgen Brinkmann) proves with his works in many parts, for example *Die stummen Götter (The Mute Gods)* (1978), and *Andromeda* (1983).

In the 1970s it became more common for scientists and other specialists to try their hand at science fiction. Such authors include the physician Wolf Weitbrecht, with *Das Orakel der Delphine (The Dolphins' Oracle)* (1972) and its sequel *Die Stunde der Ceres (The Hour of Ceres)* (1980), *Der Stern der Mütter (Star of Mothers)* (1980), and the short-story collection *Die Falle von Alderamin (The Trap of Alderamin)* (1982); Alfred Leman and Hans Taubert, who work in collaboration; Richard Funk; Heinz Hüfner; Ernst-Otto Luthardt, and others. Among the most successful authors to make their debut recently are Bernd Ulbrich with *Der Unsichtbare Kreis (The Invisible Circle)* (1977), and *Störgrösse M (Disruption Magnitude M)* (1980), Erik Simon, with *Fremde Sterne (Strange Stars)* (1979) and Angela and Karlheinz Steinmüller with *Andymon* (1982), *Pulaster* (1986) and some tales, all of whom demonstrate certain aspects of science fiction that raise their work above that of most others.

The most important of the publishing houses of entertainment literature in the German Democratic Republic (East Germany), the Verlag Das Neue Berlin, has started a paperback library "SF—Utopia," consisting of some four titles a year, mostly drawn from works in heavy demand that are then republished. Since 1980 this house has also published the fantasy almanac *Lichtjahr (Lightyear)*, especially valued for the quality of its graphics. Apart from the children's book publishers Verlag Neues Leben, and Verlag Volk und Welt, which specializes in important international literature—including the work of Lem and the brothers Strugatsky—a large number of other publishers in the GDR have in recent years included in their lists occasional works of science fiction literature, of which Verlag Der Morgen (books), Greifen-

Lichtjahr 2

The science fiction almanac of the publishers Verlag Das Neue Berlin, 1981.

verlag Rudolstadt, and Mitteldeutscher Verlag Halle/ Leipzig deserve mention. This demonstrates how the interest shown in science fiction in recent years has risen in various areas of readership. It is also a fact that in mainstream literature there is now a tendency for important authors to learn to use fantasy as a way of appropriating the world, evaluating it, and communicating ideas about it. The publishers Hinstorff Verlag Rostock have brought out an anthology under the title *Blitz aus heiterem Himmel (A Bolt from the Blue)*, edited by Edith Anderson, in which four male and three female authors all work from the idea of a sudden change of sex in order to explore the role-related problems of our time both critically and

185

amusingly. Christa Wolf's contribution to this book, *Selbstversuch (Experiment on Oneself)* is also to be found in her volume *Unter den Linden* in which she experiments with fantasy in three stories.

Anna Seghers (1900–83) plays about with time in *Die Reisebegegnung (The Journey Meeting)*, postulating a meeting between Gogol, E. T. A. Hoffmann, and Kafka. Their various conceptions of poetry and writing become clear in the discussions on art and life. *Sagen von Unirdischen (Legends of the Unearthly)* seem to be primarily a mixture of medieval Germany and space travel, of Christian legend and science fiction. In the masterly hands of its authoress the work becomes a hymn to our imperfect, sorely afflicted, and yet incredibly beautiful world—a song of praise on the necessity for art in human existence.

Irmtraud Morgner (born in 1933) employs numerous fantastic ideas, even science fiction motifs and subjects, in her Salman trilogy, of which only two volumes have so far been printed: *Leben und Abenteuer der Trobadora Beatriz nach Zeugnissen ihrer Spielfrau Laura (The Life and Adventures of the Troubadour Beatriz as Related by Her Assistant Player Laura)* (1974) and *Amanda—Ein Hexenroman (Amanda—A Witch's Book)* (1983). Beatrix the troubadour wakes after an eight-hundred-year sleep in present-day Europe. Thus the author alienates our own age (an inverted version of *A Connecticut Yankee in King Arthur's Court* by Mark Twain, one of Morgner's influences.)

Franz Fühmann (1922–84) wrote his story "Ohnmacht" ("Helplessness") (1974) during an intense personal crisis, "in order to overcome an existential paralysis, and [he] found in that unreal world and method the . . . form, otherwise unavailable, to . . . put into words what was torturing [him]."[26]

Similar backgrounds reappear in stories about the three characters in the book—Janno, Jirro, and Pavlo. After the first edition was published, Fühmann was informed by an "expert" that his work "fell completely outside the genre of science fiction."[27] In order to remove such misunderstandings, he named his collection of stories *Saiäns-Fiktschen* (1981). It is included however among science fiction works as material of high literary quality, whose many-layeredness and symbolism are rather beyond what normal science fiction fans are used to unraveling. *Saiäns-Fiktschen* does not sketch a utopian system, only perhaps a closed one, and it does not claim to be prophetic. How can one know what the year 3456 holds in store?

> *Saiäns-Fiktschen* then: a hermaphrodite;
> not to be taken seriously as science fiction,
> as *Saiäns-Fiktschen*, perhaps as seriously as the
> script of something spoken, say: as estrangement.
> It shows results, not processes, though these
> results are what are achieved by processes.
> They are, the stories, a general end point in
> the area of faltering contradictions, where stagnation appears as a motive force. Development
> as lack of development. The sleep of reason,
> says Goya, produces monsters; the faltering
> of contradictions produces monsters. I can
> offer very little defence when people say
> these stories are monstrous.[28]

186

THE AMERICANIZATION
OF WESTERN SCIENCE FICTION

In the period immediately before America entered World War II, there were, apart from many fanzines, some sixteen regular science fiction magazines published. More than half of these were forced to cease publication by 1943 because of the war.[1] But only a few years after the end of the war a new upturn of unprecedented proportions began. Some twenty-nine new periodicals were launched after 1948, and by 1955 there were approximately thirty-five science fiction and fantasy magazines published regularly in the United States. The most important were those founded under Hugo Gernsback, including *Amazing Stories*, John W. Campbell's *Astounding* (renamed *Analog* in 1960, and carried on under Ben Bova after

Frederik Pohl.

Campbell's death in 1971 until 1978, and then by Stanley Schmidt from 1978 on), Herbert Gold's *Galaxy Magazine* and *The Magazine of Fantasy and Science Fiction*. *Astounding* came strongly under the influence of L. Ron Hubbard's dianetics and other pseudoscientific and mystical teachings; because of this Campbell began to lose his hitherto impregnable leadership, giving way to *The Magazine of Fantasy and Science Fiction* and *Galaxy*, and, later on, *OMNI*. This is not to say that readers suddenly altered their allegiance; according to the statistics, *Analog* was still at the head of the league in 1968–69 with a publishing run of some 92,000 copies while *Galaxy* was at about 75,000 and *The Magazine of Fantasy and Science Fiction* only about 50,000.[2]

The well-established team of *Astounding* was joined by new authors who helped define the developments that were taking place in science fiction: the decline of the space opera and the avoidance of the lowest standards of adventure clichés—that is, the inevitable recourse to blood and violence. These authors also proved themselves less reliant on scientific and technological problems, and began to introduce questions of morality and ethics, the psyche of mankind, the relations of the individual to society, and the future hopes for humanity. Indeed, some books were referred to as "social fiction." The short stories of the 1950s are of equal significance. The lift in science fiction during the 1950s has led commentators to designate this decade as the second golden age of American science fiction (the first being Campbell's). The zenith came around the year 1953.

The middle of the century witnessed major changes in publishing and printing processes. Apart from the magazines, accompanied by anthologies and collections, an increasing number of hardcover books of science fiction was issued. Classic works from the past were republished and novels that had been successfully serialized were produced in novel format. The most important change, however, was the development of the paperback book, which made production of huge quantities of very inexpensive books

187

A journey through time—back to the legendary island of Atlantis.

of only about thirty American novels and anthologies had been published in England, in the ten years following that date the number rose to about four hundred.

Following on the heels of this widening of interest, the non-English-speaking world soon showed a similar broadening of interest. In 1953 in France, two science fiction magazines were founded, one of which was a French edition of *Galaxy*, the leading American magazine. Other similar periodicals appeared, with critics (Jacques Giomard and, especially, Michel Butor) beginning to dispute problems of the genre. The fan movement spread, and new fanzines appeared. In France as in America the paperback book trade soon pushed the magazines into the background. A handful of French authors were able to de-

Serial from the Federal Republic of Germany (West Germany).

possible. The consequences of this development was the demise of most science fiction magazines, leaving only a handful to survive into the 1960s. The reading habits of the public changed so radically that by the 1970s, some 90 percent of all science fiction writings were being published in paperback editions, usually as part of a "collection."

The general influence of this new publishing phenomenon began to spread over the world. The English-speaking market opened up first of all. J. F. Clarke gives in his book *The Tale of the Future from the Beginning to the Present Day. A Checklist*[3] convincing evidence of this. While before 1950 a total

188

The American film *Planet of the Apes* was adapted from Pierre Boulle's science fiction novel.

velop their country's traditions: René Barjavel, Gérard Klein, Jacques Sternberg, Pierre Barbet (pseudonym for Claude Avice), Francis Carsalc, Julian Verlanger, Michel Jeury, Pierre Pelot, André Ruellan, Daniel Walther, Charles Henneberg, Alain Dorémieux, Philippe Curval, Michel Demuth, and so on. Pierre Boulle (born in 1912) achieved world fame with his science fiction novel *La planète des singes (Planet of the Apes)* (1963) and the film version that followed it. He also wrote *Le pont de la rivière Kwai*, filmed as *The Bridge over the River Kwai*. Gradually French science fiction became the domain of translations of English and American books.

A similar tale could be told of many other countries. In the Federal Republic of Germany (West Germany), for instance, science fiction magazines met with only limited success: *Utopia-Magazin* lasted from 1955 to 1959; *Galaxis* only from 1958 to 1959; and *Comet*, founded in 1977, closed again in 1978. The old futuristic novels and technological fantasies that had followed the lead of Hans Dominik had during World War II and its aftermath become suspect owing to their strong nationalist emphasis; another problem was that the technological invention and anticipation was now thought homespun, drab, and lacking in excitement. All the same, new editions of Hans Dominik's books were published. The project begun by the Dusseldorf publishers Karl Rauch Verlag—to publish the classics of science fiction under the series title of "Weltraum-Bücher" ("Space Books")—was,

189

Pierre Boulle's novel, creating a fantasy world peopled by apes, spawned a number of popular and money-making films for Twentieth Century-Fox.

Apart from Fischer and Rowohlt, all the main paperback publishers today have in their lists special series of science fiction and/or fantasy novels. In every instance, these series are built around a core of English-language works. At the same time, these publishers do make an effort, however great or small, to discover or encourage novels and tales by authors from other countries, especially those where German is spoken. Since the market for science fiction is largely made up of young people with limited financial resources, it is not expected that there will be a glut of science fiction.

The list of the publisher Wilhelm Goldmann includes many variations of the genre. The "Science Fiction" series accords with the principles already outlined. More recently, German authors like Werner Zillig and Gerhard R. Steinhäuser have introduced a little more originality into the genre. Thomas le Blanc edits a special series for original works in German. New emphases are discernable as this paperback series celebrates its twenty-fifth anniversary. For ex-

despite the inclusion of such names as Asimov, Campbell, and Williamson, a resounding flop.

Instead, however, there blossomed an original production in the form of lending library books and cheap periodicals serializations. From 1953 the Erich Pabel Verlag of Rastatt produced a utopian novel of the future describing the actions in outer space of "superman" Jim Parker. Another serial followed featuring Rex Corda, and then another with Ren Dhark, and so on, culminating in the "heir to the universe," Perry Rhodan, from 1961. This path was leading "to the Neanderthal, at the speed of light."[4]

The establishment of a paperback series by the publishers Heyne and Goldmann in the 1960s broke the spell. Other publishers soon followed suit. The end result of this has been that in the Federal Republic of Germany (West Germany), as elsewhere, Anglo-American science fiction has predominated.

190

ample, multivolume books at the lower end of the market and of less literary worth are published in a "Science Fiction Adventures" series. This includes the "Star Wars" books and stories based on "Battle Star Galactica." The titles indicate both its target and its aesthetic value and limitations.

As a kind of optimistic response to balance Orwell's *1984*, Goldmann published a twelve-volume *Edition '84*. These newer, and more positive searches for utopia were the works of such authors as Isaac Asimov, Harry Harrison, Frederik Pohl, Poul Anderson, and Pauline Gedge, as well as Werner Zillig and Gerhard R. Steinhäuser. In 1968, the normal science fiction series were resumed.

"Heyne SF" follows similar principles to those exemplified in the Goldmann series. Again, there is a predominance of Anglo-American works in spite of the introduction of anthologies, the promotion of certain German-speaking authors, and the inclusion of titles from other countries. Heyne's "Library of Science Fiction Literature" publishes important works of sig-

A German-language fanzine.

nificance in the history of the genre, or works that treat topical themes. A series of reprints in the form of three novels per volume, published under the title of "Chronicles of the Future," is now airing works that have been out of print for many years.

Heyne and Goldmann both publish special fantasy series alongside their science fiction publications. Droemer/Knaur, on the other hand, combine the two in its paperback series "SF/Fantasy," which covers writing ranging from the literary mainstream to the lower echelons depending only on excitement for effect. The authors featured include Philip K. Dick and Joanna Russ, as well as Robert Silverberg and Philip José Farmer. Each year sees the series expanded by one volume in which three novels are brought together and published at a special price.

191

Suhrkamp's "Fantastic Library" emerged from the series "Science Fiction of the World" (from 1971 to 1975, fifteen volumes, edited by Franz Rottensteiner) and from the mystery/fantasy of the "Library of the House of Ascher" (Insel-Verlag). Names such as Stanislaw Lem, Herbert W. Franke, J. G. Ballard, Günter and Johanna Braun, and Arkadi and Boris Strugatsky, confirm that this publishing house in particular brings out works of a higher literary quality that break through the ghettolike world of entertainment science fiction. The anthology *Polaris* also reflects this basic concept.

The "Black Fantasy Series" of "dtv" (German paperback publishers) also brings out interesting titles, as does the Swiss firm, Diogenes.

The highly diversified paperback publishers of Ullstein, Bastei-Lübbe and above all Moewig/Pabel

Cover for Swedish science fiction magazine of a later era.

Kapten Frank
och
Rymdkejsaren
En hel science fiction roman
med spännande äventyr i
rymden
Av Edmond Hamilton

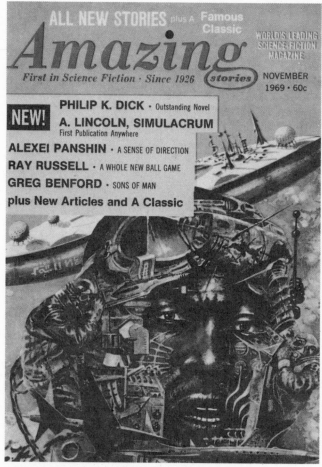

Cover for 1969 revival of *Amazing Stories*.

make more concessions to public taste, including in their lists not only mainstream literature of international repute and good popular works, but also the more trivial efforts.

Moewig/Pabel also publish, in their series "Moewig Science Fiction" under the subseries "Analogue" and "Copernicus," collections of short stories. In addition, the *Moewig SF Yearbook* comes out annually; there is also a *Moewig SF Almanac* dedicated primarily to German-speaking authors. The series "Playboy Science Fiction" has recently established itself in the market, perhaps as a result of the associations inherent in its title. It is for the most part a collection of science fiction short stories, dominated by classic authors.

The "Heir to the Universe" in a film version.

192

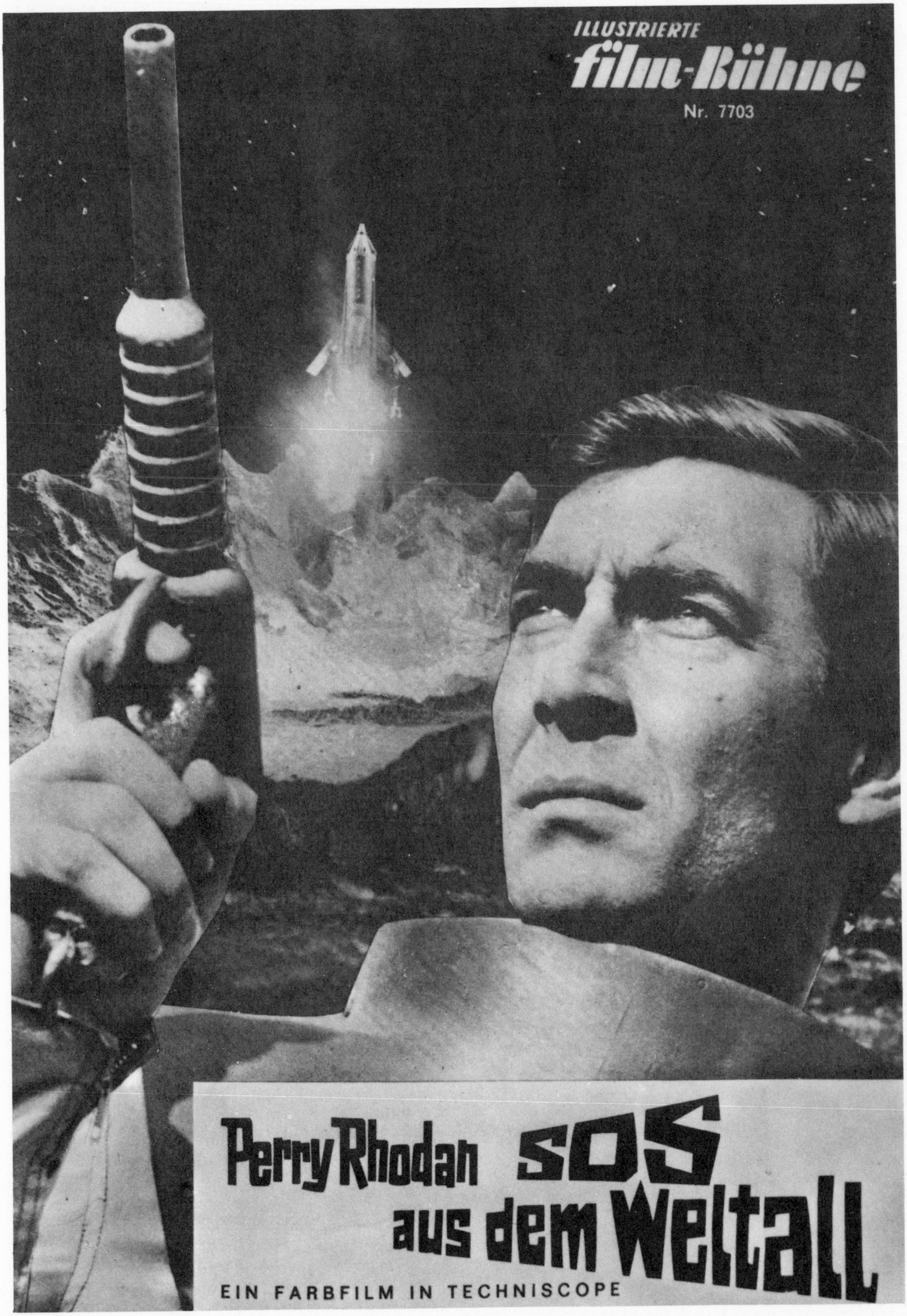

ILLUSTRIERTE
film-Bühne
Nr. 7703

Perry Rhodan SOS aus dem Weltall

EIN FARBFILM IN TECHNISCOPE

Die Dritte Macht

Das erste
Perry-Rhodan-Buch

Im Herbst 1978 erscheint der erste Band der ungeduldig erwarteten Buchausgabe von **Perry Rhodan:**

ca. 400 Seiten Vorsatz bedruckt mit Rißzeichnungen Ski-vertex-Einband mit dreidimensionalem Bild Prägung auf Vorderseite und Rücken.

Dieser Band enthält die ersten fünf Hefte der original **Perry-Rhodan**-Serie, die 1961 gestartet wurde. William Voltz, Herausgeber der Buchausgabe, hat die einzelnen Hefte neu überarbeitet und zu einem großen, in sich geschlossenen SF-Roman zusammengefaßt. In seiner einzigartigen, repräsentativen Aufmachung darf das Buch in keinem Bücherschrank eines SF-Fans und **Perry-Rhodan**-Lesers fehlen.

500 Exemplare der Gesamtauflage wurden von den Autoren K.H.Scheer und C.Darlton handsigniert. Diese Bände werden in der Reihenfolge der Bestellungen ausgeliefert. Deshalb sofort den Bestellschein auf der letzten Seite ausfüllen und einsenden!

Legen Sie mit diesem ersten Band den Grundstein für Ihre eigene

Perry-Rhodan-Bibliothek

Die nächsten Bände sind bereits in Vorbereitung! Der Moewig Verlag beabsichtigt, im Laufe der Jahre die gesamte **Perry-Rhodan**-Serie in Buchform herauszubringen.

Die Weltauflage der **Perry-Rhodan**-Serie hat die 300-Millionen-Grenze weit überschritten und erscheint in sieben Sprachen.

Die Dritte Macht

Das erste
Perry-Rhodan-Buch

DM 19,80

From the serial to the hardcover book.

Alongside standard Anglo-American works, Ullstein sets particular store by its publication of the writings of non-English speaking authors. Included in its list are the Swedish writer Sam Lundwall and the French writer Daniel Walther, as well as German authors like Andreas Brandhorst, Michael K. Iwoleit, Horst Pukallus, and Thomas Ziegler.

For the Orwellian year of 1984, Ullstein began its *Oceanic Library 1984*. Edited by Herbert W. Franke, it brings together the important dystopias, and thus operates, in a sense, as a kind of opposing force to Goldmann's *Edition '84*.

Also in West Germany, the fan movement suddenly took off and specialist amateur magazines were launched. One noteworthy fanzine of the German-speaking world was *Quarber Merkur*, published in Austria by Franz Rottensteiner.[5] *Science Fiction Times* is also well known.

Few native writers in German-speaking countries were able to resist the absolute dominance of American and British writers in the science fiction book market in the Federal Republic of Germany, Austria, or Switzerland. One West German author expressed his opinion on the matter in 1975 thus:

Since the American science fiction writers dominate practically 100 percent of the market—at least in hardcover and in paperback—the opportunities for publishing our own work are very limited. For us there are only the collections

194

Terra-Astra and *Zauberkreis-Science Fiction.*
Some dozen authors are sitting snugly at Heinrich Bauer's publishing house Pabel Verlag, where, according to reports by a chief editor, they work away at numerous weekly serials, and have practically an in-house status. Every year they have to write a predetermined number of contributions and need have no fear that the editorial board will fire them for merely failing to produce an episode in a serial.

Asked to name them, he continued:

Karl Herbert Scheer, Walter Ernsting, Horst Gehrmann, Willi Voltz, Claus Mahn, Hanns Kneifel, Hans Frankiskowsky, and Dirk Hess. These are not authors any more, but paid scribblers. Their single privilege is, apart from their high wages, that they are allowed to work at home. They are professionals. All others—perhaps two dozen—are just part-time science fiction writers.[6]

A small group of people earn a mention here less through their work as writers than through their activities as publishers, translators, or literary agents. They come mainly from the ranks of the science fiction fan movement, and often have experience of working on the fanzines. Most are now employed at publishing houses on science fiction series or books. They include the Austrian Dr. Franz Rottensteiner (born in 1942), Hans Joachim Alpers (born in 1953), Werner Fuchs (born in 1949), Ronald M. Hahn (born in 1948), Wolfgang Jeschke (born in 1936), and others.

These people have managed to help bring about a situation where German-speaking authors in western countries can have their work published.

The most important German-speaking science fiction author today is the Austrian physicist Herbert W. Franke, born in 1927 and now a resident of the Federal Republic of Germany (West Germany). Franke wrote a dissertation on theoretical physics for his PhD in 1950. His wide variety of interests, even apart from his specialist's knowledge in physics, has given great impulse to his science fiction writing: he has done cave research, he has investigated and written specialist books on cybernetics and related problems in the field of aesthetics, he has become involved in computer graphics, and is a passionate exponent of science fiction both as a critic and publisher. Above all, however, he is an author. His first contacts with the genre date back to the 1930s; it goes without saying that as a youth he, like the rest of his generation, devoured *Sun Koh* and similar publications.

Franke became a free-lance writer in 1957, and since then has published many short stories, tales, and novels. The most important of his books are the story collections *Der grüne Komet (The Green Comet)*

Cover of a Franke novel. Illustration by Hans Ticha.

195

(1960), sixty-five sketchlike short stories, *Einsteins Erben (Einstein's Heirs)* (1972), and *Zarathustra kehrt zurück (Zarathustra Turns Back)* (1977), and the novels *Das Gedankennetz (The Thought Network), Der Orchideenkäfig (The Cage of Orchids), Die Glasfalle (The Glass Trap), Die Stahlwüste (The Steel Desert), Planet der Verlorenen (Planet of the Lost),* and *Der Elfenbeinturm (The Ivory Tower),* all written between 1961 and 1965. After a break, more novels appeared in the 1970s, among them *Zone Null (Zone Zero)* (1970), *Ypsilon Minus (Y Minus)* (1976), and *Sirius Transit* (1979).

Most of Franke's work explores the relationship between scientific and technological progress, and social development. He combines the roles of scientist and sociologist as an author, and he knows how to use the interdependence and interpenetration of these points of view to create exciting and at the same time

Herbert W. Franke.

effective and parablelike situations. He moves freely around all contemporary areas of conflict and those of the future, and juggles hope, danger, and possibility. The novel *Einstein's Heirs* recalls at first *Fahrenheit 451,* but Franke extends the idea: "The development is unstoppable. If it were halted in one place, it would simply break out somewhere else."[7]

Franke's short-story plots are usually designed so that only at the last moment is an answer given to the question that has been set to puzzle the reader through the course of the work. For instance in "Cleopatra III" the utility of lifelong research is questioned; the champion of "Wir wollen Darius Miller sehen" ("We Want to See Darius Miller") turns out to be a robot; the result of brain surgery in *Präparat 261 (Preparation 261)* is to banish everything except fear; *Die Pfauen (The Peacocks)* live on electrical power; and also, for the age-old triangular problem of one woman and two men, *Tiefkühlschlaf (Deep-Frozen)* finds a quite new solution.

"Ein Kyborg namens Joe" ("A Cyborg Named Joe") ends in nightmarish fashion and warns against the loss of specifically human relations and attributes. The hope in "Der Traum vom Meer" ("The Dream of the Sea"), in which there is some chance of life having survived somewhere on the exhausted and destroyed Earth, ends in the water glass of the "Transformation Institute." Franke offers no calculated optimism or prophecies, nor does he offer nihilist warnings or pessimism that dismiss every further step as the work of the devil. He is concerned at getting to the heart of things through fantasy and to reveal the truth, however bitter it may prove to be. In this connection, he can be seen as standing alongside the most valuable traditions of bourgeois critical realism.

The features that make Franke's trenchant short stories so attractive are equally compelling in his novels. He uses the full range offered by the form, especially in his writings of the 1970s. Paradoxical ideas are used to warn against the destruction of humanity, and to caution against the loss of the individual in a cybernetically driven and motivated system of dynamics. Again and again destructive tendencies are presented as possible outcomes of undirected scientific and technological evolution. The author makes clear that he is a committed "spiritual brother" of the best writers of science fantasy in our century. Reverberations of the warnings depicted by Huxley, Orwell, Bradbury, or Le Guin of a totally manipulated and administered world are just as unmistakable as the moral rigor of Lem or the brothers Strugatsky. *Zone Zero* and *Y Minus* reflect the picture of the world and humankind as seen by Herbert W. Franke with particular clarity. Despite the tragedy, hope of a humane application of scientific and technological progress shines through. According to Franke, this can be achieved by the commitment of the emancipated individual.

It must however be realized that Franke is far from portraying technology as absolutely diabolical, as do some individuals today among environmentalists, like the "greens." Just as Franke presents his considered views on cybernetics problems in the field of aesthetics in books and articles, he likewise attempts to set down in his literary work a vision of the unity of technology and beauty in the modern world. This is the case in his depiction of Ben's place of work in *Y Minus*, where he plays with countless variants on this theme. Again, in *Zone Zero*, he writes of spaces that can transform themselves and that are full of fluorescent lights and fantastic techniques of illusion and television.

Franke writes freely of many topoi, subjects, and motifs of present day science fiction literature, mostly taking up preexisting subjects and finding new sides to them.

Close to Franke in writing elevated and yet at the same time entertaining science fiction literature is Carl Amery, born in Munich in 1922. This is the pseudonym of Christian Mayer, author of *Das Königsprojekt (The King's Project)* (1974), *Der Untergang der Stadt Passau (The Decline of Passau City)* (1975), and *An den Feuern der Leyermark (To the Fires of Leyermark)* (1979). Other such authors deserving of mention include Jürgen vom Scheidt, a doctor of psychology born in 1940, Horst Pukallus (born in 1949), whose greater commitment to social themes is evident in his short stories, especially "Das Rheinknie bei Sonnenaufgang" ("The Sharp Corner in the Rhine at Dawn"), and Thomas Ziegler (pseudonym for Rainer Zubeil, born in 1956). Some authors have specialized in children's books, for instance, Eva-Maria Mudrich, Michail Krausnick, Jo Pestum, or Rolf Ulrici.

Dieter Hasselblatt is not only the foremost West German writer on the theory of the genre, but is also a supporter of many science fiction radio plays. Through his efforts dozens of such plays have been brought to an audience of millions. This has undoubtedly helped to dispel public prejudice against science fiction.

The position is similar in many countries to that described above relating to France and West Germany. Well-loved authors in Italy include Inisero Cremaschi, Vittorio Curtoni, Gustavo Gasparini, Gianni Monatanari, and Piero Prosperi; in Belgium, Eddy C. Bertin, and Hugo Raes; and in Sweden the Nobel prize winner Harry Martinson (1904–78), who in his verse epic *Aniara* (1956) describes the flight of the last survivors of a world catastrophe in a spaceship towards nothingness. But everywhere the domination of Anglo-American science fiction in all its forms was felt. This had the effect, mainly, of flooding each country with shallow and trivial products, having a decisive impact on the great mass of the readership. Science fiction all over the world was placed alongside a large output of commercial fiction that concentrated on action and external elements. Concerted efforts to renew national science fiction was unable to stem the tide.

At the end of the 1950s and the beginning of the 1960s, several authors, mainly of the younger generation, set to work against these all-conquering conventions, standard situations, and stereotyped settings, against the lack of inspiration and the never-ending supply of banalities, and tried to effect a thorough transformation of science fiction. When the young British author Michael Moorcock took over the publication of the English magazine *New Worlds*, he gathered around him a group of writers who were to go down in the history of science fiction as a "New Wave." Franz Rottensteiner said that there was not in fact so very great a difference between the old and the new science fiction, and that the quarrels surrounding the group could be traced back to the contradictory, somewhat vague though heavily polemical leading articles of Moorcock himself rather than the actual contents of the magazine.[8] Much attention was attracted

Michael Moorcock.

by "scandals" like questions raised in the House of Commons concerning subsidies given to *New Worlds* when Norman Spinrad's *Big Jack Barren* was printed. This included obscene words that shocked some people.

Moorcock's 1964 attempt to redesign the magazine *New Worlds* as a periodical of the science fiction avant-garde was successful for only a few years. The "New Wave" reached its crest in the middle years of the 1960s. This was the time of growing protest against the Vietnam War, of student unrest, and turmoil among the young. As this movement's vigor abated in the late 1960s, enthusiasm for the renewal of science fiction declined also. The magazine was forced to close in 1970, and even the quarterly *New Worlds* collections produced later by Moorcock and his erstwhile colleagues found only limited favor.

Moorcock's own writings were unable to stimulate any new impetus. *An Alien Heat* (1972) is quite probably his most popular work, but his series of "Jerry Cornelius" novels, featuring what he called the "myth figure of the twentieth century," was his breakthrough. Beginning the series with *The Final Program* (1968), he continued with four follow-ups—*A Cure for Cancer* (1971), *The English Assassin* (1972), *The Lives and Times of Jerry Cornelius* (1976), and *The Condition of Muzak* (1977)—to make up *The Cornelius Chronicles*. Eventually Jerry Cornelius appeared with the Moorcock character "Miss Brunner" in a comic strip in *International Times*, drawn by Mal Dean. The adventures, chronicled by various other writers as well as Moorcock, were collected in book form in *The Nature of the Catastrophe* (1971), edited by Michael Moorcock and Langdon Jones. Moorcock's main influence on science fiction was felt mostly in the editorial vein, although his fictional works were entertaining and well received in a critical sense.

The most significant member of the so-called Moorcock group was J(ames) G(raham) Ballard, born in 1930 in England. Ballard's short stories and some of his novels have succeeded in attracting readers through their rich style and sharp inventiveness of language and form. Ballard's work shows a movement away from traditional science fiction towards what may be termed "inner space," the exploration of the psychic events in the progress of mankind. This is especially true of his short stories dating from the middle of the 1960s, but is also observable in his two novels *The Drowned World* (1962) and *The Crystal World* (1966). He himself has called his type of writing "fiction of psychological fulfillment." Generally recognized as his best works, these two books involve individual reactions to doomsday catastrophes that have overtaken humankind. In *The Drowned World*, for example, the hero winds up traveling south towards the Sun—and towards certain death. Nevertheless, Ballard points out that this move is "a sensible course of action that will result in absolute psychological fulfillment" for the hero.[9] *Crash* (1973) is a departure from his earlier books, set as they are in distant landscapes. It takes place in the world of today, and is an ugly and neurotic story, almost in the horror genre. Two years later *High-Rise* appeared—equally con-

198

temporary, but certainly more fun to read. The *Unlimited Dream Company* (1979) is a fantasy of life fulfillment, full of surreal images and odd-ball events.

As to writing technique, Ballard uses all the well-established and traditional literary devices familiar to mainstream literature at the beginning of the twentieth century: present-tense narration, interior monologue, abandonment of linear description of events in time sequence, and stream-of-consciousness. Ballard says that science fiction, primarily a prospective literary genre dealing with the immediate present in terms of the future rather than of the past, demands narrative techniques that reflect its themes. Until now, he argues, all authors (not excepting himself) have ignored this because they have failed to realize that the foremost narrative technique of retrospective prose—namely the relating of a tale in a continuous, orderly development recording a predetermined complex of

Brian W. Aldiss.

events—is wholly unsuitable to the creation of pictures of a future that has not yet arrived. *The Best Science Fiction of J. G. Ballard* (1977) serves as a good introduction to his works in the short-story form, including brief forewords by the author to elucidate each piece. He considers his novels "condensed novels" rather than simply novellas. He claims that the length of the ideal science fiction novel should be closer to 40,000 words than 60,000, the accepted conventional wordage. He seems most comfortable writing in this truncated length.[10]

Such a lifting of the aesthetic quality and adoption of the narrative techniques of modern "genuine" literature should in turn have led to a renewal of subject matter and content and the rejection of the old clichéd ideas. This demanding program was however only partially achieved in practice. Most science fiction literature remained immune to the new theory, or those writers who tried harder tended to be met with blank stares and were commercial failures.

In connection with Ballard, Brian W(ilson) Aldiss must also be mentioned. Born in Norfolk, England, in 1925, he was already an established writer when he became enthused by the Moorcock group's ideas and wrote some experimental texts of his own. His first science fiction novel was *Non-Stop* (1958), published in America as *Starship*. It was the author's attempt to "humanize" a genre that he felt had become remarkably *de*humanized and inundated with clichés and claptrap. He selected the classic science fiction motif of a society enclosed in a spaceship on a voyage destined to last for generations, and tried to breathe life into it. Although the book was not generally considered a tremendous success, it did contain bits of vivid imagery and a sense of compassion. Later he came out with *Hothouse* (*The Long Afternoon of Earth* in America), a fantasy of the future in which mankind has been reduced to primitivism, forced to live in a world dominated by gigantic and threatening vegetation. A novel composed of various incidents—it was actually a series of short stories strung together—the book won a Hugo Award in 1962. In *The Dark Light Years* (1964), mankind comes to terms with friendly aliens who are, disgustingly enough, coprophiliacs. *Greybeard* (1964) poses an interesting problem: what happens to a world in which there are no children?

199

One watches with some apprehension as each old person dies, one by one. *Cryptozoic* appeared in 1967. *Report on Probability A* (1968) analyzes the process of observation and its effects on the essentiality of realism; *Barefoot in the Head* (1969) is a series of short stories set in a future in which weapons of destruction are hallucinogenic drugs. Mary Shelley herself appears in *Frankenstein Unbound* (1973) as the hero indulges in a bit of time travel. *The Malaca Tapestry* (1976) is a simple romance set in an eternal mystic city of the future.

An American author who agreed with Moorcock's and Ballard's aims, as well as those of Aldiss, was Thomas M(ichael) Disch, born in 1940 in Des Moines, Iowa. Typical of his "New Wave" work is *Camp Concentration* (1968), in which a group of leftist intelligentsia are locked up in a concentration camp to be exploited by the state. The novel is in the form of a diary of a man fed a drug to heighten his intelligence—all as an experiment in the service of the state. The drug has the unfortunate side effect of inducing death within a matter of months. It is a tricky piece of stylistic narrative; Disch had to write the diary of a man who knows he is going to die, and whose intelligence is steadily increasing to superhuman levels as he faces death. The result is a most interesting study in style and analysis. The book is of course a sharp attack on the misapplication of modern medical methods—something out of Mary Shelley. In this work Disch maintains the tradition of world literature exemplified by Thomas Mann's *Doctor Faustus*, which is quoted in the book, and which confronts the problem of intensified intellectual and creative talent through the pathogens of syphilis. Disch's first science fiction novel, *The Genocides*, was published in 1965, describing the unknown arrival of alien plant life that turns the Earth's ecology upside down and renders civilized existence impossible. The human survivors who try to rid the Earth of this alien life form are immediately exterminated as pests. Disch is interested in studying the human psyche in relation to odd pollutions and poisonings of its environment—not always with happy results for the human race. Equally dangerous to Disch is the pollution and poisons in the social conditions that mankind allows to grow up around him. *On Wings of Song* (1979) is a fantasy

that deals seriously with the question of freedom, creativity, and the human spirit. His novel *334* is a gloomy vision of the America of the future, condemned by some as nihilistic. It presents a world, according to Disch, in which problems like "death and taxes are considered insoluble, and the welfare system is *not* seen as some totalitarian monster that must call forth a revolt of the oppressed masses."[11] Disch points out that most problems in life cannot be solved by a hero in some symbolic act of rebellion. "That's not what the world is like, so there's no reason the future should be like that."[12]

Other American New Wave writers include John T. Sladek, born in 1937 in Waverly, Iowa. It seemed almost as if Sladek was indulging in practical jokes when he turned his characters loose on the science fiction genre and pulled it inside out to laugh at it. His humor has a dark side that is constantly present. *The Müller-Fokker Effect* (1970) is the story of a man, Bob Shairp, who becomes reduced by a computer to data stored on a tape. By playing around with this concept, Sladek is able to indulge in satirical thrusts at various familiar targets like evangelism, journalism, the media in general, the United States army, religion—almost everything that suits the arsenal of the average satirist. Another character who inhabits numbers of Sladek novels is Roderick, an almost-human machine. He appears in *Roderick: Or, the Education of a Young Machine* (1980) and *Roderick at Random: Or, Further Education of a Young Machine* (1983).

Another New Wave figure is Samuel R(ay) Delany, born in New York City in 1942. In his early novel, *The Ballad of Beta-2* (1965), Delany began to probe the truth about normality. In other words, what are the parameters of normality in such things as human beings or animals? When does the freak cease to be a human? Does he ever cease to be a human? Are these parameters existential and ever-expanding and contracting? In the closed "locked-room" milieu of the spaceship *Beta-2*, Delany's characters are forced to redefine normality to solve political and sociological problems that crop up during a long space flight. Delany, reaching maturity during the strife-torn years of the 1960s—with that period's emphasis on ethnicity and racial differences—perceived "normality" as

200

a function of coercion, manipulation, and corruption. In 1971 Delany produced his trilogy *The Fall of the Towers*, composed of *Captive of the Flame* (1963), *The Towers of Toron* (1964), and *City of a Thousand Suns* (1965). From this he moved on to his novel *The Einstein Intersection* in 1967, which he made his own eloquent statement of the science fiction genre. *Intersection* is a complex and mind-boggling literary experiment. Its problem is manifold. Not only does it involve a story line that is different, but it also involves many levels of different kinds of symbolism and allegory. In addition, the story utilizes a number of standby science fiction motifs—that of alienation, for example, in the form of a physical "difference." In fact, whole groups of characters are "different." The hero Lobey is a twenty-three-year-old freak. So are his companions. But there is not time to linger on that fact: almost immediately the novel breaks into separate parts, with figures of certain symbolism emerging. The villain is Kid Death, an obvious representation of Billy the Kid; but also Kid Death is a specific monster out of mythology, and in one episode even becomes the Bull of Minos. Lobey in turn takes on various characteristics. In the Bull of Minos sequence, he becomes Theseus, and strangles the Bull in a cave, later meeting Kid Death on a color television screen, recognizing him for what he is. When Lobey's girlfriend Friza is suddenly murdered Lobey is obliged to find her killer. Eventually another figure enters the story—this one called Green-eye. Green-eye is a Christ figure, the only one Kid Death cannot control. The interplay of these levels of story is too complex to go into here, but suffice to say that there is the realistic level, the mythological level, the religious level, and the scientific level. Lobey—and Delany—are forever trying to discover the "norm" and eventually they find that the norm must keep changing perpetually. Thus the "Einstein line" intersects the world and human life, to carry it on to manifold divergences. There are bits and pieces of all types of literary genres and subgenres in the writing—Kid Death in one small interlude acts out the Western fiction genre from which he came. Lobey finally manifests his own power—as great in its way as Kid Death's and Green-eye's: Lobey can play music. It is the creation of music—read, art—that makes Lobey/Delany triumph in

the end. Even Green-eye/Christ must use the artist to guide and instruct. A "mythic science fiction bildungsroman," one critic calls it.[13] Implicit in the entire reading process, and indeed in the wanderings of the hero Lobey, is the difficulty of distinguishing reality from illusion. The difference between the real and the illusive during the 1960s was a most important daily consideration. The inability to differentiate between the two—because of the drug culture, the Vietnam War experience, and ethnic struggles, the assassinations, the unreality of the world—led to the destruction and self-destruction of many people during that time. Delany's work reflects that and elaborates on it—in a "new" kind of science fiction vein. *Nova* (1968) is Delany's multiplex reading of a future galactic society. *Dhalgran*, which appeared in 1975, involves a study of the lost city of Bellona, looking at the characters, their various relationships, at art and reality, and at the entire fictional world of the "lost city" through Delany's eyes.

The name of Roger (Joseph) Zelazny, born in 1937 in Cleveland, Ohio, is frequently linked with Delany's in retrospectives of New Wave science fiction writing in America. However, Zelazny's brand of "new" was actually a return to the purer kind of storytelling initiated by Edgar Rice Burroughs in his Mars, Pellucidar, and Venus stories. Like Delany, Zelazny preferred to construct his stories on typically familiar mythologies. *This Immortal* (1966) is a hodgepodge of various old Greek myths, used as underpinning for a tale about aliens from a distant planet who mean to take over and operate Earth as a kind of enlarged Disneyland. The hero, a muscular and ingenious Ulysses type named Conrad Nomikos, has intellectual insight and spouts poetry as well as practices the martial arts against his enemies. The idea is that he is one of the old Greek gods returned to life to save humankind. *The Dream Master* (1966) concerns psychiatrists of the future who learn the art of manipulating dreams and thereby cure their patients of various neuroses and psychoses, but capture their initiatives. The hero, Charles Render, dominates the story line, with undertones of Regnarok, the Quest of the Holy Grail, and the Tristan and Isolde legend—lending mythology to Zelazny's topos. For the literary cognoscenti there is a great deal of allusion in this modern tale. *Lord of*

Light (1967) takes place on a far-off planet in the distant future—and yet concerns an exploration of Hindu mythology in a society in which the gods are real people. The hero, Hamasamatan (known as "Sam") liberates the masses repressed by an evil, rigid, hierarchical religion. *Creatures of Light and Darkness* (1969) features the Egyptian gods in another mythological story line. Zelazny's work more or less reflects the sixties individual's search for a style, for a cultural entity—through experiment with old mythic patterns. Lately, Zelazny turned to a new project, the Amber mythos. The five Amber books are: *Nine Princes in Amber* (1970), *The Guns of Avalon* (1972), *Sign of the Unicorn* (1975), *The Courts of Chaos* (1978), and *The Chronicles of Amber* (1979).

Another writer identified with the New Wave of science fiction is Harlan Ellison, born in Cleveland, Ohio, in 1934, where, as he constantly repeats, he was the object of a "lot of violence" and "an awful lot of hatred and bigotry and alienation." In turn this led him to write about alienation and bigotry and disillusion. Primarily not a science fiction writer—he has said to assert angrily "that he doesn't write science fiction"—he began writing about teenage gang life in Brooklyn in the late 1950s and early 1960s. *Web of the City* (1958) and *Memos from Purgatory* (1961)—in no way science fiction novels—are still in print, attesting to their documentary power and authenticity. Mainly his stories during the sixties and seventies involved themes of rebellion, alienation, and violence—very characteristic of that period. In spite of his derogatory attitude toward science fiction, Ellison's stories frequently crop up in anthologies, and he occasionally visits a science fiction convention if only to collect another award or two. Typical of Ellison's output is the short story "I Have No Mouth, and I Must Scream" (1967), anthologized in *Science Fiction: A Historical Anthology*, edited by Eric S. Rabkin. The title is almost the explication of the story. It explores the relationship of humanity to machinery, using biblical allusions involving the story of Jonah and the whale. The machine—read, giant computer—is, in Ellison's eyes, a monster that mankind had invented. It has no limbs, and no organs, but is pure intelligence: a focal point, a bull's-eye of human obsession. A line from the story evokes the general mood of the piece: "Perhaps Benny was the luckiest of the five of us: he had gone stark, staring mad many years before."[14] Here's another, from the non-mouth of the "monster"—read, computer intelligence—"HATE. LET ME TELL YOU HOW MUCH I'VE COME TO HATE YOU SINCE I BEGAN TO LIVE."[15] The narrative ends with the story's title. Needless to say, the machine-monster has once again won, swallowing up the modern Prometheus who created it.

Cover illustration for Kurt Vonnegut, Jr.'s *Cat's Cradle* and *The Sirens of Titan.*

THE SECOND HALF OF THE TWENTIETH CENTURY

Inspired by the New Wave writers, a number of other Americans helped to introduce a "fresh" tone to science fiction at the beginning of the 1960s. One of them—perhaps the foremost—is Kurt Vonnegut, Jr., born in Indianapolis, Indiana, in 1922. Ironically enough, Vonnegut is really a mainstream writer whose works were for some reason categorized and marketed as science fiction at the beginning of his career. It was obvious early on that Vonnegut had an antic sense of fantasy and allegory, but it was hardly typical science fiction stuff. His first novel, *Player Piano* (1952), is an ironic commentary on automation, on technological breakthroughs, and on the evils of American big business: hardly the kind of thing to excite a science fiction fan. However, his second book, *The Sirens of Titan* (1959), is almost pure science fiction—conventional, at least, in structure and insight. By the time *Cat's Cradle* (1963) was published, it was obvious that Vonnegut was being erroneously categorized. *Cat's Cradle* has an invented religion, acceptable to the science fiction genre, but its unconventional structure and its ending—complete catastrophe with irreversible results—is scarcely in the conventional genre. Of course, *Cat's* interesting concept of "foma"—the telling of lies to make for human happiness—certainly fits into the satiric science fiction vein, but the book was a bit surrealistic for proper sci-fi fantasy. As science fiction, these Vonnegut books were received by the fraternity with somewhat lukewarm acclaim. By now Vonnegut was confident and gaining power as a writer himself, and when *Slaughterhouse-Five: The Children's Crusade* appeared in 1969, it was obvious that he was actually a mainstream author with only slender claim to fame as a category writer. Nevertheless, many of the science fiction genre's favorite elements continued to appear in his works—time warps, doppelgängers, utopian and dystopian worlds, space travel, and so on. After 1969, Vonnegut's early works suddenly appeared in reprintings—this time being reviewed by the publishing establishment in New York! It had taken *Cat's Cradle* ten years to be "received." After his breakthrough into the mainstream, Vonnegut continued to write the same kind of books he had always written, but now they were reviewed by mainstream reviewers and Vonnegut was suddenly an *in* figure. *Breakfast of*

Champions appeared in 1973, and *Slapstick* in 1976—both featuring characters created earlier but now involved in the irony of the future. Vonnegut's novels are all basically pessimistic, although he does not necessarily *admit* that they are. He came into science by the back door, working for General Electric as a publicist in his early years. His brother is a full-fledged scientist, hardcore. "It's just superstitious, to believe that science can save us all," Vonnegut once said. "We're starting to back down on a lot of our technology now."[16] Generally, his attitude towards humanity is the same as that depicted in *The Sirens of*

Titan—a blind mob pursuing high aspirations secretly manipulated by "higher forces" to satisfy trivial whims. "I get curious about—what if there was a God who *really did care*, and had things He *wanted done*. How inconvenient that would be!"[17] Typical of Vonnegut's capricious style and sly humor is the title page of *Slaughterhouse-Five*. It reads:

> Slaughterhouse-Five
> *or*
> *The Children's Crusade*
> A DUTY-DANCE WITH DEATH
> BY
> Kurt Vonnegut, Jr.
>
> A FOURTH-GENERATION GERMAN-AMERICAN
> NOW LIVING IN EASY CIRCUMSTANCES
> ON CAPE COD
> [AND SMOKING TOO MUCH],
> WHO, AS AN AMERICAN INFANTRY SCOUT
> *HORS DE COMBAT*,
> AS A PRISONER OF WAR,
> WITNESSED THE FIRE-BOMBING
> OF DRESDEN, GERMANY,
> "THE FLORENCE OF THE ELBE,"
> A LONG TIME AGO,
> AND SURVIVED TO TELL THE TALE.
> THIS IS A NOVEL
> SOMEWHAT IN
> THE TELEGRAPHIC SCHIZOPHRENIC
> MANNER OF TALES
> OF THE PLANET TRALFAMADORE,
> WHERE THE FLYING SAUCERS
> COME FROM.
> PEACE.

One writer unmistakably in the science fiction genre who brought in a sense of "newness" in the 1960s was Frederik Pohl, born in New York City in 1919, who began his career in concert with another writer, C. M. Kornbluth. Together, the two of them pioneered and developed a completely new kind of science fiction that might be called "sociological sci fi" with alternative futures here on Earth, satirizing social forces and trends in real life that most other writers in the genre perceived dimly and cared less about. The Pohl-Kornbluth subgenre of the form was complex and sophisticated—much too difficult for most writers to handle and for many readers to assimilate. The team produced probably the best sociological science fiction published to that date. It involves insights into economics, into mass media, into big business, into advertising—into almost every facet of modern life. *The Space Merchants* (1953) was the first collaboration of the two writers and is the book most associated with Pohl's name. A cynical and accurate visualization of space travel as a commercially exploitable enterprise, it remains a classic of its kind. In 1959, the collaborators produced *Wolfbane*, another classic. *Gladiator-at-Law* (1955) is a satirical look at the legal profession and its logical future. Pohl himself published his first work in 1937, at the age of sixteen. When he was eighteen he became a magazine editor. A working professional from the start, he turned out a number of stories and books on his own before teaming up with Kornbluth. One of his most important shorts is "The Midas Plague" (1954). A collection of his short material appears in *The Best of Frederik Pohl* (1975). Pohl's early novels include *Slave Ship* (1957), *Drunkard's Walk* (1960), and *A Plague of Pythons* (1965). In 1977 he won the Nebula Award for his novel *Man Plus*. This deals with a biological adaption of a human being for life on Mars. Pohl won both Nebula and Hugo Awards for *Getaway* (1977), and brought out *Jem* in 1979. He once observed: "In science fiction one can say a great many things that are unpalatable that people normally prefer not to think about. Because it's expressed as fiction, you can slip it through their defenses."[18] Thus, science fiction can provide all kinds of new insights into technology, natural resources, space travel, and much more—including inner space. Science fiction, Pohl points out, allows the writer to change the world and not be forced to depict it as it actually *is*. "Most of the problems of the human race are human inventions," he believes. "I'm not as convinced as I once was that political solutions are possible, but some sort of social solutions are necessary."[19]

In France there were parallel moves in the 1960s towards a renewal of the genre. The country was alarmed at two events in particular, each of which contributed to the transformation of the national

204

science fiction scene: the war in Algeria; and the student rebellion of 1968. The changed national psyche led to the introduction of new themes and problems into science fiction that until then were unheard of in the French version of the genre. In place of noncommittal entertainment there was now, albeit distanced or disguised, criticism of current conditions (Daniel Walther, René Sussan, Dominique Douay, and so on). An understanding of this background is necessary for a true appreciation of the well-known writer Robert Merle (born in 1908) to science fiction subjects, problems, and motifs, which he employs so convincingly in his entertaining exposés of our century: *Un animal doué de raison (A Reasoning Animal)* (1967), *Malevil* (1972), *Les hommes protégés (The Protégés)* (1974), and *Madrapour* (1976).

After the upheavals and soul-searching in international science fiction caused by the emergence and activities of the New Wave, science fiction settled down to a more sedate life in the 1970s. Writers like Walter M. Miller (short stories, "Anyone Else Like Me?," "Dumb Waiter," "Command Performance," and a best-selling novel, *A Canticle for Leibowitz* [1960]), Robert Sheckley ("Trap," and other stories), Damon Knight ("To Serve Man" [1950], "Four in One" [1953], and "Country of the Kind" [1956]), and other writers, continued to consolidate the gains made by the introduction of this "new" tone in the science fiction genre. Still unbroken, however, was the sway that Anglo-American science fiction held over all the western countries, despite the growing numbers of authors in non-English-speaking countries who were achieving international reputations. A random selection of such authors and books might include Japan's Sakyo Komatsu's *Nippon Chinbotsu*, published in America under the title *Japan Sinks* (1973), and his compatriot's Kobo Abe's *The Fourth Interglacial Period*, or Denmark's Anders Bodelsen's *Frysepunktet (Bruno's Frozen Days)* (1969). Major authors of the younger generation have come now to be counted among the (still living) classics of science fiction and are of crucial importance in directing the future of the genre.

Even though the New Wave cannot be said to have succeeded in all its aims, it cannot be denied that it did contribute to the fact that nowadays some science fiction is of far higher literary standard than formerly. That, in spite of the fact that the continuing popularity of the bug-eyed-monster motif and the alien conquerors from space topos in motion pictures drove and drives many intelligent science fiction fans up the wall. The concern for writers to move beyond conventional clichés and standard situations is now an intrinsic aim of many authors today.

Most popular among these, especially with the student intelligentsia, were Thomas Pynchon, author of very attractive books that played freely with ideas,

Illustrated cover of Damon Knight's doomsday novel
The People Maker.

Kobo Abe.

Sakyo Komatsu.

and Philip K. Dick. Pynchon, born in 1937 in Long Island, New York, wrote elaborately conceived mainstream books that were distinguished by complex plots combining the techniques of the mystery genre with that of the science fiction genre. In the larger sense, the metaphors of his works show a decaying world degenerating into chaos and aberration. In *V* (1963) its anti-hero hunts alligators in New York's sewers with his friends, the Whole Sick Crew. The novel's alter-ego, its hero-hero, searches the world for V, the mysterious female spy and anarchist—Venus, Virgin, Void. *Gravity's Rainbow* (1973) won the National Book Award, and features mood swings from black humor to lyrical glee, with fantasies elaborately interwoven with the realities. The point in all these complexities is purposeful ambiguity—with the "rainbow" of human happiness sinking inexorably into Pynchon's oblivion and despair.

As for Philip K(indred) Dick, nothing in his novels is ever quite what it seems to be. Born in Chicago, Illinois, in 1928, he spent his maturing years in Berkeley, where he went to college and worked in a bookstore. Addicted to science fiction from the age of twelve, he also found himself involved with the reading of Proust and Joyce. His books, of which he has written scores, have not all been published. Some deal with the drug culture of the 1960s, religious fan-

tasy, and so on. He won the Hugo for *The Man in the High Castle* (1962), which pictures a world in which World War II was won by the Axis Powers. Hawthorne Abendsen is a novelist, the "man in the high castle"—because he lives in the Rocky Mountains. The novelist's vision of life is a somber one that permeates the story. In 1964 Dick published *The Three Stigmata of Plamer Eldritch*, a book seemingly about acid heads and the drug culture, but actually about an alien invasion and takeover in a true science fiction vein—chillingly conceived and executed. *The Zap Gun* appeared in 1967. *Flow My Tears, the Policeman Said* (1974), is one of Dick's best, a book in which Jason Taverner, a television "personality" crosses over from reality into another "reality" that is drug-induced, and in which he does not even exist! The following year Dick produced his autobiography, *Confessions of a Crap Artist*, offering interesting points of view on his thoughts and his feelings. "The greatest menace in the twentieth century is the totalitarian state," Dick has said. "It can take many forms: left-wing fascism, psychological movements, religious

The popularity of "bug-eyed monster" science fiction thrillers such as *Gorgo* on the big screen in the 1960s caused paperback novelizations of these works to flourish.

206

The Gripping Story Of A City Threatened With
Annihilation By A Raging Prehistoric Monster

MM603
MONARCH BOOKS
35c

MONARCH
MOVIE
BOOK

GORGO

Carson Bingham

This classic thriller is now on the screen as a
spectacular King Brothers' Technicolor Production

Robert Silverberg.

became worthy of much more serious attention—for example, Brunner's *Stand on Zanzibar* (1969) and Silverberg's *Towers of Glass* (1970). John (Killian Houston) Brunner, born in Preston Crowmarsh, Oxfordshire, England, in 1934, produced his best work mentioned above at the close of the sixties—using the country Zanzibar simply as an area of land to which millions of people could be shipped in his novel of overpopulation, pollution, and human congestion. The novel is triple-layered, each story zeroing in on a popular discontent of the 1960s. One involves a hyperactive computer called Shalmaneser. Another is a think piece on modern morality, expressed by a "hippie"-type philosopher. A third has to do with international terrorism—predicted by Brunner as far back as 1969. His *The Sheep Look Up* appeared in 1972.

Robert Silverberg, born in New York City in 1935, began to change his direction in *Thorns* (1967), a novel in which he started the painful process of self-evaluation. In *Nightwings* (1969), he explores a future world that is entering its fourth cycle of civilization. This is a work actually about rebirth and metamorphosis, about aberration, and its cure. *Up the Line* (1969) is a tongue-in-cheek exercise in the time-warp motif. *Towers of Glass* (1970) is a new slant on the old theme of androids. *Downward to the Earth*, also 1970, shows man's isolation, and explores guilt, sin, punishment, and expiation, in Silverberg's terms. In his 1971 Nebula Award winning novel, *A Time of Changes*, Silverberg's messianic hero, Kinnall Darival, takes on Bortham, a puritanical, stern world in which civilization has become frozen into a cold, Calvinistic type of existence—an exaggeration of Early Colonial Puritanism in the WASP sense. The "covenant" by which people live forbids them from using the terms "I" or "me." An Earth alien, noting Darival's inability to express his love in any way, feeds him a mind-expanding drug, which transforms him and is the beginning of the change in his rigidly controlled society. Silverberg's intent is obviously to prod man into coming out from behind the masks one is forced to adopt in any social milieu. *The World Inside* (1971) is a new look at the old bugaboo of overpopulation. *Dying Inside* (1972) centers around telepathy as a natural function of the hero, David Selig. Because of what he knows about his acquaintances, he be-

movements, drug rehabilitation phases, powerful people, manipulative people; or it can be in a relationship with someone who is more powerful than you psychologically. Essentially, I'm pleading the case of those people who are not strong."[20] Dick's worldview is one of strange contradictions and not-entirely-pleasant eventualities. It is a world in which no one can tell the real thing from the false, in which no one can tell the drug-induced hallucination from the vision of reality. It is a world of people beset by problems from within and from without—but who nevertheless struggle gamely onward towards a glimpse of hope or the hope of a glimpse of hope.

In the 1960s John Brunner and Robert Silverberg both made astounding alterations in their previous output of science fiction; from prolific producers of conventional goods they became authors whose books

208

comes alienated from everyone as an object of fear and dread. His godlike powers are his curse. *Time Enough for Love* (1973) is a story involving incestuous relationships.

And now for probably the "biggest" sci fi writer of the sixties and seventies—Frank Herbert. Born in Tacoma, Washington, in 1920, this prolific and best-selling science fiction author died in 1986. Fame did not come to him quickly. Although he had dabbled in science fiction for some years and had published a novel as early as 1955, Frank Herbert never came into his own until the publication in 1965 of *Dune*, the first novel of what was originally to be a trilogy called *Dune World. Under Pressure*, his 1955 novel,

John Brunner's *Stand on Zanzibar.*

was a more or less routine story, without the impressive combination of elements that would make up the complex and solid *Dune*. Herbert was a newspaper reporter on the West Coast for a number of years during which he covered science and ecology. It was from this background that he drew on details that finally became the *Dune* concept. Mixing political intrigue and strange religions was nothing new in the science fiction writer's bag of tricks, but Herbert seemed to work the combination better than anyone else. Predicating a dry planet in need of water to support life, and paralleling that idea with the fact that the three great religions of Judaism, Christianity, and Muhammadanism all came out of the desert, Herbert constructed a solid mythos to support his fictional idea. Using Greek mythology as well—his hero Paul Atreides gets his name from the doomed house of Atreus in Greek mythology—Herbert built an "epic" that depicted the development, the expansion, and the diversification of a religion and a political struggle set in an alien world. Paul Atreides's mother, for one story twist, proclaims herself as a new messiah; Paul leads his people on a *jihad* to conquer a planet to support life, for another. The first two works, *Dune* and *Dune Messiah* (1969), complete this part of the fable, with *Dune Messiah* relating the overthrow of the "god" created in *Dune* to weld the people together. The third book, *Children of Dune* (1976), is a tale of ecological struggle and political intrigue, with religious mysticism, the lore of the desert, and extremely complex intrigue and chicanery moving the story along. These three books completed the *Dune* trilogy, published together in 1979 as *Dune Trilogy*. Then in 1981, Herbert returned to his old theme with *God Emperor of Dune*, followed by *Heretics of Dune* (1983), and *Chapter House Dune* (1985). In all, the eventual six books about Dune World comprised 2,300 pages, and almost a million words of writing. This is a massive and powerful work—with both good and bad in it. The first two titles are the most artful, and complete in most ways the author's vision of religion, politics, and ecology—the message he knew best how to deliver. The remaining four books depend on plot—particularly political machinations—to make them go. Nevertheless, the whole is a monumental undertaking and achievement.

209

(1966) studies an interesting idea of cyborgs, or robots, who re-invent man after mankind's wipeout. *The Green Brain* (1966) explores man's dependence on insects, with some mutating to giant sizes after an attempt to destroy them all. *The God Makers* (1972) is a kind of codicil to Dune World.

During this period of strong science fiction production, mainstream authors continued to utilize elements of the genre in an effort to infuse life into their own works. In England (John) Anthony Burgess (Wilson) conceived a daringly original environmental en-

Anthony Burgess's *A Clockwork Orange* contains plug for upcoming film of novel by Stanley Kubrick.

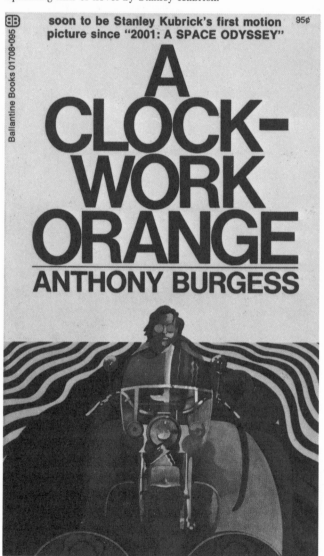

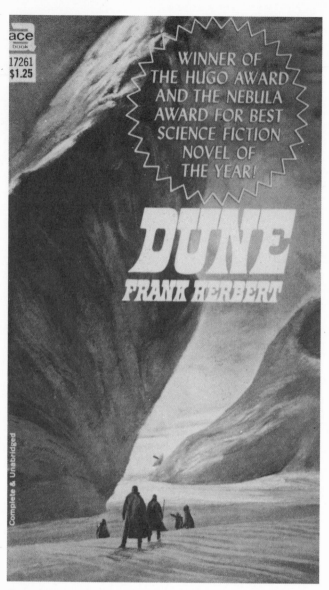

Cover for Frank Herbert's acclaimed award-winning novel, *Dune.*

At the same time he was writing his *Dune* books, Herbert continued to turn out novels with no connection to them. *The Dragon in the Sea* (1956) concerns an attempt to steal oil from the bottom of the sea held by an enemy state. *Destination: Void* (1966) is a story of a rocket trip to seek an Eden in place of the doomed Earth, but a computer fails and . . . *The Jesus Incident* (1979) is a sequel to *Destination: Void*, with clones and test-tube babies squared off against natural birth and natural intercourse. *The Eyes of Heisenberg*

210

tity in *A Clockwork Orange* (1962). Born in 1917 in Manchester, Lancashire, Burgess conceived a dystopian world of the future in which youth gangs rape women and attack the helpless and the aged. The people in this "world," apparently the result of Russian invasion, speak in a kind of fractured Russian slang, or "Nadsat." A reader has almost to learn a new language to wade through the dialogue, although most of the Russian-oriented words are fairly obvious in context. It was Stanley Kubrick's motion picture version of this book that made Burgess a household name in America and the world—as well as in Great Britain. In the same year as *Clockwork*, Burgess wrote *The Wanting Seed*, another dystopian novel, in which overpopulation causes propagation to become suspect, and homosexuality the proper modus operandi. In the end the hero effects a return to heterosexuality.

In America, (John) Michael Crichton, born in 1942 in Massachusetts, used his medical background to explore several important science fiction elements in various novels. *The Andromeda Strain* (1969) was his breakthrough. In this thriller, later made into a riveting motion picture, a mutating microorganism accidentally loosed upon the Earth from a satellite high in the atmosphere threatens the entire world with destruction. After killing all but two people in an Arizona town, the microorganism is isolated, but in the action, a fail-safe mechanism is initiated, which will send nuclear bombs to start a worldwide atomic holocaust. It is now up to the survivors to disarm the mechanism to prevent the destruction of the world. *Binary* (1972), written by Crichton under the pseudonym of John Lange, involves the imminent assassination of the President by a mad millionaire who has tapped into a closed-code computer mechanism to free a lethal nerve gas. John Gray, an intelligence agent, is deployed to prevent the killing. Crichton's script for *Westworld* (1971) became a motion picture starring Yul Brunner in 1973. *Zero Cool* appeared in 1972. The Robin Cook thriller *Coma*, with screenplay written by Crichton, was released in 1978; the plot involves the disappearance of a number of people and the eventual discovery of an organ-transplant bank—a kind of bizarre updating of Burke and Hare's body-snatching orgy in nineteenth-century Edinburgh. Crichton's writing style—clean, brisk, full of

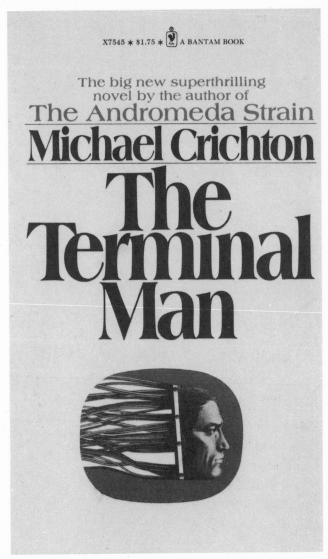

X7545 ★ $1.75 ★ A BANTAM BOOK

The big new superthrilling novel by the author of *The Andromeda Strain*

Michael Crichton
The Terminal Man

Paperback version of *The Terminal Man*, a Michael Crichton science fiction novel.

action, and fast-paced, with nicely etched characters, snapping dialogue, and surprising plot twists that keep the reader (and viewer) guessing—has proved ideal for the screen, both large or small.

Although (Edmond) Rod(man) Serling started out as a radio and television writer, he became known primarily for his two fantasy and science fiction series on television. Born in Syracuse, New York, in 1924, he moved from radio and television scripts to television production, inaugurating in 1959 a series called *The Twilight Zone*. This half-hour anthology ran for five

Scientists watch spellbound as robot machinery tries to isolate killer microbe from outer space called *The Andromeda Strain.*

years, through 1964, using scripts written by Serling himself and by other well-known authors such as Richard Matheson, Charles Beaumont, and Ray Bradbury. Generally, the scripts concentrated on the story values inherent in the characterizations themselves, with fantasy and science fiction elements usually relegated to a supporting background. A time-warp concept would simply back up the *real* story of two characters caught in this kind of impossible situation. In some, a science fiction element might predominate. Typical is "The Fever," in which a slot machine acts as the villain intent on destroying a compulsive gambler. When the show was cancelled in 1964, Serling came up with a new series—*Night Gallery*—in the

same year, which won an Emmy Award. Printed collections of Serling's own stories for the two series appeared in the 1960s. It was Serling who, with Michael Wilson, wrote the eminently successful screenplay for Pierre Boulle's fantasy novel *Planet of the Apes* (1968). Serling's dialogue has been considered convincing and serviceable, with its focus on story and character, rather than on fantasy or science fiction. In effect, Serling wrote science fiction for people who might actually hate science fiction without really knowing what it is.

One of the brightest of all the new American talents is Ursula K(roeber) Le Guin, born in 1929 and therefore no longer to be reckoned among the

212

"younger" generation of authors. Le Guin began writing in the 1960s and was immediately recognized as a major writer at the forefront of science fiction. She has received many honors confirming her unusual position in the history of science fiction. Apart from tales and children's books, she has published long novels which have been translated into many languages. *The Left Hand of Darkness* (1969) is a book that, according to Stanislaw Lem, is to be counted among the great books of literature. She probes important questions of human existence from a liberal and humanist

Cover for a collection of Rod Serling's short stories adapted for his television series *Night Gallery*.

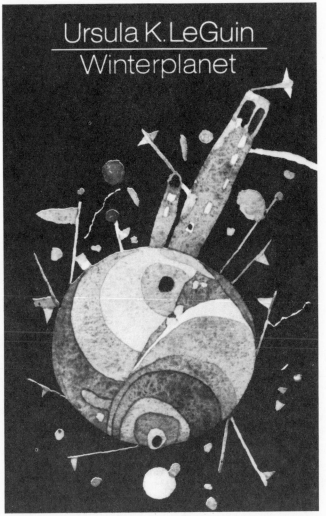

A new German-language edition of Ursula K. Le Guin's novel *The Left Hand of Darkness*. Illustration by Horst Hussel.

point of view. The strangeness of the planet Winter, whose inhabitants are hermaphrodites, raises large questions for the reader on the basic conditions of human life and social evolution.

The Dispossessed (1974) tells the story of the tragic Shevek, a brilliant physician. He lives on the dry and barren planet of Anarres, which, 160 years previously, opened its doors to the rebellious anarchists migrating from the rich neighboring planet of Urras. Anarres is too poor to realize Shevek's inventions, but on the other hand, the temptation to accept an invitation to the well-endowed parent planet con-

213

tradicts all his sense of morality. The harsh conditions on Anarres can only be survived if all inhabitants are absolutely equal.

Shevek however decides to accept the invitation, and is able to continue and expand his work in the generous conditions of the institutions on Urras. He sees much in this comfortable society, reminiscent of modern consumerism, to reject—especially the disrespect accorded women. In the end Shevek discovers his hosts are planning to utilize his work in a plot to subdue the cosmos. The ambassador of Earth is able to offer him the opportunity to return home. Shevek has learned that the society of Urras can offer nothing that the inhabitants of Anarres are lacking. He is fully aware that on his return home he will be called a traitor and stoned. He also understands that, even if his life is saved, he will not be able to continue his work as a scientist without any materials. This "open" ending provokes the reader into considering the alternatives. Ursula K. Le Guin has set new standards for western science fiction in these books and shows herself and the humanism she represents to be at one with the aims of the important authors of science fiction literature in the socialist countries.

Attempts to expose the position of women in modern bourgeois society, as seen in Le Guin (and in Robert Merle's *The Protégés*) are also to be found in the so-called feminist utopias[21] of the 1970s. These include *The Female Man* (1975) by Joanna Russ, and *Woman on the Edge of Time* (1976) by Marge Piercy. Russ, born in New York City in 1939, started out as a professor of English in the early sixties, but also at the same time became an ardent feminist. She entered the science fiction field—in her case call it more properly a battlefield—in the early seventies, after the sixties were done. Her first two major feminist works in science fiction were *The Female Man* and the short story "When It Changed" (1972). The short story won a Nebula Award. It features Janet, the protagonist, who lives on the planet Whileaway, a colony of humans out in space, where all the men have died of a plague nine hundred years before. The women now fill all the roles of life, are married to one another, and produce children by ovum-sharing. Janet and Katy have a daughter, Yuki. Earthmen land on Whileaway, and cannot understand why the women do not welcome them as saviors—and lovers. Now their lives will be complete! Janet, saddened at the thought of knowing that the men will indeed join them, sits forlorn and morose at the loss of the world she has always loved and cannot imagine changed. Likewise, at the end of *The Female Man*, Russ looks forward to the day when her book will hopefully become irrelevant, its work will be done, and in her words: "Rejoice, little book! For on that day, we will be free."

Piercy, born in 1936 in Detroit, Michigan, started out as a poet, in fact, a "radical feminist lesbian" poet. *Dance the Eagle to Sleep* (1970) was her first science fiction novel. It depicts a society like the intense and fractionated 1960s. A group of teenagers drop out to become a "tribe of Indians," as their leader Corey puts it. The society "outside" is a dystopia, with rock music used by the state to control minds. Women have no rights. The "Indians" mount an attack on New York City, and a band of National Guards are sent out to hunt them down and destroy them. Piercy intends this situation to be a parallel to the sixties. *Woman on the Edge of Time* (1976) takes place in the year 2137. This is more a utopia than a dystopia, with the scene of the action an agricultural village in which families are composed not of people related by blood, but of people related by love. Children are incubated, born to three mothers, either male or female. There is no sexist language at all. "He" and "she" become "per"—obviously a substitute for the unisex word "person." In the story, Connie, the thirty-seven-year-old heroine, is a mental patient: she is Everywoman Who Suffers, she is Madwoman, and she is Time Traveler. Her trip takes her to an alternate future, this one a dystopia where genetically altered women are kept in tiny apartments waiting to serve the males who come to them for their sexual favors. The point is obvious.

Among other feminist writers in the science fiction genre is Alice Hastings Sheldon. Born in 1916 in Chicago, Illinois, she was the daughter of an explorer and a writer; she went on a 2,700-mile trek across Africa when only ten years old. After some time spent in US intelligence, she and her husband helped shape the CIA, for which she did photo-intelligence work for some years. In the 1970s she began writing science

214

Judith Merril.

fiction with a definitely feminist slant. But she did it as an alter ego, a man named James Tiptree, Jr., whom she made up as a CIA agent who might make up a cover for her true identity. "Houston, Houston, Do You Read?," written in the seventies, is typical of her work in the short-story field, and a neatly dramatic offering it is. Three male astronauts, returning from an orbit of the Sun find themselves unbelievably caught in a three-hundred-year time warp, returning to Earth in the future. As they run out of fuel above the atmosphere, a spaceship piloted by women rescues them. They learn what a future they have come back to! All males have been wiped out by a plague. Females reproduce by cloning. After the males recover from their shock, they begin fantasizing on their unbelievable luck. Only three men alive—and all those women! But the women turn the men down, pointing out that with no aggression in their lives women are much happier *without* men.

In another story, "The Women Men Don't See," a woman opts to go to a distant planet with aliens rather than stay on Earth with its typical man-woman problems. "I'm used to aliens," the protagonist finally explains to the man she is leaving at the end of the story. *Up the Walls of the World* (1978) involves a government research project into ESP. *Brightness Falls from the Air* is a sort of extraterrestrial whodunit.

Short story collections of Sheldon/Tiptree's work include: *Ten Thousand Light-Years from Home* (1973), *Warm Worlds and Otherwise* (1975), *Star Songs of an Old Primate* (1978), and *Out of the Everywhere* (1981).

Zenna Henderson (née Chlarson), born in Tucson, Arizona, in 1917, began writing science fiction fantasies in the 1950s about a humanoid alien race that resembles mankind and that has fled its own planet to come to Earth. Paranormal and far advanced mentally and psychologically, the humanoids became persecuted as witches by the inferior humans with whom they make contact. Writing in the short-story form, Henderson collected these stories about "The People" in 1975 from the two volumes: *Pilgrimage: The Book of the People* (1961) and *The People: No Different Flesh* (1966). In 1971 William Shatner (Captain Kirk of *Star Trek*), Kim Darby, and Dan O'Herlihy made a film called *The People*, taken from Henderson's stories.

(Josephine) Judith Merril (née Grossman) was born in 1923 in New York City. Although she is usually considered a reviewer of science fiction, an anthologizer, and an editor, she has produced her own works as well. "That Only a Mother" is a short story about the effects of radiation and the power of love to blind the lover to flaws in the loved one. Her novel *Shadow on the Heart* (1950) points up the dangers of atomic energy. In it a suburban woman and her two daughters cope with the aftermath of a nuclear attack, with the woman's husband trapped in Manhattan. Merril is quietly feminist, focusing simply in this story on the domestic ability of the heroine to cope with atomic radiation and eventually to fend off the unwelcome advances of a male neighbor. *Daughters of Earth* (1968) is a collection of Merril's short stories, featuring six generations of female space explorers. "Home Calling" involves a girl and her baby brother shipwrecked on a planet where there is no human life. She eventually allows the two of them to be adopted by a grossly repulsive alien "mother." "Project Nursemaid" is a story about the selection of candidates to run a foster-mothering house for babies born in space. Merril collaborated with C. M. Kornbluth in two novels, using the pseudonym Cyril Judd: *Gunner Cade* (1964) and *Outpost Mars* (1952).

Women writers in the mainstream of literature, like men, sometimes try to weave science fictional elements into their works for freshness and vitality. Margaret Atwood, the distinguished Canadian poet and novelist, recently did so in *The Handmaid's Tale* (1986). Born in 1939 in Ottawa, Atwood had written a number of novels—*The Edible Woman* (1969), *Surfacing* (1972)—a feminist classic!—*Lady Oracle* (1976), and *Life Before Man* (1979) before trying a modern fantasy-utopian novel in 1986.

Atwood's vision of the future can be called dystopian at best. The country will be ruled by right-wingers and religious fundamentalist fanatics. Males will be warriors; females will be child-bearers, child-rearers, and cooks. Yet the world is run by women, although policed by men. Females are divided into classes, color-coded: green for housemakers; blue for wives; red, blue, and green stripes for workers; red for "handmaids" who bear children for the heads of households; brown for aunts, the agents of thought control. Books have been banned. Magazines are verboten. Even word games are forbidden. Homosexuals are hated, shunned, banned. There is no pornography allowed in this superbiblical puritanical world. Infertility is a general problem. Mutant syphilis and AIDS have lowered the birthrate considerably. "The regime," the author has remarked in a discussion of the book, "gives women some things the women's movement says they want—control over birth, no pornography—but there's a price."[22]

216

THEMES, SUBJECTS, AND MOTIFS IN MODERN SCIENCE FICTION

In science fiction there are well-established science fantasy situations; to express it more simply, certain literary elements—a situation, a device, interest, or incident—appear again and again. They are used in varying degrees and are joined with a wide range of other elements to form science fiction plots.

Such situational building blocks—called "motifs"—always have a structural function in the text as a whole. When removed from context, they can, in isolation, easily lead to incorrect conclusions, especially when made to stand alone. If one bears in mind that all literature, including science fiction, is basically about human beings, a study of human motifs can be a worthwhile, if incomplete, exercise. Attention must be paid to their particular meaning in the text, the expression and nuance given to the motif, and its development by the author—including the way it is incorporated, and the way in which any and every piece of literature may be reduced to a motivic framework.[1]

In science fiction certain situations are favored for a period of time, and are then replaced by others, so that one or other motif might appear in a spate of works and then fade away forever. These in themselves give clues to the story's historical, cultural, and literary background—for example, the prevalence of utopian stories, the dominance of technological euphoria in the space opera, or the theme of doomsday or catastrophe. Certain authors tend to prefer particular motifs and can handle them especially convincingly—space travel, robots, rockets. When the social situation alters or when a new level of technological development is attained particular motifs lose their potency or become entirely irrelevant in serious science fiction—for example, the use of birds' wings as a method of flying, or the discovery of human inhabitants on the Moon, Mars, or Venus, which has all but disappeared from science fiction in recent years.

It is unnecessary to trace all the motifs drawn together in any single work; such an analysis would serve no purpose. But each work has main motifs that are central to it, either in structure or in plotting.

Closely related to the motif is the "topos"—a theme or topic. In science fiction this means a typically formal situation that at some time has been added to the common stock of science fiction and has in the meantime come to be regarded as a tradition in the genre. The topos is usually associated with a number of motifs that are customarily all brought together in the same fashion. In some cases a topos may be reduced to the status of a motif, so that the terms motif and topos merge.

One well-known topos in modern science fiction is the Adam-and-Eve situation in which a group of people have survived an atomic blast or other doomsday incident and must now begin humanity anew.

To bait buyers of books and to apprise readers the topos and main motifs of a book may be indicated in a subtitle, blurb, or annotation on its cover. Specific

217

Nr. 888

DM 2,-
Österreich S 18,-
Schweiz sfr 2,20

Italien Lire 1400
Frankreich FF 6.-
Niederlande hfl 2,50
Spanien Ptas 100,-

Perry Rhodan
der Erbe des Universums

**Die grosse WELTRAUM-SERIE
von K. H. Scheer und Clark Darlton**

2. Auflage

Überfall der Malgonen

Die Welt des LARD in Gefahr – die Ungeheuer kommen

motifs and topoi in modern science fiction are widely recognized.[2] Some authors and literary theorists fight against the more obvious ones in their attempts to renew the genre, especially when uncreative and imitative settings recur in the more popular literature.

They landed on the Earth—and buried themselves in the depths of the ocean.

They believe the space pilot to be a murderer—all the same they give him the chance to unravel the secret of the evil flower.

Only when a young man led the people of his race from the dingy jungle into the light of day did a new future begin for the forgotten people of the planet without a name.

He came from an alien world and turned humans into monsters.

The Terranian empire is in danger—a skirmish in space is the first whisperings of a struggle for the continued existence of mankind.

They are the forgotten soldiers—their quarters become ghost ships.

They want to compel the universe—and they vanquish eternity!

A signal awakens him to life—then he broaches the sun and begins his work of destruction.

A call from the stars—but who is calling Terra?

Rex Corda hunts the telepathic strangler of the dark stars.

They come from the void—but they don't return to the void.[3]

In the above quotes, Franz Scheck shows that he fully agrees with the American author John T. Sladek, to a certain extent the mouthpiece of the whole western New Wave group. Sladek says in his attack on the

An "alien" from a science fiction serial.

usual run of science fiction that he has long detested stories glowing with nineteenth-century scientific optimism, stories about space merchants, time tourists, and horrific "alien" races. How many new such ideas can be set before the public Sladek does not profess to know, but he supposes they may take the following forms:

(1) The telepathic superchild.
(2) The robot (or slimy extra-terrestrial) who saves a life.
(3) In a thousand-year war of the pangalactic empire, the space ranger Jack is just carrying out his routine patrol, when suddenly . . .
(4) The hero's time machine carries him off to the year—.
(5) "1984" revisited.
(6) The steel grey eyes of the hero see the solution to a technical problem by which he will rescue the girl, the spaceship, or even Earth itself.
(7) The strangers rule despotically over the enslaved Earthlings, until the hero discovers the well-kept secret of their vulnerability.
(8) One of us in the space station is in reality an android planning to destroy us all.
(9) The great computer makes just one tiny mistake.
(10) The last human being on Earth.
(11) The new feudalism after the GREAT ATOMIC WAR.
(12) Woken up after a hundred years of deep frozen sleep, the hero is desperately needed.
(13) Just as he is being hounded by the black uniformed robot police, he is able to flee to the underground movement, a secret league of sweet old men and pretty young girls saves him and the universe.
(14) The leap to a parallel universe.[4]

In this attack there is much truth, but its general thrust is dubious. Only authors and publishers can claim responsibility for what is made of this. The decisive element is always the questions posed in a piece of writing and the answers offered by the author in his

219

or her particular arrangement of motifs and topoi and in their attractive and exciting presentation.

If one starts with the premise that science fiction is a branch of literature that offers metaphors of life in a pseudoscientific guise, it is possible to isolate the following important motifs and topoi: (1) Self-knowledge and human nature. (2) People and society. (3) People and technology. (4) People and time. (5) People and space. (6) Human beings and "aliens." We are going to discuss them in the following chapters.

SELF-KNOWLEDGE
AND HUMAN NATURE

Scientific fantasy literature in all its stages of development, of whatever quality, is an "imprint" of how mankind regards the world.[5] By the experience of reading it contributes to a knowledge of human nature. The reader suffers vicariously with the figures portrayed and rejoices with them, loving and hating as they do, identifying with them or feeling how distant they are. This in itself provokes reflection, engenders emotions, and perhaps even arouses passions.

In this way many complicated psychological, sociological, and aesthetic processes interact. One thing is of the utmost importance: the literary work helps the reader to understand the spiritual and intellectual content of human society.

In science fiction, as in other modern literary forms, the center of the stage is taken by the relation of the human personality to nature, to society, and to itself. It is stipulated that this genre presents the characteristics of mankind in its biological and social aspects primarily by the external means of plot and action. The main effect is one personality acting on others.

A deep study of human nature is thus precluded in science fiction because real people are shaped by everyday experience, thoughts, and feelings—not by plot and action. There are exceptions, including works influenced by the New Wave and the exploration of "inner space," and also in the recent general tendency to reflection in mainstream literature. Mankind's consciousness of its existence is portrayed mostly by stepping over the boundary of what nature has reserved for us and discovering modes of intervention in the natural rhythms of life.

Even in the early stages of social development, people understood the limits life imposed on them and dreamed of breaking through. Myths, fairy tales, sagas, religious traditions, and works of fantasy down the centuries are full of this: barren couples are suddenly able to bear the wished-for child; or special "aqua vita" heals invalids; immortality separates gods from humans; corpses are brought to life; Sleeping Beauty awakens young and fair; people are reconstructed from their bones and brought to life again; people are magically turned into animals; a suit made of swansdown enables the owner to fly; Daedalus and Wieland the smith manufacture their own artificial wings and escape confinement by flying; others fly in trunks, by magic rings, on saddles, or magic carpets; beautiful princesses live with magic fish in underwater castles; and so on.

These are all dreams of overcoming limitations. Heroes and heroines are confronted continually by the two basic limits of life: birth and death. The latter is often associated closely with its frequent precursor, illness. Science fantasy literature presents the biological nature of mankind with evidence that it too dreams of overcoming these natural limitations, the beginning and the end of each individuality. Triumph over death is a motif particularly ancient and potent.

Fantasy literature often rather fatuously bases its dreams of a longed-for future on a presumption that progress in medicine, and all other branches of knowledge, will solve the question of illness. There are examples of medical computers to which patients or even the dead persons are presented. The machine's sensors probe the subject and formulate superaccurate diagnoses, suggesting courses of treatment. Operations are carried out by fantastic instrumentaria (laser beams are the minimum for most authors), parts subject to wear and tear are renewed,

220

and after the process the patient jumps up from the operating table as good as new and ready for fresh tasks. A variation of this theme is sometimes offered in which such techniques are available to "aliens," at a higher stage of development, but not yet to humanity. Such fantasies have given rise also to visions of a stage when our biological barriers are completely vanquished and age and wisdom can flower like Methuselah. A person old by today's standards appears as still young.

Because this dreamed-of vision lies far in the future, some authors put their heroes to sleep in freezing conditions, to deliver them to an age when the art of healing is perfected. This is not only a case where time is overrun in order to portray a desired society of the future, but also where biological limits on life are overcome.

Modern science fiction now includes the expectation that many trends recognizable in the various disciplines today will be extended into the future, often expanded beyond recognition and applied in ways quite different from the expected.

Traditional love stories can be incorporated in several ways: the close confinement of men and women for many years aboard a spaceship; triangular conflicts, mostly consisting of one woman and two men; or even the love between a beautiful princess from another planet and a man from Earth. There is a short story by Pierre Boulle—"L'amour et la pesanteur" ("Love and Gravity")—in which the events of a wedding night are made the stuff of poetry under conditions of weightlessness.

On the other hand the problems of the abnormal propagation of living creations has long inspired writers of fantasy. After Mary Wollstonecraft Shelley had led the way in extending this motif to the creation of a monster from organic material in her *Frankenstein*, there have been countless variations—most merely refined or vulgarized with pseudotechnology. Ever more fancy machinery is developed, hardly understandable terminology is brought into use, and an aim is declared to create a human better, more rational, and more strictly programmed to its specific tasks than man himself. Cloning, a favorite process today, is based on the scientific discovery that all genetic information is contained within each and every cell—the operative word here is DNA (desoxyribonucleic acid)—and thus it is possible for the ingenious scientist or laboratory team to copy a genius once, twice, or even a hundred times. Breeding thus produces identical humans and a variety of humans, each containing the collected information of all input material. Fantasy has even produced a "Universal Program for the Perfection of Humans" (in Vladimir Zavchenko's *The Triple I*). Such eugenic fantasies have a dangerous side: intensive production of humans with desired qualities necessarily involves a culling of those with less desirable properties. This work often becomes a testament to social manipulation—in effect, a kind of fascist ideology. Many authors use this motif to sketch out social warnings. They show the possible mistakes that could follow such genetic engineering.

This is at the root of the connection drawn by so many writers between genetic engineering and the motif of the sorcerer's apprentice. The challenge of biological law redounds on the originator who has blindly seen only his research work and not its consequences. A favored variant is the case where a computer decides that the scholar is not worthy of life and isolates him from the community.

In the antiutopias of the twentieth century, an important role is played by overstepping biological limits. This device reinforces the dystopian message—for example, the programming and determination of test-tube babies in Huxley's *Brave New World*.

Another common motif is that of transplantation. In science fiction this process was anticipated long before the first such operations actually took place, though the interest for literature was not so much in the events of the operation itself as in the literary opportunities it presented and its possible results and effects. For instance, after the loss in an accident of his hands a musician is given those of a murderer—which turn out to have their own will, acting in total opposition to the wishes of their new owner. Similar variations—the amphibious man who breathes through gills, or the caped human who flies like Batman or Superman—crop up again and again. Especially beloved is the most complicated transformation of all—brain transplant. From this idea authors have developed enormous offshoots: the total personality change; the development of human attributes in ani-

221

mals; and, most popular of all, the continued existence of the brain after the death of the person.

The obverse of such motifs is experimentation with new forms of birth, such as virgin births (parthenogenesis), or sex change. These are rare and for the most part take place on other planets.

In recent years the motif of mutation has played a major role in science fiction. It is not commonly used now as it was in the beginning to describe possible developments in the future, but rather to show the horror of a nuclear war and the changes such a conflict could set into motion. In humanist works of science fiction, mutation serves as a warning about the dangers of atomic energy, and pleads for a well-thought-out policy for its use. In western science fiction an atomic war is often the means by which the social system is changed in the future. In socialist scientific fantasy works the premise is that human reason will prevent the outbreak of a nuclear war. Earth-based space travelers on foreign planets may be forced to face the results of an atomic blast. Usually there is an attempt to aid the affected inhabitants who may be horrendous mutant forms, or to establish a development by which the inhabitants may become normal again.

Experimentation with other possibilities of crossing the bounds of human nature arise less frequently—for example, the increasing miniaturization of the personality subjected to an unknown radioactive ray.

In a science fantasy from the German Democratic Republic (East Germany), seven generations of progressive miniaturization have reduced the people to the size of a normal thumbnail. Alongside this is a corresponding miniaturization of all machinery—including everything from helicopters to atom bombs. This "miniaturization" is described as taking place under the aegis of an apostle of imperialism. The "minis" begin to fight in the bill of a swallow, landing on the nipples of "normal people." They successfully obtain help, and ensure a future of gradual normalization.[6] Such fantasies are prefigured in the work of Lasswitz *On a Soap Bubble*, though with the distinct aim of imparting popular science, and, to take the classic case, in Swift's *Gulliver's Travels*, which plays so effectively with the idea of altered sizes in human nature.

Another ploy to track down the essence of human nature is the distortion of biological rhythms. The question addressed in these stories is this: How would it be if everything continued in its present normal pattern except for the biological rhythms of one individual, accelerated or slowed down by experiment or chance? The classic presentation of this idea is H. G. Wells's *The New Accelerator*. More modern variations offer little that is new in this area, other than new effects and gags.

Very popular in Anglo-American science fiction are so-called supernatural effects. Invisible beings, telepathic people, and the like abound, mostly emanating from foreign stars or created in the aftermath of future wars fought with terrifying weaponry. Equally popular are situations in which every movement made on Earth is traced by an alien life form that inhabits another planet and that is preparing to attack Earth. Space travelers in the region of the alien planet are rendered helpless. The author is more often than not tempted to deliver a bombshell in the form of some entanglement or other that somehow produces a happy end for the Earth.

A close relative of the "telepathic" hero, or villain, is the figure who possesses extrasensory perception, differing from his or her neighbors because of these supernatural insights. The abilities of these detectives can be lifted into the realm of the unbelievable, especially in the more popular literature. In other books, the terrible lamentable isolation of such persons is featured. Ideas like soul transplants and other supernatural phenomena are to be found only in western science fiction.

Other motifs involve the influencing of people's thoughts and feelings. Stony-hearted ogres are transformed into mild creatures capable of love and anxious to be generous, their changes in character described in terms of pseudoscience rather than mythology.

Most recently fantasy story lines have included the alteration of personality by means of drugs, intoxicants, and other pharmaceutical preparations. In the last twenty years especially, as the drug-trafficking industry has grown, these plot elements have become ever more widespread. In science fantasy literature from the socialist countries this motif is used to in-

222

dict the dangerous machinations of multinational drug manufacturers.

There has also been an increase in the number of science fiction works that explore the dimensions of the "inner space" of human beings, awakening consciousness of psychic areas, describing associations and reflections to detail stream-of-consciousness and questions of the ultimate meaning of life. These motifs belong to the more demanding science fiction titles and often meet with incomprehension in mass-circulation works of the genre. But it is these very stories that help us, through the aesthetic experience of reading, to approach a true understanding of life possibilities and their limits. The most recent works of Stanislaw Lem and the brothers Strugatsky, and even Vonnegut's *Slaughterhouse-Five* and the works of Ray Bradbury, Ursula K. Le Guin, and Herbert W. Franke belong to this group.

THE INDIVIDUAL AND SOCIETY

If one attempts to penetrate, evaluate, and give a literary description of human nature (apart from its biological parameters), it is of course necessary to recognize the inseparability of the individual and society. Even in stories dealing with the isolated individual such as Robinson Crusoe or Caspar Hauser, his relationship to society is always part of his thinking even in his separatedness.

Works of authors who subscribe to an unscientific view of society—for example, those who base their works on myth or religion—consider the relationship between the individual and society, even if only in answer to an intuitive prompting. Very often contemporary society, as the author experiences it, is felt to be unsatisfactory, inhuman, and restricting to the growth of the human personality. The author's imagination sets itself the task of describing a dreamed-of society, oftentimes vague, but sometimes delineated down to the last detail. Again one can identify here a case of overstepping borders, not of the natural extremes of individual life (birth and death), but in real historical situations. Dreams of a better life, or fears of an inhuman existence have been part of mankind's thoughts since its earliest days. In myths and religions there are Golden Ages, paradise, the prevision of a millennium under the sovereignty of God, and hints of the world's demise, a biblical flood, hell, the Last Judgment, and the Twilight of the Gods. In fairy tales one finds fabled countries where wishes are fulfilled, and where sleepyheads inhabit the Land of Cockaigne. Apostles of salvation in all ages tempt their audiences with the promises that they alone know the way to a better future, and offer a picture of this improved world that answers the hopes and aspirations of those they address.

This is similar to the pattern described earlier, where sociological portraits have been presented in works of science fiction and its precursors, where there was no thought of fantasies set in distant places or times but where the starting point was and is always the author's present-day world. He or she recognizes the negative influences of contemporary social, and tries to offer criticism of existing conditions by presenting an alternative idealized picture that embodies his or her intentions. Such an author will always be fully aware of the fact that the idealized picture can be shown only as an aim to be striven for, which may hardly be realizable in the foreseeable future.

For these reasons, the dreamed-of society was for some centuries set at a distance from the author's world—in a place remote from the author's own, or upon the Moon or Sun. As the world was increasingly explored and opened up, fewer uncharted places were left, and thus the opportunity for setting up an idealized society removed in place was diminished. Consequently, there was an increase in the number of shipwrecks and chance landings on unknown islands, where survivors experienced a better way of life. They then penned "reports" after their return home. Later there were portrayals of fantastic alternative states in the interior of the Earth or hidden behind a

223

range of mountains. Since the turn of the twentieth century, the possibility of an inaccessible setting on the Earth itself has become virtually nil. And so began the change to a setting on other planets, even in other galaxies, whenever the author's choice fell on a spatial displacement in the action of the story.

Since the last thirty years of the nineteenth century, the idea of temporal rather than spatial displacement of setting, already experimented with in the eighteenth century, has become the traditional mode of presenting an ideal society. The hero whose destiny it is to pass on knowledge of the new world no longer travels to a strange and distant country, but now stays in his own domain and witnesses life a hundred years or more hence, and is therefore able to critique his own time by comparing it with this vision of the future.

This literature was given its name by Thomas More in *Utopia*, which contains his own program of social reform. Utopian literature has for a long period of its history concerned itself basically with social criticism. That is the reason the more important of such books were viewed up to the nineteenth century primarily as works of politics and philosophy, and only secondarily as belletristic literature.

Most of the classical utopias from the sixteenth to the eighteenth centuries bear traces of utopian-communist thinking and depict societies that have in common the essential ownership of the means of production and of land, despite their differences in detail. With the development of Marxism, and therefore with, as Engels put it, the "development of socialism from Utopia to a science," utopian dreams became less convincing. From that time on hardly any philosophical utopias have deserved to be taken seriously. The most superior works, for instance those by Bellamy and Morris, represent attempts to carry on the line of socialist sketches of the future. Very often the means by which problems are solved is technological and scientific progress. It was popular belief that through as yet unguessed scientific discoveries, through inventions and machines, mankind would be automatically led into a wonderful state. But even before the turn of the century some voices were raised for varying reasons, telling of the other side of unbridled technological advance.

In the twentieth century the tradition of delineating positive social development declined sharply. Utopian communities figure hardly at all in modern science fiction. An approach to this is made by B. F. Skinner in his 1948 novel *Walden Two*, in which he refers to Thoreau's *Walden*. All the same, it seems questionable whether this book by the world-famous behaviorist psychologist should be counted as a utopian work, since its emphasis is on a nostalgic and idyllic solution to the problem.

The utopian threads in socialist science fiction derive from the concept of social development along specific lines towards communism. Socialist writers therefore confine themselves in the main to describing the details of communist society: towns laid out on generous and at the same time efficient lines, machinery placed at the service of mankind, massive progress in health care, and a plenitude of wonderful people all acting reasonably. Concrete details of social institutions on the other hand are signally few, often being present in outline only or simply taken for granted.

In a few cases the utopian society reaches beyond the bounds of the Earth. The archetype of this is Yefremov's *The Andromeda Nebula*, with its ring of the galaxy.

The last great bourgeois utopias came from the pen of H. G. Wells, who also wrote important works that emphasized the swing towards social experiment in scientific fantasy. There began the development of the great antiutopias, or dystopias (Greek: *dys* = bad, rotten; *topos* = place; horror land). In such works authors expressed their anxieties, their mistrust, their pessimism. The most famous of these, famous far beyond the boundaries of science fiction interest, include Zamyatin's *We*, Huxley's *Brave New World*, and Orwell's *Nineteen Eighty-Four*.

But dystopian threads are not confined to modern antiutopias. Many other works that profess a quite other thematic direction, or which do not concern themselves primarily with the portrayal of imagined worlds, contain antiutopian elements. At the root of this there is the fundamental connection between dangerous tendencies in the development of society and the rise in the number of warnings. Thus in the 1950s, in the period of McCarthyism in America and

224

the cold war, there appeared important dystopian sketches of the future, in which a fully developed social system is depicted, as in Kurt Vonnegut's *The Sirens of Titan* or Ray Bradbury's *Fahrenheit 451*. With the easing of political tension the whole world over, dystopian works faded from popularity, or were displaced in fictive parallel worlds—for example, in Ursula K. Le Guin's "Ambiguous Utopia" (according to the sub-title) in her novel *The Dispossessed*. Most authors of science fiction in the 1960s and 1970s limited their critique of society to one or two particular aspects, creating specific warnings about, for example, youth crime, environmental pollution, over-population, hunger, discrimination of races, dealing with unpopular people, and so on.

Utopian and dystopian works figure again and again in the history of science fiction even in the form of fake specialist books such as R. C. Churchill's *Where Is the World Going?—Shorter History of Tomorrow and the Next Day 1957–6601*[7] in which the author extrapolates the ideas of *Nineteen Eighty-Four* and pictures a possible future for mankind in the seventh millennium. Robert A. Heinlein offers in more than twenty novels and stories a picture of human development over some 550 years (1960–2500).

In toto this "future history" and the similar cycles of Cordwainer Smith, Poul Anderson and other authors offer a future with elements of both utopia and dystopia, with plots full of tension that bear witness to the particular outlook of the particular author.

Antiutopian works of socialist science fiction are set mainly on far distant planets, and offer analyses of dangerous tendencies in human development. In the 1940s the main point of attack was fascism on distant stars. The terror of certain types of rule was expounded and suggestions were offered as to how it could be defeated by the revolution of humanoids—sometimes with the help of the more advanced inhabitants of Earth. In more recent works, one finds space travelers meeting fascist or medieval feudal forms of society that are described in all their cruelty. Nowadays, however, the tendency is to reject the idea that revolution may be exported beyond the frontiers of the solar system. History must develop according to its own laws. An attack by a more highly developed civilization would supposedly meet with no sympathy for the mass of inhabitants of distant worlds, and so the Earth's explorers now content themselves with observation and analysis of the situations they discover.

THE INDIVIDUAL
AND TECHNOLOGY

Next to the social utopia the most important subgenre in science fiction is technological fantasy. Throughout the whole history of the genre, two primary roles have been assigned to technology. The first is technology as the aid to mankind in its path to the future, and the second is technology as the demon, allowing the loss of humanist nature, reducing humans to the level of slaves to so-called progress.

Even dreams of overcoming nature and subduing society have their roots in the early forms of fantasy literature. There are genies in bottles, magic rings, invisible caps, magic belts, hard-working brownies, and devilish power. Gods hurl lightning bolts and fly through the air; splendiferous castles appear overnight, with Satan's help; the wonder pot never runs dry of gruel. Science fiction takes over these themes and develops them in the guise of pseudoscience. While the early literature of fantasy includes remarkably few exact details of technical feats—one of the most exact such descriptions was the fact that Daedalus's wings were held together with wax—this was all changed by the Renaissance.

It was above all the Industrial Revolution of the eighteenth and nineteenth centuries that became the basis for the technological gullability of readers in the nineteenth century. The works of the first classical writer of science fiction, Jules Verne, is permeated through and through with limitless euphoria concerning advances in technology. Even in an apparently impossible situation, the hero always thinks up some

225

way out of his difficulties, which, in the most lucky cases, is the clue to a massive new technological advance—the most obvious example of this being *The Mysterious Island.*

Verne paid close attention to the newest technological trends, and from them developed a wealth of fantastic inventions. This approach to the relationship between people and technology was adopted by followers of Verne after his worldwide success with all classes of readers, and thus technological fantasy came to occupy a dominant position and inspire an ever-growing number of exciting books until after World War I.

American science fiction under the influence of Gernsback also adopted technological fantasy as the favored subgenre of science fiction. Technology was also, in its role as helper, the mainstay of science fiction during the Campbell phase, even while in individual books one may trace gloomy scenarios and foreshadowings of negative influences.

Socialist science fiction, in its early phase up until the 1950s, is notable for its "technological optimism." The creation of a new social order was only to be envisaged in the company of parallel technological progress. By conquering nature, by exploiting known processes, by realizing gigantic technological aims (even to the point of moving mountains, irrigating wide deserts, draining oceans, creating artificial ice flows, and launching satellite cities in space) anything and everything was possible for mankind. In the following decades to the present technological optimism informs a great proportion of science fiction the world over, especially in the trivial popular-level works of the west, and in those socialist works designed mainly for the entertainment of the young.

Notwithstanding the above, however, the warning voices of the last twenty-five years have become more and more difficult to ignore, especially in the light of the oil crisis of the early 1970s, the worldwide exhaustion of raw materials, and the by now obvious negative consequences of technological development at any price. The poisoning of rivers and lakes, the pollution of the air, acid rain and the death of forests, the increase in certain diseases in industrial regions—these are all alarm signals not only sounded by the environmentalists but sketched in technological fantasies.

Baron Münchhausen's flight. Pen and ink drawing by Theodor Hosemann.

An especially "rampant" brand of current fantasy lives on the invention of ever more complicated and horrific weapons of destruction and war—rays making one invisible, laser pistols, killer satellites, and similar ingredients of an arsenal of technological innovation. Ample opportunity is offered here for the description of total victory, mostly over "lesser" races inhabiting some distant star, with the authors indulging in lust for aggression and offering cataclysmic visions of battles on a galactic scale.

Science fiction authors and their fans often point to sensational anticipations made in science fiction

226

that have in fact come true in order to prove that science fiction *does* indeed offer a glimpse into the future. This is pure nonsense; science fiction is *not* future literature. Science fiction is a game, the starting point of which is the present day and whose purpose can be seen only in terms of today. Particular trends are discernible in their very early days, and invite a fantasy extrapolation of where they may lead, and give indications of possible technological off-shoots. But if one reads the technological details of the works of science fiction authors more closely, then it quickly becomes obvious that *real* developments have taken other paths. The submarine of Captain Nemo is as impossible as the helicopter of Robur. The music machines of the nineteenth century have as little in common with today's radio as their methods of transmitting pictures have to do with television. It must also be recognized that science fiction that concentrates heavily on technological invention and development betrays its age most quickly, becoming obsolete in the wake of actual developments.

There are scientific facts that were adopted into literature very early with dramatic and effective results—for instance, the problems of weightlessness during the space flights of Verne, the effects of rocket blast-off in the books of O. W. Gail or A. Belyayev (in both cases based on hints from a rocket engineer or theoretician). But always most dear to the hearts of science fiction readers are those cases where there appears to have been uncanny anticipation: the explosion of an atom bomb before Hiroshima in Cleve Cartmill's *Deadline*, the depiction of a satellite network covering the whole world, and so on. Such bull's-eyes must be expected by the working of chance amongst the many thousand of predictions that do not materialize.[8] One must also not forget that a great number of science fiction authors write only on the side, their main profession being scientists or engineers. For them literary play is a way of putting together abstract ideas and concrete situations and exploring their potential—negative and positive—and their consequences and outcomes.

"One can call science fiction the more lighthearted, more romantically inclined sister of science (though not to be taken as seriously as her sibling discipline), because it represents a complementary component in a common effort. Here, the possible lines of development in reality are realized in sketch form; there, they are stretched even further and—if circumstances permit—brought into existence, or—which is far more important—avoided, as a result of the conscious recognition and thorough discussion of the negative consequences."[9]

The eminence over years and decades of the explorer and the inventor in science fiction is very understandable in light of the predominance of technological fantasy. The scientist, a genius, possessed by his idea and working to no other end than its realization, is one of the basic ingredients of scientific fantasy, and forms one of its most inviolable topos. The scientist's naïvité in other areas of life is seized upon by rogues who want to steal the results of the experiments in order to put into practice their own evil

Science fiction—a favorite theme for caricaturists: love among robots. Drawing by Andrzej Podulka.

227

plans, anything up to and including the subjugation of the world. Only at the very last moment are the scientist's eyes opened so that the new invention may be turned against the enemy and used to destroy him, often with the hero losing his life; a classic example of this is Jules Verne's *Face to the Flag*. Another equally popular variant of the scientist motif is the figure of the mad professor. This version offers an opportunity of combining the genius of scientific insight with the endangerment of all mankind.

Since the 1950s attention has also been paid to the nonscientific branches of life, leading in the 1960s to the experiments of the New Wave and the new importance accorded to inner space. The scientist figure has lost something of its attraction in science fiction, and with it much of its importance. This must however have happened partly as a result of the fact that the negative aspects of so many technological inventions are clearly in evidence around us, and that today research work is nearly all teamwork with the influence of the individual diminished.

Some special technological inventions have built up a tradition of their own as motifs in science fiction, a prime example being of course robots—named, as mentioned above, after Čapek's play *R.U.R.*

In the course of time, standard topoi have grown up representing the various relationships between humans and robots. At the beginning, robots were almost always companions and helpers, suitable for dangerous work, functioning as servants and household helpers. Slowly they became, with progressively dynamic programming, cleverer and more independent. As military robots they were used by power-hungry humans in warlike conflicts to "fetch the chestnuts from the flames." Thus robots learned the use of weapons, and the meaning of destruction, which they soon turned to their own ends.

The next step was the introduction of mechanisms beyond the control of humans: robots become able to evolve their own communities and states, and eventually were in a position to threaten the very existence of mankind.

In stories and novellas humanized robots appear which are capable of thinking and feeling, loving and hating, which are lonely and which long for security and warmth; under such conditions, fictional automatons become endowed with hopes and fears, they are estranged human forms that should help us to know ourselves more deeply.

Originally such objects were also given human external features; today toy robots seen in exhibitions and the like are still presented in this fashion. But with the development of microelectronics and computer technology many authors abandoned the formal likeness of robots to humans and began to concentrate on the formidable electronic brain as the power and coordination center of great social organizations. These were in part used to portray, in a kind of dystopia, the ever-increasing subjugation of the individual by these technological "aids" that they themselves invented and constructed.

Androids are especially popular, being artificial beings like robots, but constructed out of organic material; "Cyborgs" (CYBERNETIC ORGANISMS) are a mixture of organic and inorganic parts. These too are very often connected with the motifs of threat and play the same role as do robots, the only difference being that cyborgs are on the whole even more dangerous because externally they are indistinguishable from humans.

PEOPLE AND TIME

Everything that exists does so in terms of space and time. These two concepts are philosophical categories that enable us to describe material objects as being next to one another (in a wider sense, so as to include distance, stretching, relative position) and processes as being after one another (the sequence of events, the causation linking a series of events, the duration of and development of processes). Owing to the special nature of each, it follows that space is three dimensional and that time is one dimensional—and irreversible. There is always a fascination in playing with the impossible. What would it be like if the fun-

228

damental properties of all existence were altered? How would it be if we could overcome the irreversibility of time and explore the future and the past at will? This hypothetical quest is the basis for one of the most interesting motifs in science fiction: the journey through time.

Mankind has always been interested in stepping over the boundaries of temporal existence. The desire to know what the future holds has given rise to armies of seers, magicians, medicine men, auguries, readers of tea leaves, crystal-ball gazers, clairvoyants, prophets, and so on. Even today periods of special stress and danger cause people to visit tarot readers, astrologists, and the like to strengthen their hopes into a better future.

But even when dealing with the past it is not at all as easy as it appears.

Although certain facts are established beyond doubt, to understand their relevance and interconnections necessitates taking into account fully the individual concerned. Each person and each generation forges its own attitudes to the past, works out its own interpretation and judgment, and is forced to determine from this knowledge its own understanding of contemporary processes. No definitive history is correct for once and for all. This in itself makes the subject of the past highly attractive to science fiction authors. They may play as they will with historical facts and derive their own meaning.

Though even as early as the eighteenth century dreams of an "unnatural" sleep (a development of the ideas of the Sleeping Beauty) have been used to allow literary figures to remove to different periods, time travel as such first appeared in science fiction in H. G. Wells's novella *The Time Machine*. Wells, the undisputed giant of scientific fantasy, here created simultaneously two fundamental elements of the tale of time travel: first, that a fantasy machine can travel through the fourth dimension, and second, that travel into the future means revealing a weltanschauung, or worldview.

The success of the book left other authors with no choice but to conduct their own experiments. To date great waves of "chrononauts" have visited all eras of world history, delving back into the very beginnings of human evolution and stretching into the slow freez-

Bastiné's time travelers fly to the Middle Ages where an alchemist takes them for the Devil.

ing over—or meltdown—of the final demise of the world.

At first authors preferred to write continuations of Wells's story, making a new hero discover the whereabouts of the lost vehicle and take new journeys in it—for instance, Carl Grunert's *Pierre Maurignac's Adventure*, Wilhelm Bastiné's *The Recovered Time Machine*, and Friedell's *The Return of the Time Machine*. In the meantime, a variety of means had been propounded for travel through time in science fiction literature, becoming more and more complicated (no longer to be likened to a bicycle), including cagelike rooms, time tunnels with spheres filled with some milky fluid, and time rays. Time warps can be caused by atomic bomb explosions, or come in the form of

229

The twin paradox as seen by an illustrator of 1928: The departure of the space pilot from his brother and sister. But they meet again after the flight.

biological time travel, or may be the result of deep-frozen sleep. Brian Aldiss invents a drug for the purpose. Most favored today are pseudoscientific apparatuses that stand in enormous laboratories, remaining in the present, with the traveler being propelled through time and recalled back now and then.

The presentation of the future reflects a point of view as regards the development of humanity. In western science fiction, dystopian fear of the future predominates; in socialist science fiction the orientation is towards utopian notions of the communist world already on its way.

Journeys to the past have proved far more stimulating as a field to writers. They normally begin as an attempt to describe what really happened at some date in the past, or they describe tourist journeys, often in the form of adventure safaris, or sightseeing tours. There is hardly an episode in our history, real or legendary, that has been left unexplored by literary time travelers: the hunting paradise of prehistory and

the wonderful island of Atlantis are as popular as Troy, Hellas, Rome, or the Middle Ages. The Peasants' Revolt is witnessed again, as is the French Revolution, or the American. A particularly popular theme is the "clarification" of biblical stories. Here there is a huge variety, including for example the Jesus phenomenon. Moorcock's *Behold the Man* is a blasphemous presentation, regardless of religious feeling, while Ilya Varshavski, an aesthetically minded Russian author, shows with delicate humor how a time-traveling postgraduate student is forced to play the part of Jesus, even though the traveling through time is merely imitated.

The motif of time travel offers, through the confrontation of peoples from different epochs with different knowledge, much opportunity for gags and special effects that reach their peak in the popular literature of science fiction. Carl Grunert's time traveler is mistaken by an alchemist for the devil. Such cheap antics permeate science fiction.

THEMES, SUBJECTS, AND MOTIFS

Another variant is the visit of people from the future to our time, which has proved more productive a theme than visits by people from the past.

Trivial science fiction seems to have an insatiable appetite for the thrill of the chase through time, for time-warp antics, for time wars, for time policemen, and for time agents.

Experiment with turning the course of time around seems to be useful only as a structure for a story, as for instance in Philip K. Dick's *The Counter-Clock World*, set in the year 1998, in which after World War III and the terminations of World War IV, corpses in churchyards begin to make their presence felt, and have to be disinterred as living beings. Thus time starts to flow in reverse. Another example is Fredric Brown's short story "The End," in which an experiment to reverse the direction of time meets with success, and in which the text itself turns around in the middle and, like a film shown backwards, winds itself back to its own beginning.

Time travelers' stories are also popular for demonstrating what sort of far-reaching effects any alteration of the past would have on the present. This sort of aim presents a particular problem in that authors must seek out a suitable turning point in history where intervention can fail, so that the course of real events can proceed unhindered.

An indispensable utensil of many space-travel tales is the twin paradox. The theory of relativity states that for objects traveling close to the speed of light, time will be stretched and spatial dimensions diminished. The effects of these changes were incorporated without delay into human adventures, with authors readily describing how space travelers race through the cosmos at the speed of light in their photon rockets. When they return home, they have aged only a few years, while on the Earth decades or even centuries have passed. Their return then affords them no reunion with old friends; it is a case instead of *The Ancestors' Return*, as del'Antonio has it.

Many fine works have been written on the time-travel topos, leading to quite bizarre situations as heroes move through the fourth dimension. A classic example of this, by Robert A. Heinlein, is *By His Bootstraps*. The hero of the tale meets ever new characters, who all turn out to be versions of himself at different periods. And in *All You Zombies*, a young woman becomes pregnant by a man who leaves shortly afterwards. She bears a child, born by Caesarian section. During this operation it becomes clear that she is in fact a hermaphrodite and must undergo an immediate sex change. She leaves the hospital as a young man, having just given birth to a child. She searches for a long time for the father, until it turns out to have been herself.

But this is by no means all! The newborn child is transposed from its own time, and set down twenty years into the past at the door of a children's home. It grows up. And thus Heinlein is able to complete his story: the same person is at one and the same time mother, father, and child. An interesting parallel to the holy trinity.

More such playing with time occurs in Lem's *The Star Diaries*. In the seventh journey, the space traveler Tichy is rescued by himself as a child. The twentieth journey is set in the twenty-seventh century, when attempts are being made to correct mistakes in the history of the world. Famous personages and events from history are set on their heads in an amusing and satirical manner. Lem gives the figures symbolic names (H. Ohmer = Homer; Harry S. Tottle = Aristotle).

Especially important is Memoir Number 4, in which Tichy sees the inventor of a time machine take off and age extraordinarily. The ideas here expressed embody themes valid in all forms of time travel: A traveler in time moving through a period of twenty years must naturally age accordingly. How could it be otherwise? Lem queries.

But such amusing assertions as to the impossibility of time travel is by no means the swan song of this motif. Authors of the future will continue to employ it and, it is to be hoped, continue to find new ways of writing literature describing such escapades.

231

While the question of the relationship between people and time encourages far-reaching fantasy denying the irreversibility of temporal direction, the three-dimensional nature of space offers a wider variety of starting points. Essentially, the main motifs that come to the fore in dealing with spatial problems may be divided into three groups: mankind and the blue planet Earth; mankind and the microcosmos; mankind and the macrocosmos.

Even in ancient times, the attraction of exploring new regions unknown to mankind seemed irresistible. Widely traveled people such as Herodotus told of observations, and hearsay and legends, exciting descriptions of such geographical areas. The prose writing of later antiquity concentrated on travel tales, as they are called today.

Scientific fantasy too likes to incorporate descriptions of space into stories of journeys. The classic utopian works very often open with this motif, having the hero survive an interruption of travel in a shipwreck. Thus he comes across the utopia that forms the subject matter of the work. Jules Verne owed much to the French tradition of the *"voyage imaginaire."* In almost all the books of this most often translated classic science fiction author, a journey of some sort plays a dominant role. He relates how people can, with the aid of natural science, traverse a space allotted to them on Earth. Unknown countries are investigated; major technological feats are performed (for example, the building of a railway through Siberia); travels are made around the world in what were then unbelievably short periods; and explorations of polar regions are made. But Verne also let his imagination take his heroes into the interior of the Earth, into the ocean's deeps, and indeed to the Moon; Verne's heroes do not even think twice about traveling through the solar system with a meteor.

Many authors following in Verne's footsteps tackled the problem of how to adapt the world to mankind's aims. For some years a favorite concern was the successful creation of new lands in the ocean, or the draining of the sea; or blocking the Strait of Gibraltar by a wall diverting the Mediterranean so as to irrigate the Sahara desert; or melting the polar caps to gain huge land masses. The means of transport often incorporated heady inventions that enabled the Earth to be opened up. While in earlier times the railways, motor cars, and the new flying machines sufficed for traveling, the science fiction of the twentieth century makes use of a multitude of devices driven by magnetism, antigravity, and a wide variety of other propulsive means. The joining of islands and continents was soon achieved. A projected tunnel between Dover and Calais was only the beginning, as tunnels were soon dug out in authors' imaginations linking Europe and America, or Alaska and Asia—these appealed to the tastes of genuinely "scientific" fantasy. Of course such feats of engineering could always be enlivened by the addition of adventure and detective elements to widen their appeal.

A large subgenre of space fantasy concerns itself with the exploration of natural resources and raw materials. Because of the world economic situation of

The *Minerva*—fantastical sketch of future air transport to Asia, by E. G. Robertson, 1804.

the 1970s and 1980s, Wolfgang Jeschke's novel *Der letzte Tag der Schöpfung (The Last Day of the Creation)* (1980) presents this problem along with a variety of the time warp, the western countries having ventured *into the past* to purloin all the oil of the Arab world, pumping it into the present day by means of time transport.

Adventures set in the interior of the Earth are still popular. Very often this motif is not used so much to investigate the Earth as a physical object, but to construct a parallel world. This variant has earned its own particular place in the utopian tradition ever since Ludvig Holberg. It is used also to depict contact with a world that lags far behind our own in historical development, that enables people from the present day to experience contact with dinosaurs, cave bears, and Neanderthals, and the wildest jungles—all without introducing time travel in any way.

As with adventure in the Earth's interior (using for example fantastic technical instruments that burrow like moles underground), recent years have also witnessed an increase in fantasies that depict the use of ocean riches. These include underwater farms, whales transformed into domestic pets, and submarine cowboys and wild underwater rogues. The taming and use made of dolphins has become a motif in its own right, based on the advent of dolphinariums and the astounding facts that have been established by research into the intelligence of these animals.

Clearly it was not simply the new developments in surface transport that repeatedly produced new sensation, but also the leaps forward in air and underwater transport. After many centuries of dreams of bird flight, thinking that motion through the air was possible only by means of wings, the advent of the first balloon flight made this new method of travel very popular for a short time. This was soon overtaken by the development of airplanes, helicopters, and rockets in literature which are fueled by antigravity devices and of course the ubiquitous "photon." Without these a fantastic journey into other galaxies would be unthinkable. Thus they became the favored pseudoscientific methods of propulsion in spite of their technological impossibility. In the lowest reaches of the genre, the superheroes dart about the universe just like children rollerskating down a street.

The prototype novel of utopia by Thomas More, who invented the term, remains in print—and popular—to this day.

As a substitute for this, new ideas have been developed for traveling across the greatest distances of the universe, one of which is teleportation. This involves the disintegration of the traveler at the point of departure into the tiniest particles that are beamed to the destination where all the particles are reassembled. There the hero can commence another adventure. "Beam me up, Spock!" as Captain Kirk of *Star Trek's Enterprise* would have it.

Many early science fantasies were marked by an attitude that laid particular value on a world serving hu-

233

manity—a world that took care of the aspirations of individuals and society as a whole and one that was at the same time pleasing to the eye. In more recent years this situation has changed; the subject matter has become more a question of the problems inherent in a negative alteration of the world through the actions of mankind. In this connection, particular emphasis has been placed on the abuse of natural environment as an important aspect of the relations between people and space; science fiction has seen a marked increase in themes related to the less desirable consequences of technological development, including changes in the climate caused by the destruction of forests; the drying up of large areas formerly lush and fertile through the diversion of watercourses; the alteration of biotopes by the effects of industry; and the results of acid-rain pollution.

Modern science fiction has seen a proliferation of inhuman scenarios depicting wholly technical systems that are based solely on the rational, on the laws of mathematics and logic. The impoverization of the citizens of such a sterile environment are presented as warnings, and emphasize the importance of the emotions, the arts, and beauty for mankind.

Besides this concentration on the negative changes in the world by mankind's own hand, there are also many works of science fiction based on natural catastrophes affecting large areas or even the whole world, where no blame can be apportioned. In some cases such a theme will afford an opportunity for demonstration of thinking and acting in solidarity with others, as with Komatsu (the Japanese archipelago that sank below the waves). This branch of science fiction draws on all imaginable natural disasters: floods, earthquakes, drought, epidemics, cracks in the Earth's surface, and even collisions with other celestial bodies.

Most dominant are the disasters caused by mankind's own actions, especially through the destructive force of immensely sophisticated, ever more fearsome weapons systems that could make of our beautiful Earth a desert waste devoid of life. Since total destruction is good as a warning, but poor from the point of view of plotting (how to continue the story when all are dead?), the survival of a small group of chosen persons has become an important subgenre of science fiction dealing with the relations of humans to their surroundings—be it in the form of a new Adam and Eve who are sent off to another galaxy to allow humanity a rebirth there, or a group surviving doomsday by chance. The new subgenre, known as the "doomsday" type story, flourishes today. The destruction of Earth is the starting point for the tale, the main thrust of the story being the question of the existence of the survivors, and their deliverance and mode of living in their new conditions in space. Often, as the result of exposure to radiation, the problem of genetic disturbance and mutation arises.

Catastrophes are also caused by the advent of hitherto unknown viruses and bacteria, especially those that astronauts contract by accident or that they stupidly collect from other planets, as in D. G. Compton's novel *The Silent Multitude*, in which a concrete-destroying pathogene is brought back from space, reducing all the mightiest buildings to dust within days. This inspires vivid descriptions of the extraordinary consequences.

In a relatively small group of works of scientific fantasy, the problem of the relationship of humanity to space is approached by a leap into the microcosmos. In its simplest form this involves simply the diminution in size of the people in the story, as in Lasswitz, who wanted to use this motif to make clear how very thin the crust of the Earth in fact is—no stronger than a soap bubble. Changes in relative proportions have potential for marvelous visual effects, and are therefore popular in science fiction films. It also is a field in which science fiction draws heavily on the two basic motifs of the fairy tale—giants, and dwarfs.

But far more popular in science fantasy literature, and a major factor in a great number of science fiction works, is the problem of the relationship between humanity and the macrocosmos. In a vast number of works, especially in the field of popular trivia, this has become a way of easily introducing far-reaching adventure, militarism, criminality, and horror. The authors make unsparing use of such "tension-inducing effects."

Among the thousands of space fantasies existing today there are of course some strikingly original and imaginative works. First of all there is what can be called the flying fantasy, in which the problem is to

THEMES, SUBJECTS, AND MOTIFS

overcome opposition to the construction of the flying vehicle, the blast-off, and the solving of technical and scientific hitches during flight. The developments that recent years have seen in flying technology have had an impact. So long as a moon landing was the desired aim, literary fantasy could indulge in rockets and lift-offs and the detailed description of the relatively short journey. The researches of the last twenty-five years, however, have conclusively shown that not only is the Moon uninhabited, but also Mars and Venus, and that it is quite improbable that other bodies in our solar system should be capable of supporting life. Thus it has become safer to leave our system altogether and begin to explore the Milky Way. But now this no longer suffices for the authors and readers of science fiction. Astronauts now seek fellow beings and Earth-like planets in deepest space, notwithstanding that these are many millions of light years away! Even to reach Pluto, the planet of our own system most distant from the Earth, takes light some 5.5 hours, and the North Star of our Milky Way is some 650 light years distant from us. The constellation of Andromeda, to take an example of a distant group of stars that are still visible to the naked eye, is some 210,000 light years away. In other words, the light that we see in the sky left the stars that many years ago. This must be viewed with reference to the span of human history: remember that the famous Egyptian pyramids were built a mere 5,000 years ago. This may help to illuminate the problems of intergalactic travel. This also explains the need for photon rockets—but even with these powerful vehicles, it would take over 200,000 years to reach the Andromeda constellation! In order that space travelers may reach such destinations without mishap, they must now be set into a deep frozen sleep. The tricks employed in this process by authors are ever more refined in their efforts to ensure that their heroes come into contact with other humanoid life forms and are able to experience foreign worlds.

Against this background of travel, innumerable cosmic adventures take place. All the clichés and established standard situations of adventure stories reappear in these space operas, along with new ideas born of the invention of other life forms and other conditions on far distant planets. There is the danger of meteor storms, accidents, antigravity protection plates, emergency landings on strange stars, and the lonely life of astronauts traveling through space, capture and imprisonment, and of course love itself in many varieties. For all these features a new terminology has been developed. There is some kind of an inverse proportion evident here: the weaker the literary merit of a book, the more enthusiastically pseudo-scientific "specialist" words are incorporated into the text, in order to lend the whole an air of scientific authenticity.

The problem of close living conditions for protracted periods claims some attention. The responses range from the simulation of Earthlike conditions in the spaceship to the succession of generations during the mission, and the biological transformation of the cosmonauts, and to conflicts with robots, cyborgs, and androids.

Space flight is of course the background for the subgenre of the "space opera," to which authors return again and again during the history of the genre.

A subject frequently met with in the course of space adventure is that of colonization, the taking over of other planets by mankind. Stations in space are set up and stars and planets are used as sources for raw materials. The colonizers attack in the frontier manner of the western and obliterate the inhabitants of the star or planet or capture them and use them as slaves or cheap laborers. As opposed to this, however, there are some stories of peaceful cohabitation. One meets on an impoverished star lost colonizers whose connection with Earth has withered away over the centuries and who have therefore developed independently, or perhaps paid particular attention to preserving the older moral system. Or, perhaps, the whole population of Earth must be evacuated to avoid impending catastrophe.

And lastly, there are the many fantasies, sometimes in more than one volume, that deal not simply in the story of single planets, but that span whole galaxies.

In the last few years, there has been an increase in the number of visions that portray the conqueror from the Earth as meeting with complete success at first, only to find in the course of time that the newly colonized planet is not after all suitable for human

235

habitation. The intruders are finally driven off by circumstances and the former path of development can then be taken up again and continued.

Other very popular variations on the space travel fantasy are the attempted invasion of the Earth and the war of the worlds. These involve an attack on Earth (the archetype being Wells's *War of the Worlds*) and the counterattack of the Earth's forces. Gigantic wars proliferate between different civilizations, with battles and engagements using highly fantastic technology in dozens of manifestations. These works are prone to deliver details with sadistic superfluity, with, perhaps, racial hatred and twisted ideology. In more serious science fiction such scenes and themes occur overwhelmingly in the form of warnings against the terrors of war.

Sometimes in the space wars the ideological conflict between two social systems is presented. This is especially true of the few works of socialist science fiction that address the theme of war between worlds.

There are among these works some readable and worthwhile satires of the invasion motif in which the present-day social system, the morality and the behavior of our contemporaries, is set on its head—for example in the Strugatskys' *The Second Martian Invasion*. Even earlier examples are the satires of Ray Bradbury, written in the period of the Cold War at the beginning of the 1950s.

Lastly in this section dealing with the relationship between people and space come visions of parallel worlds and antiworlds, most of which offer utopian or dystopian visions.

HUMANS AND ALIENS

From time immemorial, humankind has tried to gain a better understanding of its own existence by imagining encounters with other life forms that differ in externals from ours. Giants and dwarfs, water sprites and mermaids—these are just a few of the strange beings described in myths, religious stories, and folk tales. These are in no wise depictions of strange beings just for their own sake, but are inevitably presented as comparisons with humanity. Hopes and fears, virtues and vices, the normal and the extraordinary, the essential and the peculiar, the credible and the improbable, the irrefutable and the contestable—all aspects of human behavior are transposed into that of the other beings. The prime concern is the portrayal of human characteristics and the moral outlook peculiar to the time or considered generally valid through the ages. There are beings who are good, beautiful, courageous, and clever, and also beings who are evil, ugly, cowardly, and stupid. The first group represents an attempt to complement the nature of mankind and act as an aid to revelation of the correct path. They are ideal pictures of true humanity. The second group represents attempts to divert mankind from its proper course, and thus the representative of true humanity must struggle against such a

force. Often the aliens are possessed of wonderful powers, so that the battle seems almost hopeless and many are about to give up. But always at the last moment a human hero appears, crushing the opposition through wit, cunning, and sheer intellect. Odysseus's triumph over the giant cyclops and David's victory over Goliath are classic examples of this tradition, as is the story of the brave little tailor.

Science fiction contains many references to intelligent life forms, and uses them to illuminate humankind by observing them in unusual confrontational situations. The range of possibilities thus opened up is enormous. In the area of popular science fiction, supermen/astronauts bustle around under whatever names their creators give them—be it Perry Rhodan or Buck Rogers, Flash Gordon or anything else (often with characteristics so beloved of the Nazis, the "Nordic" racial features of blond hair, blue eyes, a muscular body full of power, and of course possessed of fabulous weaponry), thundering through the galaxies, in each story meeting a new set of slimy monsters, more insects, blood-smeared vampires, and wreaking havoc among them.

In more serious science fiction such aggressive dreams are differently disposed, and cruelty, horror, and sadism are not included gratuitously but to play their own part in the whole.

An important and as yet unsolved problem is the question whether we exist as a unique species in the cosmos or whether somewhere beyond our present knowledge there exist other intelligent beings. Scientists in recent years have tended to answer the riddle negatively, but two centuries ago there was unmistakable euphoria concerning the issue. Because we think of all life as in the form of the life familiar to us, we take it that particular physical and chemical conditions must exist on planets' surfaces before any organisms can develop. With such a premise, it is obvious that in our own solar system no planet or moon other than the Earth is capable of supporting higher forms

Two modern King Kong adaptations.

of life. It has been estimated that in the Milky Way a maximum of 5 percent of the stars are surrounded by planetary systems that may include conditions favorable to the development of life.

Since 1960 radio telescopes have been searching for signals that could be emanating from extraterrestrial life or distant civilizations. In 1967 the English astronomer Jocelyn Bell isolated in a band of rays at the Cambridge telescope a very weak and mysterious beam, the so-called Pulsars, which were later proven to come from natural sources. Sir Martin Ryle said at the time that the rays came from Little Green Men, and ever since then this idea has proved extremely popular with journalists.

In 1974 a so-called Information Program was sent out from the Earth into space. The possibility that humans may one day establish radio contact with other

237

François Truffaut, right, playing scientist Claude Lacombe, questions Richard Dreyfuss, left, about strange experience that has changed his life in *Close Encounters of the Third Kind.*

planets is almost negligible. The possibility of direct contact must, therefore, be even less.

Precisely for these reasons, inventions based on aliens are extremely attractive to science fiction authors who imagine to themselves: what would happen if . . . ? An early question to be answered is exactly how the aliens will appear. Only a few science fiction authors take the line of the Soviet writer and paleontologist Ivan Antonovich Yefremov, who said,

> The external side of humans, the single life form blessed with intelligence on our Earth, is not arbitrary. It follows the need for maximum adaptability, for the possibility of shouldering heavy demands, and has developed around the extraordinarily active nervous system. . . .
>
> An intelligent being from another world, if it should reach our cosmos, would be to the highest degree perfect, universal—in other words, beautiful! It is impossible that there should be thinking monsters with horns and tails, there cannot be people in the form of fungus, or the Kraken.[10]

Thus, Yefremov finds it impossible to imagine intelligent beings other than in human form.

Similarity to human form is only one possibility. The alien spectrum ranges through many variations, from the one-eyed, three-eyed, many-legged, or animal-like, right through to the so-called bug-eyed mon-

ster, which has insectlike eyes. There is also the colloidal ocean of Lem (in *Solaris*), or even tentacled beings, or beings that continuously alter their form, or slimy masses, or invisible forms, or particles that can join together at will into organisms and function as an entity. The horrors of myth and legend reappear here in coarsened form—even updated dragons and the like. There is also an element of threat from such monsters— for example, the Kraken, huge apes such as King Kong, and dinosaurs reawakened by atomic blasts.

Two main story variants come to the fore among the many forms meeting and making contact between people and aliens and in the consequences of this contact. On the one hand the strangers may appear as an antitype exposing the inadequacies of life on Earth. They embody a much higher civilization, with their order deeply utopian. Thus they are cleverer, have left far behind them the age of warlike conflict, and are able to come to the aid of mankind in overcoming the cruelties of life and achieving a similar high state. Often their function is to warn. They and their earlier history demonstrate where particular processes of present-day Earthly development could lead. Through this objective point of view, dangers

A variation of the "alien" in a science fiction film.

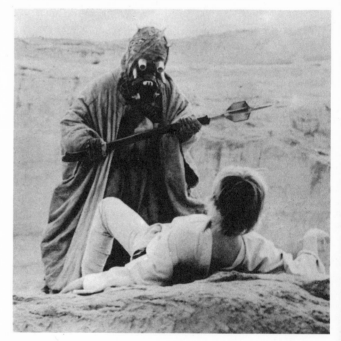

238

"E.T." ("The Extra-Terrestrial") from Steven Spielberg's film.

can be seen more clearly. Visitors to the Earth often issue such warnings.

There are also variants in which specific negative aspects of the at-first apparently superb world of the aliens are revealed: a thoroughgoing technology may have killed imagination, or the perfection of their world may have led to the end of dynamic development, to sterility, or to the threat of extinction. The second main variant deals with situations in which the aliens have reached a similar stage as humans (or are perhaps still subhuman in their behavior). Then science fiction depicts scenes in which the Earth is threatened by anything from individual aggression to the traditional "war of the worlds" topos. Sometimes the aliens send reconnaissance groups before them,

which mingle among us in order to find out the weaknesses of mankind and prepare to invade. Stories of this sort tend to concentrate on the discovery of the "spies," their ploys, and their defeat and downfall. There are of course innumerable outcomes to such situations, including quite tendentious eventualities, with the strangers delighting in the Earth and rejecting their original intentions to remain here.

An important problem is the making of contact. In earlier works, meetings between different characters took place without major complications. In more recent science fiction, lack of identification or belated identification have become important motifs. In the Strugatskys' short story "The Hunter," for instance, a traveler from the stars is accidentally killed.

A very popular scenario is that in which humans are anxious to make contact with members of a higher civilization, but instead find themselves ignored. Equally favored is the case where contact is impossible owing to too fundamental differences between the beings: size, for example, or respiratory requirements, responses to gravitational forces, or radiation.

The concept of "alien" naturally incorporates beings originally produced by technical means—that is, robots—which have since begun to develop their own evolution. It also includes combinations of organic and mechanical beings, and synthetic creatures.

A special place in modern science fiction is occupied by Stanley G. Weinbaum, for his pioneering descriptions of aliens. In his *Martian Odyssey* he wrote of drivers of strange vehicles, of pyramid builders, of hypnotic plants, and of the ostrichlike, intelligent Martian Tweel, offering in all a wealth of fruitful ideas that has inspired countless authors of science fantasy and that continue to influence science fiction up to the present.

The main criterion for estimating the value of aliens in science fiction must be in the authorial intentions that underlie the story.

240

CONCLUSION

Our historical journey through the very wide field of scientific fantasy has now reached its stated destination, the present day. Much that is worthy of observation lay waiting to be discovered in this landscape, some things that had hitherto stood overshadowed by other works were revealed in their true colors, and there was of course much that was rank growth and weeds. There is no one eternally valid definition of the historical phenomenon of science fiction. Underlying the genre, as life itself, is a constant process of change. There are particular aspects and features that last, that alter only slowly, and there are also short-lived branches that endure perhaps only through one epoch, or are even confined to one phase of development. The science fiction of the future will in any event be different from that of today. One thing certain is that the sheer breadth of science fiction is not going to alter perceptibly. As long as there is business to be transacted in marketing inexpensive reading material, there will be new space operas of ever more fantastic places farther and farther away, deep-frozen astronauts in their photon rockets visiting ever more exotic galaxies, gigantic wars between worlds, E.T.s will land on Earth and sex bombs will continue to be rescued from slimy monsters by supermen, telepathic beings, androids, and robots will threaten the Earth, time travelers will explore the past and the future, and authors will of course continue to lay before the public their versions of better, and worse, worlds.

Today much has come true of which our ancestors did not even dare to dream. Satellites cruise around the Earth, the first space probes have left the confines of the solar system, the nature of Mars and Venus is no longer a subject for speculation, nuclear energy is a part of our everyday lives, and microelectronics is making new breakthroughs all the time. All this creates however not less but more grounds for new anxieties and fears. The rationalization and improvement of productivity are causing redundancies among the workers of a large area of the world, so that the ranks of the unemployed are growing. The wasteful use of technology has led to massive disruptions in the relationship between humankind and nature. The vast primeval forests of South America are exploited without a thought for the consequences, despite the dreadful experience of similar abuse in other parts of the world. Acid rain is disrupting forest growth, rivers deteriorate into cesspools, the biological balance is disturbed. Throughout the world, the major cities attract more and more people as if by magnetism, resulting in chaotic transport, social problems, noise, and smog.

Until the middle of the present century science fiction heaped praise on technology and urban life; in the immediate past in the best science fiction this is no longer the case. The most literary works in the genre no longer strive to describe exotic adventures in distant climes, but tend to explore fantasized ver-

241

Imperial stormtroopers interrogate Ben Kenobi, played by Alec Guinness, and Luke Skywalker, by Mark Hamill, about their robots in *Star Wars*.

sions of contemporary problems, seeking to bring new consciousness to the reader. Authors want to live up to the responsibility we all bear towards succeeding generations. Again and again, the self-destruction of humanity by terrible weapons systems occupies the core of fictional concern. Speculation about truly fraternal social systems in which hunger, unemployment, slavery, and misery are forever banned, and which therefore have no further place for war, are on the increase. The real subject matter of science fiction is not technology, but human personality. For this reason, I am convinced that the science fiction of the future will anticipate social, psychic, ecological, and biological discoveries and developments that today lie at the very frontier of knowledge, testing the facilities of mankind.

The science fiction of coming years will bring as much pleasure to its public as science fiction today does to its fans now. Undoubtedly it will seek more than it does today, not only to give readers amusement, but also more food for thought as to how our planet can be preserved as a home for our grandchildren. This hope is to be approached by processes that have become visible throughout the last several decades. Important works of world literature have chosen to deal with the motifs and topoi of scientific fantasy; at the same time, the original fantasy arrangement has radically altered the literary and aesthetic quality and the humanist intention of a great number of science fiction authors. The gulf that for a century has separated mainstream literature from science fiction, dubbing the latter mere "amusement," has begun to be bridged. And one day perhaps science fiction will in its entirety again be a recognized and essential part of our literature as it was in its utopian phase a century ago.

242

APPENDIX

NOTES

PREFACE

1. Aleksandr Herzen, *Mein Leben, Memoiren und Reflexionen 1852–68*, vol. 3 (Berlin, 1962), p. 14.

BEGINNINGS

Chapter 1.
SCIENCE FICTION OR SCIENTIFIC FANTASY: WHAT IS IT?

1. Eike Barmeyer, Introduction, *Science Fiction—Theorie und Geschichte* (Munich, 1972), p. 9.

2. Kingsley Amis, *New Maps of Hell* (London, 1961), p. 18.

3. *The Reader's Encyclopedia of American Literature*, ed. M. J. Herzberg (London, 1963), p. 1005.

4. Dieter Hasselblatt, *Grüne Männchen vom Mars: Science Fiction für Leser und Macher* (Dusseldorf, 1974), p. 19ff.

5. Darko Suvin, "Ein Abriss der sowjetischen Science Fiction," in *Science Fiction—Theorie und Geschichte*, ed. Eike Barmeyer (Munich, 1972), p. 27.

6. Hans-Jürgen Krysmanski, *Die utopische Methode* (Cologne, Opladen, 1963).

7. Bernd Ulbrich, "Die sogenannte utopische Methode oder Vehementes Plädoyer für eine SF," in *NDL (Neue Deutsche Literatur)*, no. 11 (Berlin, 1981), p. 163.

8. Ibid., p. 162.

9. Peter Wilfert, "Phantastica—Literatur für Grüne und Alternative?" (interview by Knut Hansen), in *Börsenblatt für den Deutschen Buchhandel—Science Fiction, Krimis, Phantastica*, vol. 37, no. 61 (Frankfurt/M, 1981), p. 1862.

10. Stanislaw Lem, *His Master's Voice* (London, 1983), p. 106.

11. Ibid.

12. Michael Pehlke and Norbert Lingfeld, *Roboter und Gartenlaube: Ideologie und Unterhaltung in der Science-Fiction Literatur* (Reihe Hanser 56) (Munich, 1970), p. 16.

13. Robert Jungk, "Wo sind die Erfinder einer menschenwürdigen Zukunft? Plädoyer für eine neue Zukunftsliteratur: Science Creation" in *Pardon*, vol. 8, no. 2 (1969), p. 27.

14. Inge von Wangenheim, *Genosse Jemand und die Klassik: Gedanken eines Schriftstellers auf der Suche nach dem Erbe seiner Zeit* (Halle, Leipzig, 1981), p. 39.

15. Stanislaw Lem, *Phantastik und Futurologie*, part 1 (Frankfurt/M, 1977), p. 5.

16. Chingis Aitmatov, *Der Tag zieht den Jahrhundertweg* (Berlin, 1982), p. 7ff.

17. Ibid., p. 8.

18. Cf. Ursula K. Le Guin, "Vorwort zum Roman 'Winterplanet,'" in *Lichtjahr 1: Ein Phantastik-Almanach* (Berlin, 1980).

Chapter 2.
CLASSIC SOCIAL UTOPIAS AND FANTASIES

1. Boris Suchkov, *Historische Schicksale des Realismus* (Berlin and Weimar, 1972), p. 19.
2. Cf. Thomas More, *Utopia* (London, 1910).
3. Ibid., p. 15.
4. Ibid., p. 15.
5. More, op. cit., p. 49.
6. Ibid.
7. Ibid., p. 111.
8. Ibid., p. 119.
9. Rosemarie Ahrbeck, *Morus—Campanella—Bacon* (Leipzig, Jena, Berlin, 1977), p. 82ff.
10. Ibid., p. 82ff.
11. Karl Marx/Friedrich Engels, *Werke*, vol. 2 (Berlin, 1957), p. 135.
12. Friedemann Berger, "Robinson oder Die Reise in die Wirklichkeit," in *Robinson Crusoe*, Daniel Defoe, part 2 (Leipzig and Weimar, 1981), p. 353ff.
13. Cyrano de Bergerac, *Journeys to the Sun and the Moon* (London, n.d. [after 1921]), p. 199.
14. Ibid., p. 200.
15. Ibid., p. 207.
16. Ibid., p. 207.

THE INDUSTRIAL REVOLUTION AND ITS REFLECTION IN FANTASY

Chapter 3.
ANIMAL MAGNETISM, MONSTERS, AND AUTOMATONS

1. Cf. E. T. A. Hoffmann, "Die Serapionsbrüder," part 1, in *Gesammelte Werke in Einzelausgaben*, vol. 4 (Berlin and Weimar, 1978), p. 417.
2. *Der Born Judas*, part 1, "Legenden, Märchen und Erzählungen." Collected by Micha Josef bin Gorion. New edition with afterword by Emanuel bin Gorion (Leipzig, 1978), p. 663ff.
3. Cf. *Künstliche Menschen, Dichtungen und Dokumente über Golems, Homunculi, Androiden und lie-*

bende Statuen, ed. K. Völker, Bibliotheca Dracula, vol. 9 (Munich, 1971).
4. Mary Wollstonecraft Shelley, *Frankenstein, or the Modern Prometheus* (London [Penguin], 1985), p. 85.
5. Ibid., p. 98.
6. Johann Wolfgang von Goethe, *Werke* (Berlin Edition), vol. 1 (Berlin and Weimar, 1965), p. 153.
7. Edgar Allan Poe, *The Science Fiction of Edgar Allan Poe*, ed. Harold Beaver (New York, [Penguin], 1976), p. 37.

Chapter 4.
JULES VERNE AND HIS "VOYAGES EXTRAORDINAIRES"

1. Manfred Nagl, *Science Fiction in Deutschland* (Tübingen [Schloss], 1972), p. 54.
2. F. P. Freyberg, "Ein Besuch bei Jules Verne," in *Lichtjahr 2* (Berlin, 1981), p. 83.
3. Ibid.

Chapter 5.
THE GIANT OF SCIENCE FICTION: H. G. WELLS

1. H. G. Wells, *The Scientific Romances of H. G. Wells* (London, 1933), p. 12.
2. Ibid., p. 52.
3. Ibid., p. 75.
4. Ibid., p. 21.
5. H. G. Wells, *The Invisible Man* (London and Glasgow, 1959), p. 126.
6. Ibid., p. 214.
7. Wells, *Scientific Romances*, p. 450ff.
8. Ibid., p. 617.
9. H. G. Wells, *The Science Fiction of H. G. Wells* (London [Penguin], n.d.), p. 314.
10. Ibid.
11. Wells, *Scientific Romances*, p. 813.
12. Ibid., p. 814.
13. Ibid., p. 1195.

Chapter 6.
THE REVIVAL
OF SOCIAL UTOPIAN LITERATURE

1. Samuel Butler, *Erewhon* (London [Penguin], 1970), pp. 35–6.

2. Edward Bellamy, *Looking Backward*, ed. Cecilia Tichi (New York [Penguin American Library], 1982), p. 47.

3. Ibid., p. 202.

4. William Morris, *News from Nowhere* (London, New York, and Toronto, 1912), p. 121.

Chapter 7.
TECHNOLOGICAL FANTASY AND
PLANET STORIES

1. Cf. Nagl, op. cit., p. 80.

2. Aleksandr Kuprin, "Der Trinkspruch," in *Die Entdeckung Riels* (Berlin, 1980), p. 5.

3. Ibid., p. 6.

4. Ibid., p. 10.

5. Ibid.

6. Cf. Kurd Lasswitz, *Über Tropfen, welche an festen Körpern hangen und der Schwerkraft unterworfen sind* (Breslau, 1873, Research Library Gotha, Chart. A 1917 Bl. 1–77, Druck Nr. 19).

7. Kurd Lasswitz, *Bis zum Nullpunkt des Seins* (Berlin, 1979), p. 27.

8. Kurd Lasswitz, *Auf zwei Planeten*, 39.–41. Tsd. Volksausgabe, vol. 2 (Leipzig, n.d. [c. 1921]), p. 387.

9. Bernhard Kellermann, *Der Tunnel* (Berlin, 1981), p. 355.

10. *Geschichte der deutschen Literatur von den Anfängen bis zur Gegenwart*, vol. 9, *Vom Ausgang des 19. Jh. bis 1917* (Berlin, 1974), p. 471.

Chapter 8.
THE DESCENT INTO
THE TRIVIAL

1. Cf. Otto Hartmann, *Die Entwicklung der Literatur und des Buchhandels* (Leipzig, 1910), p. 94.

2. Hans Joachim Alpers, "Lendenschurz, Doppelaxt und Magie," in *Die triviale Phantasie: Beiträge zur "Verwertbarkeit" von Science Fiction*, ed. Jörg Weigand (Bonn, Bad Godesberg, 1976), p. 31.

3. Ruth Koder, *Die Presse als Quelle für die Literaturgeschichte: Versuch einer ersten Klärung des Problems* (Munich, 1952), p. 351.

4. Sam Moskowitz, *Explorers of the Infinite: Shapers of Science Fiction* (Cleveland and New York, 1963), p. 108.

5. Nagl, op. cit., p. 131.

6. Ibid., p. 132.

7. Ibid., p. 135.

THE GROWTH OF
SCIENCE FICTION AFTER
WORLD WAR I

Chapter 9.
DREAMS OF WORLD REVOLUTION
AND THE "FANTASY OF THE NEAR FUTURE":
SOVIET SCIENCE FICTION
BETWEEN 1917 AND 1956

1. Yuli Kagarlitski, *Was ist Phantastik?* (Berlin, 1977), p. 7.

2. Valentin Katayev, *Lob der Dummheit: Humoristische Prosa* (Berlin, 1976), p. 434.

3. Vivian Itin, "Die Entdeckung Riels," in *Die Entdeckung Riels: Eine Anthologie klassischer Phantastik-Erzählungen aus Russland und der Sowjetunion* (Berlin, 1980), p. 383.

4. Ilya Ehrenburg, *Die ungewöhnlichen Abenteuer des Julio Jurenito und seiner Jünger/Trust D. E. oder die Geschichte vom Untergang Europas* (Berlin, 1975), p. 6.

5. *The Golden Age of Soviet Theater*, ed. Michael Glenny (London, 1981), p. 34.

6. Ibid., p. 75.

7. Aleksandr Belyayev, *Der Amphibienmensch*, part 20, in *Junge Welt* (Berlin, 1978).

8. *Handbuch der Sowjetliteratur (1917–1972)* (Leipzig, 1975), p. 52.

9. Aleksandr Fedorov, "Sowjetische wissenschaftliche Phantastik in der DDR," in *Sowjetliteratur*, vol. 34, no. 1 (Moscow, 1982), p. 176.

10. Ibid., p. 176ff.

11. Ivan Yefremov, "Aufstiegsspirale der Evolution," in *Sowjetliteratur*, vol. 34, no. 1 (Moscow, 1982), p. 157.

Chapter 10.
Hugo Gernsback and after:
Anglo-American Science Fiction
to the 1950s

1. Stanley Grauman Weinbaum, *A Martian Odyssey and Other Science Fiction* (Westport, CT, 1974), p. 6.

2. Isaac Asimov, *I, Robot* (London, Glasgow, Toronto, Sidney, Auckland, 1986), p. 11.

3. Isaac Asimov, "Runaround," in *Machines That Think*, ed. Isaac Asimov (London, 1984), p. 8.

4. Ray Bradbury, *The Martian Chronicles* (London, Canada, 1977), p. 176.

5. Ibid., p. 180.

6. Ibid., p. 220.

7. Ray Bradbury, *Fahrenheit 451* (London, 1957), p. 7.

8. Ibid., p. 62.

Chapter 11.
Robots, Warnings, and Rockets:
European Science Fiction
between 1918 and 1955

1. Karel Čapek, *The Insert Play/R.U.R.* (London, 1961),

2. Ibid., p. 24.   [p. 5.

3. Cf. Karel Čapek, *Das Absolutum oder Die Gottesfabrik: Utopischer Roman* (Berlin, 1955), p. 13.

4. Ibid., p. 22.

5. Ibid.

6. Karel Čapek, *Krakatit: Ein klassischer Science-fiction-Roman.* Afterword by Eckhard Thiele (Berlin, 1981), p. 280.

7. Ibid., p. 274f.

8. Karel Čapek, *The War with the Newts* (London, 1985), p. 234.

9. Ibid., pp. 235–36.

10. Valeri Bryusov, "Die Republik des Südkreuzes," in *Die Entdeckung Riels* (Berlin, 1980), p. 173.

11. Ibid., p. 174ff.

12. Yevgeni Zamyatin, *We* (New York, 1972), p. 12.

13. Ibid.

14. Ibid.

15. Dmitri Bilenkin, *Sowjetliteratur*, vol. 34, no. 1 (Moscow, 1982), p. 24.

16. Ibid., p. 41.

17. Ibid., p. 192.

18. Zamyatin, *We*, p. 42.

19. George Orwell, *Nineteen Eighty-Four* (London [Penguin], 1954), p. 151.

20. Ibid., p. 167.

21. Ibid., p. 150.

22. Ibid., p. 7.

23. Ibid., p. 167.

24. Hasselblatt, op. cit., p. 188f.

25. Nagl, op. cit., p. 159.

26. Thea von Harbou, *Metropolis*, 1.–10. Tausend der billigen (gekürzten) Ausgabe (Berlin, 1926), p. 8.

27. Siegfried Kracauer, *Von Caligari bis Hitler: Ein Beitrag zur Geschichte des deutschen Films*, rde 63 (Reinbek/Hamburg, 1958), p. 108.

28. Jacques Sadoul, *Histoire de la science-fiction moderne (1911–1975)*, 2 vols. (Paris, 1975).

Science Fiction
in the Second Half of
the Twentieth Century

Chapter 12.
The Increasing Internationalization
of Modern Science Fiction

1. Claude Avice, "Science Fiction und Probleme des Friedens," (A conversation with the President of the European SF Committee), in *Sowjetliteratur*, vol. 34, no. 1 (Moscow, 1982), p. 155.

2. Fedorov, op. cit., p. 180.

3. Alpers, op. cit., p. 45ff.

APPENDIX

4. Cf. Johann Wolfgang von Goethe, *Werke* (Berlin Edition), vol. 18 (Berlin and Weimar, 1972), p. 634.

Chapter 13.
THE SCIENCE FICTION OF
THE SOCIALIST COUNTRIES

1. Cf. Yeremei Parnov, "Der Galaktische Ring," in *Sowjetliteratur*, vol. 34, no. 1 (Moscow, 1982), p. 170.

2. Yevgeni Brandis and Vladimir Dmitrievski, "Im Reich der Phantastik," in *Sowjetliteratur*, vol. 20, no. 5 (Moscow, 1968), p. 163.

3. Dmitri Bilenkin, *Sowjetliteratur*, vol. 34, no. 1 (Moscow, 1982), p. 152.

4. Stanislaw Lem, "Realistische Phantasie," in *Der Morgen*, 14/15 June 1975 (Berlin), p. 9.

5. Stanislaw Lem, *Phantastik und Futurologie*, part 1 (Frankfurt/M, 1977), p. 8.

6. Stanislaw Lem, in "Zukunftsgeschichten für die Gegenwart," answers questions on his book *The Chain of Chance*, in *Börsenblatt für den Deutschen Buchhandel*, vol. 144, no. 41 (Leipzig, 1977), p. 756.

7. Ibid.

8. Stanislaw Lem, in "Phantasie, die Brücken in das Morgen baut," interview, in *Junge Welt*, supplement "Du und deine Zeit," no. 33 (Berlin, 1975).

9. Stanislaw Lem, in "Der 'Magier aus Paris' und das 'Orakel von Krakow,'" in *Wochenpost*, no. 6 (Berlin, 1978), p. 16.

10. Malgorzata Szpakowska, "Die Flucht Stanislaw Lems," in *Science Fiction—Theorie und Geschichte*, ed. Eike Barmeyer (Munich, 1972), p. 2934.

11. Lem, "Phantasie," in *Junge Welt*.

12. Ibid.

13. Jutta Janke, "Comment on 'Test' by Stanislaw Lem," in *Test* (Berlin, 1968), p. 255.

14. Stanislaw Lem, "Noch zu wenig Phantasie," in *Der Morgen*, 21/22 May 1977 (Berlin), p. 4.

15. Darko Suvin, "Ein Abriss der sowjetischen Science Fiction," in *Science Fiction—Theorie und Geschichte*, ed. Eike Barmeyer (Munich, 1972), p. 319.

16. Brandis and Dmitrievski, op. cit., p. 163.

17. *Grundbegriffe der Literaturanalyse*, ed. Karlheinz Kasper and Dieter Wuckel (Leipzig, 1982), p. 199.

18. Arkadi and Boris Strugatsky, *Noon: Twenty-Second Century* (London, 1978), p. 296ff.

19. Arkadi and Boris Strugatsky, *Der Wald*, in *Rekonstruktion des Menschen: Phantastische Geschichten*, ed. Erik Simon (Berlin, 1980), p. 396.

20. Brandis and Dmitrievski, op. cit., p. 164ff.

21. Gisela Liloff, "Märchen unseres Jahrhunderts—Science Fiction in Bulgarien," in *Sonntag*, no. 9 (Berlin, 1983), p. 10.

22. Ibid., p. 10.

23. Ion Hobana, "Futuristik und Phantastik in der rumänischen Science Fiction," in *Polaris: Ein SF-Almanach*, no. 3 (Frankfurt/M, 1976), p. 123ff.

24. Peter Kuczka, "Die ungarische wissenschaftlich-phantastische Literatur," in *Raketen—Sterne—Rezepte* (Berlin, 1980), p. 235ff.

25. Ibid., p. 236.

26. Franz Fühmann, *Saiäns-Fiktschen* (Rostock, 1981), p. 5.

27. Ibid., p. 5.

28. Ibid., p. 6.

Chapter 14.
THE AMERICANIZATION
OF WESTERN SCIENCE FICTION

1. Martin Schäfer, *Science Fiction als Ideologiekritik? Utopische Spuren in der amerikanischen Science-Fiction-Literatur 1940–1955* (Stuttgart, 1977), p. 29ff.

2. Vera Graaf, *Homo Futurus: Eine Analyse der modernen Science Fiction* (Hamburg, Dusseldorf, 1971), p. 32–37.

3. J. F. Clarke, *The Tale of the Future from the Beginning to the Present Day: A Checklist* (London, 1961).

4. Willi Köhler, "Mit Lichtgeschwindigkeit ins Neandertal," in *Pardon*, vol. 8, no. 2 (1969), p. 16.

5. *Quarber Merkur: Aufsätze zur Science Fiction und Phantastischen Literatur*, ed. Franz Rottensteiner (Frankfurt/M, 1979).

6. *Kosmos und Marktkalkül*, "Gespräch mit einem Science-Fiction-Autor," in *Kürbiskern*, vol. 1 (Munich, 1975), p. 160.

7. Herbert W. Franke, *Ein Kyborg namens Joe: Uto-pische Geschichten*, Kompass-Bücherei, no. 239 (Berlin, 1978), p. 41.

8. Franz Rottensteiner, "Erneuerung und Beharrung in der Science Fiction: Über die New Wave der SF," in *Science Fiction—Theorie und Geschichte*, ed. Eike Barmeyer (Munich, 1972), p. 340.

9. J. G. Ballard, quoted in Charles Platt, *Dream Makers* (New York [Ungar], 1987), p. 91.

10. *Koitus 80*, ed. Franz Rainer Scheck (Cologne and Berlin [West], 1970), p. 40.

11. Thomas M. Disch, quoted in Platt, op. cit., p. 186.

12. Ibid., p. 187.

13. George A. von Glahn, "A World of Difference: Samuel Delany's *The Einstein Intersection*," in *Critical Encounters*, ed. Dick Riley (New York [Ungar], 1978), p. 130.

14. Harlan Ellison, "I Have No Mouth and I Must Scream," in *Science Fiction: A Historical Anthology*, ed. Eric S. Rabkin (New York, 1983), p. 473.

15. Ibid., p. 481.

16. Kurt Vonnegut, Jr., quoted in Platt, op. cit., p. 257.

17. Ibid., p. 258.

18. Frederik Pohl, quoted in Platt, op. cit., p. 108.

19. Ibid., p. 109.

20. Philip K. Dick, quoted in Platt, op. cit., p. 156.

21. James Blish, "Nachruf auf die Prophetie," in *Science Fiction—Theorie und Geschichte*, ed. Eike Barmeyer (Munich, 1972), p. 443.

22. Margaret Atwood, interviewed by Caryn James, "The Lady Was Not for Hanging," (*New York Times Book Review*, Feb. 9, 1986), p. 35.

THEMES, SUBJECTS, AND MOTIFS IN MODERN SCIENCE FICTION

Chapters 15–20.

1. Dieter Wuckel, "Stoff und Motiv," in *Grundbegriffe der Literaturanalyse*, ed. Karlheinz Kasper and Dieter Wuckel (Leipzig, 1982), p. 82.

2. Cf. Robert H. West, "Science Fiction and Its Ideas," in *The Georgia Review*, no. 15 (Georgia, 1961), p. 276ff; J. O. Bailey, *Pilgrims through Space and Time: Trends and Patterns in Scientific and Utopian Fiction* (New York, 1947), p. 216ff; and Hans Joachim Alpers, Werner Fuchs, Ronald M. Hahn, and Wolfgang Jeschke, *Lexikon der Science Fiction Literatur*, vol. 1 (Munich, 1980), p. 45ff.

3. Franz Rainer Scheck, Afterword, *Computerträume: Neue Science Fiction*, dtv-Sonderreihe (Munich, 1973), p. 178.

4. *Koitus 80*, p. 199ff.

5. Johann Wolfgang von Goethe, *Werke* (Berlin Edition), vol. 18 (Berlin and Weimar, 1972), p. 634.

6. Alexander Kröger, *Expedition Mikro* (Berlin, 1976).

7. R. C. Churchill, *Welt—wohin? Kurze Geschichte von morgen und übermorgen 1957–6601* (Konstanz, Stuttgart, 1956).

8. James Blish, op. cit., p. 118ff.

9. Wolfgang Jeschke, "Was ist eigentlich Science Fiction?" in *Die triviale Phantasie: Beiträge zur "Verwertbarkeit" von Science Fiction*, ed. Jörg Weigand (Bonn, Bad Godesberg, 1976), p. 27.

10. Yefremov, "Aufstiegsspirale der Evolution," in *Sowjetliteratur*, vol. 34, no. 1 (Moscow, 1982), p. 164.

BIBLIOGRAPHY

Selected Critical Studies

Aldiss, Brian W. *Trillion Year Spree: The History of Science Fiction.* New York, 1986.

Amis, Kingsley. *New Maps of Hell.* London, 1961.

Bleiler, Everett F., ed. *Science Fiction Writers.* New York, 1982.

Brown, Charles N., and William G. Contento. *Science Fiction in 1985.* New York, 1986.

Bucknall, Barbara J. *Ursula K. Le Guin.* New York, 1981.

Cassutt, Michael. *Who's Who in Space: The First 25 Years.* Boston, 1987.

Christopher, Joe R. *C. S. Lewis.* Boston, 1987.

Clareson, Thomas D. *Some Kind of Paradise: The Emergence of American Science Fiction.* Westport, Connecticut, 1985.

Goodstone, Tony, ed. *The Pulps: Fifty Years of American Pop Culture.* New York, 1970.

Gunn, James. *Alternate Worlds: The Illustrated History of Science Fiction.* Englewood Cliffs, New Jersey, 1975.

Jarvis, Sharon, ed. *Inside Outer Space: Science Fiction Professionals Look at Their Craft.* New York, 1985.

Johnson, Wayne L. *Ray Bradbury.* New York, 1980.

Knight, Damon. *In Search of Wonder.* Chicago, 1967.

Krulik, Theodore. *Roger Zelazny.* New York, 1986.

Lewis, C. S. *Of Other Worlds: Essays and Stories.* London, 1966.

Lupoff, Richard A. *Edgar Rice Burroughs: Master of Adventure.* New York, 1965.

Manlove, C. N. *Science Fiction: Ten Explorations.* Kent, Ohio, 1986.

McEvoy, Seth. *Samuel R. Delany.* New York, 1984.

Menger, Lucy. *Theodore Sturgeon.* New York, 1981.

Miller, Frank, with Klaus Jenson and Lynn Varley. *The Dark Knight Returns.* New York, 1986.

Morella, Joe, Edward Z. Epstein, and Eleanor Clark. *Those Great Movie Ads.* New York, 1972.

Moskowitz, Sam. *Explorers of the Infinite: Shapers of Science Fiction.* Cleveland, New York, 1963.

O'Reilly, Timothy. *Frank Herbert.* New York, 1981.

Philmus, Robert. *Into the Unknown: The Evolution of Science Fiction from Francis Godwin to H. G. Wells.* Berkeley, 1970.

Pierce, John J. *Foundations of Science Fiction.* Westport, Connecticut, 1987.

Platt, Charles. *Dream Makers: Science Fiction and Fantasy Writers at Work.* New York, 1987.

Riley, Dick, ed. *Critical Encounters: Writers and Themes in Science Fiction.* New York, 1978.

Sadler, Frank. *The Unified Ring: Narrative Art and the Science-Fiction Novel.* Ann Arbor, Michigan, 1984.

Smith, Curtis C., ed. *Twentieth Century Science Fiction Writers,* Chicago, 1986.

Staicar, Tom. *Fritz Leiber.* New York, 1983.

———, ed. *Critical Encounters II: Writers and Themes in Science Fiction.* New York, 1982.

———, ed. *The Feminine Eye: Science Fiction and the Women Who Write It.* New York, 1982.

Suvin, Darko. *Metamorphoses of Science Fiction.* New Haven, Connecticut, 1979.

Williams, Paul. *Only Apparently Real: The World of Philip K. Dick.* New York, 1986.

Ziegfeld, Richard E. *Stanislaw Lem.* New York, 1985.

Selected Novels

Many of these volumes have been reissued, some over many years. Date of first publication (if known) is given.

Aldiss, Brian W. *The Long Afternoon of Earth.* London, 1962.

———. *Starship.* London, 1958.

Asimov, Isaac. *I, Robot.* New York, 1950.

———. *The Caves of Steel.* New York, 1953.

———. *The Rest of the Robots.* New York, 1964.

———. *The Bicentennial Man and Other Stories.* New York, 1975.

Atwood, Margaret. *The Handmaid's Tale.* New York, 1986.

Bacon, Francis. *New Atlantis*. London, 1627.

Ballard, J. G. *The Best Science Fiction of J. G. Ballard*. London, 1977.

Bellamy, Edward. *Looking Backward: 2000–1887*. Boston, 1888.

Bleiler, E. F., ed. *The Best Tales of Hoffmann*. New York, 1967.

Bradbury, Ray. *Fahrenheit 451*. New York, 1953.
———. *The Golden Apples of the Sun*. New York, 1953.
———. *The Illustrated Man*. New York, 1951.
———. *The Martian Chronicles*. New York, 1950.

Burgess, Anthony. *A Clockwork Orange*. London, 1962.

Butler, Samuel. *Erewhon*. London, 1872.

Čapek, Karel. *R.U.R.* London, 1923.
———. *The War with the Newts*. London, 1936.

Clarke, Arthur C. *2001: A Space Odyssey*. London, 1968.

Crichton, Michael. *The Andromeda Strain*. New York, 1969.
———. *The Terminal Man*. New York, 1972.

De Bergerac, Cyrano. *Journeys to the Sun and the Moon*. Paris, 1656, 1662.

Defoe, Daniel. *Robinson Crusoe*. London, 1719.

Delany, Samuel R. *The Fall of the Tower*. New York, 1971.

Dick, Philip K. *Flow My Tears, the Policeman Said*. New York, 1974.

Disch, Thomas M. *Camp Concentration*. New York, 1968.

Doyle, Arthur Conan. *The Lost World*. London, 1912.

Heinlein, Robert S. *Farnham's Freehold*. New York, 1964.
———. *Stranger in a Strange Land*. New York, 1961.

Herbert, Frank. *Dune*. New York, 1965.

Hoffmann, E. T. A. *The Devil's Elixir*. London, 1824.

Huxley, Aldous. *Brave New World*. London, 1932.

Le Guin, Ursula. *The Left Hand of Darkness*. New York, 1969.

Lem, Stanislaw. *Solaris*. London, 1970.
———. *The Invincible*. London, 1970.
———. *His Master's Voice*. London, 1983.
———. *Fiasco*. New York, 1987.

Merril, Judith. *Daughters of Earth*. New York, 1968.

Merritt, A. *Dwellers in the Mirage*. New York, 1932.

Moorcock, Michael. *An Alien Heat*. London, 1972.
———. *The Cornelius Chronicles*. London, 1977.

More, Thomas. *Utopia*. London, 1516.

Morris, William. *A Dream of John Ball*. London, 1888.
———. *News from Nowhere*. London, 1891.

Orwell, George. *Animal Farm*. London, 1945.
———. *1984*. London, 1949.

Piercy, Marge. *Woman on the Edge of Time*. New York, 1976.

Poe, Edgar Allan. (Harold Beaver, ed.) *The Science Fiction of Edgar Allan Poe*. New York, 1976.

Russ, Joanna. *The Female Man*. New York, 1975.

Shelley, Mary Wollstonecraft. *Frankenstein, or the Modern Prometheus*. London, 1818.

Sladek, John T. *Roderick: Or, the Education of a Young Machine*. New York, 1980.

Strugatsky, Arkadi and Boris. *Far Rainbow*. London, 1967.
———. *Hard to Be a God*. London, 1973.
———. *Noon: Twenty-Second Century*. London, 1978.
———. *The Time Wanderers*. New York, 1987.

Tiptree, James, Jr. *Out of the Everywhere*. New York, 1981.

Twain, Mark. *A Connecticut Yankee in King Arthur's Court*. New York, 1889.

Vidal, Gore. *Messiah*. New York. 1954.

Voinovich, Vladimir. *Moscow 2042*. New York, 1987.

Vonnegut, Kurt, Jr. *Cat's Cradle*. New York, 1963.
———. *The Sirens of Titan*. New York, 1959.

Wells, H. G. *The Time Machine*. London, 1895.
———. *The Island of Dr. Moreau*. London, 1896.
———. *The Invisible Man*. London, 1897.
———. *The War of the Worlds*. London, 1898.

Wylie, Philip. *The Disappearance*. New York, 1951.
———, and Edwin Balmer. *When Worlds Collide*. New York, 1933.

Zamyatin, Yevgeni, *We*. New York, 1972.

Zelazny, Roger. *Nine Princes of Amber*. New York, 1970.

ACKNOWLEDGMENTS

Ace Books p. 210 (left)
ADN-Zentralbild, Berlin p. 100
Avon Books pp. 58 (left), 106, 112, 113
Ballantine Books p. 210 (right)
Bantam Books pp. 135, 211, 213 (left)
Bibliographisches Institut Leipzig (Archives) pp. 8, 31, 90, 91, 95 (left), 132
Ciesielski, Andreas, Berlin p. 183 (left)
Collection Karger-Decker, Berlin p. 15 (left)
Columbia Pictures pp. 40, 238 (left)
ČTK, Prague p. 130
Dell Books pp. 202, 203
Deutsche Bücherei Leipzig pp. 55 (left), 69, 229, 230
Deutsche Staatsbibliothek Berlin p. 38
Deutsche Staatsbibliothek Berlin/Grambow pp. 29, 32, 41, 52 (left), 53 (right), 65, 71, 78, 86, 136, 137, 143
Dietz Verlag, Berlin p. 7
Doubleday. pp. 118, 120, 124 (right), 125
Forschungsbibliothek Gotha pp. 73, 75
Hänse, Ingrid, Leipzig pp. 4, 5, 25, 33, 37, 42, 46 (left), 53 (left), 74, 99 (right), 115, 158, 166, 168, 175, 177, 178, 180, 182, 184 (bottom), 185
Harvard University Press p. 67
Holiday Film Productions p. 140
HS p. 36 (left)
J. B. Lippincott Co. p. 126 (left)
Literary Agency Utoprop/Jay Kay Klein pp. 114 (right), 116, 117, 119, 121, 122 (left), 149, 188 (left), 198, 199, 208, 215
Looking Glass Library pp. 85, 86
Mansfeldgalerie Eisleben/Renker pp. 2, 3

Mary Evans Picture Library London pp. 46 (right), 47, 58 (right), 59
Modern Library p. 66
Monarch Books p. 207
Narodni Muzeum v Praze p. 131
New American Library pp. 54
Paramount Pictures p. 126 (right)
Penguin Books p. 233
Pocket Books p. 127 (left)
Press Agency NOVOSTI, Moscow pp. 63, 92 (right), 94, 157
Publisher's Archives pp. 82, 83, 99 (left)
RKO Pictures p. 39
Signet Books pp. 138, 151
Staatliches Filmarchiv der DDR pp. 34, 35, 36 (right), 48, 49, 57, 61, 72, 79, 80, 95 (right), 96, 97 (left), 98, 110, 124 (left), 144, 146, 147, 148, 150, 160, 162, 171, 189, 193, 237, 238 (right), 239
Twentieth Century-Fox pp. 190, 191 (left), 242
T. Y. Cromwell and Co. p. 16
United Artists Corporation p. 64
Universal Pictures pp. 56, 212
Universitätsbibliothek Leipzig pp. 10, 11, 14, 15 (right), 18, 20, 21, 22, 43 (left)
Verlag Neues Leben, Berlin p. 176
Verlag Volk und Welt, Berlin pp. 92 (left), 161, 167, 173, 174
Wallmüller, Helga, Leipzig p. 30
Walt Disney Productions pp. 45, 50
Zenith Books p. 205